CHILDREN'S COGNITIVE DEVELOPMENT

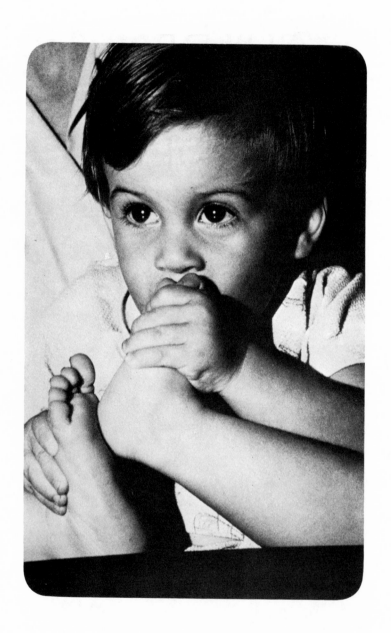

CHILDREN'S COGNITIVE DEVELOPMENT

SECOND EDITION

RUTH L. AULT
Davidson College

New York   Oxford
OXFORD UNIVERSITY PRESS
1983

Library of Congress Cataloging in Publication Data

Ault, Ruth L.
   Children's cognitive development.

   Bibliography: p.
   Includes index.
   1. Cognition in children.   I. Title.
   BF723.C5A9 1982   155.4'13   82-3529
   ISBN 0-19-503183-0   AACR2
   ISBN 0-19-503184-9 (pbk.)

The author acknowledges the kind permission of authors and publishers to reproduce material from the following sources:

R. Gelman, "Conservation acquisition: A problem of learning to attend to relevant attributes." *Journal of Experimental Child Psychology,* 1969, *7,* p. 174. Copyright © 1969 by Academic Press. Reprinted by permission.

P. R. Kingsley and J. W. Hagen, "Induced versus spontaneous rehearsal in short-term memory in nursery school children." *Developmental Psychology,* 1969, *1,* p. 41. Copyright © 1969 by the American Psychological Association. Reprinted by permission.

M. A. Kreutzer, C. Leonard, and J. H. Flavell, "An interview study of children's knowledge about memory." *Monographs of the Society for Research in Child Development,* 1975, *40*(1, Serial No. 159), pp. 9, 11, 25, 29, 43, 49. Copyright © 1975 by the Society for Research in Child Development, Inc. Reprinted by permission.

A. A. Milne, *The house at Pooh Corner.* N.Y.: E. P. Dutton, 1956, pp. 86, 94. Reprinted by permission of the following publishers: (a) E. P. Dutton & Co., Inc. Copyright 1928 by E. P. Dutton & Co., Inc. Renewal, 1956, by A. A. Milne. (b) The Canadian Publishers, McClelland and Stewart Limited, Toronto. (c) Associated Book Publishers, Ltd., London.

A. A. Milne, *Winnie-the-Pooh.* N.Y.: E. P. Dutton, 1954, pp. 86-87. Reprinted by permission of the following publishers: (a) E. P. Dutton & Co., Inc. Copyright 1926 by E. P. Dutton & Co., Inc. Renewal, 1954, by A. A. Milne. (b) The Canadian Publishers, McClelland and Stewart, Limited, Toronto. (c) Associated Book Publishers, Ltd., London.

P. A. Ornstein, M. J. Naus, and C. Liberty, "Rehearsal and organizational processes in children's memory." *Child Development,* 1975, *46,* p. 822. Copyright © 1975 by the Society for Research in Child Development, Inc. Reprinted by permission.

Illustrations by Fred Winkowski

Printing (last digit): 9 8 7 6 5 4 3 2 1

Printed in the United States of America

PREFACE TO THE FIRST EDITION

Since I had a purpose and readership in mind when I wrote this book, I ought to share that information with you, the reader. This book was designed as a supplement to college courses in child development, particularly as taught in Psychology departments, but also including Educational Psychology, Family Life, and Nursing departments in which an unspecialized course in child development is taught. The target audience is, therefore, undergraduate with not necessarily more than an Introductory Psychology course as a prerequisite. Why read a supplement at all? A glance through child psychology texts provides the answer. A majority of such texts emphasizes the child's physical and social development, relegating cognitive development to a secondary role. Often a single chapter covers both Piaget's theory and information about standardized intelligence testing. The topics of memory and perception are frequently missing or presented disjointedly. In few cases is there any attempt to compare or contrast the Piagetian approach with the approach of the non-Piagetian experimental child psychology (called the *process approach* in this book). This book, then, seeks to remedy that situation. It has been kept short enough to function as a supplement to full-length child psychology texts but is long enough to fill in the bare sketch of cognitive development painted in the primary texts. Although other cognitively oriented supplements exist, they are primarily introductions to Piaget's theory alone and are deeper treatments than is desirable for general introductory courses.

This text has a dual orientation, presenting both Piaget's theory and the research efforts of experimental child psychologists who have cognitive, but not necessarily Piagetian, interests. Such an orientation requires the presentation of research results in somewhat greater detail than is common at the introductory level. Having taught child psychology for several years, I know that the mention of research can produce sheer panic in some students. Puzzled by complicated research designs and arcane statistical analyses, introductory (and many advanced) students shy away from experimental psychology. My intention is to bring research findings to the reader in an intelligible and as nontechnical a fashion as possible. For me, that meant describing enough about an experiment that the reader would understand both its results and their significance. This contrasts with the usual treatment of listing one-sentence summaries of the results, which end up being viewed as isolated facts to be memorized. An intelligible presentation also meant excluding statistics, ignoring aspects of experiments that were tangential to the point being discussed, and avoiding the technical jargon of experimental psychology. The advantage over a book of readings that reprints journal articles is clear. For the advanced reader, reference citations indicate sources of further information: original sources in the case of journal articles and other books in the case of Piaget's theory.

The reader should also note that this book has been liberally sprinkled with footnotes. Like all good footnotes, those in this book are tangential to the basic information of the main presentation. Some provide slightly more technical information that the reader may wish to pursue. Others are what I consider to be humorous asides.* I hope the reader will read them.

I also hope that the reader will find this book both useful and enjoyable, for those were my two goals in writing it. Although it is certainly not a layman's guide to parenting or educating children, it is intended to be helpful to anyone who has contact with the younger members of our species. The underlying philosophy is that a basic understanding of normal cognitive development should help make interactions with children more sensible and, consequently, more pleasant.

Before I started this work, I read the prefaces of many other books. I was continually skeptical of the acknowledgment sec-

---

* Or snide remarks, depending on one's perspective.

tion, wondering how the author ever cajoled (or conned) so many of his colleagues into reading endless drafts of the manuscript. Having now written this book, I am amazed at, and eternally grateful for, the number who helped me. Encouragement came from faculty, students, secretaries, and friends alike. In particular, I wish to thank Donna Gelfand, Donald Hartmann, Joen Lessen-Firestone, Cindy Cromer, Christine Mitchell, and Lizette Peterson for their highly useful and detailed comments on manuscript drafts. Irwin Altman, David Dodd, and Marigold Linton helped prepare me for my initial contact with publishers (a bewildering business for novices). Janine Seely and Judie Turner served as able typists. Friends and their children provided many of the delightful anecdotes I have recounted here, but I suspect they wish to remain anonymous.

Finally, I wish to thank my husband. Not only did he suffer through the normal trials and tribulations of a spouse whose partner is writing a book, but he also tolerated such unreasonable demands as thinking up stories to illustrate some point I wished to make (usually by counterarguing that *he* did not have many years of experience studying children and mine *ought* to suffice). After laughing hysterically at my initial sketches, he drew the figures for the manuscript draft submitted to the publisher.* He also cheerfully read draft after draft, providing insightful comments and encouragement. In return for these considerations, he demanded that I become a successful author and support him in the style to which he wanted to become accustomed. A fair bargain to my way of thinking.

Salt Lake City   R.L.A.
January, 1976

---

* His laughter was quite justified, I might add.

vii

PREFACE TO THE SECOND EDITION

The timing for a second edition of a book is not difficult to predict. The author must lose the reluctance to tamper with a finished product, be sufficiently embarrassed over ill-written passages, think of new (and better) ways to express the old material, and have new material to present. The first three conditions need no further elaboration. As for the new material, readers will find that this edition has expanded coverage in three of the five previous chapters. In Chapter 2, which deals with Piaget's theory, research involving class inclusion, conservation, and Formal Operational tasks is treated more thoroughly in order to evaluate the theory more critically. In addition, the chapter expands upon the stage aspects of Piaget's theory. In Chapter 3, all three major processes (perception, memory, and the generation and testing of hypotheses) are considered in greater depth, and the research concerning them is updated. The process called evaluation has been dropped entirely since it does not seem to have stood the test of time. In Chapter 5, the educational implications of Piaget's theory and of the process approach receive much greater treatment.

My own research into the educational implications of both psychological approaches was significantly enhanced by visits to the Circle Children's Center at the University of Illinois Chicago Circle campus and to the Eliot-Pearson Child Development Institute at Tufts University. I am grateful to Maureen Ellis and David Elkind for facilitating those visits. In addition, I wish to thank the North Carolina National Bank for the faculty research support provided to Davidson College which enabled me to make those trips. I would also like to thank Christine Mitchell for discussions of Piaget and memory, Brian Nash for proofreading and checking references, and my colleagues at Davidson College for their encouragement. Marcus Boggs, editor at Oxford University Press, has been a gentle persuader, provider of good meals, and friend. I owe more than I can express to my husband for his unlimited support of both this project and my career.

Davidson, N.C.   R.L.A.
February, 1982

CONTENTS

CHILDREN'S COGNITIVE DEVELOPMENT

1

INTRODUCTION

Four-year-old Susan was asked where she got her name. She answered, "My mommy named me." "What if your mother had called you Jack?" "Then, I'd be a boy." To many children, names embody certain other characteristics; if one has a boy's name, then one must have other features making one male. Susan also claimed that if the name of the sun were changed and it were called the moon, "then it would be dark in the daytime."

A three-year-old girl, with a gleam in her eye, approached a plant. Her mother cautioned her not to touch it. "Why not?" "Because you might hurt it." "No, I won't, 'cause it can't cry." She associated crying with hurting and denied the possibility of the one without the other.

When asked to define "priceless," an eight-year-old guessed that it meant "something that's for free." Children tend to interpret words and expressions literally (see Figure 1-1).

These are just some of the numerous examples of how children's thinking is different from the thinking of adults. The study of cognitive development examines these differences in thinking and the causes of these changes as children grow older. The practical implication of cognitive development is

"Curiosity killed the cat."

clear. How a child thinks, and how his* thinking changes as he develops, has an obvious impact on his behavior at home and on what he learns at school. In addition to the practical significance, studying children's thinking can be fascinating and fun. Although the expression beginning "out of the mouths of babes" usually refers to the honesty with which children speak,

---

* Of course half of all children are "shes" and not "hes," but the English language is not well-suited to referring to a single child without assigning sex. In this book, references to a child as "he" are presumed to include "she." Similarly, parents and teachers will generally be labeled female with all due apologies to fathers and male instructors.

4

"Billy caught 40 winks."

Figure 1-1. Proverbs and metaphors conjure up childish mental images

it also serves to remind us that children say what they think and that their thinking can be amusingly different.

The purpose of this book is to describe briefly the course of cognitive development. The description will take two forms because psychologists have studied the development of thinking from two theoretical perspectives. Although initially the two approaches were viewed as incompatible, each approach has been modified by the arguments of the other so that now

5

substantial overlapping can be seen, especially in the topics which are studied and in the methods used to study them. Some of the explanatory mechanisms or constructs, however, remain in theoretical dispute.

The most complete and unified theory of cognitive development has come from Jean Piaget, a Swiss psychologist. Since Piaget's writings spanned more than 50 years, his ideas evolved, but the basic elements of the theory remained unchanged. His theory can be characterized as tracing the *qualitative* or *stagelike* changes in children's knowledge which develop out of their interactions with their world. Piaget's description of these changes is organized around four global stages which he believed occur in an invariant sequence and are correlated with a child's age, but are not caused by physical maturation alone.

The contrasting theoretical approach will be called the *process* approach because it stems from the information-processing tradition of North American psychologists. As will become apparent, no one person has proposed as unified a theory as Piaget's. Rather, the approach focuses on the development of relatively discrete cognitive processes, in particular (a) attention and perception, (b) memory, and (c) the generation and testing of hypotheses. While acknowledging that the three processes interact and depend upon each other, individual researchers have typically focused on just one process. The basic theoretical position is, therefore, less coherent, but it can be characterized as tracing the quantitative, nonstage, changes in children's problem-solving skills or information-processing capacities. The changes may or may not occur in any particular sequence. They are, to some extent, correlated with age, but not caused by age alone.

ASSUMPTIONS

Despite the differences which should already be apparent, these two approaches share many features including two fundamental assumptions. These cognitive assumptions distinguish them from theories based on the behavioral or S-R approach.

THE ACTIVE CHILD

We assume that children are *active* rather than passive participants in their own development. This assumption means that children are not merely passive recipients of whatever environmental stimulation happens to impinge upon them. Rather, they actively seek certain types of stimulation and avoid others. For example, a child may look at the bars of his crib rather than the middle of the plain mattress. He may focus on his mother's eyes instead of her ears. He may turn his head toward the sound of his mother's voice, but not toward the window when the lawn mower passes by. In being active, children help to determine what behaviors they will exhibit. A 10-month-old may babble sounds like *maah, mmmah, mahmah, may,* and *mey,* until he can produce the particular sound he desires or until he masters and controls his own behavior.

This position does not deny the importance of environmental stimuli in shaping children's behavior. Consider again children's babbling. Research has shown that the early babbling of American babies (around 10 months old) is indistinguishable from that of Chinese babies, but the sounds of those children a few years later are quite distinctive (Atkinson, MacWhinney, & Stoel, 1970). American babies learn to speak English, not Chinese. The environment must be influencing children to result in this language shaping. By the same token, children contribute to the process too. They exercise some choice regarding how much time to spend babbling in contrast to some other activity and whether to babble the *ma* syllable or the *da* one.

The assumption of an active child implies that children inherently try to make sense out of their environment. Experiences in the environment are classified, organized, and related to each other because that is the nature of the mind. These mental manipulations create problems to be resolved, and children seek new experiences to help solve them. As soon as they have figured out the solution (to their own satisfaction), they will turn their attention to other matters. In other words, children are active because they are intrinsically motivated to learn about their world. How do children decide which of the numerous problems confronting them to solve? The *moderate novelty principle* proposes that a person's attention is attracted to events that are mildly different from the old. Events that are completely familiar are boring; events that are too discrepant from the familiar are either unintelligible or frightening. Hence children and adults tend to turn to moderately novel problems.

THE INTERACTIONIST POSITION

When a behavior is universal, occurring in virtually every human being, one could postulate that the behavioral sequence is innate—a wired-in aspect of our nervous system. This position, called *nativism,* occupies one extreme of the spectrum. The people who advocate nativism are frequently called maturationists because they believe that behavior stems from physical maturation of the organism living in a minimal environment (one containing oxygen and food). The other extreme of the spectrum is *empiricism,* which postulates that some experiences are so pervasive that all people are exposed to them in every known culture. The empiricist position is advocated by environmentalists (not to be confused with conservationists) since they believe that behaviors are learned as a result of experience with the environment, given a minimally working physical body (an intact brain and spinal cord). In between the two extremes is a wide range of positions reflecting varying degrees of *interaction* between the forces of mother nature (maturation) and of nurture (learning). Interactionists maintain that the biological and cultural aspects of a person's life are so

8

intertwined that it is difficult, or even meaningless, to try to separate the impact of these two forces.

Clearly, infants are born with some innate behavioral sequences. All healthy infants cry when pricked by a pin. And some cultural experiences are so pervasive that all children are exposed to them. For example, all infants are fed by someone else, or they do not survive. Most behavior, however, results from a combination of inherent predispositions and environmentally determined influences. The interactionist position is advocated by nearly all psychologists who study cognition, and both Piaget's theory and the process approach fit into this category.

Corresponding to the three positions (maturation, environmental experience, and their interaction) are three terms, each of which describes a change in behavior over time. *Growth* is that change which arises from physical maturation of the body. *Learning* is change due to contact with some environmental experience. *Development,* the most general change, is a function of both maturation and experience. Thus, when a change in behavior is labeled as growth, learning, or development, the cause of the change has been implicitly stated as maturation, environmental experience, or their interaction, respectively. The reader should recall these implicit causes whenever these terms occur. The title of this book, *Children's Cognitive Development,* reflects its interactionist position.*

METHODS OF STUDY

To study children's thinking, cognitive psychologists rely on two major methods: observations and experiments. In a naturalistic observation, the investigator watches and records what-

* Titles such as *Children's Learning* and *Studies in Cognitive Growth* were purposely avoided for two reasons: they might imply a learning or maturation orientation which would not be intended, and two excellent books already possess those titles, by Stevenson (1972) and by Bruner, Olver, and Greenfield (1966), respectively.

ever happens as a child goes about his daily activities. If a naturalistic observation is to be thorough, the investigator must have daily access to the subjects for long portions of the day. Since even close family friends are usually unwilling to tolerate such intrusions into their lives, investigators typically observe their own children. That increases the chance that the observer will be biased in recording and interpreting events. Even the most objective observers occasionally yield to the temptation to regard their own children as little angels. It is also difficult for the observer to refrain from participating in, and thereby influencing, the course of events. Rarely can an observer remain passive when the child's curiosity leads him to investigate the properties of matches. The enormous time demands of the observational method usually limit the study to a few children. The observer then cannot determine whether some phenomenon is peculiar to the few children in the observation or whether it has more widespread generality. Conclusions drawn from small sample observations are, therefore, open to the criticism that they are not applicable to broad ranges of children. Piaget's early writings (1951, 1952, 1954) were just such naturalistic observations of the development of his own three children. His later works (e.g., Piaget & Inhelder, 1973), however, were experiments in the same tradition as the process approach research.

In an experiment, often conducted in a laboratory, children are asked to perform certain tasks as specified by the investigator. Their performance is assessed according to some predetermined standard or relative to the performance of other children. Experiments are purposely designed to be less biased because the person who tests the children is typically unfamiliar with any of them and often does not even know the purpose of the experiment. Experiments permit greater generality because large numbers of children can be tested. An additional advantage stems from systematic manipulations of the environment. Scientific statements of cause and effect can only be made when the experimenter has controlled the presence or absence of some treatments and has obtained systematic effects as a result. In observations, the investigator can describe factors as they occur, but deciding between alternative causal explanations such as maturation, past learning, or a current stimulus requires measuring and contrasting groups of children. Experiments can suffer, however, from artificiality and narrowness of scope. The laboratory setting establishes a contrived situation that may induce children to behave in an unusual manner, and because only one small facet of the child's thinking processes is studied at a time, the interrelations between processes are difficult to investigate. Observations are much richer in portraying the whole child.

Experiments and observations each provide data that the other cannot; each is a valuable method for adding to our knowledge about children. Corresponding to the observational and experimental methods are two ways to organize the collected information about children. Since a naturalistic observer typically studies all facets of the same child's behavior as that child develops, it is not surprising that the results of these observations tend to be organized by *ages* or *stages*. All of the child's cognitive skills are observed for relatively long periods of his life, such as infancy or adolescence. An experimentalist, on the other hand, usually studies the performance of many groups of children, often of different ages, on a small set of related tasks during relatively brief sessions. These techniques suggest an organization by *process*. One particular problem-solving skill, for example, memory, is discussed for all ages before the next skill, for example, perception, is examined.

Neither organization is completely satisfactory for presenting cognitive development. If information is presented according to the age of the child, then the reader lacks a concise understanding of the development of a process. If the child's problem-solving skills are discussed as units (first one skill and then another), the reader has a poor comprehension of the child's capacities at any one moment in time. To adopt one organizational framework unfortunately relegates the other to a subsid-

11

iary status, but like the observational and experimental methods, both the stage and process organizations offer valuable contributions to the study of cognitive development.

OVERVIEW OF THE REMAINING CHAPTERS

Chapter 2 presents the theory of Jean Piaget. It begins with the theoretical constructs he proposed to account for developmental change. Then the chapter sketches the four major stages of cognitive development. Piaget's writings were rich and compelling descriptions of very real children and they have stimulated a considerable amount of research. The chapter includes a small sample of that research and its implications for the theory. Chapter 3 presents a sample of the data obtained primarily through laboratory experiments derived from the information-processing tradition. Three problem-solving processes are examined: perception, memory, and hypothesis testing. Since no one theory fits all these pieces together, the account may seem disjointed, but it is a valid and valuable representation of the facts we know about children's thinking.

Because results are more understandable when the experimental procedures are also understood, brief descriptions of many experiments are presented in Chapters 2 and 3. The reader without much background in psychology should rest assured that the presentations are simplified and technical jargon has been avoided as much as possible. For the more advanced reader, reference citations indicate the original sources to which the reader can turn for more detailed information. Some of the similarities and differences between Piaget's theory and the process approach are highlighted in Chapter 4. The two approaches are now more similar than they were 10 or 20 years ago, as researchers of each perspective have tried to incorporate the ideas and data of the other, but important differences remain.

The fifth and final chapter is an attempt to make the preceding chapters relevant to parents and educators. It exemplifies how adults can evaluate problem-solving tasks in terms of the demands placed on the child's capacity to think. The underlying philosophy of this book is that each child is unique, has an individual rate of development, and has an individual set of needs. Hence, no one list of specific suggestions will suit the various situations that parents and educators meet daily in their interactions with children. Chapter 5, therefore, is not a comprehensive manual on child rearing or child educating. Nor can it be a compendium of useful suggestions for the distraught parent or teacher. Instead, it proposes that adults create their own list of solutions based on an assessment of the child's current level of cognitive development and of the task demands.

In essence, the approach is to deny two popular ideas: the concept of the "average" child and the "correct" way to handle children. The average child is as mythical as the unicorn. No person has ever seen one. His characteristics are assigned according to whatever statistical average results from measuring a sample of children. Real children have unique clusters of abilities, some above and some below the average. What is a description of the average child will not necessarily describe any one particular child.

Similarly, if each child is unique, then no one way of handling a situation can be uniformly right or wrong. Wise advice givers must always hedge their bets. They rarely have as much information about the specific situation as the advice seeker and so cannot make as informed a judgment. They can, however, tell the advice seeker what factors might be weighed in the decision. That is the function of this book's final chapter.

It is always difficult to decide how to limit the topics under consideration, especially since the maxim "Everything always relates to everything else" is particularly appropriate for the psychology of human organisms. The determining factors in this book are a combination of personal bias, traditional lines of psychological inquiry, interest for the reader, and availability of research findings, but not necessarily in that order.

2

PIAGET'S THEORY OF
COGNITIVE DEVELOPMENT

Piaget's theory concerns the development of intelligence, that is, how children construct knowledge of the world and how they put that knowledge to use. Piaget wrote extensively on various aspects of children's cognitive development, but this brief introduction cannot do full justice to such a comprehensive and complex theory. Only a few of the most basic terms and assumptions underlying Piaget's theory can be explained, and only a cursory look can be taken at the developmental stages that he proposed. More detailed information about Piaget's theory can be obtained from many excellent books, including Brainerd (1978), Flavell (1963), Furth (1969), and Ginsburg and Opper (1979).

DEFINITION OF TERMS

According to Piaget, intelligence has a functional aspect, which is how the cognitive system works, and a structural aspect, which is the knowledge the system produces.

FUNCTIONS

Piaget (1970) has said that one cannot understand his theory unless its biological basis is examined first. He "borrowed" two functions from biology—organization and adaptation—to explain both stability and change in development. Neither organization nor adaptation is directly observable; rather, each is inferred from a person's activity.

Organization refers to the tendency of behaviors or thoughts to become clustered into systems of related behaviors or thoughts rather than to remain isolated. For example, infants have several individual behaviors such as grasping, sucking, and looking, which at first function independently. If someone places an object in an infant's palm, the baby will grasp the object. If the object appears in front of his eyes, he will look at it. But the infant who has not yet organized these two behaviors will not perform them simultaneously. With development, that is, with maturation and experience, the infant will come to look at things he grasps and grasp things he looks at. Organization happens spontaneously; it is not something which takes conscious or deliberate effort. Piaget considered organization to be a mechanism of cognition because it is a basic biological principle and because he observed the combining of behaviors and thoughts into higher-order, smoother-functioning units.

The second biological mechanism, *adaptation*, consists of two complementary processes: *assimilation* and *accommodation*. Assimilation is the process of incorporating new pieces of information into old ways of thinking or behaving. Let us suppose that an infant knows how to grasp, bite, and shake various objects that are in his crib. For the first time, he is confronted with a new object, such as a stuffed doll. He will try to understand this new object by applying what he already knows how to do; he will grasp, bite, and shake the doll (probably

15

disassembling it in the process). Thus, part of the child's adaptation to a new experience is to assimilate it.

The other part of the child's adaptation is to accommodate to the object's unique features. Accommodation involves modifying some elements of the old ways of thinking and behaving or learning new ways that are more appropriate to the new object. Grasping can be modified by gripping tightly or loosely as a function of an object's weight. One of the properties of stuffed dolls is that they can be rubbed. Once the child learns to rub the doll, accommodation has occurred.

Another example of the usefulness of the concepts of assimilation and accommodation can be seen in the preschool child's early attempts to count. As Gelman (1979) described it,

> It is hard, if not impossible, to explain [young children's] tendency to count *on their own* without the notion of assimilation. A 2½ year old may say "2-6" when counting a 2-item array and "2-6-10" when counting a 3-item array. The fact that young children invent their own count lists can be explained if we assume that counting principles . . . are guiding the search for (or assimilation of) lists in the environment. Likewise, the shift from the use of idiosyncratic count lists to the conventional ones . . . makes sense if we recognize the workings of accommodation. [P. 3, italics in the original]

Piaget (1970) proposed that both assimilation and accommodation occur simultaneously whenever the child adapts to an environmental stimulus. He modeled these processes after biological systems such as digestion, in which food is assimilated by breaking it down into a form which the body can use, while at the same time the body accommodates to the food by secreting enzymes and contracting muscles. In both digestion and cognition, assimilation and accommodation always occur, but the particular balance between them can vary from situation to situation. Feedback from the environment is one important factor in determining which process is more influential. Other important factors include the extent to which the new stimulus

16

situation differs from previous ones and the kinds of behaviors or thoughts the child already has. Let us consider again the example of the child who has been given the stuffed doll. When he applies his old behaviors, he finds that grasping and shaking the doll do not produce very interesting noises. Biting a stuffed doll can be unpleasant (depending on the stuffing), so the child looks for new things to do with it and eventually comes upon rubbing. Accommodation has thus played a larger role than assimilation.

For a contrasting example, let us suppose that the child has been given rattles before, with handles one-half inch or less in diameter. Then he is presented with a new rattle with a handle one-inch in diameter. For the most part, the child will assimilate the new rattle, applying the old behaviors of grasping and shaking it. He will have to accommodate only slightly. He must open his hand wider in order to grasp it, hold on harder, and shake with more force to produce any noise. In his adaptation to the new stimulus of a one-inch handle, assimilation has played a larger role than accommodation.

Piaget stated that one of the forms of adaptation takes definite precedence over the other in two situations. In make-believe play, the child's behavior is predominantly assimilation. The child ignores the "realistic" features of an object and responds to it as if it were something else. In many nursery schools, for example, a corner of the classroom is set up for playing house. Children can be seen sweeping the floor, washing dishes, and setting the table. One child straddles a broom, pretending to be flying. The broom's sweeping capabilities are ignored while the child interacts with it as if it had wings. While we can look at such play as evidence of creativity, the child is not learning anything about brooms as sweeping instruments. Imitation, on the other hand, is primarily accommodation. The child learns new behaviors by imitating someone else's behaviors. When a boy observes his mother pet a dog and then imitates and pets the dog, he is accommodating to it. The dog could not be a completely novel object, however, because the boy needs a framework to which he can connect the newly imitated behavior. Accommodation will not occur if the behavior to be imitated is too novel. Each time a child accommodates more than he assimilates, he adds to his repertoire of behaviors and becomes a bit more mature. In other words, advances in cognitive development are greater when accommodation plays a larger role than assimilation because the child's repertoire of behavior expands. Assimilation is still very important, though, for the child understands new objects by applying old patterns of behaving to them. As Piaget (1970) has said, "Assimilation is necessary in that it assures the continuity of [mental] structures and the integration of new elements to these structures" (p. 707).

Assimilation and accommodation are, in one sense, opposing forces. Assimilation tries to maintain the child's current status and force change upon the external situation, while accommodation tries to maintain the external situation and force change on the child. Such tension between two forces must reach a balance, or the system will fail to thrive. Consequently, Piaget proposed a self-regulating mechanism, equilibration, which coordinates the actions of assimilation and accommodation. Cowan (1978) likened equilibration to a steam engine's governor "which shuts down the engine temporarily when the steam pressure builds up, and then allows the engine to switch on again" (p. 25). This analogy emphasizes that the regulatory mechanism is a property of the system (hence, self-regulatory) and not something imposed on it from outside stimulation. Piaget (1970) described equilibration as "a set of active reactions of the [child] to external disturbances" or to disturbances created by inner reflections (p. 725).

STRUCTURES

The structural aspect of Piaget's theory refers to the system of knowledge children construct out of their actions (first, physical and later, mental) with the environment. This system of knowledge takes on two forms: schemes and operations.

A *scheme* is an organized pattern of behavior. All of us engage in behavior patterns, or habits, which form part of our daily routine. Although we may never repeat any action exactly the same way, there is a similarity to the actions, and it is possible to recognize the critical, defining elements of the behavior pattern. To say that a child is sucking, for example, certain minimal criteria must be met. The cheeks and lips of the mouth must move in and out rhythmically in a drawing action, and some object, such as a thumb or nipple, is usually in the mouth. Other movements, such as the mouth opening and closing repeatedly, are the essential elements of other schemes, such as biting. In sucking, it does not matter whether the child's right thumb or left thumb is in his mouth, or whether he brought his thumb to his mouth after scratching his cheek or after brushing hair out of his eyes. The essential ingredients of the scheme are the sucking movements.

But more than just these common movements are implied in the definition of a scheme. The definition includes the idea that the scheme will be used because it is available to be used. Recall that in discussing assimilation we said that the child would grasp, bite, and shake a stuffed doll because those were schemes he already had. Assimilation occurs when old schemes are applied to new events.

The feature of schemes that highlights their importance in Piaget's theory is that by applying the schemes to various objects, the child can build up knowledge. Bottles and thumbs can be grouped together as objects-which-can-be-sucked, and they can be differentiated because one object often leads to food in the mouth and the other does not. Thus, from observing physical responses, such as an infant grasping a rattle and a bottle, Piaget inferred an underlying cognitive structure. The tendencies to grasp objects and to know objects as graspable are not, themselves, directly observable.

The other type of structure is an *operation*. Operations are

19

more difficult to understand because they are not tied to behavior in as straightforward a manner as schemes. Operations are inferred from some commonalities children exhibit when they solve a particular set of problems. We will consider this in more detail in later sections; for now, operations can be defined by two characteristics: (a) they are mental, in-the-head representations and (b) they are reversible. Reversibility refers to the capacity to undo or compensate for one mental action by taking a different mental action and arriving back at the beginning state. Reversibility distinguishes operations from other types of mental activity such as imagining and perceiving.

The structural and functional aspects of Piaget's theory are closely interwoven. First, because of the principle of organization, all the elements in a structure are interrelated. One element cannot be changed without influencing the others. Second, each act of assimilation and accommodation transforms a structure, so structures appear dynamic and changeable rather than static. Third, structures develop from simple to more complex forms. Finally, Piaget emphasized the active role of the child in constructing structures. Structures are not imposed on the child from external stimulation or experience, nor are they merely preformed in the genetic makeup to unfold with maturation. Rather, "the construction of structures is mainly the work of equilibration" (Piaget, 1970, p. 725). Equilibration is an active reaction or compensation to some cognitive discrepancy, but it does not reestablish a prior balance point by discounting some of the conflicting data. Instead, equilibration involves building a new balance which will allow the cognitive system to "integrate disturbances into wider and more powerful structures" (Lovell, 1979, p. 16).

By oversimplifying a bit, one can say that Piaget's theory accounts for cognitive development in terms of the development of structures, from the schemes of the infant to the schemes plus operations of the adult. Piaget said that this occurred in four major time divisions, variously called stages or periods (although in some articles [e.g., Piaget, 1970], the mid-

20

dle two periods are combined). We shall adopt the terminology that *stages* characterize the smallest units of change which meet certain criteria such as being qualitative (rather than quantitative) and occurring in an invariant sequence. *Periods* are broader time blocks incorporating several stages within them. A fuller discussion of the requirements for a stage theory occurs at the end of this chapter.

The first of the four periods is the Sensorimotor Period, beginning at birth and lasting $1\frac{1}{2}$ to 2 years. During this period, children have only schemes. The Preoperational Period, from $1\frac{1}{2}$ to 6-7 years, is a transition between the predominant use of schemes and the use of operations. Children begin to use such mental representations as symbols and language, but these are not true operations. In the Concrete Operational Period, from 6-7 to 11-12 years, children have some true operations, but these can only be applied in concrete, physically real situations. Finally, in the Formal Operational Period, from adolescence through adulthood, operations have developed to the point where they can be applied to abstract and hypothetical problems. Table 2-1 summarizes these periods.

Here as elsewhere in the book, ages associated with the various periods and stages are meant to be rough approximations only. In addition to describing stages and periods of general cognitive processes, Piaget described stages in the development of some specific abilities. While we shall be concerned primarily with the general periods, brief descriptions of specific

TABLE 2-1

FOUR PERIODS OF COGNITIVE DEVELOPMENT

Period	*Approximate Age Ranges*
Sensorimotor	Birth–$1\frac{1}{2}$-2 years
Preoperational	$1\frac{1}{2}$-2–6-7 years
Concrete Operational	6-7–11-12 years
Formal Operational	11-12–through adulthood

abilities (such as object permanence) will be presented as well.

THE SENSORIMOTOR PERIOD

The first period of development is called *Sensorimotor* because children solve problems using their sensory systems and motoric activity rather than the symbolic processes that characterize the other three major periods. Children's knowledge about objects comes from their actions on them. At this point we need to pause briefly to examine some perceptual-motor capabilities of the newborn. Then we shall return to Piaget's theory and see how the perceptual-motor system is used in the Sensorimotor Period.

Although infants may appear completely helpless at birth, many of their senses are functioning. From the moment of birth, when their eyes are open, infants can see. The muscular control of eye movements is not very precise, and they have sharp focus only for those objects 9-10 inches from their faces because the muscles controlling the curvature of the lenses are not fully developed. Nevertheless, newborns can perceive color and shape when there is good contrast to the surrounding visual pattern. Since infants startle in response to loud noises and quiet in response to soft voices, we know that the sense of hearing functions from birth. Babies cry when stuck with a diaper pin and fuss when too hot or too cold; thus we know that the senses of pain and temperature are operative. Touching, stroking, and rocking typically soothe a fussing infant, leading to the conclusion that the sense of touch and bodily posture cues are meaningful to newborns. Finally, controlled experiments with a baby's reactions to different odors and tastes have permitted us to learn that the sense of smell works immediately from birth but taste discrimination is delayed for several days. Thus infants are capable of receiving stimulation through the many sensory modalities they are born with.

In addition to perceiving stimulation, newborns are capable of reflexive behavior. Reflexes are responses that all normal members of a species exhibit after a particular type of stimulation. Typically, psychologists consider reflexes unlearned. That is, the species-specific response occurs the very first time the stimulus is contacted, and it is not necessary for the organism to observe anyone else making that same response or to be taught. Examples of reflexes in adults are the knee jerk when a doctor's hammer strikes the patella, and the constriction of the eye's pupil in response to bright light.

Some infant reflexes clearly have survival value. Among these are the rooting reflex, the sucking reflex, and the grasping reflex. The rooting reflex helps the infant locate his mother's breast for feeding. When a baby's cheek is stroked, he will turn his head toward the side that was touched and open his mouth. Then, when anything touches the infant's mouth, he begins sucking. Together the rooting and sucking reflexes ensure that with a little help from his mother, the infant can obtain food. The grasping reflex is triggered by any object placed in the palm of the baby's hand. His grasp is strong enough that the infant can be pulled from a lying to a sitting position just by grasping an adult's fingers. The grasping reflex was probably significant in evolution when babies were transported by clinging to their mothers. Newborns also have reflexes for yawning, hiccoughing, sneezing, coughing, withdrawing an arm or leg if pricked with a pin, and so on.

Other reflexes indicate how mature the infant is. The Babinski reflex, named after its discoverer, seems to be an indicator of the state of the central nervous system. When the outer sole of the infant's foot is stroked, the infant fans his toes apart and arches his foot. Between about four and six months of age, the Babinski reflex disappears, and the infant now curls his toes downward in response to the sole stroke, just as adults do. If an infant still has a Babinski reflex after his first half year of life, damage to the central nervous system may be indicated.

Finally, there are reflexes whose functions are currently unknown. One example of this is the "walking" reflex. If infants are held upright with their feet lightly touching a surface such as a table top, they will step in alternation, as if walking. These reflexes disappear, but the behaviors return later under voluntary control.

With the reflexes and sensory capacities outlined above, infants are ready to begin interacting with their world. Their reflexes allow their sensory systems to contact many objects. As they look at, hear, touch, taste, and smell things, they acquire valuable information about their environment. Before this interaction takes place, infants do not know whether things are hot or cold, hard or soft, smooth or rough, sharp or blunt, tasty or ill-tasting. They do not even know what belongs to their own bodies and what is part of the external world. They soon find out, though, that biting their own toes causes pain whereas biting most other objects does not.

The amount of information infants must learn is truly enormous, and they have only their reflexes and sense organs with which to begin the process. Since the infant's reflexive systems are not as precise or discriminating as they could be, Piaget observed that one of the first significant changes to occur in infant behavior is the modification of some of these reflexes. These changes characterize the first of the six stages within the Sensorimotor Period.

STAGE 1: MODIFICATION OF REFLEXES

When children are born, the sucking reflex is an automatic response to anything placed in the mouth. The reflex at first functions equally well to the stimulus of fingers or pieces of clothing as it does to nipples of bottles or breasts. During the first month of life, however, the sucking reflex is modified, enabling hungry infants to suck more quickly and vigorously for milk while simultaneously enabling them to reject nonfood substances. When they are no longer hungry, infants can reject food but will still suck on toys or pacifiers. The reflex thus becomes both more efficient and more voluntary. In other words, infants learn to recognize objects by sucking on them and then can choose whether to suck or not.

In a similar manner, the rooting reflex first becomes more efficient, turning the head in precisely the proper direction for a given stimulus, and then drops out as more voluntary movements replace it. These voluntary head-turning movements arise from a combination of factors, including a maturing neuromuscular system and a conditioning process in which hunger, the presence of mother, and being held in a particular position are paired with the rooting and sucking reflexes.

Not all reflexes change in the Sensorimotor Period or, indeed, even in a person's lifetime. Pupil constriction to bright lights and withdrawal of a limb when pinpricked remain virtually unchanged. Nevertheless, those reflexes which do change demonstrate the significant changes in the first stage of the Sensorimotor Period.

STAGE 2: PRIMARY CIRCULAR REACTIONS

The second stage of the Sensorimotor Period has been called the stage of Primary Circular Reactions. During this time, if the infant's random movements lead, by chance, to an interesting event, the infant will attempt to repeat the behavior. The term circular reactions refers to the circularity or repetitive aspects of the behavior. An example of a primary circular reaction might be thumb sucking. The infant's thumb accidentally falls into his open mouth, triggering sucking, but then falls out. The infant then attempts to get his thumb back into his mouth so that the interesting event, sucking, can be repeated. The adjective primary refers to the fact that the interesting activity involves only the infant's own body. If there is any purpose to a circular reaction, it may be to practice a scheme, in this case, sucking; or there may be no demonstrable purpose at all. In any case, there is no intention to suck the thumb to find out what thumbs are like. Such investigatory intent is hypothesized to occur only at later stages in the infant's development.

STAGE 3: SECONDARY CIRCULAR REACTIONS

The Secondary Circular Reaction Stage follows (logically enough) the Primary Circular Reaction Stage. In this third stage of the Sensorimotor Period, infants still exhibit circular reactions (repeating interesting chance-occurring events), but now the repetitions involve events or objects in the external world, secondary to the infant's body. Piaget (1952) described an incident in which his son waved his arms, thereby swinging some balls which had been suspended above the crib and attached by a string to one hand. After observing a series of arm waves followed by intense stares at the swinging toy, Piaget concluded that his son acted for the purpose of repeating an interesting event. It might be argued that the pleasure of seeing the swinging toy caused such excitement in the baby that his arms waved, which accidentally resulted in the toy swinging again, which in turn excited the baby to swing his arms once more, and so forth. Piaget rejected this explanation because he noticed that the hand which was not connected to the string stopped moving. When Piaget changed the hand tied to the string, his son changed the arm he waved. Thus, intentionality can be inferred because of the refinements that occurred in the waving.

Even though infants in the Secondary Circular Reaction Stage know there is a connection between their behavior and the interesting events, these infants still have several cognitive deficiencies. Their behavior is not fully intentional, in the sense that the goal was discovered by accident. It is only after the interesting event has occurred that the infant desires it. In addition, their behavior is aimed solely at reproducing the prior event; they are not yet inventing new behaviors.

STAGE 4: COORDINATION OF SECONDARY REACTIONS

In stage 4, children can combine two or more previously acquired schemes to obtain a goal. The name of the stage is derived from this new achievement: children coordinate several of their secondary circular reactions. One frequently cited example from Piaget's observations (1952) involves his son reaching for a matchbox Piaget was holding. Piaget held a pillow in one hand and behind it he held the matchbox, thus presenting an obstacle in front of a goal. He observed his son strike the pillow to displace it and clear the way to grab the matchbox. By putting the previously acquired striking and grabbing schemes together in a coordinated manner, the child overcame an obstacle and reached the goal. In earlier stages, the child might have given up his attempts to grab the matchbox as soon as the obstacle was imposed, or he might have been distracted into striking the pillow repeatedly. What is new about this stage is the child's continued orientation toward a specific goal. In the sense that only previous behaviors are joined together, however, there is no novelty. That accomplishment comes in the next stage of development.

STAGE 5: TERTIARY CIRCULAR REACTIONS

The Tertiary Circular Reaction Stage is the fifth stage in the Sensorimotor Period. As the term *circular reactions* implies, events are still repeated, but the child has progressed to the point of actively seeking novelty. Actions are no longer repeated in exactly the same manner from trial to trial, as was done in earlier stages. Now children purposely vary their movements to observe the results. Infants perform actions as if they were learning about the properties of objects as objects or actions as actions, not merely acting on objects to obtain some goal. This involves novelty for its own sake, but the novel actions still develop by trial and error. Children do not know the outcome of their behavior until they try it.

To clarify the distinction between the stages of secondary and tertiary circular reactions, consider a child in his playpen with a variety of toys. A secondary circular reaction might involve the child dropping a block from shoulder height and watching it bounce off the floor. In repeating the action, the child would continue with the blocks and always release them from shoulder level. In the Tertiary Circular Reaction Stage, the child might vary the height of his release from his head to just barely above the floor. He might vary what he dropped, trying out all the toys available, or he might vary both the height and the toy simultaneously.*

The change from secondary to tertiary circular reactions can be illustrated with an episode from *The House at Pooh Corner* (Milne, 1961a). Pooh is walking in the forest holding a fir-cone when he trips, dropping the cone into the river.

> "That's funny," said Pooh. "I dropped it on the other side," said Pooh, "and it came out on this side! I wonder if it would do it again?" And he went back for some more fir-cones.
>
> It did. It kept on doing it. Then he dropped two in at once, and leant over the bridge to see which of them would come out first; and one of them did; but as they were both the same size, he didn't know if it was the one he wanted to win, or the other one. So the next time he dropped one big one and one little one. [P. 94]

The interesting event (the fir-cone floating under the bridge) happened literally by accident, and Pooh first attempted to

---

* Parents are urged to be patient if their child, playing this dropping game, happens to pitch the toys out of the playpen. After all, what are parents for, if not to retrieve the toys so that baby can drop them again? Parents should also not be surprised when peas and meat are dropped from the highchair. It is just a way of learning how these objects behave, although it is more likely that baby will learn how parents behave.

repeat it exactly, showing secondary circular reactions. Then he varied both the number and size of the cones, showing tertiary circular reactions.

STAGE 6: BEGINNING OF REPRESENTATIONAL THOUGHT

Stage 6 is the beginning of representational thought. Before this stage, children can solve problems and learn how to act deliberately and efficiently to achieve a desired goal. But Piaget stated that children do not start to *think without acting* before entering the sixth stage of the Sensorimotor Period. Representational thinking, according to Piaget, involves mentally reasoning about a problem *prior* to acting. Children try to solve problems using their familiar schemes, but if these fail, they will not grope around in the trial-and-error fashion of prior stages. Rather, now they will consider the situation mentally, perhaps drawing an analogy from a different time and place, and then directly act on the problem with a scheme never before applied to it. Piaget (1952) described his daughter's attempts to remove a chain from a matchbox which was not open enough for her to insert her hand and grasp the chain. According to Piaget's observations, many times before she had grasped the chain, but she had always been able to insert her hand through the opening. She first applied an old scheme, pushing her fingers into the box, but that did not work. In earlier stages of development, she might have applied other schemes such as shaking the box or biting it. Now Piaget observed her to open and close her mouth a little bit, then open it a bit wider and then still wider. Finally she put a finger into the opening of the matchbox, pulled it wider, and grasped the chain. Piaget believed she solved the problem by examining her old schemes mentally, rather than by trying each of them overtly. Reasoning by the analogy with opening her mouth wider, she invented a novel solution to her problem.

29

Piaget did not believe that the Sensorimotor child's thought involved language because the child's language development was still too rudimentary in this stage. As children first learn to speak, word meanings are unstable and idiosyncratic. Children do not realize that the meaning of a word must be agreed upon by the language community, so they change the meaning to suit their own purposes. For example, a child might use the syllable *mu* to represent first his milk, then a cookie, his dog, and finally his mother, all within the span of a few hours. By the end of the Sensorimotor Period, the child is using only one- or perhaps two-word utterances to label objects and express simple desires. Language usage is thus not developed enough to be useful for the new skill of representational thinking.

The six Sensorimotor stages span the child's development from the early reflexive behaviors to repetitions of various activities involving the child's own body and other objects to the beginning of mental reasoning prior to acting (see Table 2-2 for an outline of these stages). Children in the Sensorimotor Period use their behavioral schemes to manipulate objects, to learn some of the properties of objects, and to obtain goals by combining several schemes. Their behavior is tied to the concrete and the immediate, and they can only apply their schemes to objects they can perceive directly.

OBJECT PERMANENCE

The overview just presented of the Sensorimotor Period has focused on the inferred underlying structure of infancy, that is, on the various schemes an infant can use. An alternative way to view the period is to examine the development of a specific product of using the schemes: object permanence.

Object permanence is defined as the knowledge that objects continue to exist even when one is not perceiving them. You know that this book continues to exist even if you put it on a shelf and leave the room. If it is not there when you return,

TABLE 2-2

SIX STAGES OF THE SENSORIMOTOR PERIOD

Stage	Principal Characteristics
1. Modification of Reflexes (0–1 month)	Reflexes become efficient and more voluntary movements replace them
2. Primary Circular Reactions (1–4 months)	Repetition of interesting body movements
3. Secondary Circular Reactions (4–10 months)	Repetition of interesting external events
4. Coordination of Secondary Reactions (10–12 months)	Combining schemes to obtain a goal
5. Tertiary Circular Reactions (12–18 months)	Varying repetition for novelty
6. Beginning of Representational Thought (18–24 months)	Thinking prior to acting

you might start inquiring whether another person took it. Although the idea is sometimes appealing, you do not really believe that it could "vanish into thin air." Does the child have this same knowledge of the permanence of objects from birth, or is it something the child has to learn? Piaget suggested that object permanence is learned during the Sensorimotor Period in a series of stages defined by the infant's searching behaviors.* These six stages are shown in Table 2-3.

* The stages of object permanence development cut across the stages outlined above for the Sensorimotor Period. As a guide to the reader, approximate age ranges will be given in this discussion.

TABLE 2-3

SIX STAGES IN THE ACQUISITION
OF OBJECT PERMANENCE

Approximate Ages	Principal Characteristics
1. 0–2 months	No expectations or searching
2. 2–4 months	Passive expectations
3. 4–8 months	Search for partially covered objects
4. 8–12 months	Search for completely covered objects
5. 12–18 months	Search after visible displacements
6. 18+ months	Search after hidden displacements

According to Piaget, in the first stage (from birth to 2 months), children will look at objects in their visual field, but if the objects leave the visual field, the infants stop looking and change to some other activity. This results in the world being perceived as a series of fleeting images. Mother's face appears above the infant so he looks at her. If she steps away, he looks at something else. The next stage (from 2 to 4 months) is characterized by "passive expectations." For a short while infants will gaze at the location where an object disappeared, as if waiting for it to reappear. There is no active search, however, and Piaget does not credit the child with object permanence. He interprets the child's behavior as merely continuing an on-going activity. Consider, for example, a girl waving a rattle. If the rattle accidentally slips from her hand to the floor, she will just continue waving her hand. She will not look around on the floor for the rattle.

In the next stage (roughly 4 to 8 months), children can anticipate the trajectory of an object and look for it at its landing place. This search is usually limited to looking for objects that children themselves have caused to disappear, but it shows what Piaget considered to be the beginnings of true object permanence. In this stage, children will also reach for a partially covered object. If it disappears completely, though, they will stop reaching.

From about 8 to 12 months, children will search for objects that other people have caused to disappear, but they cannot do so successfully (that is, find the object) if a series of movements (displacements) has to be considered. Piaget's demonstration of this involved showing a child a toy and then placing the toy under a cover. The child in this stage immediately lifts the cover and obtains the toy. This sequence is repeated, and again the child finds the toy. On the third trial, however, the child watches as the toy is hidden in a different location, under a pillow. Once it disappears from sight, the child turns away and looks for it under the cover where it was hidden the first two times. Although the child apparently knows that the object exists, he confers a certain "privilege of position" on it and includes in the definition of an object where it can be found.

By the beginning of the second year of life (12 to 18 months), children learn how to handle the displacements described above. They will search for the object where it was last seen. However, they have to see the displacements to be able to follow them. If the toy is hidden under the cover, the cover and the toy are both put under the pillow, and then only the cover is removed, children will not search for the toy under the pillow. Searching after hidden displacements occurs only after the final stage in the development of object permanence (18 months onward).

While Piaget's description of the child's active search for objects is accurate, one can ask whether active search is the best response to use as an indication of object permanence. A recurrent suspicion in developmental psychology is that because of lack of development in some related function, children may *know* something before they can demonstrate their knowledge. For example, children might know an object has permanence before they can actively search for it because active search involves the development of eye-hand coordination—to reach where one is looking. Or children might know an object exists but forget about it due to a limited memory span. This latter hypothesis, in fact, was offered by Bower (1971) after he conducted an experiment on object permanence in young infants.

Bower's test of object permanence

Since Bower wanted to test very young infants, who would not reach for objects, he used a simple response, the surprise or startle reaction, as the potential indicator of object permanence. The babies in his experiment were either 20, 40, 80, or 100 days old, corresponding to infants in Piaget's first two stages in the development of object permanence. Bower propped each baby up in a sitting position so that the baby faced a brightly colored object, such as a ball. As the infant looked at the ball, a screen moved in front of it, hiding the ball from the infant's view. The screen remained in front of the ball for either $1\frac{1}{2}$, 3, $7\frac{1}{2}$, or 15 seconds. Then the screen moved away. On half of the trials, the ball was visible again. On the other half, the ball had disappeared. Bower reasoned that if the babies had a notion of object permanence, they should expect the ball to be visible again when the screen moved off. Its reappearance should produce no reaction, but if the ball had disappeared, the babies should be quite surprised. On the other hand, if infants have no notion of object permanence, they should be surprised to see the ball and not surprised if it had disappeared. In this experiment, surprise was measured by watching the babies' facial expressions. In other experiments, more sophisticated measures of heart rate and breathing changes have indicated the same results. Figure 2-1 presents the alternative outcomes possible.

The results of this little experiment depended upon the age of the baby and the length of time the screen hid the ball. All age groups of babies were surprised when the ball was gone if the screen had been hiding it for only $1\frac{1}{2}$ seconds. None were surprised on the trials when the ball was still there. To-

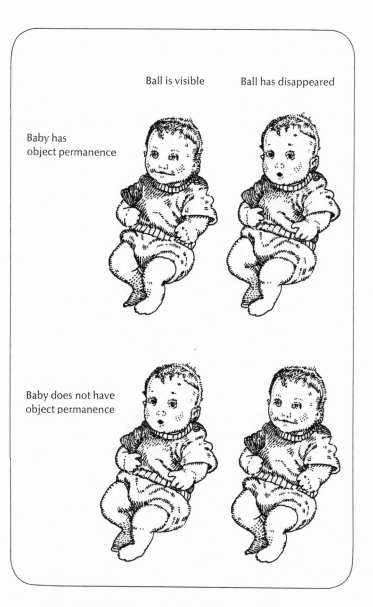

Figure 2-1. Possible reactions by babies with or without object permanence, depending on the conditions of the experiment

gether these two results indicated some object permanence by infants as young as 20 days. The oldest infants expected the ball to be there even after the longest time interval. The youngest infants, however, were more surprised to see the ball remain than disappear at the longest time interval. That is, after 15 seconds of hiding, the youngest babies appeared not to have object permanence (see Figure 2-2). Apparently, then, 20-day-old babies will show some object permanence if the conditions are proper (only $1\frac{1}{2}$ seconds of hiding), but lack of development in processes such as memory prevents the infant from having a fully developed conception of object permanence.

Piaget disagreed with Bower's interpretation of these results, saying it "only serves to prove that recognition is a very early phenomenon and in no way does it confirm the permanency . . . of the object while it is hidden" (Piaget & Inhelder, 1976, p. 32). By repeatedly looking at an object, children can form a static copy or image of it and recognize it in a limited sense, but the concept of object permanence can only come from children organizing the schemes they have used on that and other objects. For Piaget, children must form a distinction between themselves as actors and the objects they act upon to fully appreciate the permanency of the object (see Gratch, 1975, for a detailed contrast of the views of Piaget and Bower).

The object permanence test described above used a static scene. What would happen if the object was moving when it became hidden, for example, if a rolling ball went under a couch? Or what if a ball went under the couch but a doll came out? Bower (1971) performed another experiment which addressed this question, although his original purpose was to investigate which features of an object (size, shape, color, speed) help an infant to recognize that an object which reappeared is the same as the one which disappeared. Bower argued that if a ball disappeared but a doll reappeared and the infant looked around for the ball, then object permanence would be indicated.

The infants who served as subjects in this experiment were

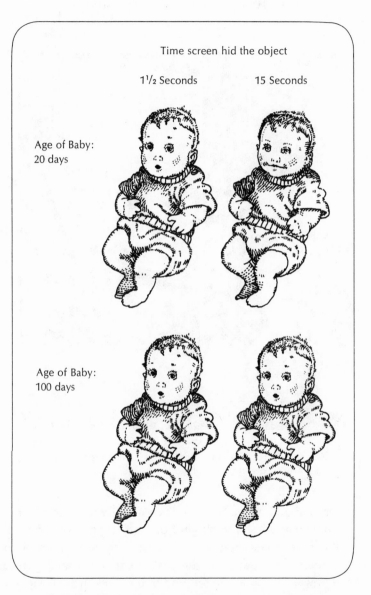

Figure 2-2. Surprise and nonsurprise reactions obtained on trials when the ball has disappeared in Bower's experiment on object permanence

Figure 2-3. Location of baby, screen, and railroad track in Bower's experiment on object recognition

between 6 and 22 weeks of age. Each infant was seated facing a screen, and a railroad track ran from left to right, passing behind the screen (see Figure 2-3). Each baby was exposed to four different situations. In the first situation, a small white mannikin was placed at the left end of the track. It then moved along the track at a constant speed, passed behind the screen, and emerged from the other side, stopping at the right end of the track. After a short pause, the mannikin reversed directions, moving back to the original left end of the track, again passing

38

behind the screen. All babies followed the movement with their eyes, tracking the mannikin.

In the second condition, the white mannikin moved along the track, and at the time when it should have reappeared from behind the screen, an entirely different object, a red lion, emerged. The red lion traveled to the right end of the track, paused, moved back behind the screen, and the white mannikin reappeared, moving to the left end of the track. Seeing a difference in size, shape, and color, adults would conclude that two objects were being used. Babies over 16 weeks old followed the motion of the lion when it emerged, but some of them glanced back at the screen. When the lion paused at the right end of the track, there were definite looks back at the screen about one quarter of the time. This was taken as an indication that many of the babies knew that two objects had been involved. Babies under 16 weeks of age showed a very different pattern of responses. They tracked the moving object with no glancing back toward the screen. If the mannikin is not a permanent object, then of course a lion can emerge.

In the third condition, the white mannikin moved toward the right and went behind the screen. According to its speed of movement, the mannikin should have been behind the screen for a certain length of time. In this condition, a white mannikin emerged "too fast." That is, just after the first white mannikin disappeared behind the screen, an identical one emerged from the far side of the screen. As in the other two conditions, the entire sequence was repeated in reverse. Adults will take this as an indication of two different but identical-looking objects. All the babies over 16 weeks of age looked back at the screen after the one object had stopped, apparently waiting for the second one to emerge. Babies under 16 weeks of age got very upset and refused to look anymore. They did not track the movement of the object that emerged.

The fourth condition was a combination of the previous two. As the white mannikin moved toward the right and passed behind the screen, a red lion emerged "too fast." The reactions to this condition resembled responses to the third condition. Babies over 16 weeks looked back at the screen after they had tracked the emerging object. Babies under 16 weeks cried and refused to look. Table 2-4 summarizes these results.

Bower's results suggest two conclusions. First, before 16 weeks, infants do not use information about size, shape, and color to make decisions about the *identity* of objects. They use speed of movement instead. Although they can *perceive* size, shape, and color differences (see Chapter 3), they do not use these features in identifying objects. Older infants, in contrast, use all the features to identify an object. Second, by 16 weeks, some infants visually searched for the mannikin by glancing back at the screen when the lion emerged. If active looking is an active search, then this evidence cannot be dismissed as mere "passive expectations." Thus Bower's results could indicate object permanence one or two months earlier than Piaget found. Why hiding a moving object should produce active searching earlier than covering a stationary object is not yet known. As we will see in other sections of this chapter, the particular task selected to demonstrate some cognitive competency affects the age at which the skill seems to emerge.

Despite disagreements about how early one can find signs of object permanence, the sequence of stages which Piaget documented have been reaffirmed in other research. In fact, the same first four stages have also been found in cats (Gruber, Girgus, & Banuazizi, 1971), and all six stages have been found in rhesus monkeys (Wise, Wise, & Zimmermann, 1974). The value of Piaget's contribution lies in the discovery that the child's concept of object permanence undergoes significant changes during the Sensorimotor Period.

It is no coincidence that the last object permanence stage, searching after a hidden displacement, occurs during the last stage of the Sensorimotor Period. To follow a hidden displacement, a child must be able to form a mental representation of the missing object and to anticipate mentally the results of moving the first cover behind the second. The emergence and

TABLE 2-4

RESULTS OF BOWER'S EXPERIMENT ON OBJECT RECOGNITION

Objects	Speed	Age of Babies	
		Under 16 weeks	Over 16 weeks
Cond. 1. Mannikin	Normal	Track moving object	Track moving object
Cond. 2. Mannikin→Lion	Normal	Track moving object	Track moving object and some glances at screen
Cond. 3. Mannikin	Too fast	Refuse to look	Track moving object and look back at screen
Cond. 4. Mannikin→Lion	Too fast	Refuse to look	Track moving object and look back at screen

use of mental representations marks the final development in the Sensorimotor Period and sets the stage for the second major period of cognitive development, the Preoperational Period.

THE PREOPERATIONAL PERIOD

The distinguishing characteristic of the Preoperational child is the development of *symbolic functions*.* Symbolic functioning is the ability to make one thing represent a different thing which is not present. The degree of correspondence between the symbol and its referent can vary from highly concrete to highly abstract. That is, if one uses a toy hammer made of plastic to represent a real metal hammer, the degree of correspondence is highly concrete. A mental picture or image of a hammer is more abstract but may retain some features of the thing represented, such as color and shape. The word made up of the letters *h, a, m, m, e, r* is a highly abstract symbol for the real object since printed letters on a page bear an arbitrary relationship to the metal tool. Piaget argued that the acquisition of symbolic functions enables children to increase their sphere of activity to include past and future events as well as present ones. That is, they can apply their schemes to nonimmediate events. This use of symbolic functions is one of the major distinctions between children in the Preoperational Period and those in the Sensorimotor Period.

SYMBOLIC FUNCTIONS

Symbolic functions have been inferred from four types of activities seen in Preoperational children: search for hidden objects, delayed imitation, symbolic play, and language. Having acquired object permanence, as discussed earlier, Preopera-

* These have also been called *semiotic functions* (Piaget & Inhelder, 1976).

tional children can follow hidden displacements. In order to guide their searching behavior, children must have some sort of mental representation of the hidden object and of the unseen movements of displacement. At younger ages when children would only search if they perceived the object, the perception of the object could be said to guide the search. Now some kind of symbolic function must take over the guidance.

Delayed imitation is, as the name implies, imitation of a behavior some time after it was observed. It is postulated that as children observe a model, they form an internal representation of the modeled behavior. Later the recall of this internal representation controls imitation. Piaget rejected the idea that language was the primary mode of internal representation used in delayed imitation and search for hidden objects because the behaviors displayed are much too complex for the child to describe verbally. He cited the example of his daughter who one day watched a playmate throw a temper tantrum, stamping his feet and howling (Piaget, 1951). The next day Piaget's daughter stood up in her playpen, stamped her feet, and howled just as she had seen the friend do the day before. Her actions had a deliberateness about them which suggested that she was trying out a new behavior, to see what it was like. Without a symbolic means of learning and then recalling the temper tantrum actions, his daughter could not have imitated them a day later.

In symbolic play, the child treats an object as if it were something else. This is readily seen in a child's use of a broomstick as a plane, a doll as a friend, or fingers as guns. One object is made to stand for another in the make-believe world of play.

In the Preoperational Period, language begins to be used symbolically, as children describe activities of the past and understand some references to the future. Their use of words is more conventional, though by no means perfectly adultlike. While the meaning of a word is now stable, the name of an object is seen as such an integral part of the object that changing the name changes the object. Recall the examples in Chapter 1 when Susan thought that renaming her would make her a boy and calling the sun the moon would produce darkness during the day. Besides giving children an efficient way to communicate with others, language has two other uses: it helps children control their own behavior, and it teaches them how to classify and organize their environment. The behavioral-control use is quite striking when children tell themselves what to do or not do. For example, a child can be seen approaching a forbidden object like a hot stove and saying out loud, "No, don't touch," just before withdrawing his outstretched hand. (Even some adults have been known to talk out loud to aid their concentration during problem solving.) The classification use of language enables children to group objects together because of shared labels. For instance, children can guess that a beanbag chair is good for sitting on, even though it does not have four legs, because it has been called a chair. Similarly, any strange offering called "candy" will probably taste good. Preoperational children thus begin to learn about the formal properties of classes.

PROPERTIES OF CLASSES

Classes are, in essence, the categories into which we divide objects. These class divisions can be made along one or more dimensions (or properties) of the objects. For example, one can classify objects according to their shapes, resulting in the classes of square objects, circular objects, and triangular objects. Alternatively, one can classify objects according to their color, resulting in the classes of red things, blue things, green things, and yellow things. One of the properties of classes is that no object may belong to two classes *along the same dimension* simultaneously. Thus a large blue square could, if classified according to shape, belong to the class of square things, but it could not simultaneously belong to a class of circular things or triangular things. It could, however, also belong to another class based on a different dimension such as color. In other words, classes along one dimension are mutually exclusive, but classes along independent dimensions may overlap.

All objects in one class have some common trait. A large blue square and a small red square share squareness. This property, squareness, gives the class its definition and is called its *intension*. Circularity is the intension of a class of circles. Blueness is the intension, the defining characteristic, of the class of blue objects.

A class can also be described by listing its members. This is the *extension* of the class. The extension of a class of flowers could be roses, tulips, pansies, and daisies. Finally, the intension of a class determines its extension. If the intension of a class is "fully enclosed, stationary structures in which people live," the extension of the class must include tents, teepees, houses, cottages, and hotels.

MULTIPLE CLASSIFICATION

During the Preoperational Period, children come to know some of the basic properties of classes. They demonstrate this knowledge by sorting objects according to various classes. One typical task, called the multiple classification problem, is to present children with an array of cards such as pink and yellow, large and small, circles and squares. Children with a firm understanding of class properties can sort the cards into two groups in three separate ways, according to each of the three dimensions, color, size, and shape. Children who do not yet have a full understanding of classes will show any of several common mistakes. The first mistake to appear is not sorting the cards at all. Children might not know what is being asked of them, they might think the task is too difficult, or they simply might not want to cooperate. Frosty the Snowman was the product of one child asked to sort cards (see Figure 2-4a). The second error to

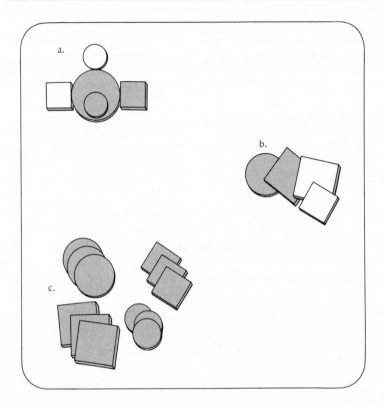

Figure 2-4. Typical sorting errors on a multiple classification task

a. "Frosty the Snowman" was created by a child who ignored the instructions to sort the cards into two piles.
b. This arrangement was created by a child who changed dimensions from pink to square for one of the two piles.
c. This arrangement was created by a child who formed discrete piles of identical objects.

appear is to change the basis of the groupings several times. One boy started out putting all pink things together. He placed two pink circles next to each other, then a pink small square, and then changed the dimension of the sort to shape and put a large yellow square next, followed by a small yellow square

46

(see Figure 2-4b). No single intension, or defining property, regulated his sorting. The third mistake is to sort according to all dimensions simultaneously, ignoring the instructions to form only two piles. One girl formed discrete groups of small yellow circles, small pink circles, large yellow squares, and so forth. Classes for this girl consisted only of identical objects rather than of objects sharing a trait (see Figure 2-4c).

By the end of the Preoperational Period, children demonstrate a basic understanding of classes. When asked to sort cards, they will choose one dimension (e.g., size) to serve as the basis for the sort. All objects having a certain value along the dimension (e.g., the intension, large) will be placed together, while those objects having another value along the same dimension (e.g., the intension, small) will be amassed. Moreover, no objects will be left out of the sort.

Thus we have seen that Preoperational children are more advanced than Sensorimotor children because Preoperational children have mental representations as well as behavioral schemes. These mental representations are inferred from various tasks (search for hidden objects, delayed imitation, make-believe play, and language) which all exemplify symbolic functions. In addition, children in the Preoperational Period show some understanding of classes. Despite these accomplishments, the thinking of Preoperational children is, as the name implies, still not "operational." Preoperational children have mental representations, but Piaget did not believe that their thinking met the second defining characteristic of operations, being "reversible." In addition, Piaget asserted that Preoperational children are unable to focus their attention on different dimensions of a problem simultaneously. For example, the matrix problem shown in Figure 2-5 is a basic classification task extended to two dimensions simultaneously. Preoperational children fail to consider both number and shape and so would find the four-triangle card as acceptable as the three-triangle one, or would find the three-X card as acceptable as the three-triangle one.

47

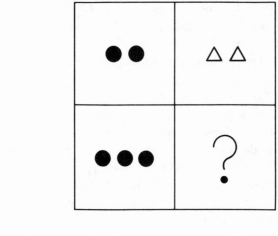

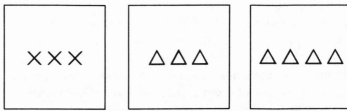

Figure 2-5. A two-dimension matrix problem. Children select one of the three lower cards to replace the question mark.

Piaget called this focusing of attention *centration* when *decentration* is required to reach the solution. Centration shows up in three tasks which Preoperational children fail but Concrete Operational children pass: seriation, class inclusion, and conservation.

SERIATION

The seriation problem asks children to put elements in a series according to one quantifiable dimension. That is, the task is to arrange objects in some order relative to each other. For ex-

48

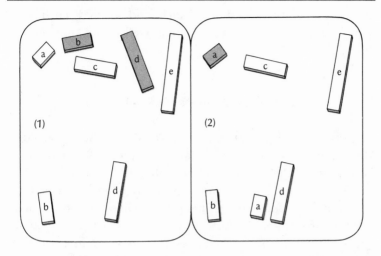

Figure 2-6. Typical error in sorting sticks according to their lengths

1. Two sticks (b and d) are randomly selected from the pile and compared. The shorter is placed to the left.
2. One of the remaining sticks (a) is randomly selected from the pile, compared to one of the previously sorted sticks (d), and placed to the left of (d) since it is shorter. No comparison is made between sticks (a) and (b).

ample, children are given a series of sticks of differing lengths and told to arrange them from shortest to longest. A Preoperational child might proceed as follows: he would take two sticks from the main pile, compare them, and put the shorter of the two on the left. Then he would take another stick from the pile and compare it with only one of the two prior sticks. If it was shorter, he would place it to the left without regard for its length relative to the other original stick (see Figure 2-6). Piaget's explanation for the Preoperational child's behavior is that he can focus on only one aspect of the problem at a time. In the previous example, the child focused on one paired comparison at a time rather than on the total array. An older child might solve the seriation problem by scanning the main pile, removing the shortest stick, scanning the pile again and removing what was then the shortest stick, and so on. Each time he would consider the entire problem as well as the arrangements he was forming.

CLASS INCLUSION (PART—WHOLE)

The class inclusion problem also gives Preoperational children difficulties. In a common variation of the task, children are shown seven blue beads and three white beads, all made out of wood. They are asked if there are more blue beads or more wood beads. Because Preoperational children have trouble focusing their attention both on the parts (white and blue) and on the whole (wood) simultaneously, they err in their judgments. The following is an interchange between a five-year-old boy and an adult.

Adult: Do you see all these beads I have? Some of them are blue and some are white. What do you think the blue beads are made of?
Child: Wood.
Adult: That's right. And what do you think the white ones are made of?
Child: Wood.
Adult: Good. Both the blue beads and the white beads are made of wood. Now I have a question for you. Do you think there are more blue beads or wood beads?
Child: Blue.
Adult: Why?
Child: Because there are more.
Adult: More what?
Child: More blue.
Adult: More blue than what?
Child: More blue than white.
Thinking that the child might have misheard the question, the adult attempted more directive questions.

Adult: But I wanted to know about the wooden beads. Are the white beads made out of wood?
Child: Yes.
Adult: Are the blue beads made out of wood?
Child: Yes.
Adult: So all the beads are made of wood?
Child: Yes.
Adult: So are there more *wood* beads or blue beads?
Child: Blue.

This child was not really being stubborn. He was just unable to make the necessary comparison across the two levels of the hierarchy, that is, across the two subordinate classes based on color (blue and white) and the superordinate class based on material (wood). Piaget maintained that children would have to focus on the two levels of classes at the same time in order to solve the class inclusion problem. Such an ability is characteristic of children in the next major period of development, the Concrete Operational Period.

CONSERVATION

In addition to their difficulty with the class inclusion and seriation problems, Preoperational children do not succeed in conservation tasks. In any of the various conservation tasks, children watch the tester change some features of a display and must decide that some other feature does not change. For example, if two quantities are equal along one dimension, such as number, but appear to be unequal along another dimension, such as length or density, Preoperational children will be mistaken in their judgments concerning numerical equality. The task can be presented as follows: on a table between the child and the tester, a row of five red checkers is placed. Below the five red checkers are placed five black ones, aligned so that each black checker is directly below a red one (see Figure 2-7a).

51

Figure 2-7. A conservation of number task with checkers

a. The starting arrangement from the child's point of view.
b. The experimenter spreads out one row.
c. The ending arrangement from the child's point of view.

The child is asked if the two rows have the same number of checkers, if the red row has more, or if the black row has more. Children above about the age of three will say that the rows have the same number. As the child watches, the black row is spread out (see Figure 2-7b) until the arrangement seen in Figure 2-7c is created. Then the child is again asked if the two rows have the same number of checkers or if one row has more than the other. Preoperational children reply either that the black row has more "because it is longer" or that the red row has more "because they are all bunched up" (more dense). In contrast, children in the Concrete Operational Period will correctly reply that the numbers have stayed the same, recognizing that perceptual changes in length or density have no effect on numerical quantity.

Piaget found that Concrete Operational children tend to offer three types of reasons for their conservation responses. The *counting* justification proves the two rows equal by counting each row. A *one-to-one correspondence* response reflects the idea that for every checker in the red row, there is a corresponding checker in the black row. In the *associativity* response, children state that rearranging the parts does not affect the whole. To put it in the words of an eight-year-old, "All you did was spreaded them out."

To make sure that the idea of conservation of number had generality and was not restricted to rows of checkers, Piaget devised several different conservation of number tasks. In one of them, children are given a pile of ten cars and shown two jars. One jar is tall and thin; the other is short and wide. Children are instructed to take a car in each hand and drop each car in the jar in front of their hands at the same time. After they do this five times, of course, there are five cars in each jar, but the tall thin jar appears to be full while the short wide one is not (see Figure 2-8). Children are then asked if each jar has the same number of cars. Preoperational children who do not conserve number either point to the tall thin jar as having more,

Figure 2-8. A conservation of number task with cars

a. The starting arrangement.
b. The child places a car in each container simultaneously.
c. The ending arrangement.

because it is taller or because it is "all filled up," or they point to the short wide jar, saying it has more because it is "fatter."

In summary, we have seen that Preoperational children use symbolic functions and begin to understand classes, but they fail to compare parts to wholes (in the class inclusion problem), do not order serial quantities well (seriation problem), and do not conserve number. Piaget attributed these limitations in thinking to Preoperational children's inability to decenter their attention and to their lack of true operations.

THE CONCRETE OPERATIONAL PERIOD

In contrast to Preoperational children, Concrete Operational children can solve a variety of tasks. When asked whether there are more blue beads or wood beads, Concrete Operational children can state that the wood beads are a larger class. They can place sticks in a series by length, and they can conserve number.

OPERATIONS

Why do Concrete Operational children succeed when Preoperational children fail? Piaget proposed that Concrete Operational children have new structures, called *operations,* which permit them to transform a mental "action" (i.e., a thought). These transformations can reverse the effect of the original action, compensate for it, or leave it unchanged. *Reversibility by inversion,* for example, involves applying two operations successively such that the original identity is regained. Addition and subtraction are inverse operations. Say that the original state is one item. After adding two to obtain three, we can subtract two and return to the original one.

Reversibility by compensation also involves applying two operations in succession, but this time an equivalent state, rather than the original state, is obtained. Cowan (1978) explained this reversibility with an example about the area of a rectangle. Say that the original area is the length, L, multiplied by the width, W. If the length were doubled, to 2L, and the width were halved, to $\frac{1}{2}$W, the area of the new rectangle, 2L × $\frac{1}{2}$W, would be equivalent to the first rectangle, L × W, but the two rectangles would not be identical in shape. Doubling and halving are compensating operations.

A third operation, called *identity*, can leave a state unchanged. Adding zero, for example, is an identity operation because the quantity does not change even though a mental action has been taken.

Piaget suggested that Concrete Operational children can solve conservation tasks because of these operations. Consider again the conservation of number task with rows of checkers. A Concrete Operational child might focus on the tester's action of spreading out one row. The child can mentally picture the opposite action, compressing the row, to get back to the original length and therefore conclude that the number of checkers has not changed. A child using this inversion operation might justify his conservation response by saying, "All you did was spread them out and you could put them back together again." It is also possible to solve the conservation problem using the compensation operation. Concrete Operational children see that one row has increased in length but decreased in density. Since length and density are reciprocal features, a change in one compensates for a change in the other, resulting in no net change for the display. Using the identity operation, Concrete Operational children see that nothing (zero) has been added or subtracted, so number has not changed. In the Preoperational Period, children tend to focus on the beginning state (the apparent equality of the two rows) and the end state (with its perceptual inequality in length) and ignore the intervening activity, or they focus on the initial action (spreading out) but cannot reverse their thinking to consider the potential inverse compressing action.

Conservation tasks

As with each new cognitive skill children acquire, it takes practice to apply that skill correctly and efficiently to new problems. Concrete Operational children, having mastered conservation of number, must also master conservation of other dimensions such as liquid quantity, mass, and length. The liquid quantity conservation task is very similar to the conservation of number task. Children are shown two identical beakers filled with identical amounts of colored water. They first judge the beakers to have equal amounts. Then, as they watch, the liquid is poured from one of the original beakers into a taller, thinner beaker. The children are next asked to compare the newly filled beaker with the other original one (see Figure 2-9a). An alternative form of the liquid quantity task involves pouring the liquid from one beaker into five smaller containers. The nonconserving child will either indicate that the original beaker has more because it is taller or that the five smaller containers have more because there are five of them. The classical problem for conservation of mass presents children with two identical clay balls. Then one is either rolled into a sausage or flattened like a pancake (see Figure 2-9b). To conserve, children must recognize that changes in shape do not indicate changes in mass. In the conservation of length task, children must judge that length stays the same even though position has shifted (see Figure 2-9c). In all, approximately ten different conservation tasks test for the recognition of preservation of equality in the face of compelling changes in spatial arrangement.

Although Piaget did not suggest that children ought to conserve colors, Milne (1961b) captured the spirit of the conservation problem in an episode from *Winnie-the-Pooh*. Piglet had a large red balloon, "one of those big coloured things you blow up," to give to Eeyore as a birthday present. On the way, he fell, and it burst.

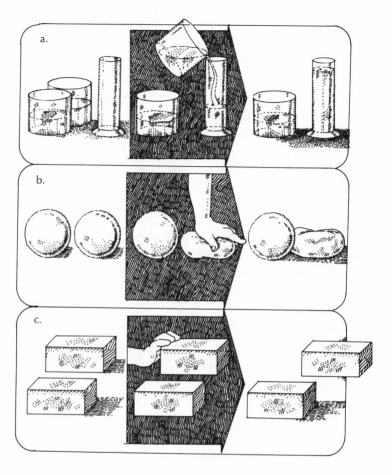

Figure 2-9. Tasks testing for conservation of liquid, mass, and length

a. Conservation of liquid.
b. Conservation of mass.
c. Conservation of length.

There was a very long silence.

"My balloon?" said Eeyore at last.

Piglet nodded.

"My birthday balloon?"

"Yes, Eeyore," said Piglet sniffling a little. "Here it is. With—with many happy returns of the day." And he gave Eeyore the small piece of damp rag.

"Is this it?" said Eeyore, a little surprised.

Piglet nodded.

"My present?"

Piglet nodded again.

"The balloon?"

"Yes."

"Thank you, Piglet," said Eeyore. "You don't mind my asking," he went on, "but what colour was this balloon when it—when it *was* a balloon?" [Pp. 86-87]

RESEARCH ISSUES

As we did for the Sensorimotor Period, we have presented the supposed underlying structures (symbolic functions and operations) and specific abilities (e.g., language and conservation) of the Preoperational and Concrete Operational periods. Piaget's descriptions and explanations of the Preoperational and Concrete Operational periods have provoked considerable research, only a small portion of which can be presented here. The first wave of research was aimed primarily at confirming (or disconfirming) Piaget's descriptions of the various stages and periods of development. It is probable that so much energy was spent in replicative research because Piaget's early methodology appeared weak in contrast to traditional American research. In brief, Piaget's approach was a flexible questioning procedure, permitting the tester to rephrase questions that the child did not understand and encouraging the child to expand brief verbal responses. The latter in particular is a delicate procedure because the tester must be careful not to suggest answers to the child. At the same time, the tester wants to be sure that the child offers his full thoughts and best reasons. Piaget was well aware of this problem, but he gave no indication of controlling for it experimentally. Also, in the books which first were translated into English, it appeared that Piaget based his conclusions on small samples of children and rarely subjected his results to statistical analysis.* One would have thought that a red flag had been waved in the face of a scientific bull. Moreover, Piaget's report of the Preoperational child's failure to solve conservation, seriation, and class inclusion problems was quite startling. This alone would have warranted replication research.

The evidence from the replicative studies is quite impressive. The response patterns Piaget noted for Genevan children were also found for other European, North and South American, African, and Asian children (Dasen, 1977). Testing with deaf, blind, and retarded children revealed the same developmental sequences as for normal children, although the rates of development are often slower for the handicapped, and the retarded may never progress very far through the stages (Brekke, Williams, & Tait, 1974; Gruen & Vore, 1972; Millar, 1976; Youniss, 1974).

Researchers then turned to other questions. One recurring question is: Do Preoperational children fail a task because they lack operations, as Piaget maintained, or because the task requires other skills or knowledge which Preoperational children lack? Note that this is the same type of question asked about Sensorimotor children's performance on the object permanence task. Can Preoperational children pass the various Concrete Operational tasks at an earlier age than Piaget suggested if changes are made in the specific task or if training is provided to make up for the specific skill deficit? The answer is clearly "yes."

* Piaget's later works rely less on children's verbal explanations, are based on larger samples, and contain comparisons between experimental and control groups when necessary.

Class inclusion studies

Gelman (1978) has reviewed the research on the class inclusion problem and has concluded that at least six factors can influence preschool children's success on it. We shall examine one factor to illustrate the general form of the argument. When we construct categories or groups of related objects, a classification can be made by *classes* or by *collections*. Membership in a class can be determined by matching an object's properties to the intension of the class. If the superordinate class of wood beads is defined by "round wooden objects with one centered hole" and a subordinate class member (a specific blue wood bead) fits that definition, then the subordinate object is also a member of the superordinate class. Inspection of the one object is sufficient to determine its membership in the class. Piaget described the stimulus materials in his class inclusion task with class nouns. To define a collection, however, the relationship between objects is important. A forest, for instance, is a collection of trees. Inspection of a single tree's attributes is not sufficient for deciding that the tree is a member of the forest. Similarly, a family is a (superordinate) collection composed of the subordinate classes parents and children. Children alone are not a family.

In a comparison of the two types of categories, the class inclusion test can be given using exactly the same stimulus materials but describing them either with class nouns or collection nouns. For example, children can be shown six oak trees and two pine trees and asked to compare the number of pine trees to all the trees (class noun) or the number of pine trees to the number of trees in the forest (collection noun). Or the children can be shown red and blue blocks and asked to compare the blue blocks to the blocks (class noun) or the blue blocks to the pile of blocks (collection noun). Kindergarten and first grade children who fail Piaget's standard class inclusion test succeed when collections are used (Markman & Siebert, 1976; Trabasso, Isen, Dolecki, McLanahan, Riley, & Tucker, 1978). "The major factor promoting successful performance seems to be unambiguous reference to the class as a whole and avoidance of procedures stressing distinctive features of the subordinate class" (Trabasso et al., 1978, p. 177). Piaget's original task with true classes seems to demand a higher degree of sophistication or knowledge than the modified versions of the task. The conclusion to be drawn is that Preoperational children can make subordinate-superordinate comparisons in some cases (with collections) before other cases (with true classes).

Conservation studies

For the conservation problem, researchers have followed the same strategy. Variations in the task have been tried, such as changing the specific stimulus materials, the words used in the questions to the children, and the children's responses (e.g., they can be asked merely to judge the stimuli as the same or different or to give a verbal explanation of their judgment). The bulk of the research, however, has used a training paradigm to see if children fail conservation tests because they are deficient in a particular skill unrelated to operations. The logic of using training studies is that some skill or knowledge, absent in nonconserving children, is provided by training. If after training children now pass the conservation tests, then one might conclude that Piaget's original tests were unnecessarily difficult or confusing. Just such a proposal was offered by Gelman (1969).

She hypothesized that young children might conserve if their attention were not so attracted to highly salient but irrelevant perceptual cues such as height, width, size, shape, and color. In the conservation of liquid quantity task, children are faced with two identical beakers containing equal amounts of water. From the child's point of view, quantity is a multidimensional concept, and decisions might be reached on the basis of any one of several salient dimensions: height, width, or shape of the beaker, water level, or actual amount. From the experimenter's point of view, only the last, actual amount, is a relevant dimension. Often equality of amount coincides with equality on the other dimensions, so the child must learn which of the dimensions to attend to. Furthermore, when the liquid is poured into the new beaker, all of the dimensions *except* actual amount are changed. It is well known that changing a dimension is one way to attract attention to it. It is likely, therefore, that younger children will attend to one of the irrelevant dimensions. If their attention is misdirected, then that will mask any attempts to find out whether they have logical operations such as addition, subtraction, or compensation.

Gelman trained children to attend and respond to actual amount and to ignore the other, irrelevant information. The subjects were children in kindergarten, about five years old. These children were chosen because they had failed to conserve on each of four conservation tasks (mass, liquid quantity, number, and length) in a pretest (a test before training). Figure 2-10 shows the tasks used in the pretest.

Training took place on two consecutive days, with eight sets of problems on length and eight sets on number each day. In each training trial, the child was confronted with three stimuli, two of which were identical and one which was different. For example, two sticks might be 6 inches long and one 10 inches. On half the trials, the child was asked to point to two things that were the same; on the other half, he was asked to point to two things that were different. The trials were arranged so as to reduce progressively the number of irrelevant cues which the child could use to make a correct response. On the first trial of a set, all cues indicated the correct response. For example, in the length problem, the two identical sticks would be placed horizontally, in parallel, with ends aligned, while the third stick might be slightly vertical with neither end aligned to the other two sticks. On trials 2-5, various placements of the sticks would make the child choose incorrectly if he used some of the irrelevant cues. On the sixth trial, none

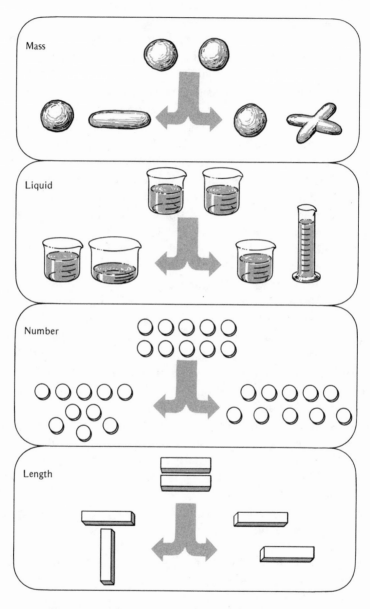

Figure 2-10. Conservation tasks used for the pretest in Gelman's experiment

of the irrelevant cues suggested a correct response. For example, the three sticks would be spatially separated, nonparallel, with no ends aligned. If the child answered correctly, it could only be on the basis of the relevant cue, actual length.* Figure 2-11 gives an example of the six trials per set for a length task.

Two groups of children, trained individually, received identical experiences with the training stimuli with one exception: whether or not they received feedback. In the experimental group, if subjects chose correctly, they were told they were correct and were given a small trinket; if they chose incorrectly, they were told they were wrong, and the next problem was presented. Subjects in the control group did not receive feedback after a trial. At the end of each session, they were told that they had played well.

All children were given two more conservation tests, one test on the day following training (the immediate posttest) and one test two to three weeks later (the delayed posttest). These posttests were comparable to the pretest and did not involve feedback. Table 2-5 shows the percentages of correct responses by the two groups of children for the four conservation tasks. On the length and number tasks, for which there had been explicit training, the experimental group got nearly perfect scores, whereas the control group got only one-quarter to one-third correct. Thus, conservation can be taught to children earlier than it typically occurs. Gelman's study also clearly showed that the experimental group improved on other conservation tasks as well (mass and liquid), even though these had not been trained.

Gelman concluded that two factors were important for training. First, children need an opportunity to work with many different arrangements of materials. This is what the control group did, and some specific learning did occur. The second important factor is feedback which indicates to the children which definition of quantity they should use. In other words,

---

* This same procedure, called *fading,* can be used to teach many different kinds of discriminations between stimuli.

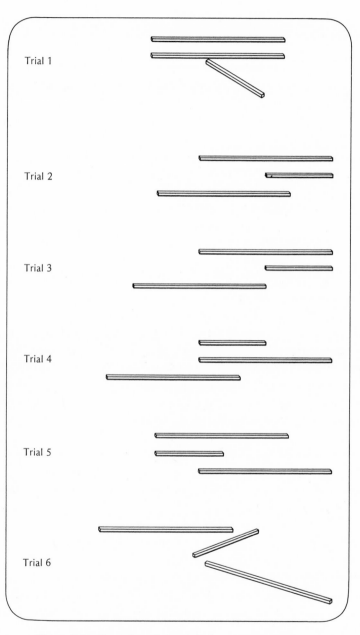

Figure 2-11. Examples of six trials for training conservation of length in Gelman's experiment

66

TABLE 2-5

AVERAGE PERCENTAGE OF CORRECT RESPONSES IN GELMAN'S EXPERIMENT

| | *Immediate Posttest* | | | |
	Length	*Number*	*Mass*	*Liquid*
Feedback during Training (Experimental Group)	95%	96%	58%	55%
No Feedback during Training (Control Group)	27%	21%	9%	4%

| | *Delayed Posttest* | | | |
	Length	*Number*	*Mass*	*Liquid*
Feedback during Training (Experimental Group)	90%	96%	65%	71%
No Feedback during Training (Control Group)	31%	29%	14%	3%

they need information about which dimension is relevant. With both feedback and opportunity, the experimental group learned a considerable amount about conservation tasks which were like the tasks on which they had trained (length and number), and they transferred this knowledge to two other conservation tasks (mass and liquid quantity).

Gelman's experiment demonstrated that some children do not give correct conservation responses because their attention is drawn to irrelevant aspects of the task. As soon as their attention is redirected, through training, they quickly solve the conservation problems. Does this mean that the children already had mental operations? That question cannot be answered because mental operations are not directly observable; like any hypothetical construct, they can only be inferred from performance. Was an attentional deficit the only factor impeding the expression of conservation? Probably not, because many other kinds of training studies have been successful, including teaching a generalized rule to express the conservation principle, providing an opportunity to watch peer models who conserve, and staging debates between conserving and nonconserving peers (see Brainerd, 1977, and Brainerd & Allen, 1971, for reviews of the training literature). The training results suggest that many different factors play a role in the development of conservation in children and/or that children can achieve an understanding of conservation by a variety of paths.

It is not particularly damaging to Piaget's theory to have children develop conservation earlier than he noted, as long as the sequence of development remains constant. Piaget's writings do mention typical ages when he observed the various conservation and classification tasks to be solved. Only those who misinterpret Piaget's position to be strictly maturational would insist that hard-and-fast age ranges should be established. Piaget himself did not take that position. He was interested in describing the sequences and processes of cognitive development, not in establishing norms of development or in rank-ordering children as the intelligence-testing movement has done. It was the characteristic errors children made that guided Piaget's research. Age was of secondary importance, serving only as a general guideline to the probable level of development of a child.

As Beilin (1981) remarked, it is ironic that critics of Piaget fault him for underestimating young children's knowledge when he was responsible for focusing researchers' attention on the cognitive accomplishments (and deficits) of young children. Those accomplishments in the Concrete Operational Period, in solving conservation, seriation, and class inclusion problems, are outstanding in comparison to Preoperational children's skills. Nevertheless, Concrete Operational children are limited to applying their mental operations to problems which they have personally experienced or which have some physical manifestation (such as sticks to move or liquid to pour). They do not readily solve purely verbal, abstract, hypothetical problems, and they tend to reject hypotheses which violate known

68

facts. For example, one can ask the following question: If all dogs were green, and I had a dog, would it be green too? Concrete Operational children will balk at such a question, rejecting the initial supposition by stating that dogs cannot be green. Formal Operational children, in the last major period of cognitive development, are more likely to solve the problem.

THE FORMAL OPERATIONAL PERIOD

Children (or adolescents) in the Formal Operational Period can construct contrary-to-fact hypotheses ("if dogs were green") and reason about them. Premises are taken as "givens" regardless of whether or not they are true in experience. Formal Operational thinkers can separate the process of reasoning from the specific content, thus enabling them to solve many different types of syllogism problems. Moreover, the adolescent's own beliefs and thoughts become valid objects of inquiry. Thinking becomes just as much a subject to be reasoned about as other, more concrete problems. Mussen, Conger, Kagan, and Geiwitz (1979) reported an adolescent who said, "I was thinking about my future and then I began to think about why I was thinking about my future and then I began to think about why I was thinking about why I was thinking about my future" (p. 177).

Formal Operations are like Concrete Operations in that both are mental representations that can be reversed. Formal Operations are more advanced, though, because the representations can apply to potential as well as to actual actions, and the various reversibilities can be coordinated to permit a higher-order thinking. This coordination is derived from the basic organization principle in which isolated operations become clustered. Formal Operational thinking thus has three distinguishing characteristics: (a) generating multiple hypotheses, (b) systematic checking of all possible solutions, and (c) operating on operations.

69

GENERATING HYPOTHESES

Because potential hypotheses are as valid as experience-based hypotheses, Formal Operational thinkers are likely to believe that a problem might have more than one solution. Concrete Operational children may generate one solution, and if it is at all reasonable, they will stop. Formal Operational children will generate multiple alternatives. For example, if children are asked why a man was lying in the middle of the sidewalk, the Concrete Operational child might propose that the man was drunk and fell down. The Formal Operational child will consider that the man may be drunk, or had a heart attack, or was hit on the head by a robber, or is playing a joke.

SYSTEMATIC SOLUTION TESTING

The more possibilities that exist, the more children need a systematic rather than a trial-and-error approach to testing their hypotheses. The second characteristic of Formal Operational thinking is, thus, the systematic checking of all possible alternative solutions to a problem. To demonstrate this in an experimental setting, a type of chemistry problem can be presented (Inhelder & Piaget, 1958). Children are shown five colorless, odorless liquids in test tubes and are asked to discover what combination of the five will produce a yellow mixture. Concrete Operational children attempt to solve this problem through trial and error. They merely start to combine the liquids. But without an overall plan of action, one which is systematic, they soon become hopelessly lost—not remembering which combinations they have already tried and which remain to be tried. Formal Operational children proceed in a more systematic fashion, often first mixing the test tubes two at a time in a logical order (first and second, first and third, first and fourth, first and fifth, second and third, and so on). Then they try combinations of three at a time, four at a time, and all five. Moreover, if Concrete Operational children stumble upon a combination which works, they will be satisfied that the problem is solved without considering that one of the liquids may be inert and hence unnecessary. Formal Operational children will continue testing even after one solution is found, isolating the relevant factors and discarding the irrelevant.

OPERATING ON OPERATIONS

Formal Operational thinkers appreciate the fact that hypothetical problems can be solved by applying the same rules as would be applied to concrete problems. In addition, they realize that the same systematic approach of isolating and testing factors can be used over a variety of contents. Therefore, they begin to generate rules which are abstract enough to cover many specific instances. Thus, the third characteristic of Formal Operations is the organization of single operations into higher-order ones. This has also been referred to as "operating on operations" in contrast to operating directly on objects as Concrete Operational children do. One way to illustrate this characteristic comes from mathematics. Given a problem such as "What number plus 20 equals twice itself?" Concrete Operational children will use the operations of addition and multiplication on various numbers in a trial-and-error way. They might, for instance, think of the number 5, insert it in the equations $5 + 20 = 25$ and $2 \times 5 = 10$, and decide that 5 was incorrect. They would continue to try other numbers in this manner until they found the correct one. Formal Operational children will develop an abstract rule, $X + 20 = 2X$, and solve the formula algebraically, $20 = 2X - X = X$. The separate operations of addition and multiplication would be combined into the higher-order algebraic operation.

One of the consequences of the ability to combine operations is that many different aspects of a problem can be dealt with simultaneously. Concrete Operational children think sequentially, considering only one aspect of a problem at a time. When several aspects can be considered together, in the Formal Operational Period, the logic of a set of beliefs can be examined.*

Adolescents are likely to consider their own beliefs about religion, politics, morality, and education in terms of logical consistency. Kagan (1971) provided the following example:

(1). God loves man.
(2). The world contains many unhappy people.
(3). If God loved man, he would not make so many people unhappy. [P. 1001]

While adolescents might resolve the inconsistency among these three statements by supposing that man is made unhappy for some hidden motive, current American adolescents tend to resolve the contradictions by denying the existence of God (often to the distress of their parents). Once one belief is challenged, all other beliefs become suspect and fair game for further attack. Adolescents are likely to challenge the adults around them to explain the inconsistencies they have suddenly found in a variety of previously accepted ideas. One can readily see where the image of an argumentative and rebellious youth comes from.

The pendulum problem

The three characteristics of Formal Operational thinking described above should be applicable to a variety of reasoning tasks. Many of Piaget's examples come from physics and mathe-

---

* Just because a person has the capacity to examine his own sets of beliefs does not mean that he always does so. This might explain why one's own children commit only harmless pranks while the neighborhood urchins engage in malicious mischief.

matics problems in inductive reasoning, in which specific facts are given and a general law must be induced. One example is referred to as the pendulum problem (Inhelder & Piaget, 1958). The setup involves a wooden stand, various lengths of string, and several weights. The experimenter suspends, one at a time, different string and weight combinations from the stand and starts the pendulum swinging by pulling the weight back to different heights and releasing it with different forces. Thus specific instances are given in the problem. Once children understand that sometimes the pendulum swings faster than at other times, they are asked to generate the law governing pendulum swinging. The correct response is that the length of the string determines the speed (short strings swing faster). Concrete Operational children generally try several combinations of weights and string lengths in a random, unsystematic fashion without proposing or testing hypotheses. Formal Operational children, on the other hand, exhibit the three characteristics of thinking outlined above. First they isolate the factors which could affect the pendulum's speed, generating multiple hypotheses about the events they have witnessed. Although the solution happens to depend on just one factor (length of string), children must eliminate the possibility that two or more factors in combination affect the pendulum's speed. Thus they must deal with multiple dimensions simultaneously. Finally, the presence of so many factors and combinations of factors requires children to systematically explore all possible solutions, not just try a few unsystematically.

The Formal Operational Period is the culmination of intellectual development for Piaget. By the time children are 15 or so, they should have all the cognitive structures necessary to do the most intellectually challenging tasks. After Formal Operations are achieved, Piaget claimed that no new kinds of structures develop; intellectual progress after adolescence consists mainly of the accumulation of new contents, or topics, for thought.

RESEARCH ISSUES

A number of researchers have challenged the accuracy of Piaget's description of the Formal Operational Period, especially children's performance on syllogism problems. In one form of the problem, valid implication reasoning, subjects must draw a correct conclusion from two premises. For example:

Premise 1: If Judy is a lawyer, then she is smart.
Premise 2: Judy is a lawyer.
Conclusion: Judy is smart.

Children who are nominally in the Concrete Operational Period (first to third grade) pass between 77 percent and 90 percent of these problems (Ennis, 1971; Kodroff & Roberge, 1975; Paris, 1973). In another syllogism form, invalid implication reasoning, subjects must avoid drawing an incorrect conclusion. For example:

Premise 1: If Judy is a lawyer, then she is smart.
Premise 2: Judy is not a lawyer.
Incorrect conclusion: Judy is not smart.
Correct conclusion: Judy may or may not be smart; one cannot say.

Adolescents, college students, and college-educated adults pass only 5 percent to 25 percent of these problems, roughly the same percentage as Concrete Operational children pass (Brainerd, 1978). Broad samples of adolescents and adults fare just as poorly on Piaget's other Formal Operational tasks (Neimark, 1975).

As the lack of empirical support became evident in the literature, Piaget (1972) advanced a number of explanations for the performance failures without really changing his conception of the underlying structures of Formal Operations. The explanation Piaget favored suggested that Formal Operational skills are more dependent on the content used in the tests than is the case in tests used for earlier stages. Extra task demands, such as knowledge of particular scientific principles, and lack of motivation or interest in the problem could produce the apparent lack of Formal Operations in adolescents and adults. Critics have argued instead that Piaget's description of the fourth period is just not appropriate for the general adult population, and they have called for new conceptualizations of mature intellectual functioning (e.g., Arlin, 1975; Greenfield, 1976; Riegel, 1973). In addition, some critics have challenged the very foundation of Piaget's theory—the idea that development proceeds by stages.

STAGE THEORY

Piaget claimed that his theory of cognitive development is a stage theory. "We have seen that there exist structures which belong only to the subject [the child], that they are built, and that this is a step-by-step process. We must therefore conclude there exist stages of development" (Piaget, 1970, p. 710). What does it mean to call a theory a stage theory? At a descriptive level, it summarizes children's capabilities at certain ages. When children at one age are regularly capable of some behaviors but not others (such as object permanence but not conservation at two years), then we can say that they are in one stage of development rather than another (Sensorimotor, not Concrete Operational). This is probably more accurate for describing cognitive development than referring to the children's chronological age, but it is of limited value because it is merely descriptive. A descriptive theory does not explain why certain behaviors change in a systematic way with age.

Stage theory gains explanatory power (and simultaneously becomes more controversial) when it proposes reasons why certain behaviors are grouped together and why those groups develop in a certain order. Piaget argued that certain behaviors constitute a stage because they share a common underlying structure, and that they develop in a particular order because the more advanced behaviors depend, in a logical way, on the more primitive ones. These requirements, of a common underlying cognitive structure and of an invariant sequence, are two of five criteria Piaget (1960) proposed to justify the identification of stages during development. Other requirements have been proposed by other researchers (e.g., Flavell, 1977) with some consensus that the following four requirements are reasonable (though not necessarily provable scientifically): (a) concurrent appearance of skills in one stage produced by a cognitive structure; (b) invariant sequence of stages; (c) qualitative differences between stages; and (d) abrupt rather than gradual transitions between stages.

Cognitive structures (Concurrence)

It seems reasonable to group behaviors together in one stage if they all depend on the same underlying cognitive structure. For example, to say that a child is in the Concrete Operational Period implies that he should be able to solve various concrete problems (e.g., conservation and class inclusion) which depend on operational thinking. Similarly, the behaviors of the Sensorimotor Period are grouped together because they use sensory and motor schemes rather than mental schemes. The same should be true for the smaller stages within the major periods; they each should have a common underlying skill which justifies grouping the various observed behaviors into the same stage. For example, if children are in the fourth stage of the Sensorimotor Period, they ought to be able to obtain any goal if the coordination of two circular reactions will solve the problem. Thus cognitive skills controlled by a common structure ought to appear concurrently rather than sequentially.

But do they? Empirical evidence for the various conservation tasks reveals consistent *decalages*—Piaget's term for the sequential appearance of logically related skills which ought to have appeared simultaneously. Conservation of number develops before conservation of liquid and solid quantity (Brainerd & Brainerd, 1972; Gruen & Vore, 1972), and quantity develops before weight, which in turn develops before volume (Uzgiris, 1964). As we have seen above, the various Formal Operational tasks are also solved (or not solved) across a wide age range, which raises questions about the validity of Piaget's stage theory. The difficulty in accepting the critics' conclusion (or in accepting Piaget's theory) is one of measurement (Brainerd, 1978; Flavell, 1977).

No test is ever a pure measure of just one skill or just one underlying operation. When a test demands extra skills or knowledge, children may fail the test because they do not have that extra skill even though they may have the skill that defines the stage. In part, this measurement problem was the basis for Bower's research on object permanence and Gelman's study on conservation. Piaget referred to these extra demands to rationalize the lack of success on Formal Operational tasks by adults.

The *decalages* in conservation might also be explained by identifying components of the test which facilitate or impede solution. For example, Siegler (1981) hypothesized that conservation of number, with a small set of items in the array, develops first because children can count to verify the results of the transformation the experimenter makes. No such verification is possible when balls of clay or beakers of liquid are transformed, so conservation is slower to develop in these areas. While all of these post-hoc justifications seem reasonable, they clearly indicate the difficulty in requiring evidence of concurrent development within a stage or in finding a common cognitive structure.

Invariant sequence

A second requirement for a stage theory is to have an invariant sequence of development between stages. The very connotation of stages is a progression from less mature to more mature behaviors. If behaviors developed in a random order for each individual, a stage description would seem inappropriate. To explain the sequence, a stage theory should show why that particular sequence was the only possible one, for example, by showing that the cognitive skills of the first behaviors are prerequisites for the later behaviors. Piaget's theory aimed to do this by showing the logical necessity of the lower stage for a higher one. A child must have mental representations (in the Preoperational Period) before the representations can be reversed (in the Concrete Operational Period). They must be able to classify objects (on the multiple classification task) before they can compare two classifications (on the class inclusion test). Or, for the stages within the Sensorimotor Period, children must have individual circular reactions (stage 3) before they can coordinate those reactions to obtain a goal (stage 4).

Qualitative differences

The existence of a fixed behavioral sequence is necessary to a stage theory, but it is not sufficient for defining a stage theory because fixed sequences occur on continuous scales as well as on discontinuous (stage) ones. Therefore, a third requirement for a stage theory is that the behaviors defining a stage be qualitatively different from other stages, that is, different in kind, not just in amount (or quantity). Piaget thought that applying circular reactions to objects was qualitatively different from applying circular reactions to the infant's own body, thus warranting the designation of separate stages. The mental schemes of the Preoperational Period are qualitatively different from the behavioral schemes of the Sensorimotor Period. But what one researcher calls a qualitative change, another might reinterpret as a quantitative one.

McLaughlin (1963), for instance, claimed that the changes Piaget saw as qualitative are really quantitative changes occurring on two dimensions at the same time. These two dimensions are the abstractness in the objects of thought and the number of concepts that can be used simultaneously. As Flavell (1977) pointed out, "What looks like a qualitative change at one level of analysis may not at another" (p. 246). The closer one gets to day-to-day behavior, the more quantitative a change will look. Piaget's theory, by virtue of being more general and abstract, sees more qualitative changes.

Abrupt transitions

Finally, a stage might be identified if many behaviors change in a short period, thus forming a natural grouping. If behavioral change is slow, it becomes difficult to form meaningful separations between behaviors. Flavell (1977) commented that behavioral change will look quite abrupt if a researcher defines the onset of the stage by the first appearance of a behavior, while the change will seem very gradual if the child is required to use some behavior with ease in many different situations. Thus the definition of the onset of a stage will dictate the abruptness of the transition.

The four requirements for defining a stage theory are difficult for any theory to fulfill, and Piaget's stage theory is no exception. Whether or not cognitive development proceeds in stages remains one of the most controversial questions in developmental psychology. To get a better understanding of a nonstage theory of cognitive development, we turn our attention in the next chapter to the process approach. First, however, let us summarize the main points of Piaget's theory.

SUMMARY

Piaget proposed the functional constructs of organization and adaptation (assimilation, accommodation, and equilibration) to account for the basic ways in which children build their own cognitive structures. Since at every age, children organize and adapt to their environments, these functional aspects remain invariant over age. Although the particular balance between the functions depends on several factors (including maturation and experience), the functions themselves are viewed as unchanging. What does change with age in Piaget's system are the cognitive structures, that is, the systems of knowledge created by children's physical and mental actions on their world. Piaget identified four stages in the construction of these structures: the Sensorimotor Period, in which children have only behavioral schemes; the Preoperational Period, in which mental representations are formed; the Concrete Operational Period, in which mental representations can be reversed, yielding operations; and the Formal Operational Period, in which operations can be coordinated and applied to abstract reasoning problems, thus permitting contrary-to-fact hypothesis generation and systematic hypothesis testing.

The results of extensive research efforts have been mixed. The widespread replication of children's performance on the tasks of Piaget's first three periods is balanced by the equally widespread failure to substantiate the Formal Operational Period. Praise for the novelty and cleverness of Piaget's tasks (such as conservation and class inclusion) is balanced by criticism that the tasks are unnecessarily complicated with distracting elements. This results in a serious underestimation of children's abilities and in a more stagelike characterization of developmental change than may be warranted. The training studies and other research call into question Piaget's model of operations as an overarching general structure guiding children's problem-solving efforts. Nevertheless, the impact of Piaget's theory is without question. As Gelman (1979) summarized it, "Piaget has given us some fundamental theoretical insights as well as some fundamental phenomena" (p. 3).

3

A PROCESS APPROACH
TO COGNITIVE DEVELOPMENT

The domain of interest for cognitive psychologists is the acquisition, organization, and processing of information so that accurate (i.e., valid or useful) knowledge is achieved and can be used to solve a problem or make a decision. The preceding chapter traced Piaget's conceptualization of cognitive development. This chapter presents a different system for organizing and describing the course of cognitive development, a system arising from the American experimental research tradition in child psychology. This approach draws on experimental evidence accumulated by many investigators, working on a variety of topics, and sometimes using rats, pigeons, and even adults, rather than children, for experimental subjects. Research is, therefore, a more integral aspect of this approach. Since no one person has developed a theory that encompasses the entire experimental literature, we shall refer to this body of information as the *process approach*. The discussion is not about a single process, however, but actually covers three processes, each of which contributes to the activity we call thinking: *perception, memory,* and the *generation and testing of hypotheses*. Perception deals with the translation of raw sensory data into a form more useful for the cognitive system.

Memory concerns the storage and retrieval of information. The generation and testing of hypotheses involves proposing and evaluating possible solutions to some problem.

Generally speaking, the process approach does not utilize stages, as Piaget did, but rather views the three processes as occurring at all ages to a greater or lesser extent. For example, the number of items which children can remember and their techniques for trying to put items explicitly into storage might change with age, but at any age, memory is a process for storing and retrieving information. Similarly, the other two processes of thought are common to people of all ages, but their specific levels of functioning change, so that problem solving appears to differ with age.

The three processes have to process something. Memory has to store some event; perception has to perceive some item. These items or events are the elements of thought, the cognitive units on which the processes of thought operate. We will describe four cognitive units (schemata, symbols, concepts, and rules) before we consider the three processes which use these units.

UNITS OF THOUGHT

SCHEMATA

The first unit of thought, called a *schema* (plural: schemata), is a mental representation of events in the world. Note that this is different from *scheme* (plural: schemes), which was Piaget's term for an organized pattern of behavior.* It is intuitively obvious that adults and older children have mental representations. In response to a simple question, older, verbal children (and many adults) will produce a voluminous catalog of their knowledge. But we need to ask whether younger infants can

---

* The similarity of these terms is unfortunate but cannot be avoided. I remember schema by thinking that the last two letters start the word *map*, which is a type of representation of the world.

also represent events mentally. The answer is not easy to obtain because the behavioral repertoire of young infants is quite limited. The preverbal infant rarely responds to our questions, so we must infer what infants know by measuring phenomena we believe are determined by their knowledge. Jeffrey (1968) and McCall (1971) have suggested that a phenomenon called *habituation* could be used as an indication that infants have schemata.

In experiments using habituation, infants are presented with a stimulus, say a black circle on a white background. Infants attend visually to (look at) this stimulus. Some physiological changes also indicate that they are attending, such as changes in heart rates and breathing rates. Each time we repeat the presentation of the stimulus, however, infants spend less and less time looking at the circle. Changes in their breathing and heart rates also decrease as the stimulus is repetitively presented. The stimulus has become familiar to the infants and, in technical terminology, we would say that they have habituated to it. In nontechnical terms, we would say that they are bored. The decline in interest is not just due to general fatigue because presenting a new stimulus, say a red square on a blue background, will evoke the same magnitude of response that infants showed to the original black circle. The renewed attention is called *dishabituation*. We infer that infants have some idea of the black circle, some way of mentally representing that event, for otherwise they could not remember from one presentation to the next what they had just seen. They would not show habituation to the black circle and dishabituation to the red square unless they could represent at least the most distinctive or important elements of the two events. The term *schema* refers to this elementary memory.

The habituation experiment has been used to test systematically for which features of a stimulus are critical to an individual's schemata. The general procedure is to allow a person to habituate to a stimulus. Then one feature is changed, such as size or color or shape, and the experimenter sees if that change results in dishabituation. If it does, then that feature would be part of the person's schemata. In a typical experiment for this, Cohen, Gelber, and Lazar (1971) presented four-month-old infants with pictures of red circles for 16 trials. Then they presented 2 trials each with a new color but the old shape (green circles), a new shape but the old color (red triangles), and a new color with a new shape (green triangles). Dishabituation was greatest when both shape and color were changed, but it was also produced by the new color alone and by the new shape alone. From a later experiment, Cohen (1973) concluded that infants stored individual stimulus components (colors and shapes) rather than specific color-shape combinations because infants who had habituated to red circles and green triangles did not dishabituate to red triangles and green circles.

Cohen and Gelber (1975) reviewed research using the habituation paradigm described above and also using a preference test, in which the amount of time infants look at one or another stimulus is recorded. They concluded that "as early as 6 or 8 weeks of age a long-term exposure will produce recognition 24 hr later, and as early as 4 or 5 months of age an exposure as short as 1 or 2 min will lead to recognition 2 weeks later" (p. 368). This recognition must be controlled by schemata of the remembered stimuli. As we saw in Chapter 2, Bower's research on object permanence also addressed the issue of infant schemata. Recall that when 20-day-old infants saw a ball reappear after it had been hidden by a screen for 1½ seconds, they were not surprised, but if it had been hidden for 15 seconds, they were surprised. Both Bower and Piaget would agree that under the former condition, a schema of the ball must have been formed (and also quickly faded).

Schemata, then, are stored conceptualizations of experiences, ways of organizing or classifying prior sensory events. They are not necessarily pictorial representations (as are images), nor are they tied to language. They are probably made up of the most important or distinctive elements from an experience, perhaps like a caricature or blueprint of distinguishing features. Recall that in Bower's second experiment of object permanence, infants under 16 weeks of age used speed of movement of an object to determine its identity, not such features as size, shape, or color. Because schemata are closely related to direct sensory impressions, they are used primarily by infants and very young children. The other three units of thought (symbols, concepts, and rules) are more abstract mental representations, accessible to older children and adults. We shall now consider each of them in turn.

SYMBOLS

Symbols are arbitrary expressions or representations which stand for other things. Language is our most pervasive symbol system, and most of the sounds we produce bear only an arbitrary relation to their referents. For example, *book* is no more like the object you are currently reading than is *livre*, the French word for book. Although a few words like *buzz*, *chickadee*, and *bow-wow* are onomatopoetic, most words are not.

Nonlinguistic symbols include the red cross to stand for hospital aid; yellow lines to divide highway traffic flowing in opposite directions; and a red bar over a picture of a cigarette to indicate that smoking is prohibited. You might recall that symbolic functions were discussed in some detail under Piaget's Preoperational Period. The theme of that discussion was that the presence of symbolic functions can be inferred from delayed imitation, language, symbolic play, and the search for hidden objects.

CONCEPTS

Symbols generally represent specific things, including events, objects, concepts, and rules. *Concepts,* on the other hand, characterize what is common across several different events or objects. Concepts are abstractions for the common elements among a group of schemata or symbols. If you use *car* to represent the first automobile you ever owned, then the symbol *car* represents a specific object. If, however, you use *car* to mean four-wheeled vehicles of a given size, then the symbol *car* represents the concept of car. Proper names are nearly always symbols for specific individuals (Samantha Snorkelfinger is probably one of a kind), but names can also represent concepts (John Q. Public).

The classical or componential view of concepts is that a short list of necessary and sufficient attributes completely defines a concept.* The concept of bird, for instance, might be described by the mental attribute list "animal, two wings, feathers." In order to decide if a particular instance, say a robin, fits the concept, the attributes of the robin are compared to the attributes of birds to see if they match. One should, therefore, be able to decide categorically, yes or no, if a particular instance is an example of a concept, and one example which has all and only the attributes of the concept should be just as good as another example for representing the concept. Unfortunately, many concepts do not seem to have a clear intension, and some instances are judged as better examples than others.

The lack of a clear intension can be seen with the concept *chair*. The short list of defining attributes would probably include "four-legged object with seat and back which can be sat upon." The chair shown in Figure 3-1a clearly fits these attributes. But the attribute four-legged surely is not necessary, because three-legged chairs are common. Benches would also fit the list of chair attributes, so the list is apparently not sufficient to enable us to distinguish between concepts. Although everyone can agree that the picture in Figure 3-1a is a chair, everyone would not agree just where the concept *chair* ended

---

* Note that this is identical to the definition of a class discussed in Chapter 2. If classes are particular collections of objects, concepts are particular collections of symbols.

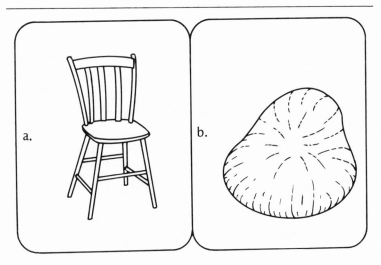

Figure 3-1. Two examples of the concept *chair*

a. A prototypical chair.
b. A beanbag chair.

and the concept *bench* began. The borders between concepts seem to be fuzzy rather than categorical.

That some instances of a concept are better than others can be demonstrated by comparing the beanbag chair shown in Figure 3-1b with the other chair in the figure. Rosch has argued that instead of being defined by a small set of necessary and sufficient attributes, concepts are defined by prototypical exemplars (Mervis & Rosch, 1981; Rosch, Mervis, Gray, Johnson, & Boyes-Braem, 1976). That is, no small set of attributes is necessary or sufficient. Rather, concept attributes are probabilistic; some subset of attributes must be present for an instance to be judged an example of a concept, but the overlap in attributes varies between any two instances of the same concept. Most concept members that are not at the fuzzy borders have a high number of shared attributes. Those exemplars which share the most attributes with other members of the conceptual class also turn out to have the fewest shared attributes with contrasting concepts and therefore make the best examples of the concept. These are called the *prototypes* for the concept. The picture of the regular chair is a good example of "chairness" while the beanbag chair is not because it does not have distinct legs. The absence of legs means that the beanbag shares one fewer attribute with other chairs and shares one more attribute with other sit-able nonchairs (such as rocks and countertops). Similarly, a robin is a "birdier" bird than a penguin.

Although we can force a list of attributes onto a concept to define it formally, with an intension, this happens developmentally after an informal, prototypical definition is created. That is, children learn the prototype of a concept before they learn about the formal defining properties separating two concepts, and they can categorize instances into concepts before they can verbalize the defining attributes for the categorization. Apparently even concepts which have clear, categorical intensions, such as "odd number," are treated prototypically because adults will rate some odd numbers, 3 and 7, as better exemplars than other odd numbers, 447 and 501, even though all of the numbers meet the definition of not being evenly divisible by two. Similarly, triangles and squares are rated as better plane geometry figures than trapezoids and ellipses (Armstrong, Gleitman, & Gleitman, as reported by Gleitman, 1981).

Because children use symbols and concepts in their speech, adults are often lulled into thinking that children are speaking "their language." That children are not is apparent when we examine four developmental changes in the use of concepts. These changes involve a concept's validity, status, accessibility, and relativity.

Four developmental changes

Validity is a measure of how well the child's use of a concept agrees with the usage by the larger social community. It has been suggested that children who do not give a conservation of number response to Piaget's tasks have concepts of number and equality different from those of adults. The adult's concepts are based on numerosity; the child's may be based on perceived length or shape. As children develop, their understanding of a concept approaches the adult meaning; the concept becomes more valid.

The second way that concept usage shows developmental change involves *status,* how precisely and exactly the concept is used. Three-year-old Bob's concept of time is likely to be vague and imprecise. When his mother tells him that they will go to the zoo "in two hours," he might go off and play for ten minutes and then ask if it is time to go. He has a valid concept of time since he knows that "in two hours" is some time in the future, but he does not know exactly how much time is indicated. Bob's ten-year-old sister Alice may be no less impatient to go, but she knows more precisely when "two hours" have elapsed.

The third change in usage involves the *accessibility* of a concept, that is, how easily children can use it in their thinking and how well they can communicate with others about it. Consider this variation on the children's game of Twenty Questions. Children are shown a set of pictures (see Figures 3-2, 3-3) and told to find out which one the experimenter has in mind by asking questions that can be answered by "yes" or "no." Young children about six years old typically just guess specific items: "Is it the zebra?" or "Is it the balloon?" When the pictures are rearranged, as in Figure 3-4, the children are more likely to ask questions involving concepts: "Is it yellow?" or "Is it a toy?" (Ault, 1973; Van Horn & Bartz, 1968). Obviously, six-year-olds have the concepts of yellow and toy, but these concepts are not as readily available as they are for older children. Increasing a concept's accessibility means increasing the chances that children will use the concept as they solve problems. An increased accessibility of concepts is also apparent in the greater verbal skills of older children who can talk about

Figure 3-2. Typical cards used in Twenty Questions

eagle	spoon	orange	dog
apple	zebra	shovel	pitcher
teapot	ball	duck	banana
kite	sprinkling can	monkey	balloon
rake	owl	wagon	bucket
cat	pear	knife	sparrow

Figure 3-3. Twenty Questions pictures in a random array

one concept by using others. For example, older children are likely to discuss the concept of justice by referring to the concepts of fairness and truth. Younger children might discuss justice in terms of the movie they could not go to because they argued with someone.

Finally, as children develop, they learn to employ concepts that are *relative* rather than absolute. If one person is taller than another, he can simultaneously be shorter than a third person. To young children who think in absolute terms, the expression "dark yellow" is contradictory because yellow is a light color. They do not understand that there are many shades of yellow, some of which are darker than others.

Differences between children's and adults' uses of concepts can also be seen in situations involving word associations. The free-association technique ("Say the first word you think of in response to my word") has been used in psychoanalysis, as a parlor game, and as a method of assessing children's language and conceptual development. Researchers have identified a progression in the types of responses children will give in the free-association situation. In the early preschool years, children will try to find a rhyme to the stimulus word, without regard for

91

brown eagle	brown sparrow	brown dog	brown monkey
black owl	black duck	black cat	black zebra
round apple	round orange	round ball	round balloon
yellow pear	yellow banana	yellow kite	yellow wagon
straight-handled spoon	straight-handled knife	straight-handled rake	straight-handled shovel
round-handled teapot	round-handled pitcher	round-handled bucket	round-handled sprinkling can

Figure 3-4. Twenty Questions pictures in an ordered array

the meaningfulness of their response. For example, in response to *sun,* the preschooler might say *run* or *lun.* A few years later, the child's typical response is to answer with a word that logically follows or precedes the stimulus in a sentence, such as *sun-shine* or *sun-hot.* Still later, the adult pattern emerges. That pattern is to respond with the same part of speech, frequently a synonym or antonym. To *sun,* most older children and adults respond *moon.* These adult responses are conceptually related to the stimulus word.

In addition to learning about individual concepts, children must learn to relate two or more of them. This results in rules, the fourth unit of thought.

RULES

Rules are statements which specify the relationship between two or more concepts. We have several different dimensions for describing rules. One distinction is between formal and informal rules. Informal rules express relationships which are generally true ("Mommy is nice") but which can be violated

("Mommy won't let me watch TV now"). Formal rules are always true under certain specified conditions. In base-10 arithmetic, $2 + 2 = 4$. Conservation of number can be expressed by the formal rule: number changes only when something is added or subtracted, not when shape is manipulated.

Language acquisition illustrates two important features of rule learning. First, rules simplify enormously the task of generating a solution to a problem. In forming proper grammatical sentences, consider trying to learn by rote the past tense form of all verbs. Without a rule, children would never know how to conjugate a verb they had not heard before. Second, informal rules are common. Grammatical rules are seldom always applicable. Rather, they seem made to be violated. The following pattern is typical of grammar-rule acquisition (Kuczaj, 1978). First, situations are handled idiosyncratically, without rules. Children learn some past tense verbs such as "went" and "came," apparently by rote. Then they appear to know that a rule can govern past tenses ("Add *ed* to the present tense") because they begin to produce correct regular forms (e.g., I walk; I walked), and they overgeneralize the rule in many situations (I goed; I comed). Eventually these overgeneralized cases drop out. If children do not know the proper form for a particular verb, even if they know the verb is irregular, they may produce an incorrect but rule-governed form. Recall the eight-year-old who said, "All you did was spreaded them out." In fact, even college students, who know that "bring" is an irregular verb (and will not say "bringed"), will incorrectly generalize from such words as "sing" to produce the past tense "brang."

In addition to being categorized as formal or informal, rules can be classified as transformational or nontransformational. Transformational rules prescribe an action to be taken on the related concepts or specify the outcome of some action. The following statements are examples of transformational rules: "Mix flour, water, and eggs to make a cake" and "Multiply the length by the width to obtain the area of a rectangle." Non-

93

transformational rules, like "Fire is hot" and "A square has four equal sides," do not prescribe any action. One major developmental change in the use of rules is to acquire more rules, both formal and informal, and to make these rules more accurate. A second major developmental change is a shift from using no rules or only nontransformational ones to using transformational rules.

Conceptual sorting test

Despite the increase in transformational rules, nontransformational rules remain quite common and come in many different forms. One way to relate two concepts is a class inclusion relation. If one concept is the superordinate for another (e.g., furniture is the superordinate concept for chair), the relationship is *categorical-superordinate*. Three other relationships are *functional-locational*, in which the concepts share a location; *functional-relational*, in which one concept acts on the other; and *analytic*, in which both concepts share a detail or feature. The Conceptual Sorting Test was designed to measure children's preferences for relating concepts (Kagan, Rosman, Day, Albert, & Phillips, 1964). In this test, children are shown sets of pictures, each containing three items. They are asked to pick the two things which "are alike in some way" and to explain the basis for the choice. One set of pictures from the test shows a man, a watch, and a ruler. A categorical-superordinate grouping would join the watch and the ruler because both are measuring devices. A functional-relational response would group the man and the watch because the man wears the watch. If a child groups the watch and the ruler because both are found in the house, a functional-locational response is indicated. An analytic response, based on similarity of some detail, would group the watch and the ruler because both have numbers. Thus the reasons given by children for their particular groupings are important for determining how children relate concepts to each other.

The first research using the Conceptual Sorting Test with American children seemed to indicate an age-related change in the basis of the sorting (Kagan et al., 1964). Preschool children preferred to make functional-relational groupings whereas older children formed categorical-superordinate and analytic groupings. Extensions of this work to other cultures led to some surprising results. Glick (1969) presented Kpelle (West African) rice farmers with an array of familiar objects and asked them to sort the objects into groups that belonged together. The farmers tended to sort on the basis of the functional-relational dimension. For example, a gazelle and a leaf were placed together because the gazelle eats the leaf. The farmers formed very few categorical-superordinate groups, such as a gazelle and a zebra because both are animals. While some investigators might have drawn the conclusion that Kpelle adults were at a low level of cognitive development (equal to American children), Glick was not convinced that Kpelle adults were any less developed than American adults. Therefore, he asked them why they had sorted as they did. They replied that "this was the clever way to do it, the way that made 'Kpelle sense.'" Glick then asked them to sort the items the way a stupid Kpelle might, and they made perfect categorical-superordinate categories comparable to those made by American adults.

Obviously, each culture has its own definition of cleverness and teaches its people to respond in the clever manner. Furthermore, other tests with American children have systematically varied some aspects of the testing situation, such as whether the stimuli were pictures or words, and obtained different proportions of categorical, analytic, and functional responses (Olver & Hornsby, 1966). The conclusion seems to be that children learn several rules for relating concepts to each other, but not in any specific age-related manner.

In summary, cognitive processes operate with four units of thought: schemata, symbols, concepts, and rules. Several major shifts occur in children's use of these units. One such developmental change is from using primarily schemata to using symbols, concepts (especially language), and rules. In another change, concepts gain increased validity, status, and accessibility, and children learn to use them relatively as well as absolutely. A third shift with age involves the particular rule (formal or informal; transformational or nontransformational) children will use to solve a problem. These developmental changes in the units of thought are closely related to the development of the processes of thought, which we shall examine in the next section.

PROCESSES OF THOUGHT

It is virtually impossible to discuss as complex a phenomenon as thinking in a single unit; but it can be misleading to separate the phenomenon into its components, especially when the pieces are so interwoven. In this chapter, thinking is divided into three processes—perception, memory, and the generation and testing of hypotheses—but you should remember that the distinction between them frequently blurs.

PERCEPTION

Our physical sensory receptors for vision, hearing, touch, and so forth make information contained in the environment available for further processing, but assigning meaning to that information depends, in part, on perception. Two major views of perception have guided research on *how* we perceive. After we outline these two views, we will examine the end product of perception, *what* we perceive.

Enrichment theory

According to the *enrichment* (or *schema*) theory, physical stimulation from the sensory receptors is relatively poor in information value and cannot be interpreted without considerable ad-

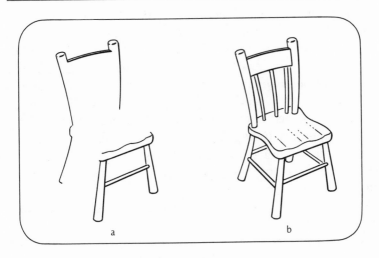

Figure 3-5. Two drawings of a chair

a. The older child is likely to recognize the partially completed picture as a chair.
b. The younger child must see a more complete picture to recognize it.

ditional information enriching the sensations. The additional information can come from biases and expectations governed by prior experiences similar to the current one and from memory, in the form of prior schemata concerning the object or event. Both sources of additional information predict that older children will have faster and more accurate perceptions than younger children. Because older children have experienced more than younger children, they will have more information to choose from to enrich a current stimulus. If information is incomplete, older children will have more accurate expectations for what will complete it. For example, they have a higher success rate in identifying a picture when only parts of the drawing are made visible (Gollin, 1960, 1962) (see Figure 3-5 for an illustration of partial and complete drawings).

The enrichment theory proposes that each time an object is perceived, a small amount of information is added to the previous schema for that object (Bruner, 1957; Vernon, 1955). Because older children have more experiences, they have better schemata (in the sense of being more detailed and more accurate) than younger children. These better schemata can be retrieved from memory to add to the current stimulus, thus enriching current perception. Any task such as discriminating between two objects requires comparing the schemata associated with each object. If the schemata for the two objects are identical, the person should not be able to distinguish between them. If the schemata are different, a discrimination can be made. The more information associated with the schemata, the more likely a comparison of them will yield the correct decision (that the objects are, in fact, the same or different).

Let us consider a common example from school in which children are presented with the letters *b, d, p,* and *q.* For younger children who have had little exposure to letters, identical schemata might be formed for each stimulus, as shown in Figure 3-6a. With more experience, children should form the second set of schemata, shown in Figure 3-6b. This set has the added information that the loops are at the top or bottom of the straight line. This set would not allow the children to distinguish *b* from *d* or *p* from *q,* but it would allow them to distinguish *b* or *d* from *p* or *q.* Finally, children might construct the schemata in Figure 3-6c, adding the information about the left-right orientation of the loop relative to the line. Now all four letters can be distinguished.

One point about this example needs to be clarified. The drawings in Figure 3-6c have been oversimplified and could give the incorrect impression that the schemata are exact images of the stimuli, but that is not the intention. Schemata are not simple graphic images.

Differentiation theory

The alternative *differentiation* or *distinctive features* theory proposes that sensory stimulation is a very rich source of infor-

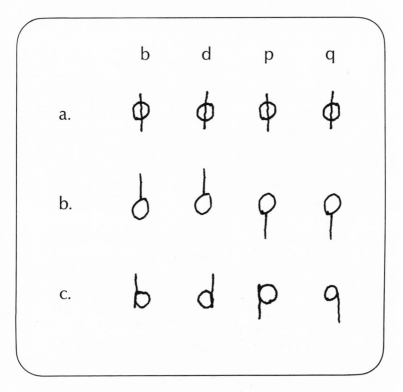

Figure 3-6. Schemata of the four letters b, d, p, and q

mation, instead of a very poor one. The process of perception is to extract the distinctive features or the invariant patterns contained within the complex, variable flow of stimulation (Gibson, 1969; Gibson & Levin, 1975). Three principles govern this view of perception: the differentiation of distinctive features by abstraction, the ignoring of irrelevant information, and the systematic search for relevant information. The last two principles are facets of attention and will be considered shortly. The first principle is the one which most clearly distinguishes the differentiation theory from the enrichment theory. It proposes that each time a person perceives an object, new features or relationships can be detected which were not noticeable before. Practice or prior experience teaches a person which features or patterns of features are distinctive and therefore critical for identification of the object. Perceptions thus become more differentiated, increasing the degree of correspondence between the potential stimulus information and the perception of that information.

Let us return to the example of learning the four letters to see how the differentiation theory interprets children's acquisition of this discrimination. Children with little prior exposure to letters might decide that the distinctive features of these stimuli were the presence of a line and a loop, as diagrammed in Figure 3-7a. These two characteristics would not help distinguish the four letters in the set. With more experience, children might select the position of the loop at the top or bottom of the line as an important feature (see Figure 3-7b). Finally, the feature of left-right orientation for the loop would be noticed (see Figure 3-7c), and all four letters could be distinguished.

Attention

Both the enrichment theory and the differentiation theory acknowledge the importance of the mechanism of attention in perception and seem to accept the same account of it, with a few exceptions which will be explained below. Both ignoring irrelevant information and deliberately scanning for relevant information are components of active attention. Gibson called these two components central and peripheral attention, respectively (Gibson & Levin, 1975). Attention does not begin with these components, however. Rather, it seems to have a passive nature first.

In early infancy, attention is characterized by such terms as *captured* and *stimulus-controlled* because certain stimuli automatically trigger an orienting reaction. Just as the behavioral reflexes of the first Sensorimotor stage initiated motor re-

a. b → straight line and loop

d → straight line and loop

p → straight line and loop

q → straight line and loop

b. b → loop at bottom of line

d → loop at bottom of line

p → loop at top of line

q → loop at top of line

c. b → loop at bottom-right of line

d → loop at bottom-left of line

p → loop at top-right of line

q → loop at top-left of line

Figure 3-7. Feature sets associated with the letters *b, d, p,* and *q*

sponses, the orienting reflexes engage the visual system.* Allik and Valsiner (1980) proposed that this is "a specific evolutionary adaptation that allows the motorically very immature human infant to extract the kind of stimulation from the environment that is necessary for the functional development of the visual system" (p. 6). Later, a more voluntary side of attention develops, so infants can control what they look at and how long they look (just as many reflexes give way to voluntary motor movements).

* We will use vision to illustrate attention since most research has been done with that sensory modality.

Cohen (1973) distinguished between two phases of attention: attention getting and attention holding. In early infancy, what gets attention in infants is a function of the size and movement of objects, while what holds their attention is a function of the complexity and familiarity of the pattern. We have encountered the importance of familiarity or novelty of a pattern twice before, when we discussed the habituation phenomenon under the topic of schemata and when we mentioned the "moderate novelty principle" as a basic assumption of the cognitive perspective. The measure of the formation of a schema was the change in attention that occurred as a stimulus was repeatedly presented. If an object continues to match the infant's schema, no new information can be extracted, so attention drops off. If the object is changed, dishabituation (renewed attention) occurs. Yet, if the novel object is too discrepant from old schemata, the infant will have no way of understanding it and so will not attend to it.

The enrichment theory would describe this by saying that no old schemata will be added to the new stimulus and so it will be relatively meaningless. Differentiation theory would say that the distinctive features of the new stimulus would not be detected. (And Piaget would describe the phenomenon in terms of the inability to assimilate and accommodate to the stimulus.) All of these explanations are circular, though, because we measure the degree of discrepancy by the amount of attention a child shows, and we claim the amount of attention is dictated by the degree of discrepancy. Nevertheless, data supporting the habituation evidence comes from measuring infants' preferences for certain stimuli, as determined by the length of time they will look at one stimulus compared to another. When the stimuli are pictures of human faces, the data seem to fit the following pattern:

> Initially, presumably before the infant has had sufficient experience to have developed a schema for human faces, there is no preference for either regular or scrambled face stimuli. However, at around 4 months, when a schema for faces is

102

inferred to be developing, infants come to prefer regular faces, which presumably provide a moderate degree of discrepancy from the developing schema. Once the face schema becomes firmly established, regular faces become too familiar and scrambled faces present an optimum amount of discrepancy. [Cohen, DeLoache, & Strauss, 1979, p. 425]

Central attention As the infant's attention becomes less captured and more voluntary, the central and peripheral components can be noted. *Central attention,* also called selective attention, refers to the active selection of some information and the rejection or ignoring of the rest. The amount of physical stimulation available to a person is truly overwhelming. Sights, sounds, odors, and touches are continually available for our sensory organs, yet we seem to take notice of only a fraction of them because we have the ability to attend selectively. At a very noisy cocktail party, we can listen to the one conversation directed at us while we ignore all the others. Selective attention is also demonstrated when children are so engrossed in a game that they do not hear their mother calling them (although parents might prefer the explanation that children show selective oblivion).

The constructivist or enrichment theory explanation is that the available information is just not processed. As Neisser explained it, "The perceiver ignores information simply by not doing anything with it. Such information is just not perceived in the same sense that objects currently lying on my desk are just not being grasped and my pipe is not currently being smoked" (1979, p. 203). The differentiation view is that information is filtered out, actively rejected after a minimal amount of processing has indicated that it is not desired.

Although children of all ages exhibit some selective attention, the capability becomes refined with increased age, permitting the older child to eliminate highly attractive distractions better than the younger child. An experimental task which shows the superior selective attention of older children was

103

developed by Stroop (1935). In one variation of the task, children are shown a card printed with various color names. Sometimes the names are printed in black ink, and sometimes they are printed in different colors. Thus, the word *red* might be printed in yellow letters. The children are asked either to name the color of the letters (ignoring the word) or to read the word (ignoring the colors of the letters). The words are a powerful distracting cue, especially for the younger children, who make more naming errors than older children when they are asked to name the color of the letters. Santostefano and Paley (1964) have demonstrated the same phenomenon using normally or incongruously colored pictures of fruit.

Because older children are not as distracted by irrelevant information, their attention span is longer. Thus the length of time that a child will remain at a task increases with age. For this reason, teachers often program only 10 minutes of an academic activity with nursery school children, 30 minutes with grade school children, and 60 minutes with high school students. But as you know from your own experiences, some activities are more interesting than others, so the length of time you attend to them varies accordingly. Most children will play outside much longer than they will play the piano. An infant will play with a rattle longer than will a college professor (at least, most college professors), but if one takes into consideration the appeal of an activity for an individual, then the older child's attention span is, on the whole, longer.

Attention should not necessarily be focused on just one thing. It is useful in problem solving to be able to shift attention between various aspects of the task. As children gain more control over voluntary central attention, they increase the speed with which they can redirect their attention. A very rapid shift in the focus of attention may result in the perception of a relationship that might otherwise not be apparent. Perhaps this is equivalent to saying that a person can hold two facets of a task in mind simultaneously. Piaget explained successful performance on the class inclusion problem by stating that children attended to both the parts and the whole at the same time. An alternative explanation is that successful children shift their attention between the parts and the whole so rapidly that they perceive a new relationship between the two.

The pattern that emerges for children's central attention is an increasing ability to take the demands of the task into consideration. In tasks where one stimulus dimension is relevant and the rest are irrelevant, older children are more successful at ignoring the irrelevant (they focus more). In tasks where two or more dimensions are relevant, older children tend to split their attention across dimensions while younger children do not consistently attend to both. Thus, older children are more responsive to the demands of the task (Shepp, Burns, & McDonough, 1980).

Peripheral attention   Attention is considered *peripheral* when it is used to scan the environment, to explore for important or relevant information. Peripheral attention can be seen for the sense of touch by the manual exploration of an object. Young infants clutch an object; older children systematically run their fingers over the contours (Gibson, 1970). With vision, scanning can be detected if children's eye movements are carefully photographed. Major developmental advances occur in such areas as selecting the more informative parts of a picture for fixation, covering the entire display, comparing parts more systematically, and maintaining a scanning strategy across changes in the stimulus (Day, 1975).

What is perceived

The process of perception involves obtaining meaning from sensory stimulation. What is the end product of that process? According to Gibson's differentiation theory, we perceive (a) distinctive features of static objects, (b) invariant relations of events over time, and (c) relations between distinctive features or between events (Gibson & Levin, 1975). Distinctive features of objects were discussed under the topic of habituation and included such features as size, shape, color, and movement. The invariance of events over time can be exemplified by the perception of a closing door. We see one door moving in time, not a series of discrete stationary doors. The ability to perceive relations between features or events (or both) enables the perception of spatial relations (e.g., one thing is to the left of another) and two-dimensional representations (e.g., pictures of three-dimensional objects). Pattern perception enables a person to identify one particular example from a class of similar objects. For example, the avid birdwatcher can identify the pattern which is the yellow-bellied sapsucker even in a tree full of other birds. Relational perception also facilitates the identification of symbolic codes. The two most prominent symbolic codes that children must learn are the phonemes which make up spoken language and the graphemes of written language. A girl must perceive the difference in sounds between *Tad* and *Dad* when she has to decide whether to throw a ball to her brother or her father. Similarly, she must perceive the difference between *b* and *d* to read *bed* and *deb* correctly.

What is perceived changes with experience and maturation. In general, more features are distinguished and more higher-order relationships are identified with increasing exposure to a stimulus. In infancy, a clear developmental trend has been identified (Cohen, 1979). It begins with the primitive ability of newborns (up to the age of about one and one-half months) to detect edges, that is, a relationship between a figure and its ground. Between two and four months, infants perceive the relations among edges (which is, thus, the perception of angles), and they process simple forms. From five to seven months, they perceive relations among forms, thus producing simple pattern perception. This allows, among other things, the recognition of one human face as distinct from others.

We have seen that differentiation theory and enrichment theory provide different interpretations of some phenomena and parallel interpretations of others. Some psychologists believe the two theories are complementary rather than conflict-ing. Stevenson (1972) offered the explanation that people can both build up a schema and pick out the distinctive features of a stimulus. When children must make an identification of one stimulus, they can compare it with various schemata and pick the best match. When they must distinguish among several stimuli simultaneously, they can isolate the distinctive features. Recall that schemata are not exact images of a stimulus. It may be that "schemata are composed of distinctive features and . . . when many distinctive features have been stored, one has a 'refined' schemata" (Caldwell & Hall, 1970, p. 7).

Other psychologists focus on the differences between the theories. Lewis and Brooks (1975) pointed out that in differen-tiation theory, finding distinctive features precedes the devel-opment of a schema whereas in enrichment theory, a schema is built first and later refined by adding distinctive elements. Cohen et al. (1979) concluded that "taken as a whole, the evi-dence does not unequivocally support any one global theory" (p. 428).

No matter what theory of perception eventually proves to be true, it is clear that perception does not function in isolation of the other processes of thought. Perception and memory are particularly intertwined since perceptions are stored in memory (be they in the form of schemata or relations or distinctive fea-tures), so we turn next to the process of memory.

MEMORY

When we encode and store some aspects of an experience and then, after a period of time, retrieve part of that stored repre-sentation, we have engaged the process of memory. Many of our memory efforts, especially in a school setting, are delib-erate. We know ahead of time that some information will need to be retrieved later, so we employ deliberate strategies to facilitate that later memory attempt. Other memories are inci-

107

dental by-products of some other cognitive activity. For example, we may have the task of sorting pictures of birds and trees into two classes, and afterward, we are asked to recall the pictures. Our memory for the pictures is incidental to the primary sorting task and hence nondeliberate or involuntary. The distinction between deliberate and involuntary memory has recently been accentuated by the publication of some Soviet research on children's memory and by the formulation of the levels of processing model of adult memory, which challenges the traditional multistore model. We will use the dichotomy between deliberate and involuntary memory as an organizing principle as we describe children's memory development.

Deliberate memory

Whenever a person deliberately encodes a list of words, a collection of pictures or objects, the spatial location of items, and so forth, with the explicit intention of retrieving that information later, memory is the goal of the cognitive activity. By far the majority of memory research has concerned deliberate memory and has been set in the theoretical framework of the multistore model of Atkinson and Shiffrin (1968). The multistore model has two basic components: (a) three structural storage systems (or stores) which are "hard-wired" into the brain and (b) "control processes" which are factors influencing the selection and maintenance of information within and between the structural stores (Hagen & Stanovich, 1977). We will first consider the three structural stores which are called the sensory, short-term, and long-term stores. Then we will turn to three control processes: strategies, metamemory, and general world knowledge.

<u>*Sensory store*</u>　The *sensory store* is the briefest of the three storage systems, lasting only about $1/4$ of a second. To demonstrate the existence of this store, Sperling (1960) used a device called a tachistoscope to show subjects a stimulus for a very brief period (50 msec). The stimulus in this particular experi-

ment consisted of nine letters, arranged in three rows of three each. After the letters flashed off, subjects would typically report four or five of the nine possible letters. Two explanations for this level of performance seemed probable. Either subjects had seen four or five letters and reported everything in their memory, or the subjects had seen all nine letters but forgotten some of them before they could report them all. The latter hypothesis was supported when Sperling changed the procedure slightly. He prearranged a signal system with the subjects so that a high tone indicated they should report the top row of letters, a middle tone indicated they should report the middle row, and a low tone indicated the bottom row. Then, *after* the visual stimulus was turned off, one tone was played. Subjects were able to report the one appropriate row quite easily. Thus they must have seen all nine letters. When the tone sounded, they scanned their sensory memory store and reported the letters in that row. The memory image must fade very quickly though, because even a delay of $1/4$ second in sounding the tone resulted in much poorer performance.

When children from the age of five years and older have been contrasted with adults, few if any differences have been found in either the amount of information available to the sensory store or the rate of decay of information in it (see reviews by Hoving, Spencer, Robb, & Schulte, 1978; Kail & Siegel, 1977). The procedure Sperling used is obviously unsuitable for infants, and we have no other way for testing their sensory store. It does not appear likely, however, that interesting developmental changes will be found in the sensory store. Since we know that our memories last longer than $1/4$ second, a distinction can apparently be drawn between the sensory store and the two longer-lasting ones.

Short-term store Memories in *short-term store* last longer than sensory memories, up to 30 seconds, but they are also transitory in the sense that information can be lost during that time. We use the short-term store when we need to remember

109

a phone number just long enough to dial it, or to remember the purchase price of an item just long enough to get out our money. The features of short-term store have been explored with two different retrieval situations, recognition and recall.

In its simplest form, recognition is that "gee, your face looks familiar" or "don't I know this from somewhere" feeling we get when we reencounter a person or object. In a more complex situation, recognition involves choosing one stimulus from a set as the solution to a problem, as students do on multiple choice tests. The possible alternatives are limited, and the person merely has to recognize the correct one. In contrast, in recall situations, a person must generate the stored representation for himself. Fill-in-the-blank and essay tests are common recall situations in school.

In laboratory experiments, the two types of retrieval can be compared for children of many ages. In one experiment, for example, 4-year-olds and 10-year-olds were shown 12 pictures to be remembered. At both ages, the children could select the 12 pictures out of a set of 100. On a recall test, however, when they were asked to name the 12 pictures they had seen, the 4-year-olds could recall only 2 or 3 pictures whereas the 10-year-olds could recall about 8 (Kagan, Klein, Haith, & Morrison, 1973). When even younger children are first shown 18 objects and then asked to pick them out of a set of 36 objects, 4-year-olds are correct 92 percent of the time and 2-year-olds are correct 81 percent (Perlmutter & Myers, 1974). Thus short-term memory tested by recognition is quite good across all ages, but when tested by recall, striking developmental changes are seen. If adults try to remember a random sequence of digits or nonsense syllables, they usually recall about 7 items (Miller, 1956). Five-year-olds recall at most about 5 items, and younger children recall even fewer. Does this difference represent a capacity difference in the structural aspects of the short-term store? Researchers initially interpreted the data in that way, but the recognition data argue against it, and now researchers are pointing instead to age changes in the use of strategies (a control process), such as chunking information into larger, meaningful units (Chi, 1976, 1978). This point will be discussed again when we examine the control processes.

Long-term store   *Long-term store* is different from the sensory and short-term stores in at least two important ways. First, its capacity is clearly enormous. All the memories we have of our childhood, of last year, of last week, of language, and so on are represented in long-term store. Second, items do not automatically disappear from the long-term store in a short period of time. Whether items can ever be permanently lost or are just temporarily inaccessible is a long-standing, unresolved topic of debate.

Does the structure of the long-term store change with age? That is, do children and adults differ in the capacity of long-term store or in the rate of losing information from it? Everyone knows that adults and older children have much better memories than do younger children. But researchers have a hard time deciding whether to attribute the changes to structural development or to the control processes, especially the strategies for encoding and retrieving information. Some evidence of structural development is that neurons in the brain continue to grow for as long as seven years postnatally. That growth is seen in the myelinization of axons and branching of dendrites which is correlated with memory (Kesner & Baker, 1980), but the specific effects of biological brain maturation on memory performance are not well specified. Moreover, three control processes are good candidates for explaining long-term memory performance differences between children and adults. These control processes are (a) deliberate strategies for encoding and retrieving, (b) knowledge about memory situations and memorizing (called metamemory), and (c) general world knowledge.

Strategies

> Piglet had got up early that morning to pick himself a bunch
> of violets; and when he had picked them and put them in a

111

pot in the middle of his house, it suddenly came over him that nobody had ever picked Eeyore a bunch of violets, and the more he thought of this, the more he thought how sad it was to be an Animal who had never had a bunch of violets picked for him. So he hurried out again, saying to himself, "Eeyore, Violets," and then "Violets, Eeyore," in case he forgot, because it was that sort of day. [Milne, 1961a, p. 86]

Strategies such as rehearsal, imagery, and chunking are deliberate procedures for trying to put information into the memory stores or to retrieve that information. These are "control processes" because they are under a person's voluntary control. *Rehearsal* is an encoding strategy which enhances both short-term and long-term memory. If we need to keep information in the short-term store, just long enough to perform some action (as Piglet did), we can repeat it over and over to ourselves in a rote fashion. This type of rehearsal maintains the information in the short-term store, but it is not very useful for transferring the information into the long-term store. A second type of rehearsal, which is repeating the information while thinking about it more, or elaborating on it, does increase the chances of putting the information into long-term store. Children under about seven years do not spontaneously use either type of rehearsal, which is one reason why their memory performance is worse than that of older children (Flavell, Beach, & Chinsky, 1966). When young children are instructed to rehearse, they can do so, and their recall improves correspondingly (Keeney, Cannizzo, & Flavell, 1967).

In a study of rehearsal using a serial recall task, Kingsley and Hagen (1969) first taught some nursery school children animal labels for nonsense figures drawn on cards like those shown in Figure 3-8. Then the children played a game like "Concentration." One at a time, five cards were shown to a child and then turned face down in a row. Next a cue card, identical to one of the stimulus cards, was presented (see Figure 3-9). The child's task was to select the matching card from the face-down row, thereby indicating memory for the serial position of the card.

112

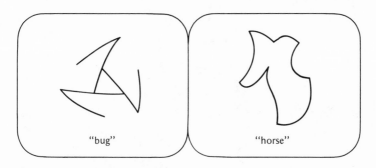

Figure 3-8. Two nonsense figures and their labels, from an experiment by Kingsley and Hagen (1969)

The experimental group relevant to this discussion was required to label each stimulus card as it was presented and to rehearse these labels, starting from the beginning of the row, after each new card was presented. In remembering the location of the matching card, children in this group performed significantly better than children in two other groups who labeled the cards as they were presented but did not rehearse or who neither labeled nor rehearsed the cards. The superiority of the subjects who rehearsed was most apparent when the matching card had been presented first (and therefore had to be kept in memory for the longest time). The authors concluded that nursery school children do not spontaneously name or repeat items to be remembered in a memory task, but if they are helped to do so, their memory scores improve.

Not only are older children more likely to use rehearsal than younger children, but the way they rehearse also becomes more effective with age. Ornstein, Naus, and Liberty (1975) asked third-, sixth-, and eighth-grade children to rehearse aloud in the free times between presentations of an 18 word list. Third graders tended to rehearse each word in isolation, or perhaps with one other word, whereas the sixth and eighth graders rehearsed four or five words as a set. Table 3-1 shows the first four words of the list and typical responses by a third

113

Figure 3-9. Procedure in Kingsley and Hagen's experiment

a. Experimenter presents third card to subject.
b. Experimenter presents cue card. Subject must turn over middle card to be correct.

TABLE 3-1

TYPICAL REHEARSAL PROTOCOLS
OF UNRELATED WORDS*

Word presented	Third-grade subject	Eighth-grade subject
1. Yard	Yard, yard, yard, yard, yard	Yard, yard, yard
2. Cat	Cat, cat, cat, cat, yard	Cat, yard, yard, cat
3. Man	Man, man, man, man, man	Man, cat, yard, man, yard, cat
4. Desk	Desk, desk, desk, desk	Desk, man, yard, cat, man, desk, cat, yard

* Adapted from Ornstein, Naus, & Liberty (1975)

and eighth grader. Notice that the third grader is speaking a word just as often as the eighth grader; it is the quality, not the quantity, of rehearsal that is helpful in making the older children's recall better.

Rehearsal is not even a preferred mnemonic strategy until children are about in fifth grade. Kreutzer, Leonard, and Flavell (1975) interviewed children from the kindergarten, first, third, and fifth grades, asking questions about what the children knew about their own memory processes.* For example, the children were asked:

(1) If you wanted to phone your friend and someone told you the phone number, would it make any difference if you called right away after you heard the number or if you got a drink of water first? (2) Why? (3) What do you do when you want to remember a phone number? [P. 9]

Even some of the kindergarten children knew that some things could be forgotten rapidly. By first grade, over half of the chil-

* This is also an aspect of metamemory, which we will consider in more detail later.

dren said they should phone first or else they might forget the number. In response to the third part of the question, the most common strategy offered for aiding memory relied on external prompts, either writing down the number or having someone else (i.e., Mother) remind them of it. The following answer from a third grader reflects at attempt to devise a self-generated prompt.

> Say the number is 633-8854. Then what I'd do is—say that my number is 633, so I won't have to remember that, really. And then I would think, now I've got to remember 88. Now I'm 8 years old, so I can remember, say, my age two times. And then I say how old my brother is, and how old he was last year. And that's how I'd usually remember that phone number. [Is that how you would most often remember a phone number?] Well, usually I write it down. [P. 11]

Only at fifth grade did some of the children think of verbal rehearsal as a deliberate memory strategy. They knew that they should repeat the number several times, and that the last four numbers would be harder to remember than the first three, which might be the same exchange as their own number.

A second encoding strategy for improving deliberate memory is *imagery,* creating a distinctive picture which either includes the item to be remembered or symbolizes it. If you need to remember that the term *Concrete Operations* refers to Piaget's third period of development, you might imagine *three* surgeons *operating* on a slab of *concrete* (see Figure 3-10). Imagery can be used more easily for some memory tasks than others because some terms evoke images more readily. For example, most Americans probably form a similar image of the Washington Monument (see Figure 3-11), but their images of freedom depend on their perspectives (see Figure 3-12). Like rehearsal, imagery is not spontaneously used by young children, but when an experimenter tells them to generate images, kindergarten and even nursery school children can do so, and their memory subsequently improves (see Reese, 1977, for a review of this literature).

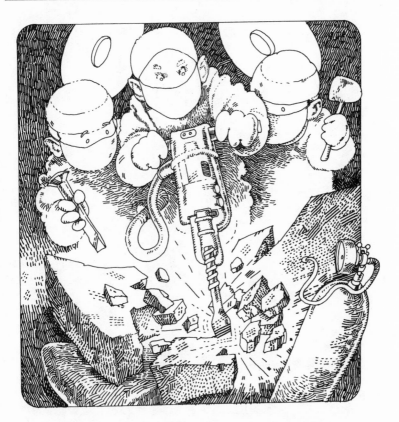

Figure 3-10. An image of three doctors operating on concrete, to symbolize Piaget's third period of development, the Concrete Operational Period

Both encoding and retrieval can be improved by a strategy called *chunking* (Miller, 1956). Chunking involves finding some higher-order category to which several of the items belong and organizing storage and retrieval of information according to these categories. Let us say, for example, that children needed to remember the following list: zebra, cow, dog, pig, horse, balloon, kite, wagon, ball, yo-yo, car, truck, plane, bus, and boat. If they tried to remember the list without any organizing

117

Figure 3-11. Image of the Washington Monument

principle, they would probably only recall 5 to 9 words, the limit imposed by short-term store. If they recognized, however, that the list included five animals, five toys, and five vehicles, they might succeed in remembering 12 to 15 words. Chunking the information into higher-order groups makes it easier to handle by providing an organized method for remembering. Kindergarten, first-, and third-grade children do not spontaneously chunk items either while they examine the stimulus ma-

Figure 3-12. Images of freedom

terials or later during recall. With instructions on chunking, however, even the kindergarten children can do so, and their memory scores improve considerably (Moely, Olson, Halwes, & Flavell, 1969).

In the studies cited above, we have seen a general pattern where younger children apparently do not think of using deliberate strategies to help them remember, but when they are induced by instructions or other task constraints to use strategies, their memory performance improves. Does the lack of strategies account for all of the memory differences between younger and older children? Apparently not. First, even with training in the use of the strategies, younger children's memory performance often does not improve all the way to adult levels. Second, as soon as the experimenter stops prompting the children to use the strategy, they stop using it. These two facts suggest that other factors are responsible for younger children's poorer memory. In particular, children's knowledge about memory (called metamemory) and their general world knowledge are probably additional sources of developmental changes in memory.

Metamemory   One factor which could affect memory performance is knowledge about memory itself. Flavell (1971) has called this _metamemory,_ while Brown (1975) used the phrase _knowing about knowing._ One example has already been presented under the topic of rehearsal, where children were asked whether a time delay makes it harder to remember a phone number. Flavell and Wellman (1977) provided a review of the current research on this topic, and this section is based on their presentation.

Metamemory can be classified into four categories. One is _sensitivity,_ which is knowing when to exert an effort to retrieve information or to prepare for some future retrieval. If you were asked to describe the clothing a friend wore yesterday, you would realize that a deliberate retrieval search is called for, but you also probably realize that you will not find the answer because you did nothing yesterday to help store this information. Yet, if you had been told yesterday that today you would be asked about your friend's dressing habits, you would have been sensitive to the need to prepare for this. No one has yet studied when or how young children deal with unexpected retrieval requests, except to document that they can smile very sweetly, look very puzzled, and say, "I don't know." If forewarned about a memory situation, children as young as three years will profit from the warning, as indicated by their remembering more than children who are told nothing or who are told merely to wait between the stimulus presentation and the retrieval time (Acredelo, Pick, & Olsen, 1975; Wellman, Ritter, & Flavell, 1975).

The knowledge that you probably will not remember your friend's clothing without forewarning illustrates a second category of metamemory, *person variables*. This includes knowing whether you are a good or poor rememberer compared to other people or compared to yourself at other times or in other situations. Even five-year-olds know their relative standings in memory situations; they are better than two-year-olds but not as good as older children and adults. Five-year-olds are not, however, very accurate in assessing their own memory in an absolute sense. They overestimate their memory span and underestimate their readiness for recall (Flavell, Friedrichs, & Hoyt, 1970).

The third category of metamemory, *task variables,* includes knowledge of what items are to be memorized and the format for item presentation. By kindergarten, children know that it is easier to memorize familiar items than unfamiliar ones and that lengthening a list increases its difficulty. On the other hand, not until the third to fifth grades do children realize that learning a list of words embedded in a story is easier than learning the list in isolation, or that learning a story verbatim is harder than learning the gist. By fifth grade, however, children can be rather articulate in explaining task differences. Kreutzer et al. (1975) reported the following interview of a fifth grader:

121

[Tester]: The other day I played a record of a story for a girl. I asked her to listen carefully to the record as many times as she wanted so she could tell me the story later. Before she began to listen to the record, she asked me one question: "Am I supposed to remember the story word for word, just like on the record, or can I tell you in my own words?" . . . Why do you think she asked this question? [P. 43]

[Child]: Because if it was word for word she would probably listen to it many times so she could memorize it. But if it was in her own words, she would not have to listen to it so much because she could get the idea, and then put it in her own words. [P. 49]

[Tester]: Would it be easier to learn it word for word, or in her own words? [P. 43]

[Child]: Be easier to learn it in her own words. You could like explain. But if you have to learn it word for word, you might forget some of the words, and that would ruin the whole story. But if you do it in your own words, you just try to get the main ideas, and then if you kind of get stuck, you could just fill it in. [P. 49]

[Tester]: If I told her to learn it word for word, what do you suppose she did? [P. 43]

[Child]: Croaked! Asked for it a second time—she can't take notes, can she? [No.] Well—she could remember it word for word and say it over again but that—how long was the story? If it's pretty long, *nobody* could remember it! [P. 49]

The final category of metamemory concerns what children know about the variety of *strategies* available to aid memory. Older children can think of more different ways to remind themselves, as the following excerpt from the Kreutzer et al. (1975) study shows.

[Tester]: Suppose you were going ice skating with your friend after school tomorrow and you wanted to be sure to bring your skates. How could you be really certain that you didn't forget to bring your skates along to school in the morning? [P. 25]

[Third grader]: I could put them in my book bag, or set them on the table. Or I could always write myself a note, and put it up on my bulletin board. Or I could tell my mom to remind me. Or I could take them to school the day before and just leave them there. [P. 29]

The topic of metamemory is too recent to allow a clear understanding of the relationship between it and actual memory performance. Preliminary research suggests two tentative conclusions. First, children who understand certain aspects of a memory task reflect that knowledge in their actual memory performance. Second, metamemory is less related to memory performance for younger children than for older children. That is, metamemory develops, memory performance improves, and the coordination between the two develops (Flavell & Wellman, 1977).

General world knowledge   Metamemory is one specific kind of knowledge which influences memory performance. In addition, memory is influenced by more general knowledge of the world, such as knowledge about language, people, places, objects, and events. Using this broader knowledge is the third "control process" which might explain developmental changes in memory performance. Younger children usually have less knowledge about most topics, and they usually remember less. (Recall that even six-year-olds know that greater familiarity with a topic enhances memory.) When children have more knowledge than adults (e.g., when comparing child chess experts to adult novices for memory of chessboard arrangements), the children remember more (Chi, 1978). Yet, even when children have some knowledge, they often fail to use it to aid their memories. In one study of this phenomenon, Paris and Lindauer (1976) read sentences to school-aged children involving a person engaged in an activity. An instrument or tool normally used in the activity was either stated explicitly or left unstated but implicit. For example, one implicit sentence was "The workman dug a hole in the ground." For the comparable explicit sen-

123

tence, the phrase "with a shovel" was added. After hearing eight such sentences, the children were asked to recall all of the sentences. To aid their recall, all children were told the instruments (e.g., "the shovel") as cues. Six-year-olds recalled more sentences when the instrument had been explicitly stated than sentences when the instrument had merely been implied. Ten-year-olds recalled the explicit and implicit sentences equally well. If a child had drawn the necessary inference at the time of encoding the sentence (as the ten-year-olds did), the instrument served as a useful recall cue. Because the six-year-olds could not make use of the recall cues for the implicit sentences, we can conclude that they were not as likely to draw the inferences about the instruments when they first heard the sentences. Similar age differences have been found in other studies; younger children are less likely to infer pre-existing conditions or consequences of actions in a story (Paris & Upton, 1976).

Involuntary Memory

In contrast to the deliberate memory described above, in which memory is the goal, memory can also be involuntary or non-deliberate, arising as a by-product of other activities. Two lines of research have emphasized involuntary memory: the levels of processing approach and the Soviet approach.

Levels of processing approach   The levels of processing model of memory started from the assumption that cognitive analysis of a stimulus could occur at several levels, each of which would produce a memory trace as a by-product (Craik & Lockhart, 1972). For example, at a sensory level of analysis, the physical properties of a stimulus would be analyzed. If the stimulus was the word *sheep,* a sensory analysis would permit a person to decide that the word was five letters long or printed in lower case letters. At a semantic level of analysis, the meaning of the word would be analyzed, permitting a person to decide that the word *sheep* represented a farm animal.

Experimentally, the phenomenon was studied by giving subjects the encoding task of answering questions about words. Sometimes the questions required a sensory analysis, such as "Is the next word printed in capital letters? BOOK," and the subject would respond "yes" or "no." Other questions, such as "Does the next word rhyme with hook? BOOK," evoked the intermediate level of phonemic analysis. Some questions required a semantic analysis, for example, "Is the next word something you can read? BOOK." Later, subjects were unexpectedly asked to recall or recognize all the words that they had seen. Typically for adults, semantically encoded words were remembered more than the sensory- and rhyme-encoded words.

Initially, the levels of processing theory proposed that the sensory analysis was a shallow processing which occurred before the deeper semantic analysis. Now the theory proposes that the different levels of analysis are qualitatively different and give rise to qualitatively different memory traces, but their time sequence is not predetermined (Craik, 1979). Under some circumstances, sensory encoding can produce better memory than semantic encoding (Kolers, 1979), so "depth" of processing is now defined in terms of the amount of attention and effort required to answer the encoding questions (Jacoby & Craik, 1979). Factors which influence the depth of encoding in the levels of processing model are analogous to those influencing the control processes in the multistore model (Naus, Ornstein, & Hoving, 1978). For example, more elaborated semantic processing enhances memory, whether it is forced through an involuntary orienting procedure or deliberately initiated by the memorizer.

In applying the levels of processing approach to the development of memory in children, three questions have been asked. The answers, however, are only tentative because very few studies have been done. The questions are as follows:

1. Do children, like adults, show the same pattern of better

memory following semantic encoding compared with sensory or phonemic encoding? Apparently the answer is "yes" (Owings & Baumeister, 1979; Sophian & Hagen, 1978), at least for adolescents down to four-year-olds (the youngest children tested so far).

2. Assuming that older children are more skilled at semantic analysis than younger ones (they have more semantic knowledge), do older children show a better involuntary memory? Although this question is easy to pose, the answer is difficult to obtain because of two major methodological problems which plague experiments. First, no age differences will appear if the task is so easy that even the youngest children do very well (a ceiling effect) or so hard that even the oldest children do very poorly (a floor effect). Several of the studies using a levels of processing task with children have had these problems (e.g., Geis & Hall, 1976; Sophian & Hagen, 1978). Second, although deliberate memory encoding strategies are presumably not operating because the subjects do not even know that they are in a memory study, deliberate retrieval strategies cannot be avoided; the experimenter has to ask the children to try to remember the stimulus words. Any age differences found in an experiment could be attributed to the better use of retrieval strategies by older children instead of to a better initial encoding analysis. The best that can be done is to compare across ages in the different kinds of retrieval situations, that is, to compare memory performance under recognition, free recall, and cued recall. A large-scale study of this kind has not yet been done, but when results from several studies are pieced together, a consistent age pattern is not suggested (Geis & Hall, 1978; Mitchell & Ault, 1980; Owings & Baumeister, 1979; Sophian & Hagen, 1978). Some researchers have already concluded that involuntary memory is very good in young children and therefore does not improve much with age (Naus & Halasz, 1979). Retrieval strategies almost certainly confound the results, though, because cued recall is generally better than free recall (e.g., Mitchell & Ault, 1980).

3. The third question that can be asked about involuntary memory is how it compares to deliberate memory. Both American and Soviet research have found that children given a "favorable orienting task" (i.e., one that evokes deep processing) remember more than children trying to memorize deliberately but without any experimenter-supplied aids as to what strategies to use (Brown, 1979; Meacham, 1977). Because younger children have fewer and poorer deliberate strategies, the gap between involuntary and voluntary memory is greater for younger children and reduces with age.

Soviet approach   Soviet researchers have concluded that involuntary memory develops before voluntary memory. They observed that the natural activities of infants and preschoolers led the children into learning some cognitive skills, such as how to label and classify objects. Only after these skills were well developed as goals in their own right could children apply them as means to some other goal, in particular, as encoding strategies in a deliberate memory task. For instance, children usually name objects during play. When this skill is well practiced in that context, it transfers to other situations, such as naming objects when an experimenter presents them during a memory test. This naming is a primitive rehearsal strategy which later changes into repeating the series of object names. (Refer to Table 3-1 for examples of rehearsal sets.) Similarly, classifying objects into categories affords practice of an organizing strategy, but it first occurs in the context of play as its own goal. Then it transfers to deliberate memory situations. During the practice of these cognitive skills, involuntary memory arises as a by-product, so it develops before voluntary memory (Meacham, 1977; Smirnov & Zinchenko, 1969).

The above description of memory development illustrates three themes which underlie Soviet research and writing: (a) what is remembered is determined by an interaction between the material to be remembered and the child's activities with that material; (b) the child's activities, in turn, are determined by social, historical, and cultural forces; and (c) activities change qualitatively with age and are marked more by change than by periods of stability and balance, that is, a dialectical model is advanced (Meacham, 1977; Vendovitskaya, 1971; Zaporozhets & Elkonin, 1971).

The first theme refers, for example, to having objects which can be named or sorted and a child trying to label or categorize them as opposed, say, to having a random collection of hard-to-name objects and a child who is interested in throwing the objects. The point can also be illustrated with a study by Leont'ev and Rozanova (as reported in Smirnov & Zinchenko, 1969). They presented children with a board containing 16 circles with a familiar word written on each circle. One at a time, in succession, each circle lit up. Children in one group were told to find the most frequent initial letter for the words and to remove those circles when they lit up. Children in a second group were told to remove each circle when it lit up if its word began with the letter s. Children in the third group were told whether or not to remove each circle as it lit up, with no explanation for the experimenter's choices. All children, in fact, removed exactly the same circles in the same order. Then the children were tested for their involuntary memory of the words and the initial letters on the circles.

The children's activities had a direct influence on what was remembered. In the first group, the children remembered all the different initial letters. In the second group, they remembered only the letter s. In the third group, none of the initial letters were remembered. As expected, none of the activities produced recall of the words because none of the activities required processing of the whole word.

The second Soviet theme, concerning sociohistorical and cultural influences, refers primarily to adult socialization pressures on children. Vendovitskaya (1971) wrote that recognition memory in infants seven to eight months old "is expressed initially by visual fixation on an object named by the adult and its shifting from object to object [depends] on [adult] verbal designation" (p. 91). Adults encourage children to name objects, and they point out what should be remembered, prompt how to do so, and reinforce the child's efforts. Children develop deliberate memory in part because of adult demands to do so.

The third theme stresses changes in children's activities. In infancy, the dominant characteristic activity is manipulating objects (equivalent to Piaget's Sensorimotor schemes). In the preschool years, the dominant activity is playing games, especially imaginary ones. In the elementary school years, school tasks set by teachers and other adults are dominant, and in adolescence, intimate personal relations and career-related activities are dominant (Meacham, 1977; Zaporozhets & Elkonin, 1971).

We have seen how the naming and sorting activities of early childhood promote the development of mnemonic skills which will later be used in deliberate memory situations. In addition, the play of preschoolers gives contextual support for early deliberate memory attempts. For example, in building a toy boat, children might need to get several items off a shelf. To remember the items, the children might deliberately rehearse as they walk across the room to the shelf. This kind of practice, supported by the context of play, later enables children to use rehearsal out of any context, for example, in school, to learn a list of vocabulary words by rote (Brown, 1979).

The memory studies done by the Soviet psychologists have provided impetus for American researchers to use more naturalistic situations to study memory and to pay more attention to involuntary memory. While new discoveries are sure to be made, the distinction between deliberate and involuntary memory is primarily restricted to the encoding phase, and some researchers (e.g., Hagen, 1979) do not believe the distinction is all that clear. No matter how information gets into memory, the storage and retrieval phases do not seem to differ with encoding method (or, at least, no one has yet proposed such a distinction). With information in memory and retrievable from it, the child is ready to use perception and memory to generate and test hypotheses in the final process of thought.

GENERATION AND TESTING OF HYPOTHESES

After children recognize that a problem must be solved, they must generate a set of hypotheses (possible solutions). The size of this set and the adequacy (appropriateness) of the hypotheses depend on children's prior experiences with similar problems. If children have had many prior experiences, they can often generalize quite easily from the old problems to the new ones. Thus, older children will, in general, be better able to solve a new problem merely because they have had more experience with similar problems on which to base their hypotheses. Children with a wider variety of cognitive units (schemata, symbols, concepts, and rules) are more likely to find a solution because they can draw on more knowledge. After children think of a hypothesis (the generation phase), they must acquire information to confirm or disconfirm it (the testing phase).

Let us compare four hypothetical children, ages 3, 4, 5, and 6 years, to demonstrate hypothesis generation and testing. Each child is taken into a room and is told that when he comes out, he can play with a toy. The experimenter then leaves the room, shutting the door afterward. Each child immediately goes to the door to try to open it. The three-year-old has learned one rule about doors: they can be pushed or pulled. On the basis of this one rule, he generates two hypotheses. One is that the door should be pushed; the other is that the door should be pulled. The child tests these two hypotheses by pushing and pulling the door, but it does not open. The four-year-old has learned the same rule about pushing and pulling, but because he has had more experience with doors, he has learned a second rule: doorknobs can be turned clockwise or counterclockwise. The four-year-old tests various hypotheses by combinations of pushing, pulling, and turning the doorknob. Eventually, he finds that he should first turn the knob clockwise and

130

then pull the door. The five-year-old has more elaborate rules about opening doors. He knows, for example, that doorknobs almost always turn clockwise and that they must be turned before pushing or pulling. His problem is very much simpler than the three-year-old's and also easier than the four-year-old's because he has more exact rules. He only needs to generate and test the hypothesis about pushing vs. pulling. A still older child, say six years old, might have watched the experimenter leave the room and observed whether the door swung inward or outward. He could then open the door the very first time he tried because the hypothesis he would generate to test first would be completely appropriate.

To get out of the room, the child had to generate hypotheses about how doors open. When the hypotheses are insufficient, as in the case of the three-year-old, the child may never solve the problem.* If the hypotheses are more or less adequate but must be combined in novel ways, as in the cases of the four- and five-year-olds, we can observe complex hypothesis testing. When prior learning is sufficient, as in the case of the six-year-old, only one hypothesis needs to be generated, and it is likely to be the correct solution. As the child accumulates experience, the expectation of correctness increases until the hypothesis is considered to be a rule. If such a hypothesis turns out to be incorrect, perhaps due to an external agent like Candid Camera or a devious experimenter, considerable consternation can result.

The example above serves as a good practical illustration of hypothesis generation and hypothesis testing. Natural situations, however, usually contain uncontrollable aspects, such as the exact kind of experience with doors each child has had. Researchers generally turn to artificial problems which offer greater control of unwanted variations in exchange for some lack of naturalness. We shall now describe a few experimental studies of the generation and testing of hypotheses to illustrate

---

* Of course, he may generate and test one further hypothesis, that if he screams loudly enough, someone is likely to let him out.

the developmental changes in this process of thought. Such experiments can be divided into two categories. One is based on the child's verbal statements; the other analyzes a sequence of nonverbal behaviors.

A verbal technique—Twenty Questions

Under the topic of a concept's accessibility, we described the Twenty Questions game. Children are shown an array of pictures (refer to Figures 3-2 and 3-3) and told to guess which one the experimenter has in mind by asking questions that can be answered by "yes" or "no." The questions which children ask have been classified into four types. One kind of question has been labeled a *specific hypothesis*. The child names one of the pictures and asks specifically about it. Examples are "Is it the kite?" and "Is it the monkey?" The specific hypothesis is obviously the least efficient question that could be asked because only one picture can be eliminated from the array with each query. A general question which can eliminate more than one alternative, on the other hand, is a *constraint-seeking question*. Children can fashion constraint-seeking questions along many different conceptual dimensions. Questions can refer to some perceptual feature of the objects such as their color, size, shape, or distinctive markings. Examples of such perceptual constraint-seeking questions are "Is it yellow?" and "Does it have a tail?" Other types of constraint-seeking questions may refer to an object's function ("Can you eat it?"), classification ("Is it an animal?"), location in the array ("Is it in the first row?"), and so forth. For the sake of simplicity, these constraint-seeking questions are designated nonperceptual. Finally, it is useful to distinguish an intermediate type called *pseudoconstraint-seeking questions*. These questions appear to have the form of a true constraint-seeking question but, like a specific hypothesis, they refer to only one picture. Examples are "Is it like a horse but with black and white stripes?" (the zebra) and "Is it green with a flower on it?" (the sprinkling can).

The sequence for the types of questions that children of various ages will generate is well established. As you might suspect, specific hypotheses are the predominant type of question for children under the age of six or seven years. When children learn that guessing specific pictures is "wrong," they try to use the more advanced types, but at first only the *form* of the question is learned. Pseudoconstraint-seeking questions, therefore, play a transitional role between specific hypotheses and constraint-seeking questions. Of the two major types of constraint-seeking questions, perceptual ones appear first, perhaps because perceptual *concepts* are more accessible to younger children. As children gain experience dealing with nonperceptual categories, they use nonperceptual constraint-seeking questions more. Whether perceptual questions are as efficient as nonperceptual questions depends on the particular set of pictures used in the game. In general, however, the nonperceptual questions will be more efficient, and this fact probably explains why children come to prefer them (Ault, 1973; Mosher & Hornsby, 1966).

The Twenty Questions game is one way of measuring change in children's hypothesis generation, but it has two drawbacks. It is dependent to some extent on children's verbal skills, and it does not discriminate among children below the age of 6 to 7, or above the age of 11 to 12 years. In other words, its range of applicability is restricted. Because it is unreasonable to suppose that no differences exist in hypothesis generation between a 3-year-old and a 6-year-old, or between a 12-year-old and a college student, researchers have used nonverbal tasks which permit a wider age range to be studied.

A nonverbal technique—probability learning

The most common probability learning task presents the subject with three buttons on a panel and some method of delivering a reward, such as a hole through which marbles can be dropped. The subject is instructed to push one button at a time. If the correct button is pushed, a marble comes out. The goal is to get as many marbles as possible in a fixed number of trials (button pushes). Two of the three buttons are never correct and hence never result in marbles. The third button is partially correct. Some fraction of the time, say 33 percent, subjects get a marble if they push this button. For the other 67 percent of the time, they get nothing after pushing it. Obviously, subjects cannot obtain a marble on every trial. The best they can do is push the "correct" button all the time and get marbles after a third of these pushes. This strategy is called *maximizing* because subjects maximize their chances of getting marbles. If they push either of the other two buttons, they get fewer marbles.

Weir (1964) compiled data for 80 trials on subjects ranging in age from 3 to 19 years. The 3-year-olds adopt the maximizing strategy fairly soon after the experiment begins, and by the last block of 20 trials, they push the correct button as much as 80 percent of the time. The 19-year-olds also maximize by the last 20 trials, but they take many more trials to reach this point. At the intermediate ages, from 5 to 15 years, children push the correct button less than 50 percent of the time, even after 80 trials. This finding is surprising since 3-year-olds rarely perform better on any task than school age children or arrive at the solution (maximizing) faster than college students. To explain these startling results, we need to examine the sequence of button-pushing which children exhibit across all the trials.

The 3-year-olds spend a few trials trying all the different buttons. Then they seem to settle on the correct button and push it most of the time. The 5- to 9-year-olds tend to adopt some alternating patterns, such as left-middle-right or right-middle-left, which yield few marbles, and the 11- to 15-year-olds sometimes formulate even more complex alternations. Why do these children persist in testing elaborate patterns when the success rate for them is so low? There are many potential reasons, but two major ones are (a) the expectation which children bring to the experiment and (b) the skill which the children have for generating and testing hypotheses. If children come to the task expecting a higher rate of success than is actually available, they will look for solutions which match their expectations. In other words, they will continue to generate patterns of responses in hopes that one of these patterns will "pay off" at the expected rate, even though searching for this pattern costs them marbles. In contrast, the 3-year-olds do not seem to expect to get marbles on every trial, perhaps because they do not consider themselves very successful on such tasks. They willingly settle for marbles on only 33 percent of the trials. Older children who have expectations of finding completely correct solutions (i.e., getting marbles after every trial) continue to generate and test hypotheses, looking for a pattern of responses which they believe will earn them more marbles (Stevenson, 1972).

In addition, 3-year-olds may not generate very many hypotheses about how to push the buttons. They try each button in turn, discover that two never pay off, and so settle on the third button. Children of intermediate ages generate many elaborate hypotheses, but their ability to test these patterns is not fully developed. Their memory may not be sufficient to remember exactly which sequences have been tried and which remain to be tried. They may not organize the potential sequences in a logical way (which would help them remember where they are in their search). Moreover, they probably consider each sequence equally likely. Older subjects, such as the 19-year-olds, might decide that the experimenter is unlikely to choose highly idiosyncratic patterns, so such patterns are rejected without being tested. Older children can also organize their search in a more efficient and logical manner, and they can keep better track of where they are. Thus, many college students eventually test the hypothesis that one button is paying off at a less-than-perfect rate, and they settle for this.

In the probability learning situation, subjects have virtually unlimited numbers of hypotheses they can generate, and they must also devise some system for testing all of the hypotheses in the number of trials allowed. Hypothesis generation and hypothesis testing cannot be controlled or observed separately in the probability learning task. In order to see the influence of hypothesis testing alone, a different nonverbal task should be used. In it, subjects are given a limited set of hypotheses to choose from so that hypothesis generation is not a factor.

Levine's blank trials procedure

Tasks called *cue-selection problems* have long been used to assess adult hypothesis testing. The basic task presents subjects with a set of dimensions (e.g., shape, color, size), each of which is represented by several values. The four stimulus pairs in Figure 3-13 show four dimensions (and two values) as follows: letter (*x* or *t*), size (*large* or *small*), color (*black* or *white*), and bar location (*over* or *under*).* Subjects are asked to determine which value of one of the dimensions is correct. Since the different possible values are clearly specified, hypothesis generation is not a factor; the burden falls on hypothesis testing.

Levine (1966) developed a procedure to assess which hypothesis a subject tested in the cue-selection problem. If subjects tested the same hypothesis for each of the four pairs in Figure 3-13, they would exhibit a unique pattern of left and right choices. For example, if the hypothesis is that *t* is correct, a right-left-left-left pattern will be shown. If the hypothesis is that *white* is correct, the pattern will be right-left-right-right. In all, subjects can exhibit eight unique patterns corresponding to the eight stimulus values, each of which will have three responses to one side and one response to the other.

In another study, Levine and his colleagues showed that subjects would continue with one hypothesis if they received no feedback on that trial about whether they were correct or incorrect (Levine, Leitenberg, & Richter, 1964). If subjects could

---

* Early versions of this task used left or right position of the stimulus as the fourth dimension, but that allowed young children who show a position preference to appear to be testing hypotheses (see Gholson, 1980).

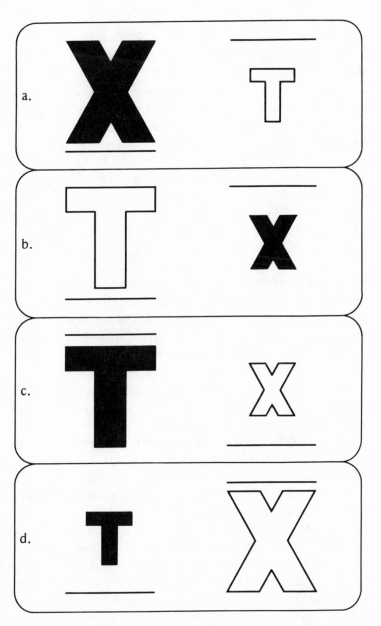

Figure 3-13. Four stimulus pairs used in hypothesis testing

137

be given four no-feedback (or blank) trials in a row (e.g., one trial on each stimulus pair of Figure 3-13), one could infer exactly which of the eight possible hypotheses they were testing. Levine's blank trials procedure incorporated this fact by giving the subjects feedback only every fifth trial. Subjects are told "correct" or "incorrect" on trials 1, 6, 11, and 16 and receive no feedback following trials 2-5, 7-10, and 11-15. Moreover, once subjects receive feedback, they should be able to discard half of the remaining hypotheses. For example, if subjects choose the *small, white, t,* and *bar over* in pair a of Figure 3-13 and receive the feedback "correct," they can eliminate the hypotheses *large, black, x,* and *bar under*. Let us say that on the next feedback trial (pair b of Figure 3-13), subjects choose the *small, black, x,* and *bar over* and again are told "correct." Now they can also eliminate the hypotheses *t* and *white;* the hypotheses *small* and *bar over* remain to be tested. If subjects always discard incorrect hypotheses and never eliminate ones which are correct, they will solve the problem in the minimum number of trials. This strategy is called *focusing*.

Two other strategies lead to a solution, although not as efficiently as focusing. In one, called *dimension checking*, subjects use feedback to eliminate one dimension at a time. For example, one subject might hypothesize that bar position is the relevant dimension. He chooses an upper bar stimulus on his first trial and is told "correct." He chooses another upper bar on his next trial and is told "incorrect." This subject will eliminate both bar positions as being unimportant, but he will not eliminate the values from the other dimensions (letter, size, and color) which were also disconfirmed. Even less efficient is the *hypothesis checking* strategy, where one value is tested at a time. A subject using this strategy might choose an upper bar, be told "correct," choose another upper bar, be told "incorrect," and then proceed to test for the lower bar on subsequent trials.

Some subjects exhibit stereotyped response sequences which are rule-governed but do not lead to a solution because feedback does not alter the rule. In the *position perseveration* stereotype, a subject will choose whatever stimulus is on the left (or right) and be correct only part of the time. A *position alternation* stereotype is shown by a simple left-right-left-right sequence, again maintained despite feedback. For the *stimulus preference* stereotype, subjects continually pick one of the four stimulus values but never drop the hypothesis when told it is incorrect.

Gholson and Beilin (1979) summarized the general developmental trends found for hypothesis testing as follows: kindergarten children (about 5½ years old) show stereotypes in 90 percent of the problems. Elementary school children (7 to 12 years old) show hypothesis checking and dimension checking 65 to 80 percent of the time and focusing 5 to 15 percent. College students focus at least 50 percent and never show stereotypes.

Rules can also be inferred on other problems, such as conservation of number or Piaget's Formal Operational tasks. Siegler (1978) tested children as young as 3 and 4 years old and reported that 4-year-olds used rules only sometimes and 3-year-olds "almost never conform to any easily describable formula" (p. 131). When asked to explain how they decided what stimulus to choose, 3-year-olds reply, "I chose the one that was special" and "I chose the one I wanted to" (p. 131). Before concluding that 3-year-olds simply do not use rules, Siegler (1981) noted that one should consider the possibilities that the children use rules on some trials but not consistently enough to be detected and that they try to use rules but fail to execute their plans accurately. In any case, it is clear that rule-governed hypothesis testing increases steadily throughout childhood.

INTERRELATIONS

One might suppose that the processes of thought operate in the same sequence as they have been presented here: perception, memory, and hypothesis generation and testing—a sequence that follows an intuitively logical order. However, it is possible that the processes do not operate sequentially. *Parallel* (or simultaneous) processing is an attractive explanation of why thinking can occur so rapidly, and current theories from the fields of information processing and computer science argue for parallel processing systems.

The interrelationship of the development of the units of thought and the development of the processes of thought is not precisely known, but it is reasonable to assume that their changes correspond over time. The functioning of each process affects the development of each unit of thought. Perception, for example, must play a central role in the development of symbols and concepts. Since symbols are arbitrary expressions for schemata, the schemata have to be refined by the perceptual process before symbols can be assigned to them. All of the units of thought are stored in and retrieved from memory; therefore, any limitation of the memory process will necessarily limit the development of the units. The units cannot be enriched, differentiated, made more precise, or validated until the old unit is recalled from memory and the new one replaces it. In a similar manner, as children generate and test various hypotheses about the meaning of certain concepts, those concepts might change in status or validity. While it might appear that fairly clear distinctions have been made between each of the units and processes, this appearance is deceptive. Instead of being discrete, the units and processes are interwoven, and it is difficult to draw fine lines between them.

In addition to the units and processes of thought, several other factors influence the likelihood that children will solve a problem. Among these factors are cultural conditioning, anxiety (e.g., fear of failure), motivation (e.g., desire to succeed, avoid errors, or to obtain a reward), and expectations for success or failure. All of these variables become more salient with age, but whether they facilitate or impede problem solving depends on the particular individual. Since these factors are neither general developmental variables nor, strictly speaking, units or processes of thought, we shall not elaborate on them.

SUMMARY

The process approach to cognitive development identifies four units and three processes of thought. Developmentally, children shift from primary reliance on schemata to the greater use of symbols, concepts, and rules. Quantitative increases occur in the number of units a child has, and the units themselves change in ways which are usually described as quantitative. For example, concepts gain validity, status, and accessibility and come to be used relatively as well as absolutely. Children gradually prefer formal and transformational rules to informal and nontransformational ones, but all remain available.

Among the more interesting changes in the development of the perceptual process are increases in children's attention span, better selectivity of attention, greater speed in shifting attention, and more rapid and more accurate final perceptions. Performance on deliberate memory tasks also increases dramatically during childhood. The multistore model suggests that most of this increase can be attributed to the control aspects (strategies, particularly organization; metamemory; and general world knowledge). It is not yet clear how much change occurs in involuntary memory. When tested in an involuntary memory situation or with recognition as the mode of retrieval, young children appear to have fairly good memories, especially in contrast to their deliberate memory performance or when recall, rather than recognition, is the retrieval mode. The third process of thought, generation and testing of hypotheses, also undergoes change with age. As children develop, they generate more adequate and sophisticated hypotheses and then test these hypotheses more systematically and efficiently. Tasks such as Twenty Questions, probability learning, and Levine's blank trials procedure for the cue-selection problem demonstrate the generation and testing of hypotheses in both verbal and nonverbal situations.

4

A COMPARISON OF APPROACHES

Some similarities and differences between Piaget's approach and the process approach have already been explored, but because they have been embedded in other contexts, they have probably not been highly salient. Therefore, the purpose of this brief chapter is to make the previous comparisons more prominent and to add some new ones. We start with a look at the interactionist and active child assumptions common to both approaches. We then examine how each approach supports the moderate novelty principle and how they differ in their stances on the nature and rate of developmental change (stage vs. nonstage theory). Then we contrast Piaget's views of perception, memory, and hypothesis testing with the process approach.

SIMILARITIES IN ASSUMPTIONS

Most cognitive psychologists consider themselves interactionists (rather than nativists or empiricists), in part because the extreme maturation and learning stances seem untenable. As Kumler (1971) expressed it:

> Imagine that you are listening to a drummer beating on a drum. Nobody would try to figure out which noises were produced by the drum and which noises were produced by the drummer. . . . Every trait results entirely from an interaction of the innate composition of the organism and the experience. [P. 184]

Neither Piagetian nor process approach researchers have spent time trying to estimate how much of some problem-solving behavior is due to heredity or the environment. While it may seem strange to say that two approaches are similar for what they do *not* do, they both stand in contrast to the third major approach to studying intelligence—the standardized IQ testing movement—which has recently been the context for a raging heredity-vs.-environment controversy (see Jensen, 1969, 1977; Scarr-Salapatek, 1971; Scarr & Weinberg, 1976). Piaget's explicit introduction of concepts grounded in biology (e.g., assimilation and accommodation) and his advocacy of a stage theory helped earn him the reputation of being a maturationist, yet he clearly subscribed to the interactionist position. The biological factors were not merely fixed bases on which the environment built its modifications. Nor were stages preformed, waiting to unfold in time. Rather, Piaget intertwined the biological and environmental factors, saying that each affected the functioning of the other. One example is that assimilation and accommodation are influenced by particular experiences, such as imaginative play or imitation. On the other hand, the child's current developmental status influences the interpretation and storing of stimulus events. The enrichment theory in perception and the constructivist approaches to memory (e.g., Paris & Lindauer, 1977) agree with Piaget on these points. Process approach researchers are, however, more likely to consider a biological base as innately given and to emphasize experiential factors (Beilin, 1981). The differentiation theory of perception, for example, focuses on what distinctive features are inherent in a stimulus. This puts process approach researchers toward the

143

environmental side of the continuum, but they are still inter-actionists.

The second common assumption, as described in Chapter 1, was that children are active rather than passive participants in their own development. Perhaps a more accurate and less sim-plistic way to state this assumption is to say that certain aspects of development begin relatively passively and become de-cidedly more active. The behavior patterns of very young in-fants in Piaget's first stage of the Sensorimotor Period are essen-tially passive. Infants cannot, for example, avoid practicing their reflexes and schemes whenever an appropriate stimulus is presented. They are, at first, bound to suck on their thumbs or grasp a rattle. Within a very short time, however, these reflexes give way to more voluntary behaviors. But for Piaget, children are active in a more important sense: they actively construct their own knowledge structures. Knowledge is not poured into an empty brain nor absorbed as a blotter draws up ink. Knowl-edge is built out of children's actions on their environment. Even though a bottle may be placed in a newborn's mouth, triggering sucking, knowing the bottle as something to be sucked results from both the bottle's physical characteristics and the child's participation. The active child assumption means that characteristics of the child are as important, if not more so, than environmental stimulus characteristics.

The process approach also describes a trend from passivity to active control, especially in the areas of attention and memory. Early attention is said to be "captured" by certain stimulus fea-tures such as high contrast and movement, which automatically provoke attention. As Neisser (1979) said, "It does 'force itself' on the perceiver . . . because she cannot help being prepared for it" (p. 213). Nevertheless, attention becomes more volitional and selective; it comes under the active control of the per-ceiver. As children develop, they show increasing ability to ignore irrelevant material and to distribute their attention ac-cording to the task's demands.

In memory, the passive-to-active trend is most obvious in

the shift from involuntary to deliberate memory. As its very name suggests, involuntary memory is not fully controlled by the memorizer. Certain encodings occur automatically; one cannot avoid storing some aspects of an experience. As we saw with the Stroop effect in which the names of colors were printed in different colored letters, the name spelled by the word is a powerful stimulus and only older subjects are able to exert enough control to prevent processing the word's name (Lockhart, Craik, & Jacoby, 1976). In retrieval too, some experiences are recognized as familiar without any active attempt to retrieve the old experience. Infants are fairly capable of this relatively passive memory. With development, however, children become skilled in the more active, deliberate memory. Strategies, such as organization and rehearsal, give the memorizer the ability to select what will be memorized and when and how it will be retrieved.

The moderate novelty principle is a third common ground between the two approaches. In Piaget's terminology, moderately discrepant events allow both assimilation and accommodation, and so yield the most change in knowledge. If an event is moderately different from previous ones, children will have old structures (schemes and operations) which can be applied (i.e., assimilated), but the structures will be modified because the new event has some novel features which must be accommodated. If an event is too familiar, children will only assimilate it. If it is too novel, children will not be able to modify old structures enough to fit the new event, so no accommodation will occur. Thus moderately novel or discrepant events are preferred.

In the process approach terminology, moderately discrepant events yield maximum attention. Events which are too familiar lead to rapid habituation. Events which are too novel do not contain enough accessible information to be meaningful. In terms of enrichment theory, no old schemata will be appropriate to be added. In terms of differentiation theory, the distinctive features of the novel stimulus will not be recognized.

145

Both theories agree that a certain amount of redundancy in information is required, especially by young children, to make sense of perceptual input.

DIFFERENCES IN EMPHASIS

Despite the similarities in assumptions, Piaget's approach and the process approach differ in some fundamental regards. Most striking is the characterization of developmental change as stagelike or nonstagelike. As was discussed in Chapter 2, Piaget believed that the interesting developmental changes were the qualitative ones which separated the four major periods. Concrete Operations, for instance, are not just more refined Preoperational mental representations. A new feature (reversibility) is added which makes Concrete Operational thinking different in kind from Preoperational thinking. Moreover, Piaget's stage theory contains an ideal end state (Formal Operations) toward which children inevitably progress (see Figure 4-1). As long as development continues, its direction is specified.

Most of the research which characterizes the process approach emphasizes the quantitative nature of developmental change. Perceptions become more efficient, more distinctive features are identified, more strategies are available for encoding and retrieving memories, more hypotheses can be generated and tested more systematically, and so forth. Stages do not seem appropriate to this conceptualization. Moreover, the end goal of development is less well specified in the process approach.

By virtue of being a stage theory, Piaget's theory takes two positions regarding developmental sequences. (a) A fixed sequence should occur for the acquisition of a concept. That is, the partial understandings of a concept like conservation should form a fixed series leading to the full mastery of the concept. (b) Within each major period, different concepts should occur simultaneously. Recall that these were the invari-

146

Figure 4-1. An ideal end state in stage theory. Piaget's "stages" of cognitive development pictured as the stages used to launch a spacecraft: (bottom to top) the Sensorimotor and Preoperational stages are jettisoned as the Concrete Operational child follows a trajectory toward the Formal Operational goal.

ant sequence and cognitive structure (or concurrence) criteria discussed in Chapter 2 under the topic of stage theory.

Because the process approach is not, in fact, as unified an approach as Piaget's, it is harder to identify a particular stance on the issues of developmental sequences. In general, process approach researchers are more likely to agree with point (a) that some conceptual development is marked by fixed sequences than with point (b) that major concepts develop simultaneously. A fixed sequence was identified for the development of attention to perceptual features, from edges to angles to simple forms, and so on. Memory researchers found that some strategies develop in a regular pattern (e.g., in rehearsal, repeating each item in isolation precedes repeating mixed groups of items). In hypothesis testing, a regular sequence of rule usage could be seen in the Twenty Questions game and Levine's blank trials procedure. To the extent that process approach researchers do not hypothesize any superordinate cognitive structures, they have no reason to predict concurrent development between concepts. As we saw in Chapter 2, the presence of *decalages* on Piagetian tasks is a serious stumbling block to Piaget's version of a stage theory. From the process approach perspective, Siegler (1981) proposed a much more complex picture of developmental sequences across concepts. When children are unfamiliar with a particular problem, they may tackle it by using one simple strategy or rule. As they gain experiences with some problems compared with others, they make irregular advances but they do *not* transfer their advances across problems because they lack critical pieces of information that would make such transfers successful. Therefore, development appears more synchronous at younger ages and less so at older ages.

Critics of the process approach continue to believe in the existence of overarching mental structures.

> It is . . . structure that gives the rules meaning, and without meaning the rules seem somewhat vacuous. . . . We should

148

> look for higher-order organizations that can predict which
> kinds of rules will emerge at different age levels as children
> cope with various tasks. [Strauss & Levin, 1981, pp. 79-80]

Critics of Piaget's stage theory counter that

> wide variation in the age of mastery of concepts that are
> theoretically within the same stage has been the rule rather
> than the exception. This has led to the serious question of
> whether there is any generality in the way that children of
> particular ages approach different problems and to the rather
> unsettling possibility that there might be none. [Siegler,
> 1981, p. 2]

Obviously, debate will continue for some time on this issue.

SIMILARITIES IN TOPICS

Because both Piagetian and process approach researchers investigate cognitive development, it should not be surprising
that the topics each studies overlap considerably. In the following comparisons, the process organization is adopted because
it was easier to bend Piaget's work to focus on processes than
the reverse. Whereas Piaget has incorporated each process into
his description of stages, the process approach has, until recently, ignored Piaget's stages, classifying children solely by
ages. Since age does not predict very accurately what stage a
child might be in, it is more difficult to fit the process approach
to Piaget's theory. The organization of the next few pages is not
intended to convey approval of one approach over the other;
it is merely a statement of the relative ease of presentation.

PERCEPTION

Piaget has suggested a theory of perception, but it is less complete and less accessible to readers than his theory of cognitive

development. Gibson (1969) has classified Piaget's theory of perception as an enrichment theory because information from schemata are added to the basic sensory data through the process of assimilation and the schemata, in turn, are modified to accommodate the specific stimulus input. The characterization of Piaget's theory as an enrichment theory focuses attention on the schemata that become enriched. Piaget's theory has an additional focus, however, on the development of certain mental operations, similar to cognitive operations, that influence perception (Elkind, 1975). Those operations are *perceptual regulations* which give children new methods of manipulating perceptual data mentally. At first, children's perceptions are centered on a few aspects of the stimulus which are highly salient and which capture their attention. The stimulus controls attention, so attention is stimulus-bound (just as it is in the process approach). According to Piaget, the development of perceptual regulations frees children's attention, allowing them to choose and control where they direct their attention. In other words, perception becomes decentered through the operation of perceptual regulations. The change from centering to decentering is directly analogous to the improvements in selective attention discussed under the process approach.

To make these ideas clearer, we can consider two abilities that arise from the development of perceptual regulations. One of them involves mentally rearranging a stimulus event by combining or separating various aspects of it to create a new perception. Some visual stimuli, for example, can be viewed as two different figures, depending on which areas are seen as central to a figure and which as the background. The young child centers on only one organization and perceives a single figure. The older child is able to decenter and reorganize the stimulus to perceive both figures. Piaget attributed the ability to reorganize the picture to perceptual regulations which allow children to add or subtract areas and contours from the picture to form all the possible figures and their corresponding backgrounds. The picture in Figure 4-2 is perceived as a vase if the

Figure 4-2. An ambiguous figure with two perceptual organizations

black area is considered the central figure and the white area (the entire image minus the black area) is the background. The picture is perceived as two faces if the white area is the central figure and the black area is the background.

The other perceptual ability involves part—whole perception. To test this, children are shown a set of pictures in which one familiar object is constructed using other familiar objects as parts. For instance, a man can be made up of pieces of fruit, with bananas representing his legs and a pear representing his body. Children who have not yet acquired the necessary per-

151

ceptual regulations will center only on the parts and report seeing the fruit, or they will center only on the whole and report seeing the man. Children who have the perceptual regulations, however, can decenter and see both the parts and the whole simultaneously, reporting a man made up of fruit. These perceptual regulations are analogous to the cognitive operations used in the part—whole (class inclusion) task. According to Piaget, in both tasks, children must consider simultaneously more than one facet of the problem or stimulus.

MEMORY

Piaget's work on memory focuses on the ways memories are influenced by general world knowledge. Thus it is compatible with the section of the multistore model concerned with general world knowledge and with the levels of processing approach. Specifically, Piaget and Inhelder (1973) suggested that the accuracy of memories should be related to children's stages of cognitive development. The levels of processing approach also "views memory as the assimilation of incoming information into one's current knowledge base [so that] a child's existing semantic knowledge determines . . . what is remembered" (Naus et al., 1978, pp. 227-28). Both positions suggest that memory performance can actually improve with time, whereas most memory theories merely try to explain memory deterioration. The levels of processing model emphasizes that the match between the encoding and retrieval environments (Tulving & Thomson, 1973) might be better on a delayed recall attempt compared with an earlier one. Piaget and Inhelder, on the other hand, stressed changes in the actual memory representation (what is stored). Memories can become more accurate over time if children acquire new operations which pertain to the memory representation.

Three types of evidence have been sought to evaluate the position of Piaget and Inhelder. The weakest evidence merely

152

shows that memory performance improves with age (as does cognitive operational level). Piaget and Inhelder (1973), for example, showed three- to eight-year-old children a set of sticks arranged in order by size (the seriation problem). One week later, the children were asked to reproduce what they had seen by drawing the sticks. Only the older children, six to eight years old (and presumably in the Concrete Operational Period), tended to draw an ordered array of sticks. The five-year-olds drew unseriated lines, although the precursors of seriation could be seen. The three- and four-year-olds drew completely unseriated lines. Although memory accuracy was thus correlated with age, the evidence is weak because operational level was not tested in each child; it was merely presumed.

The second type of evidence shows memory to be better after a lapse of time compared with immediate memory. Piaget and Inhelder (1973) retested the children described above eight months after the children had first seen the sticks. The drawings improved in the direction of increased seriation for 74 percent of the children, while the remaining 26 percent did not change. This result has been replicated by other researchers, but children's drawings have also shown increasing amounts of seriation even when a random (nonseriated) array of sticks was the original stimulus to be remembered (see Liben, 1977, for a review).

The third type of evidence that ought to be the strongest support for the Piagetian position would show a relationship between operational level and memory performance for individual children, not just for broad age groups. Unfortunately, the data produced from several different studies do not justify that conclusion at this time. Liben (1977) summarized these studies by saying,

> The Genevan position is undermined by the fact that performance on the two measures has been only weakly related, has occasionally been strikingly asynchronous (for example, children with poor performance on the operative task and perfect performance on the reproduction tasks), and has

153

not changed in parallel over the long-term retention interval.
[P. 328]

Finally, Flavell and Wellman (1977) noted a similarity between the Soviet view on memory, Piaget's view of knowledge acquisition, and their own speculations about how metamemory might develop. The Soviet position is that children learn about memory because they note the relationships between the original material, their own storage and retrieval attempts, and the final recalled product (Smirnov, 1973). Piaget proposed a process, called *reflective abstraction,* which Flavell and Wellman interpreted as follows:

> The child abstracts and permanently incorporates into his cognitive structure generalizations or regularities concerning the properties of his own actions vis-à-vis the environment. [Flavell & Wellman, 1977, pp. 29-30]

They speculate that

> since metamemory . . . primarily [entails] generalizations about people and their actions vis-à-vis objects, a process like reflective abstraction may play an important role in [its] acquisition. [P. 30]

HYPOTHESIS TESTING

Because Formal Operational thinking is the epitome of systematic hypothesis testing, it is reasonable to expect considerable overlap between the types of hypotheses children use in Levine's blank trials procedure and their level of cognitive development in Piaget's system. Gholson (1980) has interpreted Piaget's theory as predicting that Preoperational children should exhibit only stereotyped responses, never strategies. Furthermore, because Concrete Operational children neither consider multiple hypotheses simultaneously nor test hypotheses fully systematically, they should be limited to hypothesis

154

checking and dimension checking strategies. Only Formal Operational children should exhibit the focusing strategy. As reported in Chapter 3, the general development patterns found on Levine's blank trials problem fit this prediction. Kindergarten children exhibited stereotypes, elementary school children exhibited the two checking strategies with little focusing, and college students focused about half the time. Unfortunately, in those studies, the operational level of individual children was not directly measured. A study which did assess operational level produced confirming evidence (Gholson, O'Connor, & Stern, 1976). Preoperational and Concrete Operational children, all of whom were in kindergarten, were compared on a series of six blank trial problems. The Concrete Operational children solved about 30 percent of the problems; the Preoperational children solved fewer than 10 percent. On a subset of the problems, the Concrete Operational children showed a 35 percent rate of dimension checking and about 10 percent hypothesis checking, whereas the Preoperational children showed less than 10 percent of the two checking strategies combined.

Several training studies have tried to improve children's hypothesis testing (see a review by Tumblin & Gholson, 1981). In each case, children who are in the higher Piagetian stage showed more improvement than their same-aged peers in a lower Piagetian stage. The type of training also makes a difference in the amount of improvement. In fact, the type of training can account for larger performance differences than Piagetian level produces. So, although cognitive level and hypothesis testing are related, the relationship is modified by procedural features of the task (Tumblin & Gholson, 1981).

SUMMARY

Piaget's theory and the process approach are fairly similar in a number of major ways. Both take an interactionist stance, as-

155

sume that children come to play an active role in their own development, and advocate a moderate novelty principle. Piaget's theory of perception is an enrichment theory, so it contrasts most strongly with Gibson's differentiation theory but agrees with other enrichment theorists. Piaget's work in memory emphasized how the child's general world knowledge and level of cognitive development interact with what is stored in memory. This same position is adopted by Soviet researchers and is compatible with the levels of processing approach. Within the multistore model, those who emphasize the influence of general world knowledge are most similar to Piaget in focus, although they do not necessarily characterize children's world knowledge according to Piaget's stages. Finally, Piaget's description of Concrete and Formal Operational thinking resembles the description of hypothesis generation and hypothesis testing of the process approach.

The major discrepancies between the two theories center on the presence or absence of superordinate cognitive structures and whether developmental change is qualitative as well as quantitative. Piaget's theory is fundamentally a stage theory, proposing qualitative changes and cognitive structures (schemes and operations). Process approach researchers tend to adopt nonstage theories, challenging the idea of superordinate structures (especially operations) and arguing that developmental change tends to be quantitative.

5

IMPLICATIONS FOR PARENTS AND TEACHERS

IMPLICATIONS FOR PARENTING

Since the focus of this book has been on cognitive development rather than socialization, this section on parenting will not discuss such traditional parental concerns as toilet training and sibling rivalry. Instead, we hope to convey a sense of how to enjoy children by watching their cognitive development. While most grandparents expect to receive news when their grandchild sits up alone, cuts a first tooth, and crawls, they do not expect letters or phone calls relating to such milestones as coordinating secondary reactions or searching for hidden objects. Although these cognitive achievements are more difficult to observe, they can be just as exciting and rewarding for parents (and grandparents). Moreover, we hope the focus on cognitive development will present alternative interpretations for some potentially irritating child behaviors. Recall the example from Piaget's fifth stage in the Sensorimotor Period in which children repeatedly drop toys out of their playpens. While one could easily think that the children were maliciously attempting to annoy their caregivers, the alternative explanation offered here was that the dropping activity was essential practice of tertiary circular reactions.

The material in this section is organized around the broad age groups of infants, preschoolers, elementary school children, and adolescents. This is convenient because adults use age as a reference marker, often to judge whether children are acting "normally" and to know what behavior or level of performance to expect from them. This organization is not intended to deny the individual differences between children. Rather, it just reminds us that children are perceived both as individuals and as members of an age group. This same distinction is made by parents in judging their own children's actions. When their child is behaving nicely, parents offer the explanation that their love and gentle guidance produced a well-mannered child. When their child misbehaves, "he is going through a stage" or "acting like all the other 2-year-olds" (or 10-year-olds or adolescents).

One of the major themes of this section is that enjoyment is produced when challenging cognitive tasks are solved, and frustration is produced when a task proves too difficult. Children are confronted with challenging cognitive tasks every day. They have to figure out how their world functions. For parents, the challenging task is to figure out how children function. The purpose of this section is to illuminate the parents' task.

INFANCY

Everyone knows that babies enjoy playing peek-a-boo. For many adults, it is sufficient to know that baby can be amused temporarily by this game. To understand why babies enjoy it, we can examine the development of object permanence. It is a cognitive challenge for infants to figure out that objects can hide temporarily and then reappear. When such an interesting object as a mother hides and reappears, often with a smiling or playful expression on her face, infants can exercise their ideas of object permanence in an enjoyable context.

The development of object permanence can also explain situations of distress for infants. Consider the situation where a six- or seven-month-old infant has been playing happily by himself. Suddenly he begins to cry. The toy that he had held in his hand is on the floor behind his back. One might correctly suspect that his crying resulted from the frustration of not being able to find the "hidden" toy. Returning the toy to his line of vision will bring instant relief. The development of object permanence can also be related to separation anxiety which, as most parents know, is the intense distress infants exhibit when left in an unfamiliar room or with an unfamiliar person. In many instances, infants do not even seem to differentiate between mother's leaving the living room to go to the kitchen and her leaving for the evening. They still wail at the separation. People, being like objects to the infant, acquire a permanence of existence, so when they disappear, the infant may become upset if they cannot be found or made to reappear.

As soon as infants leave the immobility of their first few months and begin to creep, crawl, or walk, literally a whole new world becomes available to them. Prior to self-initiated traveling, the world for infants is severely limited to those objects that parents bring close to them. After they can navigate around the house or yard, and in spite of their parents' best efforts to babyproof the environment, they will undoubtedly get into something dangerous or forbidden. As a result, they are required to learn distinctions between permissible and forbidden activities. The difficulty for infants is that similar actions do not bring similar parental responses.

Parents generally believe that baby grasping a doll or an adult's finger is cute; baby grasping a knife, however, is dangerous. Baby reaching for a bottle will get smiles of encouragement; baby reaching for a full glass will get scolded. Baby pulling on a string attached to a toy is playing; baby pulling on a cord attached to a lamp is in trouble. From the parents' perspective, baby is alternately angelic and mischievous. From the baby's perspective, parents are alternately benevolent and malevolent. Certainly parents must teach their children which activities are permitted and which are not, but they should not be surprised that the discriminations are difficult ones for the children to make. Piaget suggested that the first classification of objects is made according to what schemes can be applied to them. Lamp cords and toy cords are both objects to be pulled, so children classify them together. By forbidding the pulling of lamp cords and permitting the pulling of toy cords, parents require their children to reclassify the objects along a different dimension. The more dimensions of difference between the two objects, the more likely that children will find one that allows them to avoid the forbidden activity. Even then, they might make the discrimination on an incorrect basis. For example, if a child decides that lamp cords are forbidden because they are brown in color whereas toy cords are permissibly white, he will successfully avoid pulling on the lamp until his parents purchase a new lamp with a white cord.

THE PRESCHOOL YEARS

A three-year-old boy drags his mother to the kitchen, opens the oven door, places his hands inside, brings them out again, and extends his arms toward his mother. Smiling, he says, "Want a cookie, Mommy?" His hands are empty. During the Preoperational Period, especially in the preschool years from three to five, children engage in a considerable amount of fantasy play. The world of make-believe is made possible because the Preoperational child has acquired the ability to use symbols. Symbols and language free children's thinking from the immediately perceptible and permit children to express their thoughts and to use their imaginations.

160

It is not a girl's vivid imagination, however, that leads her to complain about her share of dessert. If her brother's piece of pie is shorter but wider than her own, she may well believe that she got shortchanged. Similarly, once she mashes an unwanted pile of vegetables with her fork, she resists eating them all the more because the pile has gotten larger. Judging from the conservation training research, mere verbal explanations about the equality of the desserts or the unchanged quantity of vegetables are unlikely to change the preschooler's mind. It may well be simpler for a parent to cut the girl's dessert in two, so she believes she now has more, or to repile the vegetables so she believes she now has less.

With the rapid acquisition of language and concepts comes an unceasing interest in how things function, where they come from, and what they are called. "What that?" and "Why?" are nearly as frequently heard as "No, me do it!" Before parents can answer the preschooler's questions, they must figure out what was asked. That is not as easy as it might seem, as we are reminded by the familiar joke about a boy who asked where he came from. After receiving a long explanation about human reproduction from an embarrassed parent, he said, "But Johnny comes from Ohio. Where do I come from?" Elkind (1981) has suggested that young children tend to ask questions about psychological causality although the inquiries might appear to concern physical causes. A typical four-year-old might ask, "Why is the grass green?" or "Why do birds sing?" The answers that are satisfying involve psychological interpretations: the grass is green so it will look pretty; birds sing because they are happy.

In answering children's questions, it is best to remember Grandmother's sage advice to explain events in a child's own language. Even then, though, it is likely that the information will be distorted, as the process of assimilation adjusts the information to the child's current knowledge base. For example, Bernstein and Cowan (1975) reported on children's explanations of where babies come from. One child said, "They just get a duck or a goose and they get a little more growned . . . and then they turn into a baby. . . . They give them some food, people food, and they grow like a baby" (p. 87). A book read to that child about animal and human reproduction was probably too complex for the child to understand. The information about babies was assimilated into more familiar terms: ducks hatch from eggs, and feeding people helps them grow.

Perception is quite well developed in preschoolers, although they need a more complete stimulus than older children do in order to identify an object correctly. A closet door is therefore likely to become a monster as soon as the bedroom light is turned off because the partial stimulus which remains visible is not sufficient to be a convincing closet door. Moreover, showing these children that the monster is gone when the light is turned on is not persuasive. They, unlike infants, have object permanence, so the monster can easily reappear in the dark; just because they cannot see it in the light does not mean it is gone forever.

The highly limited deliberate memory abilities of preschoolers mean that they should not be expected to remember everything they have been asked to do, especially if the list is long. Face and hands might be washed, but ears are forgotten. If an interesting toy is lying in front of Father's slippers, Father's feet might get very cold as he waits for the child to remember the errand. These apparent disadvantages of preschoolers' memories are offset because they are also likely to forget some treat that had been promised by a harried parent. Distraction from a forbidden activity still works if the distractor is highly attractive, but this technique is not as successful as it is for infants. Finally, hypothesis testing will seem like unsystematic, idiosyncratic guessing rather than any pattern that could be called strategic or systematic. This might be seen in preschoolers' ideas about how a new story might end, where their shoes have been left, where pieces fit into a new puzzle, or how to fix a broken toy. The correct solution might be found, but only by trial and error.

162

THE ELEMENTARY SCHOOL YEARS

To many observers, the elementary school years are relatively quiet ones, especially because children do not need as much monitoring as preschoolers and infants. School, of course, absorbs a good deal of time as does playing games. We will look at school activity in the educational implications section, so the focus here will be on the impact of cognitive development on children's games.

We have already seen that the game of Twenty Questions exercises children's skills of hypothesis testing and that Concentration games exercise rote memory. Card games are also popular at this age, providing practice with numbers and classification. In gin rummy, for example, a number (e.g., 6) can be part of a run (5, 6, 7) or it can be part of a set of 6's, one from each suit. The child who can classify both ways and keep both possibilities in mind simultaneously will do better than the child who fixes on one classification and ignores the other. Memory is important as children try to keep track of what discards have been made and how these affect the possible plays in their own hands. They can develop hypotheses about which cards are likely to benefit their opponents. They can practice arithmetic skills in calculating the score. Frequently children will exhibit an unwarranted satisfaction with the one hypothesis they have generated instead of a thoughtful consideration of many alternative solutions, and their hypothesis testing will begin to be more systematic, but not fully efficient.

When a game can be played in many different ways, children of a wide variety of ages can enjoy it, although the older child or adult, with multiple strategies, is likely to be a better player. Consider an anagram game in which a set of letters is rearranged to form as many words as possible. A young child's strategy might be to think of a word and then see if it can be spelled with the available letters. Another strategy is to pick several letters at random and try to combine them in several orders. After the child has worked with this subset for a while, the letters can be returned to the pile and another subset drawn. A third strategy is to search for those letter combinations which are more frequent in the language as root words. Although these strategies differ considerably in their sophistication and probability for success, even young elementary schoolers can play the game with enjoyment.

If parents believe it possible to analyze their children's strategies, it is likely to occur to them that they could try to teach their children the more advanced strategies.* Two questions, however, should be raised: Can the parents teach the strategies? Should they try? The first is an empirical question. Depending on their ability to analyze the child's current level of functioning and to teach the more advanced strategies in a way that is meaningful to him, some parents will experience success. The second question is a philosophical one. What are the costs and benefits of teaching? The costs can be measured in time and motivation. If children are led to believe that their way of playing a game is wrong or stupid, and if they experience any difficulty in learning the correct or smart way, they are simply likely to avoid playing. The game will cease to be fun. If, on the other hand, they learn quickly and painlessly, the benefits may be satisfaction in solving a problem in a new manner and the competitive advantage of knowing a better way to play. Obviously no hard-and-fast rules can be made about whether or not to intervene.

ADOLESCENCE

Parents of elementary school children see that time as the lull before the storm. Adolescence is often as welcome as a sore

---

* Indeed, the search for training paradigms that accelerate children's acquisition of a particular skill seems to be a preoccupation among American researchers, educators, and parents. Piaget found this theme to recur so often that he labeled it "the American Question."

tooth because the stereotyped view of the period is as a time of rapid change, of social and sexual identity crises, of replacing parental values for peer values. That the stereotype is true for only a minority of adolescents has not weakened parental fears. Against such a background, the cognitive advances of the adolescent may not seem welcome either, for as we have already seen, Formal Operational adolescents are likely to appear argumentative as they examine their old beliefs in sets and discover inconsistencies. Profound shock awaits the unsuspecting parent who suddenly is confronted by a series of why questions: "Why can't I drink, smoke, or engage in sex?" "Why do I have to attend school or church?" "Why do I have to be home at midnight?" These why questions are much different from the four-year-old's. The psychological interpretations that satisfied the preschooler are obviously not going to please adolescents. They need detailed, factual information, often including rationalizations, for why they must engage in certain activities, especially if adults are not required to do so. Parents should expect charges of hypocrisy if their responses to their adolescents are not satisfactory.

SUMMARY

This section has offered suggestions for analyzing various problem situations and recommended that parents create their own list of solutions. The analysis that children drop food from their highchairs because of circular reactions is not advice on how to cope with the situation. Some parents will spread a plastic cloth on the floor and let their children drop as much as they please. Other parents will feed their children, denying them access to the food. Still others will ask their children to make a distinction between dropping toys, which is acceptable, and dropping food, which is not. Since most problems have a variety of potential solutions, the only real difficulty is finding one which is acceptable to parents and within the child's capability.

Unfortunately, that ideal is not always easy to meet. One

such episode occurred when a father asked me for advice on how to stop his two-year-old daughter from eating his cigarettes. I asked him to analyze the situation from her perspective. First, she watches him put cigarettes into his mouth. Imitation is a highly probable response, especially considering her age. Since she has no experience with smoking, she probably assimilates the activity into the more familiar eating scheme. The problem her father would like her to solve is a discrimination between his smoking, which she should not imitate, and his eating, which she should. That distinction may be too difficult to make. Secondly, the cigarettes are easily accessible on the coffee table. Because they are rather novel, she has a high motivation to investigate them, including shredding them and tasting them. Furthermore, she is allowed to pull apart and taste other items, especially food, that are given to her on that same coffee table. Again, the discrimination she is being asked to make is a difficult one.

Although I suggested that the father either give up smoking or at least keep his cigarettes out of her reach, for example, on the fireplace mantle, he insisted that she needed to learn the discrimination he had set up and rejected the idea that she might be too immature (both cognitively and emotionally) to learn it. Although the distinctions between eating and smoking and between eating food and eating cigarettes would be trivially easy to learn when she was a few years older, this father seemed to believe that only his solution (that the daughter be taught the distinctions now) was correct. I concluded that he was probably still in the Concrete Operational Period and resolved to stop giving advice.

EDUCATIONAL IMPLICATIONS

THE PROCESS APPROACH

The experimental tradition of process approach research includes constructing experimental tasks which resemble academic tasks, with modifications to make them "pure" measures of one or another process or subprocess. The extent to which experimental conclusions can then be applied back to class-rooms has never been very clear. When process approach re-searchers talk about educational implications at all, it tends to be in the form of broad recommendations rather than specific curriculum suggestions. The simple fact that processes are studied in isolation from each other indicates that process ap-proach researchers will not be well equipped to discuss how to put all the pieces together, as a teacher must do. Neverthe-less, it is useful to look at the recommendations because they can remind the educator where to look when difficulties arise in the educational process.

Attention

No matter what task is set before children, it is a truism that they must direct attention to the task. In the earlier grades, es-pecially, directed attention is itself a difficult task for children. Characteristics of the stimulus array can make some features so compelling that children cannot avoid looking at them (and hence fail to attend to the more relevant but less interesting features), or the entire task may be so uncompelling as to at-tract too little attention compared with the diversions any child can find around a classroom. Consider a book aimed at teach-ing young children to read. If the different letters in each word are printed in bright colors, the children might not attend suf-ficiently to the shapes of the letters, which distinguish them. If interesting pictures are printed opposite the words, children might prefer to look at the pictures. On the other hand, with no pictures or colors, children may not be attracted to the book at all.

Perception

The most extensive application of perception research has been in the area of reading, with Gibson's differentiation theory having the strongest influence (Williams, 1979). Yet after several decades of intensive reading research, we still do not have a clear picture of either the reading process or the best curriculum for teaching reading. Gibson and Levin (1975) concluded that "the reading process is rule governed and incapable of adequate description in simple terms" (p. 482). The rules which they believe govern reading are the same as those which govern perceptual development. Readers learn to select out the relevant information, ignore the irrelevant, and search for information efficiently. Selecting relevant information means that the distinctive features of letters (e.g., straight vs. curved lines, open vs. closed features) must be identified. Irrelevant information which can usually be ignored includes type font and color (except when they are used for emphasis). Visual scanning strategies refer to the control over eye movements so that (in English) words are read from left to right, preventing mistakes such as reading *saw* for *was.*

Learning to scan a page in the proper direction is sufficiently challenging that children practice it spontaneously. Elkind and Weiss (1967) demonstrated this when they asked children to name pictures that were arranged in a triangular pattern. Five-year-olds (probably not yet readers) and eight-year-olds (probably adequate readers) named the pictures by starting at the top and following around the triangular outline. Many of the young readers (six and seven years old) named the pictures from left to right, top to bottom. This was clearly a less efficient scanning strategy that was applied inappropriately, but it provided practice on a skill that was being learned. (Such spontaneous practice fits nicely with Piaget's idea that schemes are applied across many contexts merely because they are available to be exercised.) The broader implication is that teachers should be alert to the possibility that poor performance on one task may result from children's spontaneous practice of a skill they are learning in a different context.

Two other principles from perception that apply in reading are that readers will learn to process larger units of information and that they will process the least amount of information that still yields meaning. Part of the skill readers acquire is to read whole words instead of individual letters and phrases instead of individual words. The other principle means that they learn to use the many redundancies available to reduce the strain on the information processing system. Redundancies occur at many levels in reading. (a) At the level of individual letters, more than one distinctive feature helps to distinguish between letters. For example, the letter R is different from E by being curved, not straight; closed, not open; and unsymmetrical (Gibson, 1970). (b) Positions that letters may take within words are restricted. For example, ck is acceptable in English at the end of a word but not at the beginning. (c) Positions of words within sentences are constrained by what has come before them in the sentence. For example, after the article the, only a noun or adjective may follow, not a verb. (d) Words are limited by the gist of the sentence and paragraph. For example, "lightning" can "strike," but it cannot "sit." (For a more detailed analysis of redundancies, see Haber, 1978.)

Theories of perception have generally been cited as support for a phonics approach to teaching reading, under the argument that children need to learn to decode the letter patterns into sounds and to attach meanings to the sounds. The alternative position, that reading should be taught by a whole-word or sight-recognition method, is more likely to look for support in memory research.

Memory

Memory research dealing with how general world knowledge influences current information processing is applicable to the problem of reading. Whenever children encounter a new word, they can guess from the gist of the passage what that word might be. It is not uncommon for the beginning reader to come upon the following passage, "The dog said woof-woof," and read instead, "The dog said arf-arf" because prior exposure to dogs (and stories) supplied an incorrect inference about the last word. Another intrusion of prior knowledge into reading occurred when the young son of a physician laughed and said, "There's a doctor named Ugs." The sign he had read was "Drugs," but he had interpreted it as "Dr. Ugs" in keeping with his familiarity with doctors. Perhaps most importantly, though, memory is required in reading because the reader must remember the first part of a sentence while processing the last part in order to make sense of the whole thing. Many beginning readers read so slowly that they exceed their own memory spans. Each word in a sentence may be read accurately, but the words are not put together into a meaningful whole.

Although the phonics approach is frequently portrayed as the opposite of the whole-word approach, in curriculum design both are incorporated, and the debate really concerns the balance between the two. The levels of processing view of memory supports the position that both semantic and sensory analyses are needed, and in fact cannot really be separated. As Lockhart (1979) said,

> There is a tendency to regard the sensory components of a word or a picture as a kind of detachable skin within which is the kernel of meaning but that itself is meaningless. Sensory and semantic features do not possess this simple additive relationship. The sensory codes are aspects of analysis of meaning. [P. 82]

Broad recommendations stemming from memory research can be applied to nearly any educational task, not just reading. In the early grades, especially, when deliberate memory is poorly developed, teachers can work directly on improving it by teaching strategies and by teaching children to monitor their own memory efforts (Brown & DeLoache, 1978). Campione and Brown (1977) suggested teaching children to match their memory strategy to the task. Rehearsal should be used when the amount of information to be remembered is small and when verbatim (exact) recall is needed. An organizing strategy should be used when material has an inherent organization (not necessarily hierarchical) or when idiosyncratic organizations can be imposed by the child. Elaborative rehearsal is the preferred strategy when initially unrelated items must be associated (e.g., names and dates in history) and when a sufficient amount of study time is allowed.

Alternatively, as long as deliberate memory remains weak, educators can take advantage of involuntary memory by embedding memory in other meaningful tasks. The Soviets advocate a type of discovery learning to replace rote memorization. For example, Smirnov and Zinchenko (1969) recommended having children generate multiplication tables (repeatedly if necessary) instead of being given the tables to memorize directly. In the same way that general world knowledge was useful in reading, it will be useful in any school task where comprehension is desired. Understanding, and also remembering, will be automatic to the extent that new information is compatible with a child's existing knowledge (Brown, 1979).

Hypothesis testing

Hypothesis testing of the type discussed in the process approach section is directly relevant in courses where scientific reasoning is used (e.g., high school science courses) or where logical inferences are made about causes and effects (e.g., literature, history, geometry). In the earlier grades, hypotheses are still generated and tested, but children are less systematic and efficient at doing so, and the content in elementary school courses rarely calls for these skills.

A simpler kind of hypothesis generation can be seen in the rules which children acquire, especially in language and arithmetic. As was discussed earlier, children are expected to learn major rule systems, such as the grammar of their language, without formal instruction before they get to school. In school, however, teachers must correct any misconceptions children have about grammar rules and teach the more obscure rules directly. Children generate rules in other contexts on an informal basis, often in unexpected ways. One beginning reader, for example, showed me how she was to sound out the name of several pictures and circle the ones which matched the ending sound of a target word. She offered the "advice" that usually two of the four pictures were matches, but sometimes "they try to fool you and only one picture is correct." Her hypothesis was, in fact, a good one. Every set of pictures did have two which were supposed to match. Sometimes she found fewer matches because of incorrectly identifying the pictures (she called a horn a trumpet and so did not match it to the *corn* target word). It is not at all clear that her teacher would have wanted her to use the number of pictures already circled as a factor in her decision about what to circle, but the teacher can use such knowledge to diagnose the child's errors.

At other times, children can solve problems without knowing a general rule to cover the cases. One child announced to his astonished math teacher that he knew when numbers were even or odd, but only up to 999. It was frightening to think that he must have memorized each number separately instead of learning a rule to look at the last digit.

Concepts

Children might have difficulty learning if some concepts are too abstract, too complex, or lack status or validity. When children's sense of time is not fully developed, they will have as much trouble conceptualizing ancient Roman battles as the Vietnam War. Although their teacher may have vivid personal memories of the latter, the children will not, so both historical times will be difficult for them to learn. The succession of English kings or American presidents are lists to be learned by rote, since children have few personal experiences with kings or presidents. In fact, younger children's concepts of political systems and governments can be characterized as personalized, concrete, and incomplete (Adelson & O'Neil, 1966). When asked

172

the function of taxes, for example, 11-year-olds tended to reply, "to pay for the police," whereas an 18-year-old might say, "to run the government." The younger children's answers deal with highly visible services. Adolescents refer to less visible, more abstract functions; they know that there is more to government than just police or fire services.

PIAGET'S THEORY

It is easy to understand why educators hoped Piaget's theory would easily lead to specific curriculum suggestions. Despite criticisms of one or another of its aspects, the theory is the most comprehensive for intellectual development. It potentially addresses all levels of education, provides a goal to reach (Formal Operational thinking), and gives a broad timetable for reaching that goal. Consequently, educators have used the theory descriptively, by adopting Piagetian terminology to explain children's educational difficulties, and prescriptively, by setting goals and methods of education compatible with the theory.

Assimilation and accommodation

The concepts of assimilation and accommodation are particularly valuable in summarizing what children do in educational situations. Ginsburg (1977) demonstrated both concepts in the context of arithmetic. Assimilation explains why children convert the teacher-given problem into one more familiar to them, such as by changing multiplication into repeated addition. When children are learning to write large numbers, the command to write "forty-two" may produce an answer like "402," because the written system for numbers is assimilated into the spoken system. Accommodation can be seen in children's invented procedures for solving novel problems. A third grader who could do column addition correctly "solved" a new, linear addition problem as follows: $52 + 123 + 4 = 17$. The accom-

173

modation was to ignore place values (thus changing the old way of doing addition) and to add each digit individually. Kamii (1973) described the impact of assimilation and accommodation for teachers: "What we think we are teaching and what the child actually learns may turn out to be two different things" (p. 224).

Content of instruction

The first attempts to use Piaget's theory prescriptively resulted in new curriculum content aimed at moving children from one stage of development to another. Three experimental programs, all designed to change preschool children to the Concrete Operational Period, were developed in the early 1970s (Kamii, 1972; Lavatelli, 1970; Weikart, Rogers, Adcock, & McClelland, 1971). These were soon abandoned, in part because researchers decided no clear rationale existed for trying to make children attain Concrete Operations earlier than they usually did (Kuhn, 1979). At the high school level, one program has been developed to teach Formal Operational thinking in the context of biology (Lawson, 1975). Evaluation of it is hampered, however, by the difficulties in assessing Formal Operations outside of Piaget and Inhelder's original set of tasks (Kuhn, 1979).

Educators have shifted away from using Piaget's stage theory to set the content of the curriculum. DeVries (1978) expressed one reason for this: "By focusing on the stages which are the *result* of development, one misses entirely the theme of Piaget's theory—constructivism—which deals with the *process* of development" (p. 77, italics in original). Instead, educational objectives are now phrased in terms of children's mental activities and social relations. Kamii and DeVries (1977), for example, set two cognitive and three socio-emotional goals for a preschool program, which include having children generate interesting ideas, problems, and questions and notice the relationships among objects. Similarly, the "thinking games" described by

174

Furth and Wachs (1975) reflect the goals of thinking and creativity over more narrowly defined skills and factual knowledge. Educators appeal to Piaget's stage theory to argue (a) for allowing children to move from one wrong answer to another rather than from a wrong answer to the "adult" right answer and (b) for permitting them time to consolidate their gains before asking them to make new advances (Elkind, 1971; Kamii, 1973).

Methods of instruction

To derive recommendations about how teachers should teach, educational researchers have looked at various aspects of Piaget's theory. This occasionally results in conflicting advice (Murray, 1979). Generally, Piaget's theory is seen as compatible with open education, discovery learning, and Montessori's methods, because they all emphasize the self-initiated activity of the learner (Murray, 1978). In a discovery approach to spelling, for example, Duckworth (1973) recommended that children generate all possible ways for writing the sounds of the words. Thus, to spell the word *cousin,* children can suggest *c* or *k, ou* or *oo, s* or *z,* and so on. After all the alternatives are suggested, teachers can point out the usual way. Duckworth noted, "Instead of feeling stupid for creating an unconventional spelling, the children feel clever. . . . They also know . . . that there is only one correct way to write any given word" (1973, p. 152). Yet Elkind (1971) criticized discovery learning because it tries to stimulate a child's intrinsic motivation to learn by manipulating task characteristics rather than by giving the child more control over the learning environment, such as providing large blocks of time in areas of interest to him. Furthermore, Brainerd (1978) criticized discovery learning in general, and Piaget's version of it for training conservation in particular, because tutorial methods were more efficient and more likely to work with a broader sample of children.

Good and Brophy (1980) suggested that Piaget's theory is compatible with discovery learning only for the upper elementary and high school levels. Discovery learning encourages children to act mentally and physically on objects in order to discover their properties and the relationships between them. This utilizes "operative" knowing and so is only appropriate for Concrete and Formal Operational children, corresponding to the upper elementary and high school grades. In contrast, Preoperational thinking is "figurative," involving copying or reproducing the environment rather than changing it. At the preschool and early elementary grades, children are more likely to be in the Preoperational Period. Therefore, the traditional early school tasks of copying alphabet letters and memorizing simple vocabulary and arithmetic facts are more compatible with Piaget's theory for early education.

Piaget's theory has also been viewed as compatible with Montessori's methods for preschool education. Both agree that children's motivation to learn is intrinsic, and so both advocate child-initiated activities. Learning during the Preoperational Period is largely physical, rather than verbal, so children should be given many opportunities to interact with material physically. To learn about numbers, children need objects to count. To learn about colors, children can sort colored objects, not just recite names while teachers hold up colored swatches. To learn shapes, they can place shapes in a form board, copy designs, or walk patterns on a floor. Yet Piaget (1969) rejected the Montessori materials when used alone, on the grounds that the materials were too structured and too focused on sensory learning.

Two other aspects of learning which Piaget and Montessori both stressed are repetition and imitation. The need for repetition is seen in Piaget's theory in the principle of organization. Schemes and operations must be practiced in order to make them function more smoothly and efficiently. Since teachers cannot see inside a child's head to determine whether a structure is well-organized, they must allow each child freedom to practice and to set an individual pace to learning. Montessori

176

(1964, 1967; Rambusch, 1962) also recommended that children be allowed to set their own pace but warned that they might stay with a well-rehearsed skill after they are ready to move on if they are afraid of failing the next task or if no new task is available. Teachers, therefore, should have new material ready for introduction and then observe the children for signs of the proper moment to present it. Kamii (1973) warned of the difficulty in finding the right balance between intruding too much on the child's activity and being too passive.

In addition to repetition, imitation is an important tool in learning, as is readily observable in preschool children. Montessori and Piaget believed in exploiting this tendency by allowing children the freedom to move around the classroom and to observe other children's activities. In many cases, a child might provide a better model than an adult for how to perform some task. If the child uses intermediate steps toward the solution that an adult might skip, or if the child's relatively poor dexterity requires a different movement than the adult would make, then a child model will be better. Children are also more likely to exhibit incorrect problem-solving strategies which the observing child can then avoid.

The recommendation to encourage imitation can be misinterpreted in two ways, both of which the reader is cautioned against. First, it does not mean that one particular child is identified as a star and held up as an example to the other children. No child wants to be reprimanded with "Why can't you behave as well as sweet little Johnny?" The imitation described by Montessori and Piaget is spontaneous in the sense of being child-initiated. It springs from the observing child's desire to acquire the skill displayed by the other child. Second, the recommendation for imitation should not be construed as a rejection of the importance of individual differences or creativity. Learning is paced by each child and conducted according to a unique set of needs and prior experiences. The purpose of imitation is not to create similarity among children. Rather, it is to foster the learning of skills that would be accomplished more slowly through direct tuition or through trial-and-error learning.

Since the kind of imitation that Piaget suggested was child-initiated, his followers and collaborators have not exploited observational learning as a method of accelerating or teaching cognitive skills such as conservation. Instead, they have consistently advocated a type of discovery learning in which the teacher helps induce conflicts between what a child predicts might happen and what actually does happen (Inhelder, Sinclair, & Bovet, 1974). Brainerd's (1978) criticism is again appropriate here, because experimenter-directed observational learning (exposing, say, a nonconserving child to a model of another child who does conserve) is an effective training procedure according to some research.

Kamii and DeVries (1977, 1978) suggested that a teacher's methods for implementing the curriculum should correspond to the type of knowledge to be acquired. Piaget (1969) distinguished between three types of knowledge: physical, logico-mathematical, and social-arbitrary. Physical knowledge concerns the physical properties of objects and what can be done to them. Children discover these properties for themselves when they act on the objects. For example, they discover which objects float and which objects sink by placing them in water. They blow on objects through a straw to find out if that will move them across the floor. Logico-mathematical knowledge involves the child's actions on objects, not the objects themselves. For example, knowledge that the same number results when a row is counted from left to right as from right to left is derived from the counting activity, not from any property of the object counted. For both physical and logico-mathematical knowledge, the teacher does not need to provide feedback or reinforcement for learning to occur. What teachers do need to do is provide situations where the actions can take place and encourage the children to engage in the activity. For example, if children help prepare a table for eating a snack, they can count the plates, cups, and napkins each time they place an object on the table. Thus, for these two types of knowledge, a form of discovery learning is recommended.

The third category, social-arbitrary knowledge, is transmitted by the culture and includes the arbitrary rules governing interpersonal relations. Learning to take turns, to clean up after playing, and to throw balls but not blocks are examples of social-arbitrary knowledge. This information is taught directly by teachers and by other children and should be reinforced because motivation to learn these rules is not intrinsic to any situation or object. Thus many aspects of the traditional preschool curriculum are suitable for stimulating intellectual development, but the teacher's role varies according to the situation (and the child).

Most of the curriculum and method suggestions made so far have been aimed at the preschool level. This undoubtedly reflects the fact that researchers have much more ready access to preschool classrooms and fewer restrictions in implementing curriculum changes. Nevertheless, some suggestions are applicable to any grade level. Duckworth (1979) pointed out that any classroom is bound to have enormous variations in children's level of development and that designing individual programs for each child is virtually impossible. She recommended that teachers "offer situations in which children at various levels, whatever their intellectual structures, can come to know parts of the world in a new way" (p. 311). Gallagher (1981) encouraged teachers to look to Piaget's principles of assimilation and accommodation in order to decide what questions to ask children during a reading lesson. While some factual questions are necessary, teachers can also ask questions which suggest a new perspective or which prompt the children to integrate their personal experiences with facts in the story. Both Gallagher (1978) and DeVries (1978) cautioned against the common superficial application of Piagetian theory that merely gives children physical objects to manipulate. "These applications are not inconsistent with . . . Piaget's theory. Nevertheless, they have the effect of reducing it to a pale shadow of Piaget's meaning" (DeVries, 1978, p. 79).

It should be obvious by now that the connection between Piaget's theory and educational practices is far from clear. Three major reasons for this have been offered. First, Piaget studied laws of development which would have universal application; traditional American education, in contrast, is concerned with individual differences, not universality (Sigel, 1978). Second, Piaget was not concerned directly with education. His interests were in the development of knowledge, not the acquisition of skills and factual information (Murray, 1979; Sigel, 1978). Third, the theory still has major ambiguities. Kuhn (1979) identified the two most important: (a) the cognitive competencies associated with each stage are not fully specified and (b) the method for recognizing when a child is "cognitively active" is unknown.

> To the extent that developmental stages are not fully defined, the recommendation that curriculum be based on them becomes an empty one. . . . The need [is] to define . . . the nature of self-directed intellectual activity and the process by which it becomes developmentally transformed. Without such knowledge, there is no basis on which to substantiate the assertion that the ideal educational environment is one in which students are allowed to choose and direct their own activities. [Kuhn, 1979, p. 358]

SUMMARY

This chapter has indicated in a general fashion how Piaget's theory and the process approach can be useful to parents and educators. The philosophy expressed in both the parenting and educational sections was that children are fundamentally different from adults; therefore, what seems reasonable from an adult's perspective may be unreasonable from a child's point of view, and vice versa. Both previous experience and current cognitive knowledge put limits on what children can learn. Sometimes those limitations are demonstrated when the child misbehaves; other times, the limitations show as a failure to profit from classroom instruction.

The characteristics of the Piagetian stages and the developmental advances in the processes of thought provide clues to parents concerning the reasons for their child's behavior. Many actions which are annoying might be slightly more tolerable if parents could figure out what problems their children are trying to solve. Teachers were also encouraged to analyze the tasks they demand of their pupils. Successful learning is more likely to occur if the problem is within the child's perceptual, memory, and hypothesis testing skills. Moreover, the problems are more likely to be solved if their elements are familiar to children and if they are presented concretely rather than abstractly, at least for the elementary school and preschool child.

Finally, the connection between Piagetian theory and educational practice is not straightforward. While it is generally seen as compatible with discovery learning approaches, educators have varied considerably in their interpretations of how the theory is to be implemented.

REFERENCES

Acredelo, L. P., Pick, H. L., Jr., & Olsen, M. G. Environmental differentiation and familiarity as determinants of children's memory for spatial location. *Developmental Psychology,* 1975, *11,* 495-501.

Adelson, J., & O'Neil, R. P. Growth of political ideas in adolescence: The sense of community. *Journal of Personality and Social Psychology,* 1966, *4,* 295-306.

Allik, J., & Valsiner, J. Visual development in ontogenesis: Some reevaluations. In H. W. Reese & L. P. Lipsitt (Eds.), *Advances in child development and behavior* (Vol. 15). New York: Academic Press, 1980.

Arlin, P. K. Cognitive development in adulthood: A fifth stage? *Developmental Psychology,* 1975, *11,* 602-606.

Atkinson, K., MacWhinney, B., & Stoel, C. *An experiment on the recognition of babbling.* Papers and reports on child language development. Committee on Linguistics, Stanford University, 1970, No. 1.

Atkinson, R. C., & Shiffrin, R. M. Human memory: A proposed system and its control processes. In K. W. Spence & J. T. Spence (Eds.), *The psychology of learning and motivation* (Vol. 2). New York: Academic Press, 1968.

Ault, R. L. Problem-solving strategies of reflective, impulsive, fast-accurate, and slow-inaccurate children. *Child Development,* 1973, *44,* 259-266.

Beilin, H. *Piaget and the new functionalism.* Address to the Eleventh Symposium of the Jean Piaget Society, Philadelphia, May 1981.

Bernstein, A. C., & Cowan, P. A. Children's concepts of how people get babies. *Child Development,* 1975, *46,* 77-91.

Bower, T. G. R. The object in the world of the infant. *Scientific American,* 1971, *225,* 30-38.

Brainerd, C. J. Learning research and Piagetian theory. In L. S. Siegel & C. J. Brainerd (Eds.), *Alternatives to Piaget: Critical essays on the theory.* New York: Academic Press, 1977.

Brainerd, C. J. *Piaget's theory of intelligence.* Englewood Cliffs, N.J.: Prentice-Hall, 1978.

Brainerd, C. J., & Allen, T. W. Experimental inductions of the conservation of "first-order" quantitative invariants. *Psychological Bulletin,* 1971, *75,* 128-144.

Brainerd, C. J., & Brainerd, S. H. Order of acquisition of number and quantity conservation. *Child Development,* 1972, *43,* 1401-1406.

Brekke, B., Williams, J. D., & Tait, P. The acquisition of conservation of weight by visually impaired children. *Journal of Genetic Psychology,* 1974, *125,* 89-97.

Brown, A. L. The development of memory: Knowing, knowing about knowing, and knowing how to know. In H. W. Reese (Ed.), *Advances in child development and behavior* (Vol. 10). New York: Academic Press, 1975.

Brown, A. L. Theories of memory and the problems of development: Activity, growth and knowledge. In L. S. Cermak & F. I. M. Craik (Eds.), *Levels of processing in human memory*. Hillsdale, N.J.: Lawrence Erlbaum, 1979.

Brown, A. L., & DeLoache, J. S. Skills, plans, and self-regulation. In R. S. Siegler (Ed.), *Children's thinking: What develops?* Hillsdale, N.J.: Lawrence Erlbaum, 1978.

Bruner, J. S. On perceptual readiness. *Psychological Review*, 1957, *64*, 123-152.

Bruner, J. S., Olver, R. R., & Greenfield, P. M. *Studies in cognitive growth*. New York: Wiley, 1966.

Caldwell, E. C., & Hall, V. C. Distinctive-features versus prototype learning reexamined. *Journal of Experimental Psychology*, 1970, *83*, 7-12.

Campione, J. C., & Brown, A. L. Memory and metamemory development in educable retarded children. In R. V. Kail, Jr., & J. W. Hagen (Eds.), *Perspectives on the development of memory and cognition*. Hillsdale, N.J.: Lawrence Erlbaum, 1977.

Chi, M. T. H. Short-term memory limitations in children: Capacity or processing deficits? *Memory and Cognition*, 1976, *4*, 559-572.

Chi, M. T. H. Knowledge structures and memory development. In R. S. Siegler (Ed.), *Children's thinking: What develops?* Hillsdale, N.J.: Lawrence Erlbaum, 1978.

Cohen, L. B. A two process model of infant visual attention. *Merrill-Palmer Quarterly*, 1973, *19*, 157-180.

Cohen, L. B. Our developing knowledge of infant perception and cognition. *American Psychologist*, 1979, *34*, 894-899.

Cohen, L. B., DeLoache, J. S., & Strauss, M. S. Infant visual perception. In J. D. Osofsky (Ed.), *Handbook of infant development*. New York: Wiley, 1979.

Cohen, L. B., & Gelber, E. R. Infant visual memory. In L. B. Cohen & P. Salapatek (Eds.), *Infant perception: From sensation to cognition* (Vol. 1). New York: Academic Press, 1975.

Cohen, L. B., Gelber, E., & Lazar, M. Infant habituation and generalization to differing degrees of stimulus novelty. *Journal of Experimental Child Psychology*, 1971, *11*, 379-389.

Cowan, P. A. *Piaget: With feeling*. New York: Holt, Rinehart and Winston, 1978.

Craik, F. I. M. Levels of processing: Overview and closing comments. In L. S. Cermak & F. I. M. Craik (Eds.), *Levels of processing in human memory*. Hillsdale, N.J.: Lawrence Erlbaum, 1979.

Craik, F I. M., & Lockhart, R. S. Levels of processing: A framework for memory research. *Journal of Verbal Learning and Verbal Behavior*, 1972, *11*, 671-684.

Dasen, P. R. (Ed.). *Piagetian psychology: Cross-cultural contributions*. New York: Gardner Press, 1977.

Day, M. C. Developmental trends in visual scanning. In H. W. Reese (Ed.), *Advances in child development and behavior* (Vol. 10). New York: Academic Press, 1975.

DeVries, R. Early education and Piagetian theory. In J. M. Gallagher & J. A.

Easley, Jr. (Eds.), *Knowledge and development* (Vol. 2). New York: Plenum, 1978.

Duckworth, E. Language and thought. In M. Schwebel & J. Raph (Eds.), *Piaget in the classroom*. New York: Basic Books, 1973.

Duckworth, E. Either we're too early and they can't learn it or we're too late and they know it already: The dilemma of "Applying Piaget." *Harvard Educational Review,* 1979, *49,* 297-312.

Elkind, D. Two approaches to intelligence: Piagetian and psychometric. In D. R. Green, H. P. Ford, & G. B. Flamer (Eds.), *Measurement and Piaget*. New York: McGraw-Hill, 1971.

Elkind, D. Perceptual development in children. *American Scientist,* 1975, *63,* 533-541.

Elkind, D. *Children and adolescents: Interpretive essays on Jean Piaget* (3rd ed.). New York: Oxford University Press, 1981.

Elkind, D., & Weiss, J. Studies in perceptual development III: Perceptual exploration. *Child Development,* 1967, *38,* 1153-1161.

Ennis, R. H. Conditional logic and primary school children: A developmental study. *Interchange,* 1971, *2,* 126-132.

Flavell, J. H. *The developmental psychology of Jean Piaget.* Princeton, N.J.: Van Nostrand, 1963.

Flavell, J. H. First discussant's comments: What is memory development the development of? *Human Development,* 1971, *14,* 272-278.

Flavell, J. H. *Cognitive development.* Englewood Cliffs, N.J.: Prentice-Hall, 1977.

Flavell, J. H., Beach, D. R., & Chinsky, J. M. Spontaneous verbal rehearsal in a memory task as a function of age. *Child Development,* 1966, *37,* 283-299.

Flavell, J. H., Friedrichs, A. G., & Hoyt, J. D. Developmental changes in memorization processes. *Cognitive Psychology,* 1970, *1,* 324-340.

Flavell, J. H., & Wellman, H. M. Metamemory. In R. V. Kail, Jr., & J. W. Hagen (Eds.), *Perspectives on the development of memory and cognition.* Hillsdale, N.J.: Lawrence Erlbaum, 1977.

Furth, H. G. *Piaget and knowledge.* Englewood Cliffs, N.J.: Prentice-Hall, 1969.

Furth, H. G., & Wachs, H. *Thinking goes to school: Piaget's theory in practice.* New York: Oxford University Press, 1975.

Gallagher, J. M. Reflexive abstraction and education. In J. M. Gallagher & J. A. Easley, Jr. (Eds.), *Knowledge and development* (Vol. 2). New York: Plenum, 1978.

Gallagher, J. M. *Training teachers in the understanding of inferences: A Piagetian perspective.* Paper presented at the Eleventh Symposium of the Jean Piaget Society, Philadelphia, May 1981.

Geis, M. F., & Hall, D. M. Encoding and incidental memory in children. *Journal of Experimental Child Psychology,* 1976, *22,* 58-66.

Geis, M. F., & Hall, D. M. Encoding and congruity in children's incidental memory. *Child Development,* 1978, *49,* 857-861.

Gelman, R. Conservation acquisition: A problem of learning to attend to rele-

185

vant attributes. *Journal of Experimental Child Psychology,* 1969, *7,* 167-187.

Gelman, R. Cognitive development. In M. R. Rosenzweig & L. W. Porter (Eds.), *Annual review of psychology* (Vol. 29). Palo Alto: Annual Reviews, Inc., 1978.

Gelman, R. Why we will continue to read Piaget. *The Genetic Epistemologist,* 1979, *8*(4), 1-3.

Gholson, B. *The cognitive-developmental basis of human learning: Studies in hypothesis testing.* New York: Academic Press, 1980.

Gholson, B., & Beilin, H. A developmental model of human learning. In H. W. Reese & L. P. Lipsitt (Eds.), *Advances in child development and behavior* (Vol. 13). New York: Academic Press, 1979.

Gholson, B., O'Connor, J., & Stern, I. Hypothesis sampling systems among preoperational and concrete operational kindergarten children. *Journal of Experimental Child Psychology,* 1976, *21,* 61-76.

Gibson, E. J. *Principles of perceptual learning and development.* New York: Appleton-Century-Crofts, 1969.

Gibson, E. J. The development of perception as an adaptive process. *American Scientist,* 1970, *58,* 98-107.

Gibson, E. J., & Levin, H. *The psychology of reading.* Cambridge, Mass.: MIT Press, 1975.

Ginsburg, H. *Children's arithmetic: The learning process.* New York: Van Nostrand, 1977.

Ginsburg, H., & Opper, S. *Piaget's theory of intellectual development.* Englewood Cliffs, N.J.: Prentice-Hall, 1979.

Gleitman, L. *What some concepts might not be.* Invited address to the Eleventh Symposium of the Jean Piaget Society, Philadelphia, May 1981.

Glick, J. *Culture and cognition: Some theoretical and methodological concerns.* Paper presented at the American Anthropological Association Meetings, New Orleans, November 1969.

Gollin, E. S. Developmental studies of visual recognition of incomplete objects. *Perceptual and Motor Skills,* 1960, *11,* 289-298.

Gollin, E. S. Factors affecting the visual recognition of incomplete objects: A comparative investigation of children and adults. *Perceptual and Motor Skills,* 1962, *15,* 583-590.

Good, T. L., & Brophy, J. E. *Educational psychology: A realistic approach.* New York: Holt, Rinehart and Winston, 1980.

Gratch, G. Recent studies based on Piaget's view of object concept development. In L. B. Cohen & P. Salapatek (Eds.), *Infant perception: From sensation to cognition* (Vol. 2). New York: Academic Press, 1975.

Greenfield, P. M. Cross-cultural research and Piagetian theory: Paradox and progress. In K. F. Riegel & J. A. Meacham (Eds.), *The developing individual in a changing world.* Chicago: Aldine, 1976.

Gruber, H. E., Girgus, J. S., & Banuazizi, A. The development of object permanence in the cat. *Developmental Psychology,* 1971, *4,* 9-15.

Gruen, G. E., & Vore, D. A. Development of conservation in normal and retarded children. *Developmental Psychology,* 1972, *6,* 146-157.

Haber, R. N. Visual perception. In M. R. Rosenzweig & L. W. Porter (Eds.), *Annual review of psychology* (Vol. 29). Palo Alto: Annual Reviews, Inc., 1978.

Hagen, J. W. Development and models of memory: Comments on the papers by Brown and Naus and Halasz. In L. S. Cermak & F. I. M. Craik (Eds.), *Levels of processing in human memory*. Hillsdale, N.J.: Lawrence Erlbaum, 1979.

Hagen, J. W., & Stanovich, K. G. Memory: Strategies of acquisition. In R. V. Kail, Jr., & J. W. Hagen (Eds.), *Perspectives on the development of memory and cognition*. Hillsdale, N.J.: Lawrence Erlbaum, 1977.

Hoving, K. L., Spencer, T., Robb, K. Y., & Schulte, D. Developmental changes in visual information processing. In P. A. Ornstein (Ed.), *Memory development in children*. Hillsdale, N.J.: Lawrence Erlbaum, 1978.

Inhelder, B., & Piaget, J. *The growth of logical thinking from childhood to adolescence* (trans. A. Parsons & S. Milgram). New York: Basic Books, 1958.

Inhelder, B., Sinclair, H., & Bovet, M. *Learning and the development of cognition* (trans. S. Wedgwood). Cambridge, Mass.: Harvard University Press, 1974.

Jacoby, L. L., & Craik, F. I. M. Effects of elaboration of processing at encoding and retrieval: Trace distinctiveness and recovery of initial context. In L. S. Cermak & F. I. M. Craik (Eds.), *Levels of processing in human memory*. Hillsdale, N.J.: Lawrence Erlbaum, 1979.

Jeffrey, W. E. The orienting reflex and attention in cognitive development. *Psychological Review*, 1968, *75*, 323-334.

Jensen, A. R. How much can we boost IQ and scholastic achievement? *Harvard Educational Review*, 1969, *39*, 1-123.

Jensen, A. R. Cumulative deficit in IQ of blacks in the rural south. *Developmental Psychology*, 1977, *13*, 184-191.

Kagan, J. A conception of early adolescence. *Daedalus*, 1971, *100*, 997-1012.

Kagan, J., Klein, R. E., Haith, M. M., & Morrison, F. J. Memory and meaning in two cultures. *Child Development*, 1973, *44*, 221-223.

Kagan, J., Rosman, B. L., Day, D., Albert, J., & Phillips, W. Information processing in the child: Significance of analytic and reflective attitudes. *Psychological Monographs*, 1964, *78* (1, Whole No. 578).

Kail, R. V., Jr., & Siegel, A. W. The development of mnemonic encoding in children: From perception to abstraction. In R. V. Kail, Jr., & J. W. Hagen (Eds.), *Perspectives on the development of memory and cognition*. Hillsdale, N.J.: Lawrence Erlbaum, 1977.

Kamii, C. An application of Piaget's theory to the conceptualization of a preschool curriculum. In M. C. Day & R. K. Parker (Eds.), *The preschool in action*. Boston: Allyn & Bacon, 1972.

Kamii, C. Piaget's interactionism and the process of teaching young children. In M. Schwebel & J. Raph (Eds.), *Piaget in the classroom*. New York: Basic Books, 1973.

Kamii, C., & DeVries, R. Piaget for early education. In M. C. Day & R. K.

187

Parker (Eds.), *The preschool in action* (2nd ed.). Boston: Allyn & Bacon, 1977.

Kamii, C., & DeVries, R. *Physical knowledge in preschool education: Implications of Piaget's theory.* Englewood Cliffs, N.J.: Prentice-Hall, 1978.

Keeney, T. J., Cannizzo, S. R., & Flavell, J. H. Spontaneous and induced verbal rehearsal in a recall task. *Child Development,* 1967, *38,* 953-966.

Kesner, R. P., & Baker, T. B. Neuroanatomical correlates of language and memory: A developmental perspective. In R. L. Ault (Ed.), *Developmental perspectives.* Santa Monica: Goodyear, 1980.

Kingsley, P. R., & Hagen, J. W. Induced versus spontaneous rehearsal in short-term memory in nursery school children. *Developmental Psychology,* 1969, *1,* 40-46.

Kodroff, J., & Roberge, J. Developmental analysis of the conditional reasoning abilities of primary-grade children. *Developmental Psychology,* 1975, *11,* 21-28.

Kolers, P. A. A pattern-analyzing basis of recognition. In L. S. Cermak & F. I. M. Craik (Eds.), *Levels of processing in human memory.* Hillsdale, N.J.: Lawrence Erlbaum, 1979.

Kreutzer, M. A., Leonard, C., & Flavell, J. H. An interview study of children's knowledge about memory. *Monographs of the Society for Research in Child Development,* 1975, *40* (1, Serial No. 159).

Kuczaj, S. A., II. Children's judgments of grammatical and ungrammatical irregular past-tense verbs. *Child Development,* 1978, *49,* 319-326.

Kuhn, D. The application of Piaget's theory of cognitive development to education. *Harvard Educational Review,* 1979, *49,* 340-360.

Kumler, H. *Primate societies: Group techniques of ecological adaptation.* Chicago: Aldine-Atherton, 1971.

Lavatelli, C. S. *Piaget's theory applied to an early childhood curriculum.* Boston: American Science & Engineering, 1970.

Lawson, A. Developing formal thought through biology teaching. *American Biology Teacher,* 1975, *37,* 411-429.

Levine, M. Hypothesis behavior by humans during discrimination learning. *Journal of Experimental Psychology,* 1966, *71,* 331-338.

Levine, M., Leitenberg, H., & Richter, M. The blank trials law: The equivalence of positive reinforcement and nonreinforcement. *Psychological Review,* 1964, *71,* 94-103.

Lewis, M., & Brooks, J. Infants' social perception: A constructivist view. In L. B. Cohen & P. Salapatek (Eds.), *Infant perception: From sensation to cognition* (Vol. 2). New York: Academic Press, 1975.

Liben, L. S. Memory in the context of cognitive development: The Piagetian approach. In R. V. Kail, Jr., and J. W. Hagen (Eds.), *Perspectives on the development of memory and cognition.* Hillsdale, N.J.: Lawrence Erlbaum, 1977.

Lockhart, R. S. Remembering events: Discussion of papers by Jacoby and Craik, Battig, and Nelson. In L. S. Cermak & F. I. M. Craik (Eds.), *Levels of processing in human memory.* Hillsdale, N.J.: Lawrence Erlbaum, 1979.

Lockhart, R. S., Craik, F. I. M., & Jacoby, L. L. Depth of processing, recognition and recall. In J. Brown (Ed.), *Recall and recognition*. New York: Wiley, 1976.

Lovell, K. Some aspects of the work of Piaget in perspective. In A. Floyd (Ed.), *Cognitive development in the school years*. New York: Halsted, 1979.

Markman, E. M., & Siebert, J. Classes and collections: Internal organization and resulting holistic properties. *Cognitive Psychology*, 1976, *8*, 561-577.

McCall, R. B. Attention in the infant: Avenue to the study of cognitive development. In D. Walcher & D. Peters (Eds.), *Early childhood: The development of self-regulatory mechanisms*. New York: Academic Press, 1971.

McLaughlin, G. H. Psychologic: A possible alternative to Piaget's formulation. *British Journal of Educational Psychology*, 1963, *33*, 61-67.

Meacham, J. A. Soviet investigations of memory development. In R. V. Kail, Jr., & J. W. Hagen (Eds.), *Perspectives on the development of memory and cognition*. Hillsdale, N.J.: Lawrence Erlbaum, 1977.

Mervis, C. B., & Rosch, E. Categorization of natural objects. In M. R. Rosenzweig & L. W. Porter (Eds.), *Annual review of psychology* (Vol. 32). Palo Alto: Annual Review, Inc., 1981.

Millar, S. Spatial representations by blind and sighted children. *Journal of Experimental Child Psychology*, 1976, *21*, 460-479.

Miller, G. A. The magical number seven, plus or minus two: Some limits on our capacity for processing information. *Psychological Review*, 1956, *63*, 81-97.

Milne, A. A. *The house at Pooh Corner*. New York: Dutton, 1961. (a)

Milne, A. A. *Winnie-the-Pooh*. New York: Dutton, 1961. (b)

Mitchell, C., & Ault, R. L. *The development of involuntary memory*. Paper presented at the Southwestern Regional Society for Research in Human Development. Lawrence, Kan., March 1980.

Moely, B., Olson, P. A., Halwes, T. G., & Flavell, J. H. Production deficiency in young children's clustered recall. *Developmental Psychology*, 1969, *1*, 26-34.

Montessori, M. *Dr. Montessori's own handbook*. Cambridge, Mass.: Bentley, 1964.

Montessori, M. *The Montessori method* (trans. A. E. George). Cambridge, Mass.: Bentley, 1967.

Mosher, F. A., & Hornsby, J. R. On asking questions. In J. S. Bruner, R. R. Olver, & P. M. Greenfield (Eds.), *Studies in cognitive growth*. New York: Wiley, 1966.

Murray, F. B. Two models of human behavior and reading instruction. In J. M. Gallagher & J. A. Easley, Jr. (Eds.), *Knowledge and development* (Vol. 2). New York: Plenum, 1978.

Murray, F. B. The future of Piaget's theory in education. *The Genetic Epistemologist*, 1979, *8*(4), 7-10.

Mussen, P. H., Conger, J. J., Kagan, J., & Geiwitz, J. *Psychological development: A life-span approach*. New York: Harper & Row, 1979.

Naus, M. J., & Halasz, F. G. Developmental perspectives on cognitive processing and semantic memory structure. In L. S. Cermak & F. I. M. Craik

(Eds.), *Levels of processing in human memory.* Hillsdale, N.J.: Lawrence Erlbaum, 1979.

Naus, M. J., Ornstein, P. A., & Hoving, K. L. Developmental implications of multistore and depth-of-processing models of memory. In P. A. Ornstein (Ed.), *Memory development in children.* Hillsdale, N.J.: Lawrence Erlbaum, 1978.

Neimark, E. Intellectual development during adolescence. In F. D. Horowitz (Ed.), *Review of child development research* (Vol. 4). Chicago: University of Chicago Press, 1975.

Neisser, U. The control of information pickup in selective looking. In A. D. Pick (Ed.), *Perception and its development.* Hillsdale, N.J.: Lawrence Erlbaum, 1979.

Olver, R. R., & Hornsby, J. R. On equivalence. In J. S. Bruner, R. R. Olver, & P. M. Greenfield (Eds.), *Studies in cognitive growth.* New York: Wiley, 1966.

Ornstein, P. A., Naus, M. J., & Liberty, C. Rehearsal and organizational processes in children's memory. *Child Development,* 1975, *46,* 818-830.

Owings, R. A., & Baumeister, A. A. Levels of processing, encoding strategies, and memory development. *Journal of Experimental Child Psychology,* 1979, *28,* 100-118.

Paris, S. G. Comprehension of language connectives and propositional logical relationships. *Journal of Experimental Child Psychology,* 1973, *16,* 278-291.

Paris, S. G., & Lindauer, B. K. The role of inference in children's comprehension and memory for sentences. *Cognitive Psychology,* 1976, *8,* 217-227.

Paris, S. G., & Lindauer, B. K. Constructive aspects of children's comprehension and memory. In R. V. Kail, Jr., & J. W. Hagen (Eds.), *Perspectives on the development of memory and cognition.* Hillsdale, N.J.: Lawrence Erlbaum, 1977.

Paris, S. G., & Upton, L. R. Children's memory for inferential relationships in prose. *Child Development,* 1976, *47,* 660-668.

Perlmutter, M., & Myers, N. A. Recognition memory development in two- to four-year-olds. *Developmental Psychology,* 1974, *10,* 447-450.

Piaget, J. *Play, dreams, and imitation in childhood* (trans. C. Gattegno & F. M. Hodgson). New York: Norton, 1951.

Piaget, J. *The origins of intelligence in children* (trans. M. Cook). New York: International University Press, 1952.

Piaget, J. *The construction of reality in the child* (trans. M. Cook). New York: Basic Books, 1954.

Piaget, J. The general problems of the psychobiological development of the child. In J. M. Tanner & B. Inhelder (Eds.), *Discussions on child development* (Vol. 4). London: Tavistock, 1960.

Piaget, J. *Science of education and the psychology of the child.* New York: Viking, 1969.

Piaget, J. Piaget's theory. In P. H. Mussen (Ed.), *Carmichael's manual of child psychology* (Vol. 1). New York: Wiley, 1970.

Piaget, J. Intellectual evolution from adolescence to adulthood. *Human Development*, 1972, *15*, 1-12.

Piaget, J., & Inhelder, B. *Memory and intelligence* (trans. A. J. Pomerans). New York: Basic Books, 1973.

Piaget, J., & Inhelder, B. The gaps in empiricism. In B. Inhelder & H. Chipman (Eds.), *Piaget and his school*. New York: Springer-Verlag, 1976.

Rambusch, N. M. *Learning how to learn: An American approach to Montessori*. Baltimore: Helicon Press, 1962.

Reese, H. W. Imagery and associative memory. In R. V. Kail, Jr., & J. W. Hagen (Eds.), *Perspectives on the development of memory and cognition*. Hillsdale, N.J.: Lawrence Erlbaum, 1977.

Riegel, K. F. Dialectic operations: The final period of cognitive development. *Human Development*, 1973, *16*, 346-370.

Rosch, E., Mervis, C. B., Gray, W. D., Johnson, D. M., & Boyes-Braem, P. Basic objects in natural categories. *Cognitive Psychology*, 1976, *8*, 382-439.

Santostefano, S., & Paley, E. Development of cognitive controls in children. *Child Development*, 1964, *35*, 939-949.

Scarr-Salapatek, S. Race, social class and IQ. *Science*, 1971, *174*, 1285-1295.

Scarr, S., & Weinberg, R. A. IQ test performance of black children adopted by white families. *American Psychologist*, 1976, *31*, 726-739.

Shepp, B. E., Burns, B., & McDonough, D. The relation of stimulus structure to perceptual and cognitive development: Further tests of a separability hypothesis. In F. Wilkening, J. Becker, & T. Trabasso (Eds.), *Information integration by children*. Hillsdale, N.J.: Lawrence Erlbaum, 1980.

Siegler, R. S. The origins of scientific reasoning. In R. S. Siegler (Ed.), *Children's thinking: What develops?* Hillsdale, N.J.: Lawrence Erlbaum, 1978.

Siegler, R. S. Developmental sequences within and between concepts. *Monographs of the Society for Research in Child Development*, 1981, *46*(2, Serial No. 189).

Sigel, I. E. Introduction. In J. M. Gallagher & J. A. Easley, Jr. (Eds.), *Knowledge and development* (Vol. 2). New York: Plenum, 1978.

Smirnov, A. A. *Problems of the psychology of memory* (trans. S. A. Corson). New York: Plenum, 1973.

Smirnov, A. A., & Zinchenko, P. I. Problems in the psychology of memory. In M. Cole & I. Maltzman (Eds.), *A handbook of contemporary Soviet psychology*. New York: Basic Books, 1969.

Sophian, C., & Hagen, J. W. Involuntary memory and the development of retrieval skills in young children. *Journal of Experimental Child Psychology*, 1978, *26*, 458-471.

Sperling, G. The information available in brief visual presentation. *Psychological Monographs*, 1960, *74*(11, Whole No. 498).

Stevenson, H. W. *Children's learning*. New York: Appleton-Century-Crofts, 1972.

Strauss, S., & Levin, I. Commentary on R. S. Siegler's Developmental sequences within and between concepts. *Monographs of the Society for Research in Child Development*, 1981, *46*(2, Serial No. 189).

Stroop, J. R. Studies of interference in serial verbal reactions. *Journal of Experimental Psychology*, 1935, *18*, 643-662.

Trabasso, T., Isen, A. M., Dolecki, P., McLanahan, A. G., Riley, C. A., & Tucker, T. How do children solve class-inclusion problems? In R. S. Siegler (Ed.), *Children's thinking: What develops?* Hillsdale, N.J.: Lawrence Erlbaum, 1978.

Tulving, E., & Thomson, D. M. Encoding specificity and retrieval processes in episodic memory. *Psychological Review*, 1973, *80*, 352-373.

Tumblin, A., & Gholson, B. Hypothesis theory and the development of conceptual learning. *Psychological Bulletin*, 1981, *90*, 102-124.

Uzgiris, I. C. Situational generality of conservation. *Child Development*, 1964, *35*, 831-841.

Van Horn, K. R., & Bartz, W. H. Information seeking strategies in cognitive development. *Psychonomic Science*, 1968, *11*, 341-342.

Vendovitskaya, T. V. Development of memory. In A. V. Zaporozhets & D. B. Elkonin (Eds.), *The psychology of preschool children* (trans. J. Shybut & S. Simon). Cambridge, Mass.: MIT Press, 1971.

Vernon, M. D. The functions of schemata in perceiving. *Psychological Review*, 1955, *62*, 180-192.

Weikart, D., Rogers, L., Adcock, C., & McClelland, D. *The cognitively oriented curriculum*. Urbana, Ill.: ERIC-NAEYE, 1971.

Weir, M. W. Developmental changes in problem-solving strategies. *Psychological Review*, 1964, *71*, 473-490.

Wellman, H. M., Ritter, K., & Flavell, J. H. Deliberate memory behavior in the delayed reactions of very young children. *Developmental Psychology*, 1975, *11*, 780-787.

Williams, J. Reading instruction today. *American Psychologist*, 1979, *34*, 917-922.

Wise, K. L., Wise, L. A., & Zimmermann, R. R. Piagetian object permanence in the infant rhesus monkey. *Developmental Psychology*, 1974, *10*, 429-437.

Youniss, J. Operational development in deaf Costa Rican subjects. *Child Development*, 1974, *45*, 212-216.

Zaporozhets, A. V., & Elkonin, D. B. (Eds.). *The psychology of preschool children* (trans. J. Shybut & S. Simon). Cambridge, Mass.: MIT Press, 1971.

AUTHOR INDEX

194

SUBJECT INDEX

198

0

Jl

TOUCHING

TOUCHING:

THE HUMAN SIGNIFI-
CANCE OF THE SKIN

by ASHLEY MONTAGU

COLUMBIA UNIVERSITY PRESS
NEW YORK

Ashley Montagu is the author of more than thirty books and over two hundred articles in scholarly and scientific journals. He has taught at Harvard and at New York University and was formerly Chairman of the Department of Anthropology at Rutgers, the State University of New Jersey.

International Standard Book Number: 0-231-03488-1
Library of Congress Catalog Card Number: 75-151290
Printed in the United States of America

10 9 8

Clothbound editions of Columbia University Press books are Smyth-sewn and printed on permanent and durable acid-free paper.

To the Memory of
Howard Gossage

PREFACE

THIS BOOK is about the skin as a tactile organ very much involved, not alone physically but also behaviorally, in the growth and development of the organism. The central referent is man, and what happens or fails to happen to him as an infant by way of tactile experience, as affecting his subsequent behavioral development, is my principal concern here. When I first started thinking about this subject in 1944 there was very little experimental evidence available bearing upon these matters. Today a considerable amount of such evidence has been made available by a large variety of investigators, and my lonely paper of 1953, "The Sensory Influences of the Skin" (*Texas Reports on Biology and Medicine,* vol. 2, 1953, pp. 291–301) is no longer alone. This book draws upon many sources of information, and notes citing these sources have been gathered in the Reference section, pp. 293–324, where they are identified by the numbers of the pages and the line or lines on the pages where references or quotations occur. (This system seemed preferable to using note numbers which interrupt the text. When notes are amplifications, suggestions, or comments, however, rather than simple source citations, they are keyed to asterisks and appear on the same pages as the passages to which they refer.)

The skin as an organ, the largest organ of the body, was very much neglected until quite recently. But it is not as an organ as such that I am here concerned with the skin; rather, in contrast to the psychosomatic or centrifugal approach, I am interested in what may be called the somatopsychic or centripetal approach. In short, I am interested in the manner in which tactile experience or its lack affects the development of behavior; hence, "the mind of the skin."

Princeton, New Jersey   *Ashley Montagu*
8 February 1971

ACKNOWLEDGMENTS

THE AUTHOR wishes to express his appreciation to the publishers and individuals who granted permission to quote from the following sources: "The Effect of Culture on Mother-Child Tactile Communication," by Vidal S. Clay, Teachers College, Columbia University; "The Netsilik Eskimo and the Origins of Human Behavior," by R. James de Boer; "Emotional Development in the First Year of Life," by S. Escalona, in M. J. E. Senn, ed., *Problems of Infancy and Childhood* (New York: Josiah Macy, Jr. Foundation, 1953); "The Maternal Affectional System of Rhesus Monkeys," by H. F. Harlow, M. K. Harlow, and E. W. Hansen, in H. L. Rheingold, ed., *Maternal Behavior in Mammals* (New York: Wiley, 1963); *Truby King the Man,* by M. King (London: Allen & Unwin, 1948); *Alfred Kroeber: A Personal Configuration,* by Theodora Kroeber (Berkeley: University of California Press, 1970); "On the Sense of Touch," by Informant 9F, in M. Mead and R. Métraux, eds., *The Study of Culture at a Distance* (University of Chicago Press, 1953); *The Dance: From Ritual to Rock and Roll,* by Joost A. M. Meerloo, M. D., copyright © 1960, by D. Jambsten, n. d., Amsterdam, used with the permission of the Chilton Book Company, Philadelphia, pp. 14, 16, 35; and "Psychocutaneous Aspects of Persistent Pruritis and Excessive Excoriation," by P. F. D. Seitz, *Archives of Dermatology and Syphilology,* vol. 64 (1951).

CONTENTS

TOUCHING

ONE

The greatest sense in our body is our touch sense. It is probably the chief sense in the processes of sleeping and waking; it gives us our knowledge of depth or thickness and form; we feel, we love and hate, are touchy and are touched, through the touch corpuscles of our skin.*

THE MIND OF THE SKIN

THE SKIN, like a cloak, covers us all over, the oldest and the most sensitive of our organs, our first medium of communication, and our most efficient of protectors. Perhaps, next to the brain, the skin is the most important of all our organ systems. The sense most closely associated with the skin, the sense of touch, "the mother of the senses," is the earliest to develop in the human embryo. When the embryo is less than an inch long from crown to rump, and less than eight weeks old, light stroking of the upper lip or wings of the nose will cause bending of the neck and trunk away from the source of stimulation. At this stage in its development the

* J. LIONEL TAYLOR, *The Stages of Human Life,* 1921, p. 157.

embryo has neither eyes nor ears. Yet its skin is already highly developed, although in a manner not at all comparable to the development it is still to undergo. In the womb, bathed by its mother's amniotic fluid and enveloped by the soft walls of the womb, "rocked in the cradle of the deep," the conceptus * leads an aquatic existence. In this environment its skin must have the capacity to resist the absorption of too much water, the soaking effects of its liquid medium, and to respond appropriately to physical, chemical, and neural changes, and to changes in temperature.

The skin arises from the outermost of the three embryonic cell layers, the ectoderm. The ectoderm also gives rise to the hair, teeth, and the sense organs of smell, taste, hearing, vision and touch—everything involved with what goes on outside the organism. The nervous system, which has as a principal function informing the organism of what is going on outside it, is the most important of the systems to which the ectoderm gives rise.

The skin's growth and development proceed throughout life, and the development of its sensitivities depends largely upon the kind of environmental stimulation it receives. Interestingly enough, in common with chick, guinea pig, and rat, in the newborn human the relative weight of the skin, expressed as a percentage of the total body weight, is 19.7, nearly the same as in the adult, 17.8, suggesting what should be obvious: the enduring importance of the skin in the life of the organism.

In other animals it has been found that "skin sensitivity is apparently earliest and most completely developed during

* *Conceptus,* the organism from conception to delivery. *Embryo,* the organism from conception to the end of the 8th week. *Fetus,* from the beginning of the 9th week to delivery.

prenatal life." There is a general embryological law which states that the earlier a function develops the more fundamental it is likely to be. The fact is that the functional capacities of the skin are among the most basic.

The surface area of the skin has an enormous number of sensory receptors receiving stimuli of heat, cold, touch, and pain. It is estimated that there are some 50 receptors per 100 square millimeters. Tactile points vary from 7 to 135 per square centimeter. The number of sensory fibers from the skin entering the spinal cord by the posterior roots is well over half a million.

At birth the skin is called upon to make many new adaptive responses to an environment even more complex than that to which it was exposed within the womb. Transmitted through the atmospheric environment, in addition to air movements, are gases, particles, parasites, viruses, bacteria, changes in pressure, temperature, humidity, light, radiation, and much else. To all of these stimuli the skin is equipped to respond with extraordinary efficiency. By far the largest organ system of the body, about 2,500 square centimeters in the newborn and about 18,000 square centimeters in the average male, and constituting about 16 to 18 percent of total body weight, physiologically the skin has four functions: (1) as a protector of underlying parts from mechanical and radiation injuries, and invasion by foreign substances and organisms; (2) as a sense organ; (3) as a temperature regulator; and (4) as a metabolic organ in the metabolism and storage of fat, and in water and salt metabolism by perspiration. One would have thought that the remarkable versatility of the skin, its tolerance of environmental changes, and its astonishing thermostatic and tactile capacities, as well as the singular efficiency of the barrier it presents against the insults and assaults of the environment would have constituted conditions striking enough to evoke the interest of inquirers into its properties.

Strangely enough, until relatively recent years, this has not been the case. Indeed, most of what we know about the functions of the skin has been learned since the 1940's. Though much knowledge has been acquired, of both the structure and the physical functions of the skin, much more remains to be learned. Today the skin no longer languishes for want of interest.

Somewhat surprisingly, the one repository of so much of the sensitive human spirit in which one might have expected to find a sophisticated insight into the functions of the human skin, namely poetry, is found to be disappointingly barren. Poems have been written in celebration of every part of the body, but the skin unaccountably appears to have been slighted, as if it did not exist. In prose literature the case is otherwise: there are many references to the skin, perhaps the most notable being Gulliver's mortifying account of what the Lilliputians thought of the character of his skin, with its blotches and pimples and other disfigurations.

That the importance in human behavior of the tactile functions of the skin has not gone wholly unrecognized is evident from the many expressions in common parlance in which these functions appear. We speak of "rubbing" people the wrong way, and "stroking" them the right way. We say of someone that he has "a happy touch," of another that he is "a soft touch," and of still another that he has "the human touch." We get into "touch" or "contact" with others. Some people have to be "handled" carefully ("with kid gloves"). Some are "thick-skinned," others are "thin-skinned," some get "under one's skin," while others remain only "skin-

deep," and things are either "palpably" or "tangibly" so or
not. Some people are "touchy," that is, oversensitive or easily
given to anger. The "feel" of a thing is important to us in
more ways than one; and "feeling" for another embodies
much of the kind of experience which we have ourselves undergone through the skin. A deeply felt experience is
"touching." We say of some people that they are "tactful"
and of others that they are "tactless," that is, either having or
not having the delicate sense of what is fitting and proper in
dealing with others (see page 218). It is strange that, although it is the skin, of all the organs of the body, that has
most constantly occupied the forefront of man's consciousness, he should have paid little more than the most superficial attention to it.

Most of us take our skin entirely for granted, except when
it burns and peels, or breaks out in pimples, or perspires un-
pleasantly. When we think of it at other times, it is with a
vague wonder at so neat and efficient a covering for our in-
sides: waterproof, dustproof, and miraculously—until we
grow old—always the right size. As we grow older we begin
to discover qualities of the skin, firmness, elasticity, texture,
we had failed to notice at all until we began to lose them.
With the accumulation of years we are apt to regard our
aging skin as a rather dirty trick, a depressing public evidence of aging, and a somewhat unwelcome reminder of the
passage of time. No longer the good fit it once was, it grows
loose and baggy, and is often wrinkled, dry and leathery, sal-
low, splotched, or otherwise disfigured.

But these are all superficial ways of looking at the skin. As
we study the observations of numerous investigators, and put
together the findings of physiologists, anatomists, neurolo-
gists, psychiatrists, psychologists and other investigators, add-

ing to the brew our own observations and knowledge of
human nature, we begin to understand that the skin represents something very much more than just an integument
designed to keep the skeleton from falling apart or merely to
provide a mantle for all the other organs, but rather that it
is in its own right a complex and fascinating organ. In addition to being the largest organ of the body, the various elements comprising the skin have a very large representation
in the brain. In the cortex, for example, it is the postcentral
gyrus, or convolution, which receives the tactile impulses
from the skin, by way of the sensory ganglia next to the
spinal cord, then to the posterior funiculi in the spinal cord
and medulla oblongata, to the venteroposterior nuclei in the
thalamus, and finally the postcentral gyrus. Nerve fibers con-
ducting tactile impulses are generally of larger size than
those associated with the other senses. The sensorimotor
areas of the cortex are situated on each side of the central
gyrus. The precentral gyrus is largely motor while the postcentral gyrus is largely sensory. Horizontal connecting fibers
across the central fissure connect both gyri. Since it is a general rule of neurology that the size of a particular region or
area of the brain is related to the multiplicity of the functions it performs (and to the skill, say, in the use of a muscle
or group of muscles), rather than to the size of the organ, the
proportions of the cerebral tactile area underscore something
of the importance of tactile functions in the development of
the person. Figures 1 and 2 are drawings of sensory and
motor homunculi, or "little men," designed to show the pro-
portionate representations of tactile functions in the cortex.
From these figures it will be seen how large is the representation of the hand, especially the index finger and the
thumb, and the enormous representation of the lips.

Consider: as a sensory system the skin is much the most important organ system of the body. A human being can spend his life blind and deaf and completely lacking the senses of smell and taste, but he cannot survive at all without the functions performed by the skin. The experience of Helen Keller, who became deaf and blind in infancy, whose mind was literally created through the stimulation of her skin, shows us that when other senses fail, the skin can to an extraordinary degree compensate for their deficiencies. The sense of pain, mediated from the skin to the brain, provides an essential warning system designed to compel attention. The condition known as *cutaneous alagia*, in which the individual can feel no pain in his skin, is a serious malady. Those affected by cutaneous alagia have been known to sustain severe burns before becoming aware of any danger. Such persons are in jeopardy of their lives.

The continuous stimulation of the skin by the external environment serves to maintain both sensory and motor tonus. The brain must receive sensory feedback from the skin in order to make such adjustments as may be called for in response to the information it receives. When a leg "falls asleep" or grows numb the sensory cutoff results in difficulty in initiating leg movement because the impulses from the skin, muscles, and joints are not adequately reaching the postcentral gyrus of the brain. The feedback from skin to brain, even in sleep, is continuous.

As a student and teacher of human anatomy I was, in the course of the years, repeatedly struck by the largeness of the tactile area of the brain as shown, usually in green, in textbook illustrations. No one seemed to have made any significant comment on this. It was not until the middle 1940's, when I commenced to draw together the data bearing on the

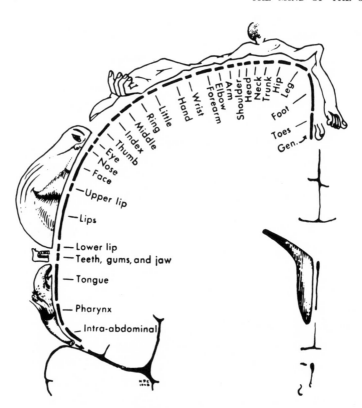

FIGURE 1. The sensory homunculus drawn upon the profile of one hemisphere. The underlying solid lines indicate the extent of cortical representation.

development of human behavior,* that the recurrence of stray bits of evidence from a large variety of different sources impressed upon me the importance of the skin not only in the development of physical functions, but also in the devel-

* Delivered as a course on socialization at Harvard University in 1945, and subsequently published in my book, *The Direction of Human Development* (New York: Harper & Bros., 1955; revised edition, New York: Hawthorn Books, 1970).

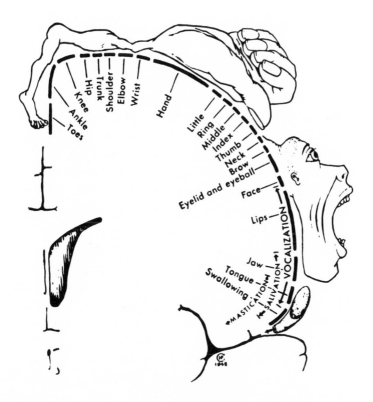

FIGURE 2. The motor homunculus. While there is a close correspondence between sensory and motor representation, the correspondence is not complete. The representation of sensation refers
to specific areas and parts, whereas the motor representation refers to the movements of those parts. (From W. Penfield and T.
Rasmussen, *The Cerebral Cortex of Man*. New York: The Macmillan Co., 1950, p. 214. By permission).

opment of behavioral ones. I delivered a lecture on this subject at the University of Texas Medical School at Galveston
in April, 1952. This was subsequently published in the journal issued by the School. The response to the lecture and to

the published article encouraged me to proceed with the
collection of the findings which are presented in this book,
and which serve, I hope, to throw some light on an aspect of
human development that has been largely underappreciated.

What is this aspect? It is quite simply the effect of tactile
experience upon human behavioral development.

Our approach to the skin in this book is quite the opposite of that which psychosomatic medicine has so illuminatingly made, the demonstration that what goes on in the
mind may express itself in the skin in a variety of different
ways. The psychosomatic approach constitutes an invaluable
contribution to our understanding concerning the influence
of the mind upon the body—for the purposes of discussion
we may preserve the artificial separation of mind *and* body
—and of the extraordinary sensitivity of the skin in reacting
to centrally originating nervous disturbances. That distress-
ing thoughts may break out as boils in the skin, that urti-
caria, psoriasis, and many other skin disorders may originate
in the mind, is no longer the novel idea it was when, more
than forty years ago, I read of this relationship in W. J.
O'Donovan's pioneering little book, *Dermatological Neuroses*. Since 1927, when O'Donovan's book was published,
considerable progress has been made, much of it admirably
set out in Maximillian Obermayer's book, *Psychocutaneous
Medicine*. The psychosomatic approach to the study of the
skin may be regarded as centrifugal; that is, it proceeds from
the mind outwards to the integument. What we shall be concerned with in the present book is the opposite approach,
namely from the skin to the mind; in other words, the centripetal approach.

The question we are most concerned to ask and answer in
this book is, What influence do the various kinds of cutane-

ous experiences which the organism undergoes, especially in early life, have upon its development? Primarily we are concerned to discover: (1) What kind of skin stimulations are necessary for the healthy development of the organism, both physically and behaviorally? and (2) What are the effects, if any, of the want or insufficiency of particular kinds of skin stimulation?

One of the best ways of discovering whether or not a particular kind of experience is necessary or basic to any particular species and its members, is to determine how widely distributed it is in the Class of animals (in the present instance, the mammals) to which the species under investigation belongs; what is phylogenetically basic is likely to be physiologically significant, and significant perhaps in other functional respects as well.

The specific question to which we seek an answer is: Must the member of the species *Homo sapiens* undergo, in the course of his early development, certain kinds of tactile experiences in order to develop as a healthy human being? If he does, what are those kinds of experiences? For some light on these questions we may first turn to the observations made on other animals.

RATS AND SERENDIPITY. What started me thinking about the skin was the serendipitous reading, in a totally different connection, of a 1921–1922 paper by the anatomist Frederick S. Hammett, of the Wistar Institute of Anatomy in Philadelphia. Hammett was interested in discovering what would be the effects of total removal of both the thyroid and parathyroid glands from albino rats of the genetically homogeneous Wistar stock. Hammett noted that following the operation some of the animals did not, as they ought to have done, die. It had been thought by many investigators that such a thyroparathyroidectomy must invariably prove fatal, presumably owing to the action of some toxic substance upon the nervous system.

Upon inquiry Hammett found that the rats that had undergone the thyroparathyroidectomies had been drawn from two separate colonies, and that the greater number of the survivors came from what was called the Experimental Colony. In this colony the animals were customarily petted and gentled. In contrast, the animals exhibiting the higher mortality rate were drawn from what was called the Standard Stock, a group whose only human contact was that incident to routine feeding and cage-cleaning by an attendant. These animals were timid, apprehensive, and high-strung. When picked up they were tense and resistant, and frequently exhibited fear and rage by biting. "The picture," as Hammett put it, "as a whole is one of constant high irritability and neuromuscular tension."

The behavior of the gentled rats was strikingly different from that of the Standard Stock animals. The former had been gentled for five generations. When handled, the gentled animals were relaxed and yielding. They were not easily frightened. As Hammett noted, "They give a uniform picture of placidity. The threshold of the neuromuscular reaction to potentially disturbing stimuli is almost prohibitively high."

With respect to their relations with human beings it was very evident that the gentled rats felt secure in the hands not only of those who fondled them, but of everyone. The laboratory attendant had raised them under conditions in which they were frequently handled, stroked, and had kindly sounds uttered to them, and they responded with fearlessness, friendliness, and a complete lack of neuromuscular tension or irritability. The exact opposite was true of the ungentled rats, who had received no attention whatever from human beings, except that involved in feeding and cage cleaning. These animals were frightened and bewildered, anxious and tense in the presence of people.

Let us see what happened when thyroid and parathyroid glands were removed in the 304 animals operated from both groups. Within forty-eight hours of operation 79 percent of the irritable rats died, while only 13 percent of the gentled rats died—a difference of 66 percent of survivals in favor of the gentled animals. When the parathyroids alone were removed, within forty-eight hours 76 percent of the irritable rats died while only 13 percent of the gentled rats died, a difference of 63 percent.

Standard Stock rats, placed at weaning in the Experimental Colony and gentled, became tame, cooperative and relaxed, and resistant to the effects of the parathyroid gland removal.

In a second series of experiments, Hammett investigated the mortality rate in parathyroidectomized wild Norway rats that had been caged for one or two generations. The wild Norway rat, it is well known, is a notoriously excitable creature. Of a total of 102 wild Norway rats, 92 animals, or 90 percent, died within forty-eight hours, most of the survivors succumbing within two or three weeks of operation.

Hammett concluded that the stability of the nervous system induced in rats by gentling and petting produces in them a marked resistance to the loss of the parathyroid secretion. In excitable rats this loss usually results in death from acute parathyroid tetany in less than forty-eight hours.

Subsequent experience and observation at the Wistar Institute showed that, the more handling and petting rats receive, the better they do in the laboratory situation.

Here, then, was something more than a clue to the understanding of the role played by tactile stimulation in the
development of the organism. Gentle handling of rats could
make all the difference between life and death following the
removal of important endocrine glands. This discovery was
striking enough. But what was equally remarkable was the
influence of gentling upon behavioral development. Gentling produced gentle, unexcitable animals; lack of gentling
resulted in fearful, excitable animals.

These important findings, it seemed to me, were worth
following up. There were innumerable unanswered questions, principally involving the mechanism, the physiology
by which handling or gentling could produce such significant differences in organismal and behavioral responses as
Hammett had recorded. Since, apart from the Wistar Institute observations by Hammett and his colleagues, there was
literally nothing in print that could throw any light on such
questions, I began to make inquiries among animal breeders,
people who had been raised on farms, veterinarians, hus-
bandrymen, and the staffs of zoos—the results were illuminating.

LICKING AND LOVING. Reading the Wistar Institute studies of
Hammett, it occurred to me that the "washing" the mammalian mother gives her young, virtually from the moment
they are born, in the form of licking, isn't washing at all, but
something fundamentally very different and very necessary;
that "washing" in the sense of cleaning was not the real function of licking, but that licking served very much more pro-

found purposes. It seemed a reasonable hypothesis that, as Hammett's observations suggested, the proper kind of cutaneous stimulation is essential for the adequate organic and behavioral development of the organism. It seemed likely that the licking mammalian mothers give their newborn, which they continue for durable periods thereafter, probably serves a basic series of functions, since it was universal among mammals with the exception of man, and the possible exception of the great apes. In that exception, I reasoned, there probably also lay an interesting story, as, indeed, we shall later see.

As soon as I commenced my inquiries among persons with long experience of animals I found a remarkable unanimity in the observations they reported. The substance of these observations was that the newborn animal must be licked if it is to survive, that if for some reason it remains unlicked, particularly in the perineal region (the region between the external genitalia and the anus), it is likely to die of a functional failure of the genitourinary system and/or the gastrointestinal system. Breeders of chihuahua dogs were particularly insistent upon this, for according to them the mothers often make little or no attempt to lick their young. Hence there is a high mortality rate among these puppies, caused by failure to eliminate, unless some substitute for maternal licking, such as stroking by the human hand, is provided.

The evidence indicated that the genitourinary system especially simply would not function in the absence of cutaneous stimulation. The most interesting observations on this matter soon became available in the form of an unpremeditated experiment carried out by Professor James A. Reyniers of the Lobund Laboratories of Bacteriology of the

University of Notre Dame. Professor Reyniers and his colleagues were interested in raising germ-free animals, and in 1946 and 1949 they published their findings in two separate monographs. In the early days of their experiments these workers' labors came to naught because all the experimental animals died of a functional failure of the genitourinary and gastrointestinal tracts. It was not until a former zoo-worker brought her own experience to bear upon the solution of this problem, advising the Notre Dame group to stroke the genitals and perineal region of the young animals with a wisp of cotton after each feeding, that urination and defecation occurred. In response to an inquiry, Professor Reyniers wrote me:

With respect to the constipation problem in hand-reared newborn mammals the following may be of some interest: Rats, mice, rabbits, and those mammals depending upon the mother for sustenance in the early days of life apparently have to be taught to defecate and urinate. In the early period of this work we did not know this and consequently lost our animals. The unstimulated handled young die with an occlusion of the ureter and a distended bladder. Although we had for years seen mothers licking their young about the genitals I thought that this was a matter largely of cleanliness. On closer observation, however, it appeared that during such stimulation the young defecated and urinated. Consequently, about twelve years ago, we started to stroke the genitals of the young after each hourly feeding with a wisp of cotton and were able to elicit elimination. From this point on we have had no trouble with this problem.

Failure of the genitourinary tract to function when newborn mammals were removed, immediately after birth, from contact with their mothers was soon also demonstrated by McCance and Otley. These investigators suggested that normally the licking and other attentions of the mother stimulated an increase in the excretion of urea as a consequence of the change in blood flow to the kidney.

Motherless kittens and other animals have been successfully raised by the appropriate cutaneous stimulation administered by a surrogate "mother." In an engaging account of his rescue of a newborn abandoned kitten from the bushes, Larry Rhine tells how he called up the A.S.P.C.A. after feeding the kitten from a doll's bottle, and having announced that Moses, as he had named him, was eating quite normally, received the reply, "Of course he is. Your problem is not with the eating. You see, a kitten's first eliminations are stimulated by the mother cat. Now, if you'd like to do the same with a cotton swab dipped in warm water you might be able to . . ." And for the next few days Mr. Rhine was up every two hours, with a cup of warm water and a cotton swab, feeding, swabbing and sleeping—and Moses, who had been found in the rushes, flourished.

Observation of the frequency with which the mother licks different parts of the kitten's body reveals a definite pattern. The region receiving most licking is the genital and perineal region; next in order comes the region around the mouth, then the underbelly, and finally the back and sides. The rate of licking seems to be genetically determined, about three to four licks a second. In albino rats the rate is six to seven licks a second.

Rosenblatt and Lehrman found that, during a fifteen-minute observation session, maternal rats lick their newborn pups for an average of two minutes and ten seconds in the anogenital region and lower abdomen, for about twenty-five seconds to the rear end of the back, about sixteen seconds on the upper abdomen, and about twelve seconds on the back of the head.

Schneirla, Rosenblatt, and Tobach mention, among the criteria defining maternal behavior in the cat, exaggerated licking of self and of young. We shall return to a consideration of the significance of self-licking later. These observers found that between 27 and 53 percent of the time was spent in licking; no other activity approached licking in the amount of time devoted to it.

Rheingold, in reporting her observations on a cocker spaniel, a beagle, and three Shetland sheep dogs (Shelties), states that licking started on the day of birth and occurred infrequently after the forty-second day. The area most commonly licked was the perineal region.

Turning to the order of mammals to which man belongs, the primates, Phyllis Jay reports, on Indian langurs observed in the field under natural conditions, that langur mothers lick their young from the hour of their birth. The same appears to be true of baboons under natural conditions. "Every few minutes she explores the newborn infant's body, parts its fur with her fingers, licks, and nuzzles it."

Interestingly enough, I can find no data on whether any of the great apes lick their young. It may be that the great apes —orang-utan, chimpanzee, and gorilla—share with man the unique distinction among the primates and the mammals generally of being the only mammals who do not lick their young. However this may be, the ubiquity of the practice among the mammals testifies to its basic nature.

The self-licking in which many mammals indulge, in the nonpregnant or parturitive state, while having the effect of keeping the animal clean, is probably more specifically designed to keep the sustaining systems of the body—the gastrointestinal, genitourinary, respiratory, circulatory, digestive, reproductive, nervous, and endocrine systems

—adequately stimulated. What this means in actual end-effects is perhaps best illustrated by the developmental failure which follows any significant restraint of self-licking. A striking behavioral feature of both the pregnant rat and the pregnant cat is intensified self-licking of the genito-abdominal region as pregnancy progresses. The functional significance of this self-licking may be conjectured as serving to stimulate and improve the functional responses of the organ systems especially involved in the pregnancy during labor, delivery, and parturient periods. It is known that suckling and other stimulation of the genito-abdominal regions of the body serve to maintain lactation and to cause growth of the structures of the breast, the mammary gland, after the birth of the infant or litter. There was, however, no evidence that sensory stimulation contributed to mammary development during pregnancy. Drs. Lorraine L. Roth and Jay S. Rosenblatt inquired into this matter experimentally. In a series of ingenious experiments these investigators put neck collars on pregnant rats in such a manner that they were prevented from licking themselves. It was found that the mammary glands of collared rats were about 50 percent less developed than those of control animals.

Since collars would undoubtedly produce some stress effect, other uncollared pregnant rats were subjected to stress effects, while still others were fitted with notched collars which allowed them to lick themselves. In none of these, nor in the normal uncollared groups, was the inhibition of mammary development anywhere nearly as great as in the collared group.

Birch and his collaborators have shown that when the female rat is fitted with a light collar that prevents self-licking of the abdomen and posterior erogenous zone, even though the collar is removed permanently for delivery and thereafter, such females make very poor mothers. They carry materials but fail to build regular nests, spreading the materials around very loosely instead. They do not nurse their young to any extent, but seem to be disturbed when the newborn pups happen to reach them, and tend to move away. The pups would invariably die were it not for artificial interference by the experimenter. Hence, depriving the pregnant female of the self-stimulation of her body that provides a normal preparation for maternal behavior seems also to deprive her of orientations that would otherwise promote the fluid-licking, afterbirth-eating, and other activities underlying the transition to the after-care period.

From such experiments it is clear that cutaneous self-stimulation of the mother's body is an important factor in contributing to the development of the optimum functioning of the sustaining systems, not only before and after pregnancy but equally so during pregnancy. The question immediately arises whether this may not also be the case during these same periods in the human female. It is a question to which the answer seems to be in the affirmative.

It is evident that in mammals generally cutaneous stimulation is important at all stages of development, but particularly important during the early days of the life of the newborn, during pregnancy, during labor, delivery, and during the nursing period. Indeed, the more we learn about the effects of cutaneous stimulation the more pervasively significant for healthy development do we find it to be. For example, in one of the most recent studies reported, it was found that early infantile cutaneous stimulation exerts a highly beneficial influence upon the immunological system, having important consequences for resistance to infectious and other diseases. The study indicated that rats who had been handled in infancy showed a higher serum antibody titre (standard) in every case, after primary and secondary immunization, than those who had not been handled in infancy. Thus the immunological responsivity of the adult appears to be significantly modified by early cutaneous experience. Such immunological competence may be produced through the mechanism of conductor substances and hormones affecting the thymus gland, a gland which is critical in the establishment of immunological function, and also through the mediation of that part of the brain known as the hypothalamus.

Indeed, the evidence showing the greater resistance to disease of subjects given early cutaneous stimulation is striking, but is perhaps complicated by the fact that the cutaneously stimulated animal enjoys a great many other correlated advantages, which undoubtedly also play a role in contributing to the greater resistance of the stimulated organism. As many investigators have confirmed, handling or gentling of rats and other animals in their early days results in significantly greater increases in weight, more activity, less fearfulness, greater ability to withstand stress, and greater resistance to physiological damage.

In sheep, although active maternal assistance is not essential in order for the newborn lamb to find the teats and suck for the first time, the process is facilitated by licking and by directional orientation of the ewe toward the lamb. In a series of experiments Alexander and Williams found that it was the combination of the two factors, the licking and the directional orientation—that is, the standing of the ewe facing the kid—that significantly facilitated the progress of the kid toward successful sucking. Neither orientation nor lick-

ing alone, which these investigators later refer to as "grooming," facilitated the drive toward sucking to any significant
extent. Licking and maternal orientation in every case resulted in significantly greater teat-seeking activity, and also
in a tendency toward an earlier increase in weight than in
unlicked lambs.

The importance of intercutaneous or reciprocal cutaneous
stimulation, or physical contact, between mother and young,
among birds as well as mammals, has been demonstrated by
many investigators. Blauvelt has shown that, in goats, if the
kid is removed from the mother for only a few hours before
she has a chance to lick it and the kid is then restored to her,
"she seems to have no behavioral resources to do anything
further for the newborn." In sheep Liddell found the same
thing, and interestingly enough, Maier observed that the same
held true of hens and their chicks. Maier found that when
broody hens are prevented from having physical contact
with their chicks, even though all other visual clues are left
intact, and they are situated in adjacent cages, the hen's
broody response quickly disappears. Furthermore, Maier
found that hens kept in close physical contact with their
chicks and unable to leave them remained broody for a
longer period of time than those hens who were free to leave
their chicks whenever they chose.

Physical contact, then, appears to act as a principal regulator of broodiness. Stimulation of the skin apparently constitutes an essential condition in causing the pituitary gland to
secrete the hormone most important for the initiation and
maintenance of broodiness, namely prolactin. This is the
same hormone associated with the initiation and maintenance of nursing in mammals, including the human mother.

Collias showed that, in goats and sheep, mothers establish the identity of their own young immediately after birth, largely by contact, and thereafter vigorously repel any alien young that may approach them. The findings of many independent researchers indicate that there exist certain types of normal species-specific behavior dependent upon particular experiences during critical periods in the life of the individual animal. It has been found that changes in the natural environment at these times often result in the development of abnormal, species-atypical behavior. Hersher, Moore, and Richmond separated twenty-four domestic goats from their newborn kids five to ten minutes immediately following birth, for periods ranging from a half hour to an hour. Two months later these mothers were observed to nurse their own kids less and alien kids more than nonseparated mothers. A most interesting and unforeseen result of this experiment was the appearance of "rejecting" behavior, that is, nursing neither their own nor other kids, among mothers of the nonseparated group. Separation of these highly gregarious animals seems to have influenced the structure of the herd as a whole, "changing the behavior of 'control' animals whose early *post partum* experiences had not deliberately been disrupted, but whose environment had been affected in turn by abnormal maternal and filial behavior produced in the experimental members of the group."

In an ingenious experiment designed to determine whether the critical period for the development of individual specific maternal behavior could be prolonged in sheep and goats, Hersher, Richmond, and Moore found that this could, indeed, be achieved by enforced contact between dam and young and the prevention of butting behavior.

In the domestic collie, McKinney has shown that, immediately after whelping, removal of the pups for little more than an hour seriously retards the recovery of the mother, a recovery which is accelerated by the rooting, nuzzling, and nursing of the young. McKinney suggests that similar undesirable effects may be produced in human mothers as a consequence of the practice of removing their babies from them at birth without permitting the continued contact that is so urgent a need in the newborn.

In the rhesus monkey Harry F. Harlow and his co-workers, on the basis of their direct observations, "postulate that contact-clinging is the primary variable that binds mother to infant and infant to mother." Maternal affection, they find, is at a maximum during close bodily face-to-face contacts between mother and infant, and maternal affection appears to wane progressively as this type of bodily interchange decreases.

Maternal affection is defined by these authors as a function of many different conditions, involving external incentive stimulation, different conditions of experience, and many endocrinological factors. External incentives are those relating to the infant, and involve contact-clinging, warmth, sucking, and visual and auditory cues. Experimental factors relating to the maternal behavior probably embrace the mother's entire experience. Here it is probable that her own early experiences are of special importance, as well as her relationships with each individual infant she bears, and her cumulative experiences gained from raising successive infants. Endocrinological factors relate both to pregnancy and parturition, and to the resumption of a normal ovulatory cycle.

Indeed, the mother's early experiences are of considerable importance for the subsequent development of her own offspring, right into adulthood. In a series of elegant experiments, Drs. Victor H. Denenberg and Arthur E. Whimbey showed that the offspring of handled rats, whether in relation to the natural or to a foster mother, exhibited a higher weight at weaning than pups reared by mothers that had not been handled in infancy; they also defecated more and were significantly less active than the offspring of nonhandled mothers.

Ader and Conklin found that the offspring of rats that had been handled during pregnancy, whether they remained with their natural mothers or were cross-fostered to other females, were significantly less excitable than the offspring of unhandled rats.

Werboff and his co-workers found that handling of pregnant mice throughout the gestation period resulted in an increased number of live fetuses and surviving offspring. The decrease in weight these workers observed may, as they suggest, be due to the increased litter size.

Sayler and Salmon found that young mice raised in a communal nest, in which females combined their litters, showed faster rates of growth during the first twenty days than young raised by single females, even when the ratio of mothers to young was the same. The investigators think that the differences in body weight are most likely related to the nutritional benefit of additional and higher quality milk provided by more than one mother. They also think that tactile stimuli may be operative, as well as thermal ones, the presence of additional littermates and mothers serving to insulate the pups so that more metabolic energy could be devoted to growth.

Weininger found that male rats gentled for three weeks following their weaning at twenty-three days had, at forty-four days, a mean weight twenty grams higher than the ungentled control group; furthermore, the growth of the gentled was greater than that of the ungentled rats. In an open-field test gentled rats ventured significantly closer to the brilliantly lit center of the open-field setup, thus showing more of a tendency to ignore the natural habit of their species to cling to walls and avoid light. Rectal temperatures were significantly greater in the gentled rats, suggesting a possible change in the metabolic rate of these animals.

When exposed to stressful stimuli (immobilization, and total food and water deprivation for forty-eight hours) and autopsied immediately thereafter, the gentled rats showed much less damage to the cardiovascular and gastrointestinal systems than the ungentled rats.

Cardiovascular and other organic damage under prolonged stress, as Hans Selye and others have abundantly demonstrated, may be considered an end-product of the action of the adrenocorticotrophic hormone (ACTH); that is, the hormone secreted by the pituitary gland which acts upon the cortex of the adrenal gland to cause it to secrete cortisone. This interactive relationship is sometimes called the sympathetico-adrenal axis. Weininger suggests that the relative immunity to stress damage exhibited by the gentled animals was probably due to their lesser output of ACTH from the pituitary in response to the same alarming situation with which the ungentled animals were confronted. If this were in fact the case, it would be expected that the adrenal glands of gentled and ungentled rats following stress would show those of the ungentled rats having been stimulated by more ACTH output, to be heavier, and upon examination this was, indeed, found to be the case. "A major change in hypothalamic functioning, involving reduction or inhibition of massive sympathetic discharge in response to an alarming stimulus (and hence decreased ACTH output from the pituitary), is predicted to account for the results mentioned above."

The process is much more complicated than that, but, reduced to its essential elements, the relation between the pituitary-adrenal secretions in gentling and stressful situations holds true. Gentled animals respond with an increased functional efficiency in the organization of all systems of the body. Ungentled animals fail to undergo organization expressing itself in functional efficiency, and are therefore in all respects less able to meet the assaults and insults of the environment. Hence, when we speak of "licking and love," or skin (cutaneous tactile) stimulation, we are quite evidently speaking of a fundamental and essential ingredient of affection, and equally clearly of an essential element in the healthy development of every organism.

Fuller found that puppies isolated from all contact shortly after birth, and subsequently stroked and handled by human beings, did better on tests following their emergence from isolation than puppies that had been neither stroked nor handled.

The workers at the Cornell Behavior Farm found that, with no licking at all (although licking for one hour after birth is sufficient) many newborn lambs fail to stand and subsequently die. While it is possible for some lambs to stand without licking, it is notable that when the newborn makes an effort to rise its mother will often keep it down with her foot until she has licked it. Barron found that lambs that had been dried-off with a towel (the equivalent of licking) rise on their four feet before lambs who have not been dried off.

The very real effects of early tactile experience have been impressively demonstrated by a series of independent experi-

ments. Karas, for example, found that rats handled during
the first five days showed a maximal effect of emotionality, as
measured by avoidance conditioning, as compared with animals handled at other times during infancy. Levine and
Lewis found that animals handled during days 2 to 5 after
birth showed a significant depletion of adrenal ascorbic acid
in response to severe cold stress at twelve days of age, as compared with nonhandled animals and animals handled after
the first five days, which did not show a significant depletion
reaction to stress till the sixteenth day of life. Bell *et al.*
found that twenty-four hours after electroconvulsive shock
blood sugar level was significantly higher in nonhandled animals and animals handled at times other than the first five
days, than in animals handled during the first five days. Denenberg and Karas found that rats handled during the first
ten days of life weighed the most, learned best, and survived
longest.

The manner in which the young of all mammals snuggle
and cuddle against the body of the mother and against the
bodies of their siblings or of any other introduced animal
strongly suggests that cutaneous stimulation is an important
biological *need,* for both their physical and their behavioral
development. Almost every animal enjoys being stroked or
otherwise having its skin pleasurably stimulated. Dogs appear to be insatiable in their appetite for stroking, cats will
relish it and purr, as will innumerable other animals both
domestic and wild, apparently enjoying the stroking at least
as much as they do self-licking.

The touch of a human hand is very much more effective
than the application of an impersonal mechanical apparatus,
as for example in milking, where it is well known among experts and dairy-farmers that hand-milked cows give more

and richer terminal milk than machine-milked cows. Hendrix, Van Valck, and Mitchell have reported that horses exposed to human handling immediately after birth developed unusual adult behavior. Among the adult traits observed in these handled horses were responsible behavior in emergencies without loss of cooperative tractability at other times, and inventive behavior for equine-to-human communication in situations of urgency.

Dolphins, as I well know from personal observation, love to be gently stroked. At the Communications Institute in Miami I enjoyed the opportunity of making friends within a few minutes with Elvar, an adult male dolphin who occupied a small tank all to himself. Because Elvar habitually splashed them, visitors were customarily attired in oilskins. Elvar adjusted his splashes to the size of the visitor: small children would receive small splashes, middle-sized children middle-sized ones, and adults, large ones. For some reason I received no splash at all. Dr. John Lilly, the director, stated that this had never happened before. Approaching Elvar with all the affection, interest, and respect he deserved, I proceeded to stroke the top of his head. This was very much to his liking. During the remainder of the visit Elvar proceeded to expose every part of his body for me to stroke, leaning over sidewards so that I could stroke him under his flippers, which he seemed particularly to enjoy. It is sad to have to record that some months afterwards Elvar caught cold from a human visitor and died.

Drs. A. F. McBride and H. Kritzler of the Duke University Marine Laboratory at Beaufort, North Carolina, have recorded, concerning a two-year-old female dolphin, that she "became so fond of being caressed by the observer that she would frequently rear cautiously out of the water to rub her chin on the knuckles of his clenched fist." The same observers recorded that "dolphins are very fond of rubbing their bodies on various objects, so a backscratcher, constructed of three stout sweeper's brushes fixed to a slab of rock with the bristles directed upward, was installed in the tank. The young dolphins took to rubbing themselves on these brushes as soon as the adults discovered their purpose."

Quite fascinating is an observation made by Mr. A. Gunner relating to the fleas carried by hedgehogs. He writes:

I have kept and observed hedgehogs for some fifty or sixty years and am convinced that de-fleaing hedgehogs is not good for them. There is some essential factor which the fleas provide. It may be—and I think it is—a skin circulation stimulus that is missing in an animal unable to nudge, massage, scratch, rub or otherwise stimulate the skin to keep its labyrinth of capillaries properly active.

A zoologist friend assures me that I may be right, as the Australian echidna, some armadillos, and particularly that mammalian curiosity the *pangolin* tolerate insect populations in the overlaps at crevices of their armoured bodies and that the cleaned up and deloused animal does not long survive.

In attempting to follow up this observation I regret to say I could obtain no further information of any kind on the subject, but, like the zoologist friend of Mr. Gunner, I rather suspect that his observation is a sound one. The close (commensal) association of birds with other animals, from crocodiles whose teeth they pick, to sheep on whose backs they often alight, picking debris and insects from their bodies with the obvious approval of their hosts, the "grooming" of monkeys and apes, or the loving embrace—all these forms of behavior indicate that a basic and complex need is involved.

What emerges from the observations and experiments reported here—and there are many more with which we shall deal in subsequent pages—is that cutaneous stimulation in the various forms in which the newborn and young receive it is of prime importance for their healthy physical and behavioral development. It appears probable that for human beings tactile stimulation is of fundamental consequence for the development of healthy emotional or affectional relationships, that "licking," in its actual and in its figurative sense, and love are closely connected; in short, that one learns to love not by instruction but by being loved. As Professor Harry Harlow has put it, from the "intimate attachment of the child to the mother, multiple learned and generalized affectional responses are formed."

In a series of valuable studies Harlow has demonstrated the significance of physical contact between the monkey mother and her infant for the subsequent healthy development of the latter. During the course of his studies Harlow noticed that the laboratory-raised baby monkeys showed a strong attachment to the cloth pads (folded gauze diapers) which were used to cover the hardware-cloth floors and cages. When an attempt was made to remove and replace the pads for sanitary purposes the infants clung to them and engaged in "violent temper tantrums." It had also been discovered that infants raised on a bare wire-mesh cage floor survive with difficulty, if at all, during the first five days of life. When a wire-mesh cone was introduced the baby did better; and when this was covered with terry-cloth, husky, healthy babies developed. At this point Harlow decided to build a terry-cloth surrogate mother, with a light bulb behind her which radiated heat. The result was a mother, "soft, warm,

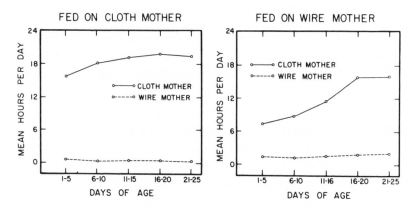

FIGURE 3. Time spent on cloth and wire mother surrogates. (From H. H. Harlow and R. R. Zimmermann, "The Development of Affectional Responses in Infant Monkeys," *Proceedings, American Philosophical Society, 102:*501–509, 1958. By permission).

and tender, a mother with infinite patience, a mother available twenty-four hours a day, a mother that never scolded her infant and never struck or bit her baby in anger."

A second surrogate mother was built entirely of wire mesh, without the terry cloth "skin," and hence lacking in contact comfort. The remainder of the story is best told in Harlow's own words. He writes:

In our initial experiment, the dual-mother surrogate condition, a cloth mother and a wire mother were placed in different cubicles attached to the infant's living cage. . . . For four newborn monkeys the cloth mother lactated and the wire mother did not; and for the other four, this condition was reversed. In either condition the infant received all its milk through the mother surrogate as soon as it was able to maintain itself in this way, a capability achieved within two or three days except in the case of very immature infants. Supplementary feedings were given until the milk intake from the mother surrogate was adequate. Thus, the experiment was designed as a test of the relative importance of the variables of contact comfort and nursing comfort. During the first 14 days of life the monkey's cage floor was covered with a heating pad wrapped in a folded gauze diaper, and thereafter the cage floor was bare. The infants were always free to leave the heating pad or cage floor to contact either mother, and the time spent on the surrogate mothers was automatically recorded. Figure 3 shows the total time spent on the cloth and wire mothers under the two conditions of feeding. These data make it obvious that contact comfort is a variable of overwhelming importance in the development of affectional responses, whereas lactation is a variable of negligible importance. With age and opportunity to learn, subjects with the lactating wire mother showed decreasing

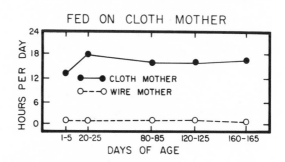

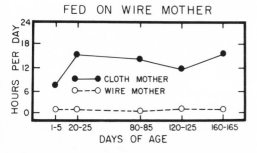

FIGURE 4. Long-Term Contact Time on Cloth and Wire Mother Surrogates. (From H. H. Harlow and R. R. Zimmermann, "The Development of Affectional Responses in Infant Monkeys." *Proceedings, American Philosophical Society, 102*:501–509, 1958. By permission).

responsiveness to her and increasing responsiveness to the nonlac-
tating cloth mother, a finding completely contrary to any interpretation of derived drive in which the mother-form becomes
conditioned to hunger-thirst reduction. The persistence of these
differential responses throughout 165 consecutive days of testing
is evident in Figure 4.

We were not surprised [writes Harlow], to discover that contact comfort was an important basic affectional or love variable,
but we did not expect it to overshadow so completely the variable of nursing; indeed, the disparity is so great as to suggest that
the primary function of nursing as an affectional variable is that
of insuring frequent and intimate body contact of the infant with
the mother. Certainly, man cannot live by milk alone. Love is an
emotion that does not need to be bottle- or spoon-fed, and we
may be sure that there is nothing to be gained by giving lip service to love.

Finally, Harlow concludes:

We now know that women in the working classes are not needed
in the house because of their primary mammalian capabilities;
and it is possible that in the foreseeable future neonatal nursing
will not be regarded as a necessity, but as a luxury—to use Ve-
blen's term—a form of conspicuous consumption limited perhaps
to the upper classes.

As we shall later see (pp. 64–88) Harlow thoroughly un-
derestimates the importance of breastfeeding in both animals
and man, but this does not in the least affect the validity of
his conclusions concerning the value of body contact between mother and infant. As Harlow and his co-workers
have shown, in their normal nursing-couple (mother and infant) rhesus monkeys, nutritional and nonnutritional nipple
contacts endure for some three months. These nipple contacts undoubtedly play an important role in the development of the individual.

A striking finding of Harlow and his fellow investigators was that when the five utter failures as mothers had their histories traced back to their early experiences it was found that they had been denied the oportunity to develop normal maternal-infant relationships, that they had never known a real monkey mother of their own, and had also been denied normal infant-infant relationships, subsequently having only limited physical association with other monkeys. Two of these mothers were essentially indifferent to their infants, and three were violently abusive. "Failure of normal gratification of contact-clinging in infancy may make it impossible for the adult female to show normal contact relationships with her own infant. Likewise, maternal brutality may stem from inadequate social experience with other infants within the first year of life." Furthermore, these investigators found that none of the motherless-mother animals ever showed normal female sex behavior, such as posturing and responding. They became mothers in spite of themselves. As we shall see, the parallel with such interrelated behaviors in man is virtually complete, and the significance of these behaviors is virtually identical.

Harlow and his co-workers comment upon the "extremely powerful social response observed throughout the monkey kingdom," namely, that of grooming. This response to their young increased throughout the first thirty days following the birth of the infant, and they suggest that this perhaps represents an intensification of the specific psychological bond between mother and infant.

Phyllis Jay reports that "from the hour of its birth" the mother langur monkey "inspects, licks, grooms, and manipulates the infant. When the newborn is nursing quietly or sleeping, she grooms and strokes it softly without disturbing or waking it. For the first week of life the newborn is never away from its mother or another adult female."

Tactile communication plays a major role in primate life. As an order, primates are, as Hediger has remarked, contact animals. The young are carried on their mothers' bodies for long periods of time. There is much clinging, riding, and contact with other members of the group. Young animals, and often adults, tend to sit and even sleep together in close contact. There is a great deal of touching and, most characteristically, grooming. Primates groom each other. Grooming not only serves to keep the body free of parasites, dirt, and the like, but it constitutes, as Allison Jolly puts it, "the social cement of primates from lemur to chimpanzee." Anthoney has described the development of grooming in the dog-headed baboon, *Papio cynocephalus,* from the infant's suckling the nipple, to grasping the specialized sucking fur, to grooming. The reciprocal pleasure enjoyed in this relation is quite probably related to the later pleasure of grooming and being groomed.

In addition to grooming, primates exhibit a large variety of other contact behaviors, such as patting and nuzzling, especially in greeting behavior. Chimpanzees will not only pat each others' hands, faces, groins, and other parts of the body, but will lay a hand on each others' backs in reassurance, will kiss in affection, and in their passion for being tickled will draw the tickler's hand to their bodies.

Grooming with the hands, which is usual among monkeys and apes, or, as among lemurs, with the specialized comblike teeth, presents an interesting seriation, for as Jolly has pointed out, the lemurine form of grooming with the teeth really represents a form of licking. This view of grooming may be extended to the finger-picking variety, and finally to the stroking of human beings. In short, it may well be that there has been an evolutionary development from licking, to tooth-combing (as among lemurs), to finger-grooming, to handstroking or caressing, as in *Homo sapiens,* and that therefore handstroking is to the young of the human species virtually as important a form of experience as licking is to the young of other mammals. This is a matter into which we shall inquire further. Meanwhile, it would seem evident that one of the elements in the genesis of the ability to love is "licking" or its equivalent in other forms of pleasurable tactile stimulation.

TWO

*There are many events in the womb
of time, which will be deliver'd.**

THE WOMB OF TIME

As WE HAVE SEEN in the preceding chapter, licking, or tooth-combing, or grooming of the young soon after they are born and for an appreciable period thereafter, appears to be an indispensably necessary condition for their survival. Such stimulations seem to be equally necessary for the healthy behavioral development of the young. If this is so, why then is it that human mothers neither lick, toothcomb, nor groom their young?

Human mothers do none of these things. Extensive inquiries over many years yielded only two cultures in which mothers sometimes washed their young by licking. In regions in which water is scarce, among the Polar Eskimos and in the Tibetan highlands, mothers sometimes resort to lick-

* SHAKESPEARE, *Othello*, I, iii.

ing their older young children as a substitute for washing them with water drawn from other sources. The fact is that human mothers, like great-ape mothers, do not lick their young, though traditional wisdom has not been insensible to the likeness between what the good human mother does and what the mammalian mother of other species does. The parallel is recognized in such phrases as *un ours mal léché,* "an unlicked cub." The French phrase is often employed to describe an ill-mannered person, "a boor," one who is awkward in his relations with others. Although the notion behind this phrase originally referred to the belief that the young of some animals were born in so undeveloped a form that they had to be licked into shape by the mother,* later usage conferred upon the phrase a meaning implicitly recognizing the importance of the mother's gentle ministrations in the development of what might be called "relatability." George Sarton, the distinguished Belgian-American historian of science, for example, wrote in his private journal, "I have now discovered that the first of August is the saint's day of the Spaniard Raymond Nonnatus (1200–1240). He was called Nonnatus because he was 'not-born,' but removed from his mother's womb after her death. My own fate was not very different from his, because my mother died soon after my birth and I never knew her. . . . Many of my shortcomings are due to the fact that I had no mother, and that my good father had no time to bother much about me. I am indeed 'an unlicked bear' (*un ours mal léché*)."

The question we have to answer here is: What, if any, are

---

* Pliny the Elder (A. D. 23–79) writes in his *Natural History,* Book VIII, 126, "Bears when first born are shapeless masses of white flesh a little larger than white mice, their claws alone being prominent. The mother then licks them gradually into proper shape."

the equivalents of "licking" which the human mother gives her child in order to prepare his sustaining systems for adequate functioning?

I suggest that one of the equivalents for "licking" is represented by the long period of labor that the parturient human female undergoes. The average duration of labor with the firstborn is fourteen hours; with subsequent-born children the average duration of labor is eight hours. During this period the contractions of the uterus provide massive stimulations of the fetal skin. These uterine contractions serve much the same functions and end-effects that licking of the newborn does in other animals. In the womb the fetus has been constantly stimulated by the amniotic fluid and by the growing pressures of its own body against the walls of the uterus. These stimulations are greatly intensified during the process of labor in order to prepare the sustaining systems for postnatal functioning in ways somewhat different from those which were necessary in the aquatic environment in which the fetus has thus far spent his life. This intensification of cutaneous stimulations is especially necessary in the human fetus because, contrary to general belief, the period of gestation is not completed when the baby is born. It is only half-completed. It will be necessary for us to discuss this matter further, in order to gain some insight into the precarious condition in which the young of human kind is born, and why it is necessary that the human neonate undergo certain kinds of cutaneous stimulation.

THE MEANING OF NEONATAL AND INFANT IMMATURITY IN MAN. Why are human beings born in a state so immature that it takes eight to ten months before the human infant can even crawl, and another four to six months before he can walk and talk? That a good many years will elapse before the human child will cease to depend upon others for his very survival constitutes yet another evidence of the fact that man is born more immature, and remains immature for a longer period, than any other animal.

The newborn elephant and the fallow deer are able to run with the herd shortly after they are born. By the age of six weeks, the infant seal has been taught by his mother to navigate his watery world for himself. These animals all have long gestation periods, presumably because animals that give birth to small litters, which they are unable to protect as efficiently as predatory animals, must give birth to young who are in a fairly mature state. A long gestation period serves to allow for such maturation.

The elephant, which has a gestation period of 515 to 670 days, gives birth to a single infant. In animals such as the fallow deer, which gives birth to a litter of two or three, the gestation period is 230 days. In the seal, which produces only a single pup at a birth, the gestation period varies from 245 to 350 days. Predatory animals, by contrast, are very efficient in protecting their young, and have a short gestation period. Their litters may vary from three at a birth upwards; the size of the young may be small at birth, and the young may be born in a somewhat immature state. The lion, for example, which generally has a litter of three cubs, has a gestation period of 105 days. Man has a gestation period of 266½ days, which is distinctly in the class of long gestation periods. Since this is so, what can be the explanation for the extremely immature state in which man is born? This is a somewhat different question from that which refers to the prolonged immaturity of the young of human kind.

Apes are also born in an immature condition, but remain

in that state for a much shorter time than does the human infant. The average duration of gestation in the gorilla is about 252 days, in the orang-utan about 273 days, and in the chimpanzee 231 days. Labor in the apes generally lasts not more than two hours, which contrasts strikingly with the average of fourteen hours for the firstborn and eight hours for the subsequent born in the human female. Like man, the apes are monotocous, that is, one infant is usually conceived and born at term, but compared with that of man the development of the young ape is somewhat more rapid, so that the infant ape takes about one-third to two-thirds of the time the human infant does to develop such traits as lifting the head, rolling, worming along, sitting alone, standing, and walking. Ape mothers tenderly care for their young for several years, and it is not uncommon for breastfeeding to continue for three or more years. Man's immaturity in infancy, therefore, may be regarded as an extension of the basic infant immaturity characteristic of all anthropoid forms, characteristic, that is, of the great apes and probably earlier forms of man. Among anthropoids the care, feeding, and protection of the young fall exclusively to the females. Only when the females and the young are endangered do the males act to protect them.

While the length of the gestation period lies within the same range in anthropoids and in man (see Table I), there is a marked difference in the growth of the fetus in the two groups. This is seen in the great acceleration in the rate of growth of the human fetus, as compared with the anthropoid fetus, towards the end of the gestation period. This is most strikingly seen in the increase in size of the human fetal brain, which by the time of birth has acquired a volume of between 375 and 400 cubic centimeters. Total body weight of the human newborn averages 7 pounds. In the chimpanzee total body weight of the neonate is, on the average, 4.33 pounds (1,800 grams), and the brain volume is about 200 cubic centimeters. In the gorilla the total body weight of the newborn is about 4.75 pounds (1,980 grams), and the brain size at birth would appear to be not much more than in the chimpanzee.

TABLE I. LENGTH OF GESTATION, POSTNATAL GROWTH PERIODS, AND LIFE SPAN IN APE AND MAN

Genus	Gestation (days)	Menarche (years)	Eruption of First and Last Permanent Teeth (years)	Completion of General Growth (years)	Life Span (years)
Gibbon	210	8.5	?–8.5	9	30
Orang-Utan	273	?	3.0–9.8	11	30
Chimpanzee	231	8.8	2.9–10.2	11	35
Gorilla	252	9.0	3.0–10.5	11	35
Man	266½	13.5	6.2–20.5	20	75

The smaller size of the anthropoid newborn is probably correlated to some extent with the shorter duration of labor in the anthropoid female. In man, however, the large body size, and especially the large size of the head at 266½ days of fetal age, necessitate the birth of the child at that time. If it were not born then and it continued to grow at the rate at which it is geared to grow, it could not be born at all—with fatal consequences for the continuation of the human species.

As a consequence of the evolution of the erect posture in man, the pelvis has undergone major rearrangement in all its parts. Among these changes has been a narrowing in the pelvic outlet. During parturition the pelvic outlet enlarges somewhat with the relaxation of the pelvic ligaments, enough to permit the head of the child, with a certain amount of moulding and compression, to pass through the birth canal. In adaptation to this situation the skull bones of the human infant, in relation to the membranes in which these bones develop, grow much less than those of the ape infant of the same gestation age. Thus the human infant's skull bones allow for a considerable amount of movement and overlapping in adaptation to the compressive forces that will act upon them during the process of birth. The human infant, then, is born when it is because it must be born at that time; otherwise the rapid rate at which its brain grows would make it impossible for it to be born at all. The brain growth of the anthropoid infant presents no such problems, particularly in view of the mother's generous pelvic arrangements.

Not only does the prolonged period of behavioral immaturity of the human infant reveal how undeveloped and dependent it is at birth, so too does its biochemical and physiological immaturity. For example, several enzymes remain undeveloped in the newborn human. In this the human shares a trait common to a number of other mammals, except that in the human infant, unlike most other mammalian infants thus far investigated, most of these enzymes are not present at all. In guinea pigs and mice, for example, the liver enzymes develop during the first week of life, but require some eight weeks for full development. It appears that in all mammals some factor is present in the uterine environment which represses the formation of liver enzymes in the fetus. In the human infant some liver and duodenal enzymes (amylase) do not appear until several weeks or months have passed. Gastric enzymes are present which are fully capable of dealing with the ingested colostrum and milk from the maternal breast, but these enzymes cannot effectively metabolize foods normally consumed by older children.

All the evidence indicates that, while the duration of the gestation period in man differs by only about a week or two from that of the great apes, a large number of other factors, all combining to lead to the much more prolonged development of the human infant, cause it to be born before its gestation has been completed. One would think that a creature developing at the rate the human fetus does, in the later stages of uterine development and during childhood, should, developmentally, enjoy a much longer period of gestation within the womb. In man, as compared with the apes, every one of the developmental periods, with the exception of the developmental period within the womb, is greatly extended in duration—why not also the period of gestation?

The explanation seems to be that the fetus must be born when its head has reached the maximum size compatible with its passage through the birth canal. This transmigration constitutes no mean accomplishment. Indeed, the passage through the four inches of the birth canal is the most hazardous journey a human being ever takes. The fact is, the human fetus is born before its gestation is completed. The rate of growth of the brain is proceeding at such a pace during the last month of pregnancy that its continuation within the womb would render birth impossible. Hence, the survival of the fetus and the mother requires the termination of gestation within the womb when the limit of head size compatible with birth has been attained, and long before maturation occurs.

The process of evolution by which the increase in the length of man's developmental periods has been accomplished is known as *neoteny*. The term refers to the process whereby the functional and structural features of the young (fetal or juvenile) of ancestral forms are retained in the developmental stages of the maturing individual, from infancy to adulthood. Man's large head, flat face, roundheadedness, small face and teeth, absence of brow ridges, thinness of skull bones, late suture closure, relative hairlessness, thin nails, prolonged period of educability, playfulness, love of fun, and many other traits all constitute evidence of neoteny.

The gestation period, then, is also greatly extended in man, except that its latter half is completed outside the womb. Gestation, as we have usually understood it, is not in fact completed at birth, but is continued from gestation within the womb, *uterogestation,* to gestation outside the womb, *exterogestation.* Bostock has suggested that the limit of exterogestation be set at the stage of the beginning of effective crawling on all fours, a suggestion which has considerable merit. Interestingly enough, the average duration of exterogestation, taking its limit here to be when the infant commences to crawl, lasts, on the average, exactly the same time as uterogestation, namely, 266½ days. In this connection it is also of interest to note that while the mother continues to nurse her infant, pregnancy will be delayed for some time. Nursing the child at the breast causes the suppression of ovulation for variable periods of time, and thus constitutes a natural, although not altogether dependable method of child-spacing. It also suppresses menstrual bleeding. Menstrual bleeding tends to be heavier and longer-lasting when the mother does not breast feed, and, as a consequence of the heavier bleeding, the mother's reserve energies tend to be somewhat depleted. The premature cessation of breastfeeding would, then, result in distinct disadvantages, especially when a mother already has other children who require her attention. Hence breastfeeding confers advantages not only upon the baby but also upon the mother, and therefore upon the group. This is to mention only the physical advantages of breastfeeding. Even more important are the psychological advantages which are reciprocally conferred upon infant and mother in the nursing situation, especially in a species in which the mother is symbiotically designed to continue the gestation of her child outside the womb. (See pp. 50–51)

To learn what the child must learn in order to function as an adequate human being, he must, then, possess a large warehouse in which to store all the necessary information, a brain, in short, of considerable storage and retrieval capacity. It is a striking fact that by the time the human child has attained its third birthday it has virtually achieved full adult brain size. The average brain-volume of the human three-year-old is 960 cubic centimeters, while the brain volume of the human adult, attained at the age of twenty years, is 1,200 cubic centimeters; that is to say, after the end of its third year the human brain will grow by only another 240 cubic centimeters to attain its full size, and that 240 cubic centimeters will accumulate by small increments over the next seventeen years. In other words, at the end of three years of age the human child has achieved 90 percent of its brain growth. Significantly, the infant brain more than doubles in volume by the end of its first year to about 750 cubic centimeters, or 60 percent of its adult size. Almost two-thirds of the total growth of the brain is achieved by the end of the first year. It will take an additional two years to add almost another third to the volume attained at the end of the third year (see Table II). In its first year, therefore, the infant's brain grows more than it ever will again in any one year.

TABLE II. GROWTH IN BRAIN AND CRANIAL CAPACITY
IN MAN (BOTH SEXES)

Age	Weight (grams)	Volume (cubic centimeters)	Cranial Capacity (cubic centimeters)
Birth	350	330	350
3 months	526	500	600
6 months	654	600	775
9 months	750	675	925
1 year	825	750	1,000
2 years	1,010	900	1,100
3 years	1,115	960	1,225
4 years	1,180	1,000	1,300
6 years	1,250	1,060	1,350
9 years	1,307	1,100	1,400
12 years	1,338	1,150	1,450
15 years	1,358	1,150	1,450
18 years	1,371	1,175	1,475
20 years	1,378	1,200	1,500

SOURCE: *Growth and Development of the Child, Part II,* White House Conference (New York: Century Co., 1933), p. 110.

It is important that most of the brain growth be accomplished during the first year, when the infant has so much to learn and do. Indeed, the first year of life requires a great deal of unobtrusive packing for a journey that will continue for the rest of the traveler's life. To perform this packing safely, the infant must possess a brain much larger than 375 to 400 cubic centimeters, but quite clearly he cannot wait until he has grown a brain of 750 cubic centimeters before being born. Hence, he must be born with the maximum-sized brain possible, and do the remainder of his brain growing after birth. Since the human fetus must be born when its brain has reached the limit of size congruent with its admission into and extrusion through the birth canal, such maturation or further development as other mammals complete before birth, the human mammal will have to complete after birth. In other words, the gestation period will have to be extended after birth.

When the uterogestation period is extended beyond the expected date of delivery for more than two weeks, the pregnancy is said to be postmature. Some 12 percent of births are delayed two weeks beyond the due date, and some 4 percent are delayed three weeks. All the evidence indicates that postmaturity is increasingly unfavorable for the fetus, as well as for its postnatal development. The perinatal mortality rate is more than twice as high for postterm infants as it is for term infants, and the incidence of primary caesarean section done because of head-pelvis disproportion is double that in term infants; severe congenital abnormalities occur in about a third more of these postterm children, and they are generally characterized by a reduced capacity to adapt. All of which underscores the importance of being born at term.

The human infant is almost, if not quite, as immature at birth as the little marsupial which, born in an extremely immature state, finds its way into its mother's pouch, there to continue its gestation until it is sufficiently matured. The human infant remains immature much longer than the infant kangaroo or opossum, but whereas the marsupial infant enjoys the protection of its mother's pouch during its period of immaturity, the human infant is afforded no such advantage. However, the human infant comprises part of a symbiotic unit; the mother, having given it shelter and sustenance within the womb, is elaborately prepared throughout the period of pregnancy to continue to do so, once the baby is born, outside the womb, at least as efficiently as the mar-

supial mother. The biological unity, the symbiotic relationship, maintained by mother and conceptus throughout pregnancy does not cease at birth; indeed, it is naturally designed
to become even more intensively functional and mutually
involving after birth than during gestation in the uterus.

If this interpretation of the gestation period is sound, then
it would follow more than ever that we are not at present
meeting the needs, in anything approaching an adequate
manner, of the newborn and infant young, who are so precariously dependent upon their new environment for survival and development. Although it is customary to regard
the gestation period as terminating at birth, I suggest that
this is quite as erroneous a view as that which regards the
life of the individual as beginning at birth. Birth no more
constitutes the beginning of the life of the individual than it
does the end of gestation. Birth represents a complex and
highly important series of functional changes which serve to
prepare the newborn for the passage over the bridge between gestation within the womb and gestation continued
outside the womb.

Because the human infant is born in so precariously immature a condition, it is especially necessary for the parental
generation of the human species fully to understand what
the immaturity of its infants really signifies: namely, that
with all the modifications initiated by the birth process, the
infant is still continuing its gestation period, passing, by the
avenue of birth, from uterogestation to exterogestation in a
continuing and ever more complex interactive relationship
with the mother, who is best equipped to meet its needs.
Among the most important of the newborn infant's needs
are the signals it receives through the skin, its first medium
of communication with the outside world. In preparation for

its functioning in the postnatal world—to afford it, as it were, a womb with a view—the massive contractions of the uterus upon the body of the fetus play an important role. It is this that we have now to consider.

ON BEING STROKED THE RIGHT WAY. The relatively short labor which nonhuman mammals experience is usually insufficient to activate such sustaining systems as the genitourinary and gastrointestinal systems, and in part the respiratory system; hence mothers must initiate this activation by licking their young. This they are designed to accomplish by an inbuilt series of reactive behaviors to odors, wetness, touch, temperature, early experience, and the like. Such inborn reactive responses are feeble in human mothers. The human mother's responses to her newborn will to a large extent depend on her own early experience as an infant and child and to some extent upon learning and maturation. If the mother has not enjoyed such experience or learned how to behave as a mother she is very likely to prove inadequate, endangering the continued survival of her baby.* Hence, a basic assurance that the baby will be adequately prepared for postnatal functioning must be physiologically automatic. This basic assurance must not be dependent upon any postnatal behavior such as "licking," necessary as that may be for further development in other species. This insurance in the human species is secured by the prolonged contractions of the uterus upon the body of the fetus. The stimulations thus received activate, or tone up, the sustaining systems for the functions they will be called upon to perform immediately after birth. In short, it is here being suggested that in the human species

* For a further discussion of this subject, see A. Montagu, *The Reproductive Development of the Female,* (New York: Julian Press, 1957).

the prolonged uterine contractions during labor represent, in addition to their other vital functions, a series of massive cutaneous stimulations calculated to activate and ensure the proper functioning of the sustaining systems.

When we ask what the function is of the ordinary uncomplicated process of labor and birth, the answer is: preparation for postnatal functioning. The process of preparation takes some time, for there are many changes which must be induced in the fetus about to be born if he is successfully to negotiate the brave new world of his immediate postnatal existence. The bridge the process of birth forms between prenatal and postnatal life constitutes part of the continuum of individual development. The initiation of the birth process is associated with a fall in oxygen saturation of the placenta and of the fetal circulation, followed by the onset of labor, that is to say, the beginning uterine contractions which average about one a minute, and the breaking of "the bag of waters." All this, and much more that is involved in these bare words, means that a baby is to be born, to which must be added that it is to be born prepared to adjust successfully to the next series of events in the developing continuum of its life. That series of events cannot be broadly subsumed under the words "postnatal existence," for "postnatal existence" refers to the whole of life outside the womb, and clearly no newborn is ever prepared to deal with the whole of that postnatal life over which, only after many years, if at all, it will achieve some sort of mastery. What the fetus must be prepared to deal with during the birth process is the *immediate* neonatal period of the first few hours, then days, weeks, and months of gradual adjustment and habituation to the requirements of early postnatal existence. Towards this end the neonate must be readied with all its sustaining systems, as well as its muscular system, prepared to function.

The sustaining systems are the *respiratory* system, which controls the intake of oxygen as well as the utilization and elimination of carbon dioxide; the *circulatory* system, which conveys the oxygen through the blood vessels to the capillaries to supply the cells, and, in turn, to take up the gaseous waste products and return them to the lungs; the *digestive* system, which is concerned with the ingestion and chemical breakdown of solid foods and liquids; the *eliminative* systems, which carry the waste products from the alimentary tract, from the urinary tract, and from the skin through the sweat glands; the *nervous* system, which enables the organism to make the appropriate response to the stimuli it receives through that system; and the *endocrine* system, which, in addition to the important role it plays in growth and development and in behavior, assists in the functioning of all these systems. The response of the respiratory center to the biochemical changes induced by the lack of oxygen and the accumulation of carbon dioxide, initiates the whole complicated process of respiration. The circulation becomes autonomous, the foramen ovale in the septum between the two atria of the heart which, in the fetus, permits blood to pass directly from the right into the left atrium, begins to close, and the ductus arteriosus, which connects the aorta with the pulmonary trunk directly below, begins to undergo occlusion. Blood is now carried by the pulmonary arteries to the lungs, there to be aerated, and returned to the heart by the pulmonary veins, and then from the left ventricle through the aorta into the general circulation. This is a very different arrangement from that which existed in the fetus. It now in-

volves the functioning of the muscles of the chest and abdomen, the diaphragm, and the heart, as well as such organs as
the lungs, and the whole of the upper respiratory tract in
quite novel ways. In addition, the temperature regulation of
the body now begins to be taken over by the newborn, the
experience of birth initiating the stimulation of the tempera-
ture-regulating centers.

Contraction of the uterus upon the body of the fetus stimulates the peripheral sensory nerves in the skin. The nervous
impulses thus initiated are conducted to the central nervous
system where, at the proper levels, they are mediated
through the vegetative (autonomic) nervous system to the
various organs which they innervate. When the skin has not
been adequately stimulated, the peripheral and autonomic
nervous systems are also inadequately stimulated, and a failure of activation occurs in the principal organ systems.

It has been an age-old observation that when the newborn
infant fails to breathe, a hearty slap or two on the buttocks
will generally be sufficient to induce breathing. The profound physiological significance of this remarkable fact appears to have escaped attention. Reasoning from the physiological relations already indicated, it seemed to me likely
that under similar conditions, that is, when the baby failed
to breathe immediately after birth, stimulation of the respiratory center and the respiratory organs could perhaps be
achieved by subjecting the baby to immersion, alternately,
in hot and cold baths. Upon inquiry I found that this was,
indeed, an old-established practice. In such cases it would
seem reasonable to assume that it is the cutaneous stimulation which activates the autonomic nervous system, with the
autonomic nervous system acting in turn upon the respiratory centers and viscera. The effect of a sudden cold shower

upon respiration is well known, and is indicative of a similar series of events.

The short, intermittent stimulations of the skin over a prolonged period of time that are produced by the contractions of the uterus upon the body of the fetus thus appear to be perfectly designed to prepare it for postnatal functioning.

How can we be sure that this is in fact one of the functions of the prolonged cutaneous stimulation? One of the things we can do is to inquire into what happens when there is inadequate cutaneous stimulation of the fetus, as in the case of precipitately born children. This often occurs in prematurity, and also in the case of many caesarean-delivered infants. In such cases what we should expect to find, according to our theory, would be disturbances in the gastrointestinal, genitourinary, and respiratory functions. Investigations made without any knowledge of or reference to our theory, but which are directly relevant to it, substantially support the theory. For example, Dr. C. M. Drillien studied the records of many thousands of prematures and found that during the early years of postnatal life they exhibited a significantly higher incidence of nasopharyngeal and respiratory disorders and diseases than normally born children. This difference was especially marked during the first year.

In 1939, Mary Shirley published the results of a study on premature children of nursery school and kindergarten age conducted at the Harvard Child Study Center in Boston. Shirley found that premature children exhibit a significantly higher sensory acuity than term children, and in comparison are somewhat retarded in lingual and manual control, as well as in postural and locomotor control. Control of bowel and bladder sphincters, significantly enough, was found to be achieved later and with difficulty in the premature children. The attention span is short; such children are inclined to be highly emotional, jumpy, anxious, and usually shy. Summarizing her findings, Shirley observed that in the preschool period, the prematures present significantly more behavior problems than fullterm children. These problems include hyperactivity, later acquisition of bowel and bladder control, enuresis, excessive distractibility, shyness, thumbsucking, negativism and hypersensitivity to sound. In interpreting this prematurity-syndrome Shirley pointed out that premature births often are cataclysmic; unduly prolonged or precipitant, both of which conditions subject the baby to birth trauma. . . . Thus, it seems possible that, through a less favorable prenatal environment or through the too early loss of intrauterine media, or through the lack of adequate time for the birth preparatory responses, or through birth injuries that are sometimes so slight as to be unrecognized or through a combination of these factors, the premature may be predisposed toward the development of a higher degree of nervous irritability than the term child.

The "lack of adequate time for the birth preparatory responses," is the critical passage here, and the finding of the later and more difficult learning of control of bowel and bladder sphincters, the significant observation.

Caesarean-delivered babies suffer from a number of disadvantages from the moment they are delivered. Their mortality rate, to begin with, is two to three times as great as that which follows vaginal delivery. At full term the rate is twice as great in caesarean-delivered babies as in vaginally delivered ones. In elective caesarean deliveries, that is to say, in nonemergency caesareans, the mortality rate is 2 percent higher than for vaginally delivered babies. In the emergency caesareans the mortality rate is 19 percent higher than in vaginal deliveries.

Death from the respiratory disorder known as hyaline membrane disease is ten times more frequent in caesarean-delivered than in vaginally delivered babies.

It may be conjectured that the disadvantages, among other things, from which caesarean-delivered babies suffer, compared with vaginally delivered babies, are to a significant extent related to the failure of adequate cutaneous stimulation which they have undergone.

Pediatricians have noted that caesarean babies tend to be characterized by greater lethargy, decreased reactivity, and less frequent crying than the vaginally delivered.

In the hope of throwing some light on the developmental history of the caesarean-delivered infant, Dr. Gilbert W. Meier of the National Institutes of Health conducted a series of experiments on macaque monkeys (*Macaca mulatta*). He compared thirteen caesarean-delivered with thirteen vaginally delivered infants for the first five days of their lives. He found that the vaginally delivered infants "were more active, more responsive to the situation, and more responsive to additional stimulation within that situation." Vocalizations, avoidance responses—the beginnings of true learning responses—and activity counts were on the average about three times more frequent in the vaginally delivered than in the caesarean-delivered infants.

Quite possibly, had the caesarean-delivered babies been given an adequate amount of caressing for some days after they were born, a significant change might have been observed in their behavioral and physical development. All the evidence clearly points in that direction.

Drs. Sydney Segal and Josephine Chu of the University of British Columbia studied twenty-six vaginally delivered and thirty-six caesarean-delivered babies, and found that the latter showed a smaller crying vital capacity than the former, a difference that persisted for the six days of their stay in the baby nursery.

A number of biochemical differences have been found between caesarean-delivered and normally delivered babies, such as higher acidosis, lower serum proteins, lower serum calcium, and higher potassium in the caesarean-delivered.

A most significant finding relates to the production of sugar in newborn infants. Normally when a small amount of glucagon, a substance thought to be secreted by the pancreas, is introduced into the digestive system, the system responds by producing sugar. In caesarean-delivered infants the amount of sugar produced in response to this glucagon factor was much less than in vaginally delivered infants, *in the absence of labor.* If, however, labor had occurred before caesarean delivery this difference was obliterated. The basic importance of labor in the preparation of the infant for postnatal functioning is thus strikingly confirmed.

In contrast, in their studies of rats, Grota, Denenberg, and Zarrow found no differences between caesarean-delivered and vaginally delivered young in survival until weaning, or in weaning, weight, and open-field activity.

Both Shirley and Drillien observed that prematures as children presented more frequent and greater feeding problems than children born at term. Such observations, abundantly confirmed by other observers, suggest the possibility that inadequate cutaneous stimulation plays a role here, and, in some cases at least, results in a greater susceptibility to infection and disorder of the respiratory, gastrointestinal, and genitourinary systems. Further contributory evidence is to be seen in the meconium plug syndrome. This is the condition in which a plug formed of loose cells, intestinal gland secretions, and amniotic fluid produces intestinal obstruction, resulting in a marked delay in the emptying of the stomach and the passage of food through the intestines. In such cases there is an apparent failure of the pancreas to secrete the protein-splitting enzyme trypsin, leading to inadequate peristaltic action of the intestines. Hence there is both a failure and a breakdown in the movement of the meconium. The whole syndrome strongly indicates a failure of action of the necessary substances upon the gastrointestinal tract.

Dr. William J. Pieper and his colleagues studied the case data from the files of a state child-guidance clinic, which enabled them to compare 188 pairs of normally delivered and caesarean-delivered children matched for age, sex, ethnic group, ordinal position, and father's occupational level. Comparisons were made in 76 variables. In most of these variables these two groups of children were indistinguishably similar, but in a small number they were significantly different. Thus, caesarean-delivered males and all caesareans eight years of age or older were more likely to have a speech defect, to have a speech defect at the time of the diagnostic examination, and to have a mother rated as behaving inconsistently in the mother-child relationship. The other six differences were as follows: normally born males were found to have more unspecified other somatic complaints; caesarean-delivered males were more likely to be rated by the psychologist as showing evidence of organic involvement; caesareans under eight years of age were more likely to present the symptoms of fear of school and unspecified other personality difficulties; and caesareans over eight years of age were more likely to present the symptoms of restlessness and temper.

Clearly, the differences found by Pieper and his colleague between caesarean-delivered and normally delivered children were largely of an emotional nature, the caesarean-delivered children being somewhat significantly more emotionally disturbed than the normally delivered children. It would be difficult to attribute such differences to the absence or inadequacy of a single factor in the development of these caesarean children, but, as we shall see, it is quite probable that inadequate cutaneous stimulation during the perinatal period, that is, the period shortly before and shortly after birth, may have been one of the factors involved.

Dr. M. Straker found a significantly higher frequency of emotional disturbance and anxiety in caesarean-delivered individuals than in normally delivered ones. Liberson and Frazier found that the electroencephalographic patterns in caesarean newborns show evidence of greater physiological stability than in the normally born. This finding, however, is difficult to evaluate as an evidence of greater or lesser general physiological stability. It is referred to here simply to make it clear that the evidence does not all point in the same direction. One would hardly expect it to.

That postpartum cutaneous stimulation can to some extent compensate for a lack of skin stimulation during the birth process is supported by Dr. Donald H. Barron's observation of twin kids delivered without the occurrence of labor, by caesarean section. If one newborn kid is left wet in a warm room, while the other is completely dried off with a towel, cleaning it well, the kid that has been dried gets up before the other. This difference in response, Barron remarks, points to the great survival value of cutaneous stimulation. "I have the impression," he states, "that the drying, licking, and the grooming are important in raising the general level of neural excitability in the kid, and thereby hasten his ability to rise on his knees, to orient himself, and to stand."

Since the head of the human term fetus is, within the womb, larger than it has ever been, and since it lies in the head-down position in the narrowest part of the womb, the stimulations received from the contracting uterus by the face, nose, lips, and remainder of the head are very considerable. This facial stimulation corresponds to the licking of the muzzle and oral region given by other animals to their young, and presumably produces much the same effect, namely, the initiation of sensory discharge into the central nervous system and the raising of the excitability of the respiratory center. As Barron has shown, there is a rise in the oxygen content of the blood associated with licking and grooming, in the newborn of goats: "Raising the excitability of the respiratory center in turn increases the depth of the respiratory effort, increases the level of oxygenation of the blood, and so enhances the capacity for further muscular movement and strength."

Insofar as the higher oxygenation of the blood is concerned, these observations have been confirmed in the normally newborn human, as compared with the caesarean-delivered and the premature. McCance and Otley have shown that when the newborn rat is removed from its mother immediately after birth its kidneys remain relatively functionless for the first twenty-four hours of its life. They suggest that normally the attentions of the mother cause an increase in the excretion of urea owing to some reflex change in the blood flow to the kidney.

The skin and the gastrointestinal tract meet not only at

the lips and mouth, but also at the anal region. Hence it is scarcely surprising, in the light of what we have already learned, not only that gastrointestinal function will be activated by stimulating this region, but that respiratory function will also often be activated by such stimulation. This method of stimulating respiration in the newborn often works when other methods fail.

That the skin and the gastrointestinal tract are often interactive has been suggested in clinical reports for many years. Disorders and diseases may simultaneously affect both intestinal tract and integument.

That the benefits of maternal-infant cutaneous contacts are reciprocal is evident from the fact that when the newborn is placed in contact with its mother's body the uterus will be stimulated to contract. This fact constituted part of the folk-wisdom of many peoples for centuries. It is, for example, reported from Brunswick, in Germany, that it is the custom not to allow the child, during the first twenty-four hours after its birth, to lie by its mother's side, "otherwise the uterus can find no rest and scratches about in the woman's body, like a large mouse." Folk-wisdom, while recognizing the fact, failed when it came to drawing the correct conclusion from it, namely, that the contractions of the uterus were of advantage to the mother.

The evidence surveyed in the preceding pages, sparse as it is, nevertheless lends strong support to the hypothesis that an important function of the prolonged labor and especially the contractions of the uterus, in the human female, is to serve much the same purpose that licking and grooming of the newborn serve in other animals. This purpose is to further the infant's development for optimum postnatal functioning of its sustaining systems. We have seen that in all animals cutaneous stimulation of the infant's body is in most cases an indispensably necessary condition for the survival of the young. We have suggested that in a species such as man, in which gestation is only half completed at birth, and in which maternal behavior is dependent upon learning rather than upon instinct, the selective advantage would lie with a reflex initiation and maintenance of uterine contractions functioning for the fetus as an automatic, physiologically massive stimulation of its skin, and through its skin of its organ systems. The evidence, as we have seen, tends to support this hypothesis, that the uterine contractions of labor constitute the beginning caressing of the baby in the right way—a caressing which should be continued in very special ways in the period immediately following birth and for a considerable time thereafter. This we may proceed to discuss in the next chapter.

THREE

I will lift up mine eyes unto the hills:
*From whence cometh my help.**

BREASTFEEDING

WHETHER OR NOT we accept the psychoanalytic view that life in the womb is normally a supremely pleasureable experience, a blissful state rudely shattered by the experience of birth, there can be little doubt that the process of birth is a disturbing one to the birthling. Having spent its prenatal life in a supporting aquatic environment, within a medium in which the second law of thermodynamics is perfectly satisfied by the constancy of the temperature and the pressure, that is to say within the amniotic fluid surrounded by the amniotic sac, the fetus is said to live a Nirvana-like existence. This blissful existence is rudely interrupted largely owing to a fall in the levels of progesterone in the mother's bloodstream, resulting in the turbulent series of changes which

* PSALMS 121.1.

the fetus begins to experience as the birth process. The contractions of the uterus in labor act as compressive forces
upon its body, so that it is pushed against the birth canal
where the repeated thrusts of its head against the maternal
bony pelvis produces the swelling beneath its scalp known as
the *caput succedaneum.* It is doubtful whether the fetus
quite appreciates that this apparently unseemly assault upon
its person is designed entirely for its benefit. Providentially,
the oxygen available to it at this time is gradually undergo-
ing reduction, so that such consciousness, such awareness of
pain as it may be capable of, is probably reduced. This may
well be the function of the anoxia or hypoxia, as this reduced state of oxygenation is called. The contracting uterus
completes its parturitive functions with the expulsion of the
fetus from the uterus. With birth the newborn moves into a
wholly new zone of experience and adaptation, from an
aquatic into an atmospheric and social environment.

At birth, atmospheric air immediately rushes into the
lungs of the newborn for the first time, inflating them, and
causing them to press against and to produce gradual rotation of the heart. There is, as it were, a competition for
space between the heart and the lungs. The ductus arteriosus between the arch of the aorta and the upper surface of
the pulmonary trunk, which in the fetus made it possible to
bypass the systemic circulation involving the lungs, begins to
contract and close. The cupolae of the diaphragm begin to
rise up and down, the chest wall to expand, all of which
could hardly be described as adding up to a pleasant experience for the newborn exterogestate. What the newborn is
looking forward to, and has every right to expect, is a continuation of that life in the womb before it was so catastrophic-
ally interrupted by the birth process. And what it receives

in our highly sophisticated societies in the Western world is a rather dusty answer.

The moment it is born, the cord is cut or clamped, the child is exhibited to its mother, and then it is taken away by a nurse to a babyroom called the nursery, so called presumably because the one thing that is not done in it is the nursing of the baby. Here it is weighed, measured, its physical and any other traits recorded, a number is put around its wrist, and it is then put in a crib to howl away to its heart's discontent.

The two people who need each other at this time, more than they will at any other in their lives, are separated from one another, prevented from continuing the development of a symbiotic relationship which is so critically necessary for the further development of both of them.

During the whole of pregnancy the mother has been elaborately prepared, in every possible way, for the continuation of the symbiotic union between herself and her child, to minister to its dependent needs in the manner for which she alone is best prepared. It is not simply that the baby needs her, but that both need each other. The mother needs the baby quite as much as the baby needs its mother. The biological unity, the symbiotic relationship, maintained by mother and conceptus throughout pregnancy does not cease at birth but becomes—indeed, is naturally designed to become—even more intensified and interoperative than during uterogestation. Giving birth to her child, the mother's interest and involvement in its welfare is deepened and reinforced. Her whole organism has been readied to minister to its needs, to caress it, to make loving sounds to it, to nurse it at the breast. From the breast it will not only take in the wondrous colostrum, the lemony-yellowish fluid which confers such benefits upon the child, but the child will also, by its nursing, confer vital benefits upon the mother. The psycho-physiological benefits which mother and child, the nursing couple, reciprocally confer upon one another in the continuing symbiotic relationship are vitally important for their further development. This is a fact which is only very slowly coming to be recognized in our highly sophisticated, mechanized, dehumanized Western world, a world in which breastfeeding is considered to be beneath human dignity. As one expensively educated young woman remarked to me when I asked her whether she was going to breastfeed her baby, "Why, only animals do that." It is a world in which there are pediatricians who assure mothers that a bottle formula is every bit as good as, and even better than, breastfeeding.

We live in the logical denouement of the Machine Age, when not only are things increasingly produced by machine, but human beings, who are also turned out to be as machinelike as we can make them, therefore see little wrong in dealing with others in a similarly mechanical manner; an age in which it is considered a mark of progress when whatever was formerly done by human beings is taken out of their hands and done by machine. It is reckoned an advance when a bottle formula can be made to substitute for the contents of the human breast and the experience of the human infant at it, especially in an age when women have so unhappily taken over the values of the masculine world.

In the widely read official manual *Infant Care,* issued by the U. S. Children's Bureau of the Department of Health, Education and Welfare, a work mainly edited by women, the 1963 edition reflects an apparently not uncommon negative attitude toward the tactile experience of breastfeeding. "You

may feel," the editors write, "some resistance to the idea of
such intimacy with an infant who, at first, seems like a
stranger. To some mothers it seems better to keep the baby
at arm's length, so to speak, by feeding plans which are not
so close."

These astonishing sentences reveal, more than whole trea-
tises could, a deep failure to understand the meaning and
importance of the intimacy which should exist, from the moment of birth, between mother and infant.

During the birth process mother and infant have had a
somewhat trying time. At birth each clearly requires the reassurance of the other's presence. The reassurance for the
mother lies in the sight of her baby, its first cry, and in its
closeness to her body. For the baby it consists in the contact
with and warmth of the mother's body, the support in her
cradled arms, the caressing it receives, and the suckling at
her breast, the welcome into "the bosom of the family."
These are words, but they refer to very real psychophysiological conditions.

Within a few minutes after the baby is born the third
stage of labor should be completed; that is, the placenta
should be detached and ejected. The bleeding of the torn
vessels of the uterus should begin to be arrested, and the
uterus should commence its return to normal size. When the
baby is put to nurse at the mother's breast immediately after
birth, and even before the cord is clamped, if the cord is
long enough, the baby's suckling will serve to accelerate all
three processes. By suckling at the breast the baby sets up
changes in the mother; its suckling increases the secretion of
oxytocin from the pituitary gland, producing massive contractions of the uterus, with the consequence that: (1) the
uterine muscle fibers contract upon the uterine vessels; (2)

the uterine vessels undergo constriction at the same time; (3) the uterus begins to undergo diminution in size; (4) the placenta becomes detached from the uterine wall, and (5) is ejected by the contracting expulsive uterus. In addition, the secretory functions of the breast are greatly augmented. Physiologically, the nursing of her babe at her breast produces in the mother an intensification of her "motherliness," the pleasurable care of her child. Psychologically, this intensification serves further to consolidate the symbiotic bond between herself and her child.

For the newborn, what better reassurance can there be than the support of its mother and the satisfaction of suckling at her breast, what better promise of good things to come? The cutaneous stimulation the baby receives from the mother's caressing, from the contact with her body, its warmth, and especially the perioral stimulations, that is, the stimulations received during suckling about the face, lips, nose, tongue, mouth, are important in improving the respiratory functions and through this means the oxygenation of the blood. As an assistance in suckling, the newborn is equipped with a median papilla on its upper lip which enables it to gain a firm hold on the breast. At the same time, at the breast the baby is ingesting the valuable colostrum, the best of all the substances it could possibly imbibe. The colostrum lasts only two days and, among other things, acts as a laxative; it is the only substance that can effectively clean out the meconium in the baby's gastrointestinal tract. Colostrum constitutes the most powerful insurance against the baby's development of diarrhea. Babies ingesting colostrum do not develop diarrhea. The fact, indeed, is that the only known successful treatment for diarrhea in babies is breastfeeding. Colostrum is richer than true milk in lactoglobulin,

70 BREASTFEEDING

which carries the factors that immunize the baby against a number of diseases. Years ago Dr. Theobald Smith of New York showed that colostrum conferred upon calves immunity to colon bacillus septicemia. In 1934 Dr. J. A. Toomey demonstrated that similar immunizing factors against this bacillus were present in human colostrum, as well as immunizing factors against other bacteria that infect the gastrointestinal tract. Colostrum encourages the growth of desirable bacteria and discourages the growth of undesirable bacteria in the gastrointestinal tract of the newborn.

In many ways the newborn calf is more mature than the human newborn. Like the calf, the human newborn has an undeveloped immunological capacity at birth; that is, it has no antibodies and little ability to make its own as defenses against foreign invaders. The antibody-rich colostrum from its mother's breast, which is some fifteen to twenty times richer in gamma globulin than maternal serum, provides the newborn with such antibodies, and confers a passive immunity upon him for the next six months, by which time he will gradually have acquired his own antibodies.

Thus breastfeeding provides a number of correlated benefits for the newborn, immunological, neural, psychological, and organic. Over the two or more million years of human evolution, and as a consequence of seventy-five million years of mammalian evolution, breastfeeding has constituted the most successful means of ministering to the needs of the dependent, precariously born human neonate.

While I am in this book principally concerned with the stimulation of the skin as an important factor in the development of the individual, and not with the immunological and nutritive properties of the substances ingested during breastfeeding, it is fundamentally important for us to understand that the colostrum which lasts for some two days, the transitional milk which lasts for some eight days, and the permanent milk which comes in about the tenth day, are all designed to meet the gradually developing metabolic needs of the infant in adjustment to its developing capacities to deal with the various substances it ingests. The baby's enzyme systems take some days to develop sufficiently to be able to deal with these substances, mostly proteins. The colostrum, transitional, and permanent milk, coming in as gradually as they do are perfectly timed and adjusted to the physiological development of the infant's digestive system.

These facts suggest that breastfeeding constitutes a fundamental requirement for the human newborn. Not that the newborn cannot survive in the absence of breastfeeding, but that he will not develop in as healthy a manner as the breastfed baby, and finally, that the breastfed baby at any rate will get a much better start towards healthy development than the non-breastfed baby.

The *development* of colostrum and of transitional milk will occur in the absence of a suckling baby, but the *giving* of these substances to the baby will depend upon the suckling of the baby. The link between *making* milk and *giving* milk is called the *letdown reflex*. When the baby begins to suckle at the breast the cutaneous stimulation in the mother initiates nervous impulses which travel along neural circuits to the pituitary gland, which then releases the hormone oxytocin into the bloodstream. The oxytocin, reaching the glandular structures of the breast, stimulates the basket cells, which surround the alveoli and milk ducts, resulting in expansion of the ducts. This, in turn, results in a greater flow of milk down into the sinuses behind the nipple, and from thirty to ninety seconds after the baby has begun to suckle the letdown reflex is completed, and the flow into the baby of the rich substances in the mother's breast will continue as long as she perseveres in breastfeeding.

While breastfeeding is maintained, pregnancy will not usually occur for at least ten weeks after the birth of the child, and often much longer. Thus during the breastfeeding period a kind of natural birth control will be in effect. The advantages of breastfeeding to the baby are enormous. In one pilot study of 173 children followed from birth to the age of ten years, including both breastfed and non-breastfed children, it was found that the children who had not been breast fed had four times as many respiratory infections, twenty times more diarrhea, twenty-two more miscellaneous infections, eight times as much eczema, twenty-one times more asthma, and twenty-seven times more hayfever.

Similarly, Drs. C. Hoefer and M. C. Hardy in a study of 383 Chicago children found that breastfed children were physically and mentally superior to those who were artificially fed, and that those fed from four to nine months were in these respects more advanced than those breast fed for three months or less. The artifically fed ranked lowest in all the physical traits measured. They were nutritionally the poorest, the most susceptible to the diseases of childhood, and slowest in learning to walk and talk.

Early weaning is a subject on which we have no data for the human species. But we do have some data on rats. Dr. Jiri Krecek of the Institute of Physiology of Prague, at an international symposium held at Liblice, Czechoslovakia, on "The Postnatal Development of the Phenotype," stated the thesis that the period of weaning in mammals is a critical one, inasmuch as several basic physiological processes are being reorganized at this time, particularly those involving salt balance, general nutrition, and fat-intake. Defining weaning as withdrawal from breastfeeding at sixteen days of age, other workers reported that rats who were weaned early elaborated a conditioned reflex less rapidly than those weaned at thirty days of age, and also that the adult of these animals showed deficiencies in ribonucleic acid, a basic constituent of all cells. It was also found that the principal electrolyte-regulating steroid was detrimentally affected by early weaning, and that even the male hormones, the androgens, are adversely affected. At the same symposium Dr. S. Kazda described a pilot study of human adults indicating that reproduction and certain kinds of pathology may be affected by early weaning.

The advantages of breastfeeding during the first year of life on subsequent development and into adulthood have been demonstrated by a number of investigators. The evidence indicates that the infant should be breast fed for at least twelve months, and terminated only when the infant is ready for it, by gradual steps in which solid foods, which can begin at six months, commence to serve as substitutes for the breast. The mother will generally sense when the baby is ready for weaning.

Drs. Francis M. Pottenger, Jr., and Bernard Krohn, in a study of 327 children, found that the facial and dental development of children who had been breast fed for more than three months was better than those who had been breast fed less than three months or not at all. They conclude their report with the following words: "These findings in our 327 cases indicate that it is advisable to nurse a child at least 3 months, and preferably 6 months. This will stimulate optimal malar [cheekbone] development. We have also observed that patients who were well nursed had better-developed dental arches, palates, and other facial structures than patients who were not nursed."

Much else could be said on the advantages of breastfeeding accruing to both mother and child; the aim is, of course, to give the child something rather more than an adequate diet, to provide it, in sum, with an emotional environment of security and love in which the whole creature can thrive. Breastfeeding alone will not secure this. It is the mother's total relatedness to her child that makes breastfeeding significant.

The experience of breast and touch can be seen, within the framework of a concept drawn from gestalt psychology, as a figure/ground perception, with body always there as ground, and reaching for the breast as figured stimulus. This figure/ground experience initiates not only the letdown reflex, but the ongoing process of socialization of two human beings, for when a baby is in this way "born," a mother is, too.

It is highly probable that the development of the skin itself as an organ is greatly benefited by the experience at the breast. While I know of no experimental data on this, there does exist some evidence from other sources and on other animals tending to support this view. For example, Truby King, the distinguished New Zealand pediatrician, was much impressed with the statements on this subject made to him by a merchant dealing in wool and hides. The piece is worth quoting in its entirety. Truby King having spoken to the merchant of the advantages of breastfeeding, the latter replied, "I don't need convincing as to what mother's milk must mean for the child—I know it already from my own business. *Why, I can tell you how your boots were fed!*" He then proceeded to explain and demonstrate his point:

"In the trade we know the highest grade of calf-skins as Paris Calf. That is because calves reared on their mother's milk to provide the finest veal for Paris, have also incidentally set the standard for the whole world as to what is best in the way of calf-skins for tanning.

"Suppose the hair has not been removed, it is smooth and glossy, not harsh or dry, and it all lies the right way. Or take the leather, it isn't patchy. The whole hide is more or less uniform, smooth and fine-grained. When you feel and handle it you find that it has a certain body and firmness, and yet it is pliable and elastic. It's nice to touch and handle—there is a kindly feeling about it. Why (pausing to think of an illustration) it's like the face of a sleek child that is doing well, compared with one that's not flourishing."

"What about the other kind?" Truby King inquired.

"Oh, you mean the 'bucket-feds,' " replied the merchant. "Of course there is every grade and degree; but speaking generally, the hide is patchy—it's not all over alike. It tends to be harsh and dry, and has a more or less dead feeling. There is not the same body in it, and it hasn't the fine grain and pliancy of Paris Calf. It's not kindly to the touch. Why, look here, when handling a first-rate calf-skin we say to one another in the trade: 'By Jove, that's a good piece of stuff—why, that's milk-fed.' "

While there can be small doubt that the "kindliness," of the milk-fed skin is in large part due to the nutrients ingested by the calf from its mother's milk, some of its quality, we will not, I am sure, be far wrong in concluding, is probably also due to the cutaneous stimulation received by the calf from the mother.

The quality of the tactile stimulation received stands in direct relation to the qualitative development of the organism in all its organ systems. As we have already noted, since the introduction of the mechanical milking of cows it has been observed that hand-milked cows give more and richer terminal milk than machine-milked cows. This appears to be true also in the lactating human female. Usually, as we know, the tactile stimulation provided by the baby's suckling at the nipple initiates the letdown reflex and the full flow of milk. But in cases in which the breast-milk is for some reason insufficient, systematic massage, starting at the abdomen and carried up to the breasts, is generally sufficient to stimulate an abundant flow of milk.

Sir Truby King states,

The value of massage of the breasts, and sponging them twice a day with hot and cold water alternately, has been abundantly demonstrated for some years at the Karitane Harris Hospital, New Zealand. It is found that these simple measures, along with an abundance of fresh air, bathing, daily exercise, due rest and sleep, regular habits, suitable feeding and drinking of extra water, rarely fails to re-establish breastfeeding in cases where the supply has been falling off—indeed where suckling has been entirely given up for days or even for weeks.

It is known that in the absence of suckling stimulation the hormone which initiates the secretion of milk, namely prolactin, will not continue to be produced by the pituitary gland in adequate quantities, and ovulation, failing to be inhibited, will resume. In order to test whether the production of prolactin would continue in the absence of suckling, but in the sight, sound, and body contact with the young, Moltz, Levin, and Leon surgically removed the nipples from female rats who were subsequently impregnated and allowed to give birth normally. When compared with unoperated control groups from whom the young had been removed twelve hours after birth, it was found that the control females began to ovulate after an average of seven days, a sham-operated group ovulated at sixteen days, while the experimental group ovulated at twenty days. The exteroceptive stimuli of sight, sound, odor, and perhaps "feel" of the young, this investigation suggests, even in the absence of suckling, are able to promote the output of prolactin in amounts sufficient to inhibit ovulation for sixteen to twenty days.

The inter-cutaneous stimulation of the nursing couple has evolved quite clearly as a reciprocating developmental arrangement designed to activate and to keep tonally at their optimum the various bodily functions of both mother and child. The areola and the nipple possess very sensitive reflexogenic capacities. When uterine irritability is at its maximum, during and shortly after labor, stimulation of the nipple causes pronounced, often violent, contractions. The center of this reflexogenic mechanism is believed to be in the hypothalamus, which stimulates the release of the hormone oxytocin from the pituitary gland. It is this hormone that initiates and maintains the contractions of the uterus during labor, and is thus believed to be the hormone responsible for the initiation of the birth process. As we have already seen, oxytocin is also the hormone which is released in abundance as a result of the baby's suckling at the breast, a reflex activity resulting in the letdown reflex and the flow of milk.

We see, then, how beautifully designed the suckling of the baby at the mother's breast is, especially in the immediate postpartum period, to serve the most immediate needs of both, and from this to grow and develop in the service of all their reciprocal needs. What is established in the breastfeeding relationship constitutes the foundation for the development of all human social relationships, and the communications the infant receives through the warmth of the mother's skin constitute the first of the socializing experiences of his life.

It is quite remarkable that in a pre-Freudian age, Erasmus Darwin—Charles Darwin's grandfather—in an extraordinary book *Zoonomia, or the Laws of Organic Life,* first published in 1794, should have suggested a relationship between breastfeeding and subsequent behavioral development. In his book Darwin wrote as follows:

All these various kinds of pleasure at length become associated with the form of the mother's breast; which the infant embraces with its hands, presses with its lips, and watches with its eyes and thus acquires more accurate ideas of the form of its mother's bosom, than of the odor and flavor of warmth, which it perceives by its other senses. And hence at our maturer years, when any object of vision is presented to us, which by its waving or spiral lines bears any similitude to the form of the female bosom, whether it is found in a landscape with soft gradations of rising and descending surface, or in the forms of some antique vases, or in other works of the pencil or chisel, we feel a general glow of delight, which seems to influence all our senses; and if the object be not too large, we experience an attraction to embrace it with our arms, and to salute it with our lips, as we did in our early infancy the bosom of our mother.

Possibly the psalmist who wrote the words, "I will lift up mine eyes unto the hills: from whence cometh my help," may have been responding to the influence of such early experiences.

Erasmus Darwin traces the origin of the smile to the experience of the infant at its mother's breast. He writes,

In the action of sucking, the lips of the infant are closed around the nipple of his mother, till he has filled his stomach, and the pleasure occasioned by the stimulus of this grateful food succeeds. Then the sphincter of the mouth, fatigued by the continued action of sucking, is relaxed; and the antagonist muscles of the face gently acting, produce the smile of pleasure: as cannot but be seen by all who are conversant with children.

Hence this smile during our lives is associated with gentle pleasure; it is visible on kittens, and puppies, when they are played with, and tickled; but more particularly marks the human features. For in children this expression of pleasure is much encouraged, by their imitation of their parents, or friends; who generally address them with a smiling countenance: hence some nations are more remarkable for the gaiety, and others for the gravity of their looks.

It is as good a theory of the origin of smiling as any that has been offered, and it is to be noted that it does not escape Darwin's attention that the readiness with which people smile is to a large extent culturally conditioned. The fact that the smile universally constitutes an evidence of pleasure, of friendliness, may at least partly be due to the origins of smiling in the infant's oral-tactile pleasures at the maternal breast.

The meaning of skin-contact with the mother, especially at her breast, is recalled most beautifully by Kabongo, a Kikiyu chief of East Africa. He was eighty years of age when he spoke these words:

My early years are connected in my mind with my mother. At first she was always there; I can remember the comforting feel of her body as she carried me on her back and the smell of her skin in the hot sun. Everything came from her. When I was hungry or thirsty she would swing me round to where I could reach her full breasts; now when I shut my eyes I feel again with gratitude the sense of well-being that I had when I buried my head in their softness and drank the sweet milk that they gave. At night when there was no sun to warm me, her arms, her body, took its place; and as I grew older and more interested in other things, from my safe place on her back I could watch without fear as I wanted and when sleep overcame me I had only to close my eyes.

"Everything came from her." These are the key words. They imply warmth, support, security, satisfaction of thirst and hunger, comfort, well-being, the very satisfactions that every baby must experience at its mother's breast.

It is through body contact with the mother that the child makes its first contact with the world, through which he is enfolded in a new dimension of experience, the experience of the world of the other. It is this bodily contact with the other that provides the essential source of comfort, security, warmth, and increasing aptitude for new experiences.

FOUR

I was a child beneath her touch,—a man
When breast to breast we clung, even I and she,—
A spirit when her spirit looked through me,—
A god when all our life-breath met to fan
Our life-blood, till love's emulous ardours ran,
Fire within fire, desire in deity.*

TENDER, LOVING CARE

IN THAT seminal book, *Psychosocial Medicine,* James L. Halliday writes:

As the first few months following birth may be regarded as a direct continuation of the intrauterine state, there is need for continuance of close body contact with the mother to satisfy the requirements of the kinesthetic and muscle senses. This requires that the baby be held firmly, nursed at intervals, rocked, stroked, talked to, and reassured. With the disappearance of the "shaley wife" and the introduction of the perambulator the need for adequate body contact is often forgotten. How readily the infant

* D. G. ROSETTI, *"The Kiss,"* from *The House of Life*

reacts to the absence of the contact is seen when a baby is laid on a flat surface such as a table without support. Immediately it reacts with a startle and a cry. Mothers who are anxious (from whatever cause) tend when holding a child to hold it loosely or insecurely instead of firmly and confidently, and this to some extent explains the saying that "anxious mothers produce anxious babies," the insecurity of the mother being, as it were, sensed by the child. The absence of accustomed mother contact has a bearing on the problem of "fretting" such as is seen when an infant is removed from a hospital. Many of us who have been resident medical officers in a fever hospital used to be somewhat skeptical of the importance of fretting, but recent observations have shown its reality and its practical importance, in that infants deprived of their accustomed maternal body contact may develop a profound depression with lack of appetite, wasting, and even marasmus leading to death. As a result of these findings volunteer women now attend some of the children's hospitals to provide infants that are fretting with periods of handling, caressing, rocking, etc. (The results are said to be dramatic.)

The results are, indeed, dramatic—and thereby hangs a fascinating tale.

During the nineteenth century more than half the infants in their first year of life regularly died from a disease called *marasmus,* a Greek word meaning "wasting away." The disease was also known as infantile atrophy or debility. As late as the second decade of the twentieth century the death rate for infants under one year of age in various foundling institutions throughout the United States was nearly 100 percent! It was Dr. Henry Dwight Chapin, the distinguished New York pediatrician, who, recognizing the emotional aridity of the children's institutions, introduced into America the system of boarding out babies instead of leaving them in institutions. But it was Dr. Fritz Talbot of Boston who brought the idea of "Tender, Loving Care," not in so many words but in practice, back with him from Germany, which he had visited before World War I. While in Germany Dr. Talbot called at the Children's Clinic in Dusseldorf, where he was shown over the wards by Dr. Arthur Schlossmann, the director. The wards were very neat and tidy, but what piqued Dr. Talbot's curiosity was the sight of a fat old woman who was carrying a very measly baby on her hip. "Who's that?" inquired Dr. Talbot. "Oh, that," replied Schlossmann, "is Old Anna. When we have done everything we can medically for a baby, and it is still not doing well, we turn it over to Old Anna, and she is always successful."

America, however, was massively under the influence of the dogmatic teachings of Emmett Holt, Sr., Professor of Pediatrics at New York Polyclinic and Columbia University. Holt was the author of a booklet, *The Care and Feeding of Children,* which was first published in 1894 and was in its 15th edition in 1935. During its long reign it became the supreme household authority on the subject, the "Dr. Spock" of its time. It was in this work that the author recommended the abolition of the cradle, not picking the baby up when it cried, feeding it by the clock, and not spoiling it with too much handling, and, while breastfeeding was the regimen of choice, bottle-feeding was not discounted. In such a climate the idea of tender, loving care would have been considered quite "unscientific," so that it wasn't even mentioned, although, as we have seen, in places like the Children's Clinic in Dusseldorf, it had already obtained some recognition as early as the first decade of the twentieth century. It was not until after World War II, when studies were undertaken to discover the cause of marasmus, that it was found to occur quite often among babies in the "best" homes, hospitals, and institutions, among those babies apparently receiving the best and most careful physical attention. It became apparent that babies in the poorest homes, with a good mother, despite the lack of hygienic physical conditions often overcame the physical handicaps and flourished. What was wanting in the sterilized environment of the babies of the first class and was generously supplied to babies of the second class was mother love. Recognizing this in the late twenties, several hospital pediatricians began to introduce a regular regimen of mothering in their wards. Dr. J. Brennemann established the rule in his hospital that every baby should be picked up, carried around, and "mothered" several times a day. At Bellevue Hospital in New York, following the institution of "mothering" on the pediatric wards, the mortality rates for infants under one year fell from 30 to 35 percent to less than 10 percent by 1938.

What the child requires if it is to prosper, it was found, is to be handled, and carried, and caressed, and cuddled, and cooed to, even if it isn't breast fed. It is the handling, the carrying, the caressing, and the cuddling that we would here emphasize, for it would seem that even in the absence of a great deal else, these are the reassuringly basic experiences the infant must enjoy if it is to survive in some semblance of health. Extreme sensory deprivation in other respects, such as light and sound, can be survived, as long as the sensory experiences at the skin are maintained.

Cases capable of throwing considerable light on the importance of cutaneous stimulation in the absence of other kinds of stimulation are represented by those few instances in which either the loss of such senses as vision and hearing occurred at or shortly after birth, or where the child has been kept in a dark room with a deaf-mute mother. The most dramatic instances of the first sort are the cases of

Laura Bridgman and Helen Keller. Their stories are too well known to be retold here, except to draw attention to the fact that, having lost both vision and hearing, these two children were, after much effort, reached through the skin and eventually learned to embrace the whole of the human world and to communicate with it upon the highest levels entirely through the skin. Until each of these children had learned the finger alphabet—in other words, communication through the skin—they were cut off virtually completely from interactive social relations with other human beings. They were isolated, and the world in which they lived held little meaning for them; they were almost completely unsocialized. But after the patient efforts of their teachers had succeeded in enabling them to learn the finger alphabet, the world of symbolic communication was opened to them, and their development as social human beings proceeded apace.

Equally interesting is the case of Isabelle. She was an illegitimate child, and for that reason she and her mother were secluded from the rest of the mother's family in a dark room where they spent most of their time together. Born in Ohio in April, 1932, Isabelle was discovered by the authorities in November, 1938. She was then six and a half years of age. Lack of sunshine and poor nutrition had produced severe rickets. As a result Isabelle's legs were so bowed that when she stood erect the soles of her shoes came nearly flat together, and she moved about with a skittering gait. When found, she resembled a wild animal more than anything else, mute and idiot-like. She was at once diagnosed by a psychologist as genetically inferior. However, a specialist in child speech, Dr. Marie K. Mason, put her through an intensive and systematic training in speech, and in spite of all prognostications to the contrary succeeded not only in teaching her to speak normally, but to achieve with speech all the usual associated abilities. In two years she covered the stages of learning that normally require six years. She did very well at school, participating normally in all school activities.

The case of Isabelle conforms to the type picture of the isolated child with malnutrition, idiocy, and muteness, who nevertheless, under intensive training, became a thoroughly normal socialized being. Malnutrition did not do any noticeable damage to the nerve cells of her brain, and her development to perfectly normal social adjustment strongly suggests that she probably received a great deal of attention, mostly of a tactile nature, during the years of isolation with her mother.

Laura Bridgman and Helen Keller communicated through the sense of touch. We are told that Isabelle also communicated with her mother in this manner and by gesture. Isabelle's disabilities and her nonsocialization were entirely due to her prolonged isolation. Her ability to recover from its effects was almost certainly due to the fact that she had been adequately loved by her mother, handled, held, caressed, and fondled.

It is recorded of Frederick II (1194–1250), Emperor of Germany, in his own time called *stupor mundi,* "wonder of the world," but referred to by his enemies in less flattering terms, that

he wanted to find out what kind of speech and what manner of speech children would have when they grew up if they spoke to no one beforehand. So he bade foster mothers and nurses to suckle the children, to bathe and wash them, but in no way to prattle with them, for he wanted to learn whether they would speak the Hebrew language, which was the oldest, or Greek, or Latin, or Arabic, or perhaps the language of their parents, of whom they had been born. But he laboured in vain because the children all died. For they could not live without the petting and joyful faces and loving words of their foster mothers. And so the songs are called 'swaddling songs' which a woman sings while she is rocking the cradle, to put a child to sleep, and without them a child sleeps badly and has no rest.

"For they could not live without the petting . . ." This observation constitutes the earliest known pronouncement on the importance of cutaneous stimulation for the development of the child. Undoubtedly awareness of the value of caressing the child is much older than that.

As Dr. Harry Bakwin, among the earliest pediatricians to recognize the importance of mothering the hospital child, has written, "Most important to the young baby appear to be the skin sensations and the kinesthetic sense. Babies are readily soothed by patting and by warmth, and they cry in response to painful stimuli and to cold. The quieting effect of keeping babies outdoors may be due, in part, to the movement of the air on the skin."

The reference to warmth and to air points to some very important influences in the immediate postpartum experience of the newborn. The baby's temperature *in utero* is probably about the same as its mother's, but during the birth process and in the perinatal period the baby's temperature is somewhat higher than the mother's, varying between 97.5° and 102.0° Fahrenheit with a mean of about 100°. Temporary exposure to cold air will stimulate the baby to cry, but is in no way damaging unless the exposure to cold is prolonged. Babies respond pleasurably to warmth and with distress to cold. Neonatal cold injury can lead to death. Normally the warmth of the mother's body flowing through to the baby will comfort him, and the absence of that warmth will distress him. When, in later life, we speak of the "warmth" of a person, as compared with those who are "cold," these are not, we may suspect, mere figures of speech. As Otto Fenichel has said, "Temperature eroticism in particular is often combined with early oral eroticism and forms an essential part of primitive receptive sexuality. To have cutaneous contact with the partner and to feel the warmth of his body remains an essential component of all love relationships. In archaic forms of love, where objects serve rather as mere instruments for gaining satisfaction, this is especially marked. Intense pleasure in warmth, frequently manifested in neurotic bathing habits, is usually encountered in persons who simultaneously show other signs of a passive-receptive orientation, particularly in regard to the regulation of their self-esteem. For such persons, "to get affection' means 'to get warmth.' They are 'frozen' personalities who 'thaw' in a 'warm' atmosphere, who can sit for hours in a warm bath or on a radiator."

The human newborn, even if he is born before term, has considerable ability to regulate his own temperature, but the range of thermal environment in which he remains comfortable, his range of thermal neutrality, is of lesser amplitude than in the adult, because he has the disadvantages of a relatively large surface area from which to exchange heat and a small body mass to act as a heat sink (a mass which absorbs heat). Hey and O'Connell have examined the neutral thermal zone in clothed babies, and concluded that a draught-free environment of 75° F is necessary to provide neutral thermal conditions for most cot-nursed babies in the first month of life. The clothed baby is at an advantage over the naked baby. The bare face and head, and especially the face, will not only provide the important sweating areas for the dissipation of heat, when that becomes necessary, but will also serve to receive the cool air which will act as a stimulus to respiration. Glass and his co-workers have shown that blanketing symptom-free low birthweight infants not only simplifies their management but also enhances their immediate and longterm ability to resist acute cold stress.

There is reason to believe that there exist two systems of temperature sensitivity, one for warmth and one for cold, and to these the newborn is particularly sensitive. Like adults, the infant tolerates high external temperatures better than he does low ones, and prefers warmth to cold, but precisely what role the early experience of differences in temperature plays in his subsequent development, except in the matter of cold injury, we do not know; we may surmise that it is not inconsiderable.

The temperature sense or senses present many complexities which are far from being well understood. The metabolic response to sudden changes in temperature can be very threatening. For example, as Hey and his co-workers have shown, while a baby may be born into a draught-free room warmed to a temperature of 82–86° F, when an exchange transfusion is performed under these conditions, the deep body temperature of the baby will fall progressively unless active steps are taken to warm the donor's blood. There is good reason to believe, as these investigators suggest, that the use of cold blood could precipitate circulatory collapse during exchange transfusion. The same is often true when it is necessary to give adults a rapid transfusion of stored blood.

Cold has a constricting effect upon the blood vessels and also tends to slow down the flow of blood, with resulting accumulation of deoxygenated blood in the capillaries, leading to cyanosis, that is, blueness of the skin, and this is greatly affected by temperature, being accelerated by warmth and decelerated by cold.

The practice of bathing babies shortly after they are born often exposes them to heat-loss and cold, especially when the cheeselike coating, the *vernix caseosa* as it is called, is removed. The vernix caseosa is composed of sebum secreted from the baby's own skin glands and shed epithelial cells from its skin. In the liquid medium of the womb, this serves as an insulating layer which protects the baby's skin from maceration. Following birth the vernix caseosa serves as an insulation against loss of heat and the penetration of cold. For this reason the practice of washing away this cheeselike substance is considered undesirable by some authorities. This would be particularly true where the surrounding temperature is less than 80° F. In general it might be a good idea to leave this substance undisturbed and the baby placed with the mother until she is ready to nurse it.*

The baby's sucking pressure at the breast is lower at 90° F than at 80° F, according to the findings of Elder on twenty-seven fullterm healthy infants. Cooke found that caloric intake in infants decreased as environmental temperature increased from 81° F to 90° F, and that caloric intake increased when temperature decreased from 91° F to 80° F. Such findings suggest that the common hospital practice of heavily wrapping infants at feeding time might benefit from review.

The obvious efforts of mothers among the mammals to keep their young warm, and broody behavior among birds, sufficiently testify to the great importance of warmth in the

---

* Since the vernix caseosa tends to dry rapidly upon exposure to air it presents no particular problems.

development of the young. The strong drive of the young to huddle together in the absence of a broody or warming mother further serves to underscore the importance of a necessary condition which can best be produced in the young through body contact.

The suggestion has been made that the basic factor in changes induced by handling may be temperature. Schaeffer and his co-workers, for example, found that rats whose temperature had been lowered showed the same drop in ascorbic acid in the blood as handled rats. The conclusions of these investigators have been criticized on various methodological grounds, without denying that temperature may be a variable in producing manifold effects in different animals.

The touch of a cold hand is not pleasant—the touch of a warm one is, an observation which brings us to the consideration that cutaneous sensation cannot be a matter simply of touch or pressure, but must in part be a response to temperature. Caressing with an ice-cold hand would scarcely be received by the recipient as comforting, but rather as an uncomfortable, if not outright painful experience. Clearly, it is the quality of cutaneous stimulation that conveys the message. A sharp, painful slap conveys a very different message from a tender, gentle caress, and differences in skin pressure may make all the difference between a painful and a pleasureable sensation. It is probably in something of this manner that infants are able to discriminate between those who care for them and those who do not.

It is the messages the infant picks up through its own muscle-joint receptors from the manner in which it is held, rather than mere pressure on the skin, that tell the infant what the holder "feels" about it. The skin belongs to the class of organs called *exteroceptors* because they pick up sensations from outside the body. Receptors that are stimulated principally by the actions of the body itself are called *propri-oceptors*. It is both through its skin and the proprioceptors that the infant receives the messages from the muscle-joint-ligament behavior of the person holding it.

The infant makes the proper discriminations in much the same way that adults do when they draw inferences about the character of a person from the quality of his handshake. At least, those individuals who have not been desensitized in their capacity to do so are able to draw such conclusions with a high degree of accuracy. Every baby is clearly born with this kinesthetic sense, and the evidence we have—experimental, observational, experiential, and anecdotal—all tends to support the view that, just as we learn to speak by being spoken to, and will speak as we have been spoken to, so we learn to respond to exteroceptive skin stimulation and proprioceptive muscle-joint stimulation largely as a function of our early experience or conditioning in these senses.

It is quite probable that something of the manner in which the individual comes to carry himself, to hold his head, his shoulders, and to move his limbs and torso, is related to his early conditioning experiences. It is well known, for example, that the anxious individual, whether infant, child or adult, tends to rigidify his movements, to tense his muscles, to over-elevate his shoulders, and even to glare with his eyes. These conditions are not infrequently associated with pallor and dryness of the skin, not to mention other cutaneous disorders.

Thoughts and feelings are often communicated in nonverbal ways, through movements of the body. The study of this subject is known as *kinesics*. Kinesics is concerned with the exploration of the constant adjustments, without their necessarily being aware of the fact that they are making them, which human beings are constantly engaged in in relation to the presence and activities of other human beings. Our leading student of kinesics, Ray L. Birdwhistell, is convinced that kinesic behavior is learned, systematic, and analyzable. "This," he writes, "does not deny the biological base in the behavior but places the emphasis on the *interpersonal* rather than the *expressional* aspects of kinesic behavior."

It is in the interpersonal relationship with the mother, exteroceptively and proprioceptively, as well as *interoceptively,* especially involving the receptors of the gastrointestinal tract —and this is very important—that the child establishes its first communicative relationships. Quite probably during this period conditioning conducive to the formation of hypertensive habits takes place. These hypertensive habits later show up in hypertensive conditions affecting the gastrointestinal tract in the form of colitis, hypermotility, ulcers, and the like, affecting the cardiovascular system in the form of psychogenic cardiovascular disturbances, affecting the respiratory system in the form of asthmatoid conditions, and, of course, affecting the skin in a large variety of disorders.

Dr. P. Lacombe has described a remarkable case of a severely neurotic female patient who manifested depressive violent behavior and neurodermatosis. The grandmother of the patient gave the latter's mother minimal tactile attention as a child, and the patient's own mother failed her in this respect also. Lacombe sees this patient's disorder as the expression of a loss of the infant-mother attachment resulting in a fixation on the mother. Loss of the mother equals loss of ego, and loss of maternal skin as point of contact reappears in the patient as weeping skin areas. The patient's pet dog also suffered from skin problems, which Lacombe interprets as due to the identification of the dog with its mistress. The ego, says Lacombe, "is the perception of the bodily self, and what one feels and knows of the body is the skin."

A striking example of specific cutaneous conditioning during the first two weeks of life, and subsequent regression to this very early age level, is illustrated by a case of trichotillomania, that is, pathological hair-pulling, reported by Dr. Philip F. Durham Seitz in a child under three years of age.

A 2½ year-old white, female child was referred for psychiatric study by a dermatologist because of scalp hair loss of one year's duration. Dermatologic examinations had failed to reveal an organic basis for the alopecia. The scalp exhibited an over-all thinning and shortness of hair, more marked on the right side.

During the initial psychiatric interview, it was observed that the child cuddled herself in the arms of her mother and sucked milk from a nursing bottle. While sucking the nipple of the nursing bottle, which was held in the left hand, she searched her scalp with the right hand for remaining hairs. When a hair or group of hairs was found, she pulled these out with a twisting motion of her fingers. The hairs were then carried in her fingers to her upper lip, where she rolled them against her lip and nose. This process was continued as long as she nursed from the bottle, but ceased promptly when the nipple was removed from her mouth. The mother pointed out that the child pulled her hair only when sucking from the nursing bottle, and that invariably sucking was accompanied by hair pulling and nose tickling. The author went to the home of this family in order to observe the child, and also observed her during play in his office. Hair pulling and nose tickling were found to occur only, and then invariably, when the child sucked milk from a nursing bottle.

Further interviews with the mother elicited the following information: The girl was the first and only child of lower middle-class parents, both of whom exhibited somewhat precarious emotional adjustments. The father was a Salvation Army musician, and both parents were devoutly religious. They had been married for five years, considered themselves entirely compatible marital partners, and had both wanted the child at the time she was conceived. However, because of the difficulty they had experienced with her, they employed contraceptives to avoid further pregnancies. The girl was born at term, delivery being uneventful. For the first two weeks the mother nursed her baby at her breast, but discontinued this abruptly during the third week because she believed her lactation to be insufficient. The child's growth and development during the first year and one-half appeared to be normal. She sat at three months, stood at seven months, walked at ten months, began to talk at eighteen months. She was weaned from the bottle when she was one year old, after which she ate solid foods and drank liquids from a cup.

When the child was eighteen months old, a punitive program of toilet training was instituted, which involved scoldings and spankings whenever she soiled herself. In retrospect, the mother realized it was following onset of this toilet training program that the child began to refuse solid foods, insist upon milk from a nursing bottle, and pull out her hair and tickle her nose while sucking. In addition, she had become difficult to manage, resisted all efforts to teach her toilet habits, and cried a great deal, would not mind, and demonstrated a desire to splash water on herself.

From observation of the child Dr. Seitz reasoned that her refusal to eat solid foods and her continued nursing from a bottle suggested an unconscious desire to return to an earlier suckling stage. Her hair pulling and nose tickling suggested that somehow she wished in some way to duplicate the original suckling situation. This raised a question: Was her nose tickled while she was at the breast? The nose tickling suggested that hair on the mother's breast might have been responsible. With this in mind the mother's breasts were examined and revealed "a ring of long, coarse hairs surrounding each nipple."

In order to test the hypothesis suggested by this association, a nipple was constructed with a ring of coarse human hairs projecting around its base. This arrangement provided an automatic tickling of the child's nose whenever the nipple was held in the mouth. When sucking at the nipple she would slowly turn the bottle, brushing the upright hairs against her nose and upper lip. Hair pulling did not occur. The automatic nose-tickling apparently satisfied the need to regress to the early experience at the breast.

The importance of this fascinating case lies in its demonstration of early psychocutaneous conditioning, within the first two weeks of life. Nursed at the hairy breast of her mother for two weeks, and then abruptly withdrawn from it, this little girl attempted to reinstate the conditions at the breast by providing herself with hair from her own head with which to stroke her nose and lip while sucking at a rubber nipple at the end of a glass bottle.

"To what other neurotic traits," asks Dr. Seitz, "and psychosomatic reactions may an individual be predisposed in later life by specific cutaneous conditioning of this type? Psychocutaneous disorders of the nose? Nose picking? Hay fever, or allergic rhinitis?" These are good questions.

NOSING, NURSING, AND BREATHING. Psychocutaneous disorders of the nose should be a fertile field for exploration, but I know of no significant studies in this area. Yet it is clear from the many different ways in which people treat their noses that early conditioning may very well have played a part in determining or influencing their kinesic behavior toward this part of their anatomy. People pull at their noses, stroke them, flatten them, compress them, wrinkle them, put their bent fingers under them, place their index finger against them, scratch them, massage them, breathe heavily or lightly

through them, or flare their nostrils. It would hardly be warranted to attribute all such habits to early conditioning, but
there can be little doubt that in many cases such habits are
in some way related to early cutaneous conditioning. The
nose, it has been said, is the gateway to life and death. This,
of course, refers to its respiratory functions. As we have already seen, it is probable that the proper development of the
respiratory function is to some extent dependent upon the
amount and kind of cutaneous stimulation the infant experiences. It is not unlikely that persons who have received inadequate cutaneous stimulation in infancy develop as shallow
breathers, and become more susceptible to upper respiratory
tract and pulmonary disorders than those who have received
adequate cutaneous stimulation. There is some reason to believe that certain types of asthmas are, at least in part, due to
a lack of early tactile stimulation. There is a high incidence
of asthma among persons who as young children were separated from their mothers. Putting one's arm around an asthmatic while he is having an attack may abort or alleviate it.

Margaret Ribble has pointed out the importance of tactile
experience in breathing.

Respiration [she writes], which is characteristically shallow,
unstable and inadequate in the first weeks after birth is definitely
stimulated reflexly through sucking and through physical contact
with the mother. Infants who do not suck vigorously do not
breathe deeply and those who are not held in the arms sufficiently, particularly if they are bottle-fed babies, in addition to
breathing disturbances often develop gastrointestinal disorders.
They become air-swallowers and develop what is popularly
known as colic. They have trouble with elimination or they may
vomit. It seems that the tone of the gastrointestinal tract in this
early period depends in some special way on reflex stimulation
from the periphery. Thus, the touch of the mother has a definite

biological implication in the regulation of the breathing and nutritive functions of the child.

To continue with the subject of breathing for a moment, before returning to the nose through which that breathing mainly takes place, it has already been pointed out that immediately following upon exposure to atmospheric air the newborn's previously unexpanded lungs fill with air and the various changes in pressure which occur at the moment of birth help to initiate the postnatal type of respiratory movements which continue throughout the life of the person. The need to breathe is so compelling that a three-minute denial of it is often sufficient to cause death. The urge to breathe is the most imperative of all man's basic urges, and the most automatic. The process of learning to breathe is an anxious one. Every breath we take, even as adults, is preceded by a faint phobic stir. Under conditions of stress many persons go into labored breathing reminiscent of breathing at birth. Under such conditions the person often regresses to fetalized activities and assumes fetal positions. In fear or anxiety one of the first functions to be affected is breathing. Yet, in spite of its automaticity, breathing or respiration is under voluntary control and under conscious control for short periods of time, as any person who has ever taken singing lessons knows, and for very durable periods of time, as every Yogi knows. This control is actually exerted during the ordinary activities of everyday life, such as speaking, swallowing, laughing, blowing, coughing, and sucking. Breathing, indeed, is not simply a physiological process but a part of the way in which an organism behaves.

That many of the elements of breathing are learned is evident from the fact that there are significant class differences in the manner of breathing. Heavy or stertorous breathing, like noisy soup- or coffee-sipping, occurs very much more frequently among members of the lower classes than among members of the upper classes. Differences in the rate of breathing and oxygen-combining capacity of the lungs, as Dill has shown, are closely correlated with occupational status. Inadequate, shallow breathing, associated with chronic feelings of fatigue in later life, as compared with healthy deep breathing, are also for the most part learned habits, and may well have some connection with early cutaneous experiences.

To return to the nose: It could be that the various forms of handling the nose in later life, including nose picking, may be related to early experiences in the feeding situation, especially the breastfeeding situation. In nursing at the breast the baby's nose is frequently in contact with the mother's breast, and it is quite possible that the rhinal experiences there enjoyed or unenjoyed may have something to do with these various later manipulations of the nose. Most monkeys and apes pick their noses, and often eat the debris they remove therefrom. Some small children do likewise, and even adults have been known to do so. The association of picking one's nose and eating in such cases suggests the possibility of some form of early conditioning, and that nose picking alone may be a form of self-gratification regressive to such an early period of experience. "The private life is above everything ... just sitting at home and even picking your nose, and looking at the sunset," wrote V. V. Rozanov, the Russian writer.

Allowing for the fact that most people carry bacteria of various sorts in their noses and that these are often irritating, and therefore induce a great deal of handling of the nose, such nose handling and especially nose picking can scarcely be altogether attributed to bacterial irritation. It would be a matter well worth further investigation.

As the prominent peninsula it is, the nose affords a convenient piece of the main upon which to make a landfall with one's hand, and to which one can cling stroking or otherwise manipulating it with that reassured feeling that comes from being able to establish contact, even though it be only with oneself. The nose seems to be a particularly favored part of the body, for purposes of reassurance. We often recognize this kind of manipulation as a nervous gesture in others without being conscious of it in ourselves.

Why should "making a nose at" or "thumbing one's nose at" another be regarded as gestures of disdain?

The lips are established as erogenous zones, that is, as pleasure-giving structures, long before the baby is born. Fetuses at five months and earlier have been observed in the womb sucking their thumbs. The experience at the breast or the bottle, very different as it is in each case, further reinforces the erogenicity of the lips. Sucking is the major activity of the baby during the first year of its life, and its lips, presenting the externally furled extension of mucous membrane that lines its mouth, constitute the instruments with which he makes his first most sensitive contacts, and incorporates so much that is vital to him of the external world. Lips, mouth, tongue, the sense of smell, vision, and hearing, are all intimately bound up with each other and the experience of sucking. If it is at the breast it constitutes suckling, if it is at the rubber nipple of a bottle it is sucking—two very different kinds of experiences. Research findings are sometimes contradictory concerning the advantages of breastfeeding as compared with bottle-feeding and the effects of each kind of regimen upon subsequent behavior. What is, however, quite clear is that it is not so much the type of feeding that is important for subsequent behavior as the over-all behavior of the mother during the feeding. Cold mothers who breast-feed do not do as well in influencing the later behavior of their children as warm mothers who bottle-feed. Such, for example, were the findings in a study conducted by Dr. Martin I. Heinstein on some 252 Berkeley, California children.

As we have already had occasion to see, the infant very quickly responds to the mother's behavior towards it, and what is most important to its own behavioral development is not so much the material with which it is fed as the manner in which it is fed. It is precisely this kind of experience that will be picked up by the skin and the specialized mucous membranous structure we call the lips. Whether children who have had cold mothers or inadequate nursing will seek further gratification in lip stimulation, and will exhibit more of it than those who have had warm mothers and have been adequately nursed, is a question for which I know of no research answers. The variability in this, as in other matters, is undoubtedly very high and probably quite complex. Many children do spend a great deal of time manipulating their lips with their fingers, often while making a humming sound to accompany the manually stimulated lip movements. They obviously enjoy doing this. I suggest that in thumbsucking or fingersucking it is not simply the sucking that is gratifying, but that a certain amount of satisfaction is also obtained from the stimulation of the lips. The hand of the baby often rests on its mother's breast during suckling or upon the bottle during artificial feeding; the baby's eyes follow every movement of its mother's face, and it grows accustomed, as well, to the sounds that both she and it make in the nursing situation. It is not difficult to understand how all these factors become closely integrated in a developing neuro-psychic complex. Hence, when in later life the individual becomes a victim of the smoking habit, he may, again at least in part, be conjectured to have become so addicted as a regression to the complex of similar pleasures he experienced during the earliest period of his life. The sucking, the lip stimulation, the handling of the cigarette, cigar or pipe, the pleasure of blowing and seeing the smoke, of inhaling it, of smelling and tasting it, it is all very gratifying—even though the long-term effects may be lethal.

Many writers on the subject have considered that the early experiences at the lips and mouth constitute the gateway to much of our understanding of later developments. The great American psychologist, G. Stanley Hall, believed the first center of psychic life to be the mouth and the sense of taste, accompanied by a "tactile pleasure truly aesthetic which arises from bringing smooth things to the lips and hard things to the toothless gums."

Freud makes the activity of the infant's lips at the breast a foundation stone of his theory of sexuality. He writes:

It was a child's first and most vital activity, his sucking at his mother's breast, or at substitutes for it, that must have familiarized him with this pleasure [of rhythmic sucking]. The child's lips . . . behave like an erotogenic zone, and no doubt stimulation by the warm flow of milk is the cause of the pleasurable sensation. The satisfaction of the erotogenic zone is associated, in the first instance, with the satisfaction of the need for nourishment. . . . No one who has seen a baby sinking back satiated from the breast and falling asleep with flushed cheeks and a blissful smile can escape the reflection that this picture persists as a prototype of the expression of sexual satisfaction in later life. The need for repeating the sexual satisfaction now becomes detached from the need for taking nourishment—a separation which becomes inevitable when the teeth appear and food is no longer taken by sucking. . . .

This interesting theory has received much critical attention, and some serious investigation. It is a theory which at present is in an equivocal state. There can, however, be not the least doubt of the existence of a profound relationship between oral experiences in infancy and later sexual competencies. Nor can there be any doubt of the intimate connection between the skin and all its appendages, including hair, glands, neural elements, and sexual behavior. A French wit has remarked that love is the harmony of two souls and the contact of two epidermes.* And indeed, it is in the sexual act that, next to the perinatal experience of labor, the individual experiences his most massive cutaneous stimulations, with the lips and tongue and mouth usually actively involved. Nor can there be any doubt that eating and love become closely interwoven in such a manner that in later life eating often becomes a substitute satisfaction for love, obesity frequently constituting an evidence of a failure to obtain love. The offering of food is often more than a perfunctory evidence of the tendering of love.

The psychoanalyst Sandor Rado has suggested that an important element in early sucking lies in the achievement of a pleasant feeling of satiety and a diffuse feeling of sensual pleasure in which the whole organism participates, and he describes this as an "alimentary orgasm."

That the mother experiences something akin to sexual stimulation by the baby's suckling is well known, and that

* A variation of Chamfort's "Love as it exists in society is merely the mingling of two fantasies and the contact of two skins." S. R. N. Chamfort, *Products of the Perfected Civilization* (New York: Macmillan, 1969), p. 170.

the baby experiences sensations which, endowed with meanings, later become perceptions of something resembling sexual gratification, is highly probable. We have already noted on an earlier page that inadequate mothering may seriously affect the subsequent sexual behavior of the offspring. The Harlows, to whom we owe this observation, have also shown that while rhesus monkeys raised by live mothers were more advanced in social and sexual behavior than those raised by surrogate mothers constructed of terry-cloth covered wire, the surrogate-raised infants developed perfectly normal social and sexual behavior if they were permitted each day to play in the stimulating environment of other infant monkeys. The Harlows rightly point out that the role played by infant-infant relationships as determiners of adolescent and adult adjustments should not be underestimated. It is more than possible, the Harlows suggest, that the infant-infant affectional system "is essential if the animal is to respond positively to sheer physical contact with a peer, and it is through the operation of this system, probably both in monkey and man, that sexual roles become identified and, usually, acceptable."

It is, indeed possible, as the Harlows suggest, that infant-infant contacts are necessary for the full development of social and sexual behavior, but that, in the absence of any kind of mother at all, such behavior would, even in the presence of other-infant contacts, not develop as well as in mothered infants. Certainly it is clear that, in man, good mothering without peer contacts has not in any way detrimentally affected the social and sexual development of innumerable individuals. Indeed, there exists an extensive literature showing how enormously important the mother's behavior is for her infant's subsequent social and sexual development.

We may be reasonably sure, when all the evidence is in, that however valuable the infant-infant affectional relation may prove to be, it will never equal the influence of the affectional relationship that exists between the nursing couple, always with the understanding that the mother is genuinely affectionate.

As Yarrow, in an excellent survey of the evidence, puts it, "The mother as a social stimulus provides sensory stimulations to the infant through tactile, visual, and auditory media, i.e., through handling, cuddling, talking and playing with the child, as well as by simply being visually present." Deprivation of such sensory stimulations from the mother are serious in their effects.

It was mentioned on the first page of this book that it is in the region surrounding the mouth that the human embryo first responds to tactile stimulation. It is not surprising, therefore, to find that the first communications with the outside world are established by the infant through the lips, and this very gradually. It has been shown that stimulation of the newborn in the lip region triggers the oral orientation reflex, that is, opening of the mouth and rotation of the head in the direction of the stimulus. This will occur when only one lip is stimulated. When both lips are stimulated the grasping or prehension of the stimulus will occur. This stimulus is normally the nipple and then the areola of the mother's breast. Rooting, that is, digging with the nose and mouth to find the breast, will occur thereafter whenever the baby is brought into contact with the breast or anything resembling it. These two reflex activities, oral orientation and lip grasping, are regarded as two stages in the development of rooting behavior. The integration of these two reflexes into "oral grasping" in suckling represents one of the first developmental advances made by the newborn toward grasping the world, in general as well as in particular. In other terms these two reflexes are known as the searching pattern on the one hand, and the orienting or suckling pattern on the other. The clinging behavior of the lips around the nipple and areola, and later the kneading, clinging, and resting of hands and fingers on the breast, represent, as Spitz has pointed out, the precursors and prototypes of object relations.

"To smack one's lips" represents an old expression for satisfaction. It is interesting that lip smacking should be used by mother baboons to pacify their young as well as others. "The mother," writes Irven DeVore, "makes almost no sound except that resulting from soft lip smacking as she grooms her infant. Lip smacking, initiated at birth by the mother, is one of the most frequent and important of all baboon gestures. For both sexes at all ages this gesture serves to reduce tension and promote tranquility in social interactions." Ordinarily the direct approach of an adult male is very frightening to other members of the troop; it is therefore of great interest to observe that when an adult male approaches an infant who is with its mother he will do so with vigorous lip smacking. To call the infant, who may have climbed a tree, the mother will stare intently in its direction and smack her lips loudly.

Human mothers will often make pacifying sounds to their babies in similar ways or by pursing their lips and producing a variety of sounds. Babies almost invariably respond with pleasure to such pacifying sounds. Making such sounds to babies, especially soft lip-sucking ones, constitutes one of the most effective means of inducing them to laugh through their tears, even to the point of hiccups. At six months or even earlier a baby's attention will be immediately arrested by such sounds, and in the absence of all else will have a tranquilizing effect upon him. This strongly suggests that he identifies the sounds and the lips from which they emerge with pleasurable experiences.

The mother's caressing, comforting, and bestowal of affection through kisses with the lips constitute experiences in which the infant is repeatedly conditioned.

TOUCHING AND FEELING. The baby's rooting behavior is exploratory, scanning, and has for its purpose and consummation the finding and engaging of the nipple and areola between the lips. While rooting will soon be abandoned for visual scanning, the rooting is nonetheless important in that it constitutes, among other things, a re-verification and a reaffirmation of the existence of a pleasure-giving other, pleasure-giving by virtue of nothing more than the other's existence, her tangibility. Her tangibility is the ultimate reassurance, for in the final analysis we do not believe in the reality of anything unless we can touch it; we must have *tangible* evidence. Even faith rests ultimately upon a belief in the *substance* of things to come or of past events experienced. What we perceive through the other senses as reality we actually take to be nothing more than a good hypothesis, subject to the confirmation of touch. Touch attests to "objective reality" in the sense of something outside that is not myself. As Walter Ong has written, "And yet, by the very fact that it attests the not-me more than any other sense, touch involves my own subjectivity more than any other sense. When I feel this objective something 'out there,' beyond the bounds of my body, I also at the same instant experience my own self. I feel other and self simultaneously."

"It is clear," observes Ortega y Gasset, "that the decisive form of our intercourse with things is in fact touch. And if this is so, touch and contact are necessarily the most conclusive factor in determining the structure of our world." And Ortega goes on to point out that touch differs from all the other senses in that it always involves the presence, at once and inseparably, of the body that we touch and our body with which we touch it. Unlike vision or hearing, in contact we feel things inside us, inside our bodies. In tasting and smelling the experiences are limited to the surfaces of the nasal cavity and palate. Thus, it comes about that our world is composed of presences, of things that are bodies. And this they are because they come into contact with the closest of all things to man, to the "I" that each man is, namely his body.

From the tangible evidence of the mother's body, the clinging of the lips, of hands and fingers to the breast, with the world at his fingertips in a very real sense, the infant will develop an awareness of its own and its mother's body which will constitute its first object relations. And what cannot be too often emphasized here is that, while much else is involved, it is through the primacy of the skin in its experience that the infant gropes its way to this establishment of object relations.

Around suckling, as the cutaneous or tactile composite of experiences, the earliest perceptions are organized. As Ribble has remarked, "As a result of mothering the child gradually combines and coordinates sucking, or food intake, with sense intake—looking, listening, and grasping—and thus a fairly complicated behavior complex is established." Movements of lips upon the mother's breast, the developing scanning of her face and eyes, hand and finger movements in relation to the mother's body, the feeling tone associated with these experiences, enable the infant to establish in its mind a code by means of which it can reconstitute and reduplicate all these and the associated experiences, and by making the proper signals, as figure upon the ground of the maternal body, evoke the appropriate responses. What it has learned by the exploration of the mother's body, through skin, lips, tongue, hands and eyes, the infant utilizes as a basis for further learning about its own body, exploring it mostly with his hands. Indeed, the earliest strivings toward the reintegration of self are commenced through the oral experiences at the mother's breast. In these the tongue plays a prominent role, for at this early stage the tongue is still entirely a tactile organ and is utterly devoid of the ability to taste.

What is the meaning of sticking one's tongue out at another as a gesture of defiance? Can it signify such feelings as "I don't love you," or "I don't care for you," the very opposite of the feelings enjoyed through one's tongue at one's mother's breast?

It is of interest to note that in the brain the area devoted to the lips, on the central gyrus of the cortex, is disproportionately large by comparison with that devoted to other related structures. (See Figure 1, p. 8). This is equally true of each of the four fingers and the thumb, which brings us to the consideration of the hand and fingers in the development of the sense of touch. The very phrase "the sense of touch" has come to mean, almost exclusively, feeling with the fingers or hand. Indeed, when one considers the various ways in which the word *touch* is employed in speech it becomes apparent that those various meanings are for the most part extensions of the meaning "to touch with the hand or a finger or fingers." Interestingly enough, when one consults a dictionary for the various meanings of the word one finds that the entry under "touch" is likely to represent the most extensive in the volume. It is by far the longest entry— fourteen full columns—in the magnificent *Oxford English Dictionary*. This in itself constitutes some sort of testimony to the influence which the tactile experience of hand and fingers has had upon our imagery and our speech.

Originally derived from the Old French *touche,* the word is defined by the *Oxford English Dictionary,* as "the action or an act of touching (with the hand, finger, or other part of the body); exercise of the faculty of feeling upon a material object." *Touching* is defined as "the action, or an act, of feeling something with the hand, etc." The operative word is *feeling.* Although touch is not itself an emotion, its sensory elements induce those neural, glandular, muscular, and mental changes which in combination we call an emotion. Hence touch is not experienced as a simple physical modality, as sensation, but affectively, as emotion. When we speak of being touched, especially by some act of beauty or sympathy, it is the state of being emotionally moved that we wish to describe. And when we describe someone as being "touched to the quick," it is another kind of emotion that we have in mind. The verb "to touch" comes to mean to be sensitive to human feeling. To be "touchy" means to be oversensitive. "To keep in touch" means that however far we may be removed we remain in communication. That is what language was originally designed to do, to keep man in touch with his fellow man. The experiences the infant undergoes in contact with his mother's body constitute his primary and basic means of communication, his first language, his first entering into touch with another human being, the origin of "the human touch."

Of "touch" the *Oxford English Dictionary* says that it is "the most general of the bodily senses, diffused through all parts of the skin, but (in man) specially developed in the tips of the fingers and the lips." It is through the lips that the infant grasps reality, as well as the body-building substances that it ingests. It is for a time the only means of judgment the infant has. That is why, as soon as it is able, it puts things to its lips in order to judge them, and continues to do so long after it has arrived at other means of perception and judgment. The other means of perception and judgment at which it ultimately arrives are through the tips of its fingers and the palm of its hand, a hand that has rested upon its mother's palpably and recurringly reassuring breast. At birth all the baby's other senses are so undeveloped that they convey very little information of value to it. It is the sense of touch on which it depends: lips, and generalized body contact, and then fingertips to whole hand. This development has been well described by Reva Rubin, Chairman of the Department of Obstetrical Nursing at the University of Pittsburgh. Miss Rubin found a definite progression and an orderly sequence in the nature and amount of contact a mother makes with her baby. She found that from small areas of contact the mother gradually moves to more extensive ones, at first using only her fingertips, then her hands including palms, and then much later her arms as an extension of her whole body.

The initial contacts made by the mother with her child are exploratory in nature. Fingertips are used also, but somewhat stiffly. This is not necessarily a graceless gesture. At this point, the mother will usually run one fingertip over the baby's hair, rather than her hand, to discover that his hair is silky. She will trace his profile and contours with her fingertip. If she turns his head toward food, she uses fingertips; if she has to support his head in bathing, she uses the index finger and thumb (no palm); if she has to turn him over, she seems to contact parts of him with her fingertips. She does use her arms and her hands to passively receive him, but her arms are not active participators in touch at this stage. Later, her arms will hold firmly, but just now she carries the baby as though he were a bouquet of flowers, in arms held so stiffly that she becomes fatigued.

In fingertip exploration, Miss Rubin points out, involvement is tenuous. As in courtship, in making contact one is not sure how one will be received. This is true in the courtship stage of tentative advances, before the handholding stage of reciprocal confidence and commitment has been established. In maternal touch the fingertip stage precedes that of commitment.

Commitment seems to await some personally evocative response of the infant. Sometimes it is a burp, more often it is the particular way he cuddles or, still more often, the way he expresses unbounded pleasure (three months later). This response must come from the baby, no one else, if the sense of partnership, of mutuality, in this kind of relationship is to progress. The particular sign that satisfies the mother's requirements may vary. It should also be pointed out that she is very vulnerable at this time to signs of rejection. But if the young mother has an essentially strong ego, she will search out, somewhat optimistically, positive signs of mutuality for a progressive relationship.

The next stage of maternal touch arrives gradually and is superimposed on the earlier stage. The whole hand is now used for maximal contact with the infant's body. The mother is more likely to support the infant's buttock with the palm of her hand. The hand on its back will be in full contact with it. Both hands will be relaxed and comfortable, coinciding with her feeling about her child, a message which the baby receives with the sense of security that is thus conveyed to it as its responsiveness to her firm comforting support creates a feeling it obtains through touch and the interoceptive sensations it experiences in this feedback relationship.

It is sometime between the third and fifth days that the mother will advance from fingertips to the whole cupped hand to stroke her baby's head. Her own body language progresses gradually from bathing its anogenital region at fingertip distance, that is, from the exploratory information-seeking phase to that of a more intimate involvement in the use of her whole hand.

Recalling here our discussion of cutaneous stimulation in mammals in the perinatal period as contributing to the improved maternal abilities of nonhuman mammals (p. 24), Miss Rubin's remarks, following, are of the greatest interest.

Mothers who have had a very recent experience of appropriate and meaningful bodily touch from a ministering person, as during labor, delivery, or the postpartum period, use their own hands more effectively. This is true of both . . . firsttime mothers and . . . mothers who have had more than one child. Conversely, if the mother's most recent experiences of contact in relation to her own body have been of a remote and impersonal nature, she seems to stay longer at this stage in her own activities with the baby.

These are most important observations, which should lead us to consider seriously whether it would not be a good idea to institute the practice of regular body caressing by the husband of his wife during pregnancy, labor, and after the birth of the baby. On purely theoretical grounds this would appear to be advisable. We have in addition the experimental evidence and the backing of such observations as Miss Rubin's to suggest not only that such stimulation should be given by the husband to his wife, but that this might become standard obstetrical practice.

Klaus and his co-workers studied maternal behavior in twelve normal mothers at the first postnatal contact with their normal full-term undressed infants one half to thirteen and a half hours after delivery, and in nine other mothers during their first three tactile contacts with their premature infants. An orderly progression was observed in the mothers of full-term infants. They commenced with fingertip touching of the infants' extremities and proceeded in four to eight minutes to massaging, and encompassing palm contact on the trunk. The rapid progression from fingertip to palm encompassing contact within a period of ten minutes does not quite agree with Rubin's observation to the effect that palm and close contact develop only after several days. In the first three minutes fingertip contact was 52 percent, with 28 percent palm contact. In the last three minutes of observation fingertip contact decreased to 26 percent and palm contact increased to 62 percent. An intense interest in eye-to-eye contact was observed at first contact.

The mothers of normal infants permitted to touch them in the first three to five days of life followed a similar sequence, but at a much slower rate.

The observations of Rubin, Klaus, and others suggest that there exists a species-specific behavior in human mothers at first contact with their infants. "Because this period of life appears so critical," write Klaus et al., "modern social and hospital practices which now separate the mother from her sick or premature infant for prolonged periods require a very thorough re-evaluation."

Indeed, there is good evidence that premature babies do much better when their mothers are allowed to handle them, after proper instruction in handwashing, masking, and gowning. Barnett and his co-workers at the Stanford University School of Medicine encouraged forty-one mothers to handle their premature infants at any time of the day or night, with considerable benefit to everyone involved: infants, mothers, nurses and doctors. There was no increase in the much feared infections and no complications of any sort. Similar observations have been made by other observers. In commenting upon these findings, an editorial in the *British Medical Journal* (6 June 1970) makes the following sage observations:

It may well be that the immediate postpartum period is the most important time for the initial contact between mother and child, as it is in animals. Many (but certainly not all) mothers feel the urge to have skin contact with the baby immediately he has been born; they think that it is important that they should be fully conscious, and not under an anaesthetic at the time of delivery; and they want to put the baby to the breast immediately.

No one has proved that it is desirable for the mother or the premature baby that this close contact should be established immediately after birth or later during the period in hospital or that absence of contact does any harm. One cannot prove everything, and not everything is worth trying to prove. Great expenditure of time and effort may go into trying to prove something for the sake of proving it: something which, though important in itself, is not worth trying to prove, perhaps because the answer seems obvious. There are occasions when one has to make medical decisions on the basis of common sense and on what seems natural and normal.

We need to understand more fully than we have yet done that the baby takes its cues from the mother's behavior towards it. Bateson and Mead, writing of Bali, state:

The Balinese child is carried either loosely on the hip, as in most of the plains villages, or in a sling, as in Bajoeng Gede, but even where the hand of the mother is substituted for the sling, the child's adaptation is the same, passive, adjusting itself by complete limpness to the movements of the mother's body. It may even sleep with head wobbling to the timing of the mother's rice pestle. The baby receives its cues as to whether the outside world is to be trusted or feared directly from contact with the mother's body, and though the mother may have schooled herself to smile and utter courtesy phrases to the stranger and the high-caste, and may display no timorousness in her artificially grimacing face, the screaming baby in her arms betrays the inward panic.

The kinesic means which enable the child to respond to its mother's inward states, no matter what her outward ones may appear to be, have already been discussed. The observation is universally confirmed that the child is able to do so in response to the messages he receives from his mother's muscle-joint behavior.

GRASPING AND LEARNING. It is evident from the child's exploratory movements with its hands that they play an important role in discovering the lineaments and boundaries of the world in which it lives. Also fascinating to observe is the way young infants will clap the palms of their hands together, at first very much as a reflex, later in obvious enjoyment. It is possible that this constitutes the origin of later clapping in pleasure or approval? *

During the first two or three months the infant's grasping is largely reflex. It is not until about twenty weeks of age that it is voluntarily able to grasp an object, and even that

* For a discussion of the problem thus raised see M. Mead and F. C. Macgregor, *Growth and Culture* (New York: G. P. Putnam's Sons, 1951), pp. 24–25.

grasping has to develop through several stages, from the ulnar grasp (on the little-finger side) in the early months to the radial grasp (on the thumb side), and then to the finger-thumb grasp at about nine months of age. At six months the infant transfers objects from hand to hand. It plays with its toes and, as it were by way of validation, everything goes to its mouth, an activity which it abandons at about the end of its first year. After that the child's progress is one of increase in manipulatory precision so that by the time it is three years old it can fully dress and undress itself.

These are skills achieved principally by means of the learning that has gone on through the skin and joint-muscle senses in the feedback interaction between mother and child and the associated experiences she provides. Learning is defined as the increase in the strength of any act through repetition, the child being constantly reinforced by the pleasurable rewards it receives in relation to its mother; the greater the satisfaction, the greater the strengthening of the bond between the stimulus and the response. The opposite is also true, namely, the greater the discomfort the greater the weakening of the bond.*

The manner of learning through these senses is illuminatingly described by Margaret Mead in her account of the Balinese child. In Bali the child spends most of its first two years first within the arms and then on the hip of another human being who is lightly conscious of its presence. The baby is carried very loosely wrapped in a cloth that is sometimes laid over its face when it is carried indoors, and sus-

* E. L. Thorndike, *Animal Intelligence* (New York: Macmillan, 1911), p. 244. For an account of learning theory see A. Montagu, *The Direction of Human Development* (Revised edition, New York: Hawthorn Books, 1970), pp. 317–45.

pended in a sling around the shoulder of mother or father or of a young adolescent. Sleeping and waking occur without the baby moving out of the arms of its mother. At about two months of age, still in the sling, the infant is set astride the hip, now securely fastened to the carrier's body. The mother feels free to pound her rice without further attention to the infant, and the latter learns to adjust to her every movement. If it falls asleep it may be laid down on a bed-platform inside the house, but when it awakens it is immediately picked up. Practically the only occasion when a child under five or six months is out of someone's arms is when it is bathed. Since the child is almost invariably carried on the left hip its right arm is pinioned under the carrier's arm or extended around the carrier's back, so that when it reaches out with the left hand for something offered it, the carrier pulls the left hand back—for it is forbidden to receive things in the left hand—and pulls the right hand out. In this manner the child's reaching behavior occurs in a supervised, culturally patterned situation. In the course of its first year the child is carried by all sorts of people, male and female, young and old, skilled and unskilled. The child enjoys a rather varied experience of the human world, of different skin surfaces, different odors, different tempos, different ways of being held, and a correspondingly narrow experience of objects. The only objects that it habitually touches are its own ornaments: a beaded necklace with a little silver box attached, on which it teethes, and its own silver bracelets and anklets.

"So the child learns life within human arms. It learns to eat, with the exception of the experience of being fed in its bath, to laugh, to play, to listen, to watch, to dance, to feel frightened or relaxed, in human arms." The child urinates in the arms of its carrier, and feels the urination disregarded.

It defecates, and feels the low concern with which a dog is called to tidy up the scene, the baby, the sling, and the body of the carrier. The child is relaxed and the carrier habitually inattentive. Since the infant spends many hours on the mother's hip while she is pounding rice, it is of great interest to learn that Colin McPhee, the leading authority on Balinese music, found that the basic tempo of Balinese music is the same as the tempo of the women's rice pounding. Ethnomusicologists do not appear to have concerned themselves with the possible relation between childhood experiences and the character of a particular culture's music. But clearly this would appear to be a promising field of inquiry.

The early conditioning the Balinese child receives in relation to its mother's body is apparently connected with the ease with which older children fall asleep leaning against other people. Some people fall asleep while standing in the midst of a tightly packed audience at a theatrical performance, relaxed and slightly swaying. The expected environment for sleep is the close proximity of other bodies. During ceremonies of various sorts people may be crowded together in a space no larger than a double bed, sitting, sleeping, dozing.

Clothing for the child means something that binds the child and its mother together. This is quite different from the meaning clothing has in the Western world, where it is used to separate child and mother. In Bali the mother's shawl serves as a sling, a wrapper for the infant, a diaper, and a pillow folded under its head. When it is frightened the mother draws the cloth over the child's face; she may also do this when it sleeps. The child is attached to its carrier by a cloth that is neither distinctively its own nor the carrier's, and since children are neither dressed nor undressed at routine times each day, neither clothes nor sleeping habits differentiate night from day for the Balinese. They develop no internalized time pattern, waking and sleeping at any hour, as impulse or interest dictates.

During infancy the child is fed in the bath, and mother and father often splash and manipulate the genitals of the male baby; thus the bath becomes a situation of heightened bodily pleasure. It is, however, a mixed kind of pleasure during which the child is manipulated as if it were a puppet capable of obstructive but not of human movement, an attitude which contrasts strongly with the closer contactual relationship with the carrier in suckling and eating snacks in the arms. When, significantly enough, the child is old enough to walk to the spring, it bathes itself, and bathing becomes from then on a solitary pleasure, performed in company but in a withdrawn manner.

In this account of the early cutaneous experiences of the Balinese child we may see, as it were in high relief, the effects of certain kinds of experiences, for which the skin represents a most important sensory receptor, upon the later behavior of the individual, even to the act of sleeping in bodily contact with another. In this connection the question may here be raised whether the increasing modern practice of husband and wife occupying separate beds may not be related to the decreasing tactile relationships between the modern mother and her child.

Separating mother and baby, dressing the baby in clothes, and similar dissociative practices certainly serve to reduce the amount of intercutaneous contact and communication between mother and infant. Instead of sleeping in another human being's arms, as the Balinese infant does, the infant of the Western world spends the greater part of its waking hours and all of its sleeping hours alone and apart from others. One will spend the whole of one's sleeping life before marriage in a bed by oneself, and when married may find it impossible to adjust to sleeping in the same bed with another, except for the purposes of making love. Hence, the popularity of twin beds may be positively correlated with child-rearing habits in which from an early age the child is conditioned to "go" to sleep alone. It "goes" to sleep. Its separation contributes to his later feeling of separateness, and to the separateness of each of the members of the family.*

To be tender, loving, and caring, human beings must be tenderly loved and cared for in their earliest years, from the moment they are born. Held in the arms of their mothers, caressed, cuddled, and comforted, the familiar human environment, to which Balinese children can always return, is found in "the known arms of parents and siblings, where fright and comfort, interest and sleep, have already been experienced. Bodies are always there, other people's bodies to lean against, to huddle together with, to sleep beside."

The close contacts and the rhythmic tactual stimulation accompanying the carrier's bodily movements, the patting, stroking, and caressing the child receives in this way or from the hands or other parts of the body of the carrier, are soothing, assuring, and comforting. The rhythm of this kind of tactual stimulation that the mother conveys to the child in her arms is almost universally reproduced in the lullabies sung or hummed to lull children to sleep. Children who are unhappy, frightened, or otherwise disturbed may usually be soothed and restored to a sense of security when taken up in the arms of a comforter. To put one's arms around another

* For an early discussion of this subject see A. Montagu, "Some Factors in Family Cohesion." *Psychiatry,* vol. 7 (1944), pp. 349–52.

is to communicate love to the other, for which another word is security. To rhythmically rock the body when emotionally disturbed is comforting.

The cradle was an admirable invention, many thousands of years old, which sophisticated societies have discarded. Why? The answer to this question constitutes a case history in itself. It serves to illustrate how our ignorance of the most elementary facts concerning the needs of infants permits us, in the name of progress, to abandon the most valuable of practices and substitute the worst for them. The answer will also serve to shed some additional light on the functional activities of the skin in maintaining physical and mental health.

THE NATURAL HISTORY OF THE CRADLE AND THE SKIN. The story of the decline and fall of the cradle is a typical one of fads, fashions, fallacies, and of ill-informed and misguided authoritarianism. During the 1880's the view developed among physicians and nurses that there was danger in over-indulging the child. It was thought that many of the complaints from which babies suffered were due to the well-meant interference of fond parents. It soon came to be "authoritatively" held that the clearest and first evidence of this spoiling of the baby was the cradle. Hence the cradle had to go. Dr. John Zahovsky of St. Louis, recalling this period, writes, "I had the opportunity to follow this attack on the cradle during my early professional career. It seemed to me then that the greatest influence emanated from the babies' hospitals in New York, Philadelphia, and Chicago, since many of the writers in the prominent women's magazines had received their training there. In the nineties all these magazines published numerous articles on the care of

the baby. Many of these contained vicious attacks on the use
of the cradle."

The well-known educator of nurses, Lisbeth D. Price, in
her textbook on nursing published in 1892, emphasized (in
italics) that the baby *"should never be rocked nor hushed on
the nurse's neck."* And this, of course, meant that mothers
should desist from such practices also.

In America during the 1890's the attack on the cradle was
widely extended through articles on child care, for the most
part published in the leading women's magazines of the day.
The greatest influence in the campaign against the cradle
was exercised by the pediatrician to whom reference has already been made in a similar connection, namely Dr. Luther
Emmett Holt (pp. 83–84). For more than a generation Dr.
Holt kept up his attack on the cradle. In the first edition of
his widely used textbook on pediatrics (1897), Holt wrote,
"To induce sleep, rocking and all other habits of this sort
are useless and may be harmful. I have known of an instance
where the habit of rocking during sleep was continued until
the child was two years old; the moment the rocking stopped
the infant would awake."

It was Holt who was responsible for writing what became
the most popular guide to the rearing of children for almost
fifty years. This was entitled *The Care and Feeding of Children: A Catechism for the Use of Mothers and Children's
Nurses* and was first issued in 1894. This booklet was read
by millions of mothers and mothers-to-be. In it, replying to
the question, "Is rocking necessary?", Holt wrote, "By no
means. It is a habit easily acquired, but hard to break and a
very useless and sometimes injurious one." Again, writing in
1916, Holt advised that the crib should be one that does not
rock in order that "the unnecessary and vicious practice may

not be carried on." One does not have to imagine the effect
that that word "vicious" had upon so many mothers.*

This sustained attack on the cradle, led by one of the most
influential pediatricians of his day, eventually succeeded in
rendering the cradle obsolete, and the outmoded model was
turned in for the new one: the stationary prison-like crib.
The very fact that, from the earliest days of human history,
mothers had rocked their babies to sleep in their arms was
taken to mean that the practice was archaic, and that rocking
babies in cradles was equally antiquated, certainly not "modern." Alas, in the headlong rush to be "modern" worthwhile
institutions and ancient virtues may be abandoned and lost.
With so many authoritative voices raised against the cradle
as "habit-forming," "unnecessary and vicious," "spoiling,"
and even ruinous of the child's health, no mother who genuinely loved her child could conscientiously disregard the in-
junction to discontinue so "detrimental" a practice.

All this was made easier for the mother to accomplish because it was at this very period (circa 1916) that the newest

* The reader who may wish to know what manner of man could have
entertained such ideas may be referred to a profile written by one of
his last assistants together with another pediatrician: Edwards A. Park,
and Howard H. Mason, "Luther Emmett Holt (1855–1924)," in B. S.
Veeder, ed., *Pediatric Profiles* (St. Louis: C. V. Mosby Co., 1957). A few
excerpts may be quoted. "His manner was more than serious, it was
earnest. There was nothing about him which could be called impressive, due perhaps to the absence of any outstanding feature; rather he
appeared a highly efficient, perfectly coordinated human machine. He
seemed to us austere and unapproachable." He is not known to have
said "good morning" to his secretary in the many years she worked for
him, nor is he known ever to have praised anyone or anything (p. 58).
Finally, of his book *The Care and Feeding of the Child,* the writers remark, "It is only fair to point out that in recent years some pediatricians have felt that through its rigid philosophy of upbringing the
booklet had had a harmful influence." (p. 53)

and most influential psychology of the day was beginning to make itself felt. This was the "Behaviorism" of Professor John Broadus Watson of Johns Hopkins University. "Behaviorism" held that the only sound approach to the study of the child was through its behavior. The basic contention was that only the objectively observable can constitute the data of science. What could not be observed—the child's wishes, needs, and feelings—were excluded from the behaviorist's interest and were therefore treated as if they did not exist. The behaviorists insisted on treating children as if they were mechanical objects that could be wound up any which way one pleased; children were at the mercy of their environment, and parents could by their own behavior make them into anything they wished. Sentimentality was to be avoided, because any show of love or close physical contact made the child too dependent upon its parents. What one should aim for, urged the behaviorists, is the encouragement of independence, self-reliance, and the avoidance of any dependence upon the affections of others. One must not spoil children with affection.

This unsentimental, mechanistic approach to child rearing greatly influenced psychology for a time and exercised a profound effect upon pediatric thinking and practice. Pediatricians advised parents to maintain a sophisticated aloofness from their children, keeping them at arm's length, and managing them on a schedule characterized by both objectivity and regularity. They were to be fed by the clock, *not* on demand, and only at definite and regular times. If they cried during the intervals of three or four hours between feedings, they were to be allowed to do so until the clock announced the next feeding time. During such intervals of crying they were not to be picked up, since if one yielded to such weak impulses the child would be spoiled, and thereafter every time he desired something he would cry. And so millions of mothers sat and cried along with their babies, but, as genuinely loving mothers obedient to the best thinking on the subject, bravely resisted the "animal impulse" to pick them up and comfort them in their arms. Most mothers felt that this could not be right, but who were they to argue with the authorities? No one ever told them that an "authority" is one who *should* know.

Giving the child too much attention, it was repeatedly emphasized, was calculated to spoil it, while the practice of rocking the baby to sleep, either in a cradle or in one's arms, was considered to belong to the Dark Ages of child rearing. And so the cradle was finally banished to the attic or lumber room and the baby consigned to a crib. Thus, it was felt, at one stroke was eliminated an old-fashioned way of caring for babies and an unnecessary piece of furniture. Mothers were resolved to be modern and unsentimental. It is sad to have to record that wherever other nations have "gone modern" they, too, have discarded the cradle.

In India and in Pakistan, for example, where the most "enlightened" people have begun to introduce Western ways, the cradle is also beginning to be considered "old-fashioned," and is being threatened with a fate similar to that which it suffered in the Western world. Dr. Brock Chisholm, the distinguished psychiatrist and former director of the World Health Organization, tells of an occasion when he was being shown over a large general hospital in Pakistan. He writes:

As we were going along a corridor which was a sort of balcony on the side of the building, we passed the screened door of a ward. Suddenly someone pointed out to me, with great enthusiasm, something away off on the horizon in the opposite direction. Now, to any old Army inspecting officer, the situation was perfectly clear; there was something nearby they didn't want me to see. Therefore I was quite sure that whatever was hidden behind this screened door I should see. If you see only what people want you to see you will never find out anything.

So I insisted, at some risk of offense, on seeing this ward, and when I insisted, my guides began apologizing, saying that I really wouldn't like to see it at all. It was of a very old pattern; they were ashamed of it; they hoped to get it changed; they hoped that the World Health Organization might help them get the money to adopt modern and new patterns for this particular ward, because it was very bad indeed. It was a pattern hundreds of years old.

However, I still insisted that even as an antiquity I would like to see it. I went in to see this ward, with the reluctant accompaniment of the train of people with me, and I saw the best maternity ward I have ever seen in any country, far better than I have ever seen in North America. Here was a big maternity ward with beds down both sides. The foot posts of each bed were extended up about three feet or so, and slung between the foot posts was a cradle. The baby was in the cradle, and I noticed as I looked down the ward that one squeak out of the baby and up would come the mother's foot, and with her toe she would rock the cradle. On the second squeak, which showed that the baby was really awake, she would reach into the cradle and take the baby into her arms, where a baby is supposed to be most of the time.

Dr. Chisholm adds:

They wanted to get rid of that perfectly beautiful arrangement, to put their babies under glass the way we do, and to keep them in inspection wards where they can be seen at a distance by their loving fathers whenever they visit, and taken to their mother if she is good and does as the nurse tells her! They wanted to do all that because we Westerners had given them the impression that all our methods are superior to theirs.

This is a sad story, for in the drive towards the admiring imitation of Western "progress" and "advancement" the peoples of the East and other technologically undeveloped countries, who have preserved so many of the ancient virtues, are slavishly bent on catching up with us, even to the extent of imitating our worst errors.

Among ourselves the cradle went out of existence when the notion became fashionable that to fondle a child, to caress or to rock it was to endanger its development as an unspoiled independent person. To rock it in a cradle came to be regarded as especially backward and reprehensible.

Unsound as this kind of thinking is, and damaging as it has been to millions of children, many of whom later grew up into disturbed persons, the behavioristic, mechanistic approach to child rearing is still largely with us. Hospital deliveries, the mechanization of obstetrics, the removal of babies from their mothers at birth, the failure to feed them soon after they are born, the elimination of breastfeeding and the substitution and encouragement of bottle-feeding, the demotion of the pacifier, and so on, constitute some of the melancholy evidences of the dehumanizing approach to the making of people, as opposed to human beings.

Having spent the whole of its preceding life snugly ensconced in its mother's womb, the baby would certainly feel more comfortable cosily tucked into a cradle than abandoned to a large crib in which it lies, either on its front or on its back, exposed to the dull and uninteresting flat white surface of either the sheet or the ceiling, with only the prison bars at the side of its crib to break the monotony of this bleak, one-dimensional landscape. As Sylvester has said, "Small infants raised in oversized cribs are frequently very frightened infants because they are too far removed from sheltering surfaces. They often appear inhibited in their courage to experiment and explore. Infants disturbed by new situations or by the prodrome [a premonitory symptom] of physical illness often draw closer to protective shelter (the mother's arms, the sides of the crib), giving spatial expression to their need to constrict the boundaries of their pre-ego protectively."

One cannot help wondering whether the unexplained occurrence of "crib death," or "the sudden infant death syndrome," that is, the finding dead in its cot of a baby who has been perfectly healthy and for whose death no cause can be found, may not, at least in part, be due to inadequate sensory stimulation, particularly tactile stimulation. Inadequate sensory stimulation may not be the only factor involved in crib deaths, but it may well be a predisposing factor. It is rare for a child over one year to be found dead unexpectedly. Most crib deaths occur in infants between one and six months. It would be interesting to know what the incidence of sudden infant death would be in cradle-raised as compared with cot-raised babies.

In a crib the baby is weighed down by a set of coverings tucked in at the sides and foot of the crib, and thus left partially surrounded by air; this is not quite what it wants or needs. What it does want and need is the supporting contact of a snugly comforting environment, as reassurance and security that it is still in contact with the world and not airily suspended in it. The baby assures itself that all is well largely through the messages it receives from the skin. The supports it receives in the enveloping environment of the cradle are very reassuring to it, for the cradle affords it something of a replication, a continuation, of the life it led so long in the womb, and this is good and comforting. When the baby feels uncomfortable or insecure it may whimper, and if its mother or anyone else rocks the cradle this will have a soothing effect. Rocking reassures the baby, for in its mother's womb it was naturally rocked by the normal motions of her body. To be comfortable means to be comforted, and for the infant this comfort is largely derived from the signals it receives from its skin. The greatest of all comforts is to be cradled in the mother's arms or lap or supported on her back. There is, as Peiper has remarked, "no better sedative." As he says, "It is necessary to rock a healthy young infant in his cradle or in the arms or baby carriage only once when he is on the verge of crying: He immediately quiets down and starts to cry again as soon as the movement stops momentarily. He will surely not cry if it is done right."

It is absurd to suggest that the cradle is harmful because the infant will develop the habit of having to be rocked before it will be able to fall asleep. If cradle rocking is habit-forming, so is breastfeeding or bottle-feeding. Yet children are weaned from breast or bottle, unless it is done too suddenly, without any serious difficulty or aftereffects. Millions of babies who had been rocked to sleep in cradles grew up to be adults who were able to fall asleep without needing to be rocked. Children outgrow the cradle as well as they do their baby clothes.

Rocking chairs are still popular among older folks, especially in unsophisticated rural areas, where "modernity" has not made such complete inroads as it has in the more worldly-wise urban areas. It is strange that no one has ever suggested that the rocking chair is "unnecessary and vicious" in adults, or that adults will be unable to relax unless they can do so with the assistance of a rocking chair. Rocking chairs, in fact, for adults, and especially the aging, are to be highly recommended for reasons similar to those which make the cradle so highly recommendable for babies. Rocking, in both babies and adults, increases cardiac output and is helpful to the circulation; it promotes respiration and discourages lung congestion; it stimulates muscle tone; and not least important, it maintains the feeling of relatedness. A baby, especially, that is rocked, knows that it is not alone. A general cellular and visceral stimulation results from the rocking. Again, especially in babies, the rocking motion helps to develop the efficient functioning of the baby's gastrointestinal tract. The intestine is loosely attached by folds of peritoneum to the back wall of the abdominal cavity. The rocking assists the movements of the intestine like a pendulum and thus serves to improve its tone. The intestine always contains liquid chyle and gas. The rocking movement causes the chyle to move backward and forward over the intestinal mucosa. The general distribution of chyle over the whole of the intestine undoubtedly aids digestion and probably absorption. Writing in 1934, Zahovsky stated that "young infants who are rocked after nursing as a rule have less colic, less enterospasm [intestinal spasm] and become happier babies than those who are laid in the crib without rocking. In fact, I have several times availed myself of this physical therapy even in recent years to relieve the dyspeptic young baby. . . . I firmly believe that the cradle assists maternal nursing." Dr. Zahovsky concludes with the words, "Someday, I believe, it will be no disgrace to rear the young baby in a cradle and even sing him to sleep by a lullaby."

More than a generation has had to elapse before anyone could be found to echo Dr. Zahovsky's words. The cradle should be restored to the infant. It should never have been discarded in the first place. The reasons that were given for

its banishment were completely unsound and wholly unjusti-
fied, based as they were on misconceptions concerning the
nature and needs of the child and the ludicrous notion that
cradle rocking is irreversibly habit-forming.

The benefits of rocking are considerable. When the infant
is too warm the rocking has a cooling effect, hastening evap-
oration from the skin. When the infant is too cold the rocking helps to warm him. The warming has a hypnotic effect
on the infant, and it is soothing to his nervous system.
Above all, the rocking motion produces a gentle stimulation
of almost every area of his skin, with consequential beneficial physiological effects of every kind.

As a first step in the ultimately possible, and much to be
desired restoration of the cradle to its rightful place, rocking
chairs have been introduced into some hospitals. For example, at Riverside Hospital, Toledo, Ohio, rocking chairs
have been in use as a regular part of the infant-care program.
In 1957 a mahogany rocking-chair was introduced as a
Christmas gift from Riverside nurse aides, who pooled
money to buy what they voted as "most needed new equipment" at the hospital. In each of the three nurseries a rocking chair is available, including one for premature infants.
Mrs. Herbert Mercurio, obstetrical supervisor, states that the
old rocking-chairs are always used by nurses and aides at infant feeding time. "It's the best way to feed a baby and put
him to sleep at the same time. It's relaxing for the nurse,
too." The rocking chairs are used to pacify crying babies.
Mrs. Mercurio feels strongly that rocking chairs are useful
and practical and encourages their use at home. "A rocking
chair," she remarked, "won't spoil a child. This is something
they enjoy, but outgrow rapidly."

Quite possibly the rocking chair used in this manner has

some advantages over the cradle. I think both might well become standard equipment in the home with a small infant —in this manner at once satisfying the need for rocking of both infant and adult.*

A fascinating account of the serendipitous discovery of the benefits of rocking for seriously disturbed mental patients is reported by Dr. Joseph C. Solomon. Dr. Solomon observed that patients taken from their rooms in hospital for transfer to another town by train, though they had earlier needed to be restrained in straitjackets and muffs, became very quiet and calm as soon as the train was in motion. Solomon reasoned that, since in the womb the child is subjected to considerable passive motion, part of the human contact these patients may have missed as children was the active rocking in the mother's arms which would, among other things, stimulate the vestibular apparatus. Purposive active motions, Solomon suggests, develop with facility and pleasure when the passive motion imparted by the mother has been satisfactorily internalized as an integrated inner function. "Conversely, when there is little chance for the internalization of the passive movements derived from the mother, the active rocking becomes a habitual device for self-containment. It is a method of defending the formative ego against the feeling of being abandoned. This follows the principle of Newton's Second Law. If you actively push against something, it is as though something is pushing against you. In this way the infant accomplishes the goal of not feeling completely alone. It

* On the advantages of the rocking chair see R. C. Swan, "The Therapeutic Value of the Rocking Chair," *The Lancet,* vol. 2 (1960), p. 1441; J. Yahuda, "The Rocking Chair." *The Lancet,* vol. 1 (1961), p. 109. For an amusing account of a club devoted to the cultivation of the rocking chair see T. E. Saxe, Jr., *Sittn' Starin' 'n' Rockin'* (New York: Hawthorn Books, 1969).

is as though somebody is always there. As such it is another self-containment device similar to thumbsucking, the security-blanket, nail-biting, or masturbation."

Dr. William Greene Jr. in the course of studying a group of patients suffering diseases of the lymphatic and blood vessels found that a large proportion of them had developed their illness following a loss, usually of the mother or mother substitute. The association of vascular ills with the loss of maternal support suggested to Dr. Greene that the fetus, far from being a passive recipient of nourishment, was really a working member of a going partnership. Within the uterus, Greene suggests, the fetus may feel and respond to "vibrations, pressures and sounds provided by the mother's vascular pulses, and emanating chiefly from the aorta, and perhaps other abdominal blood vessels." The growing fetus, stimulated by the mother's internal functions, may be aware of the presence or absence of these, their constancy and change. Intrauterine activity, for the fetus, may constitute the "outside environment," just as, somewhat later, the functioning of its own digestive system will constitute, for the newborn, its outside environment. Within the womb the fetus may perceive the mother's internal functions as a kind of outside object, and become aware of itself as a being separate from such stimuli. Dr. Greene suggests that the infant, separated from the mother at birth, is "exposed to new stimuli . . . different, less persistent, exotic, and, most important, relatively random." The change, however, need not be total. The rocking and patting a mother gives her newborn may provide it with "a kind of object perception which bridges birth and . . . is the model for all those perceptions to come later." Rocking "tends towards synchrony with the mother's and/or baby's respiratory rate," while patting "approximates the mother's and/or baby's cardiac rate." The mother, in other words, who rocks and pats her baby may in some measure recreate the stimuli of her breathing and pulse rhythms, rhythms that were significant to it before birth, and thus give the baby the reassurance of a familiar environment that it so much needs.

In this connection, the findings on premature babies, that is, on babies of low birth weight, are extremely interesting. For example, Freedman, Boverman, and Freedman in a study of five co-twin control cases found that the rocked twin, after an upward weight trend was established some seven to ten days after birth, gained weight at a greater rate per day than the unrocked control twin in every instance, although the advantage of the rocked group was only a temporary one. The experimental twin was rocked for thirty minutes twice daily.

A variety of deficits are likely to be exhibited by many prematurely born infants in later life. However, one factor that has received insufficient attention in previous research is the possibility that sensory deprivation may contribute to such impairments. The possible adverse effects of life in the controlled, monotonous environment of an isolette where the premature infant remains, receiving minimal emotional and tactile stimulation for several weeks, have been the subject of a pilot study by Sokoloff, Yaffe, Weintraub, and Blase. These investigators studied four boys and one girl of low birth weight and compared them with a similar group. The experimental group were stroked five minutes every hour of the day for ten days, while the control group were provided with routine nursery care. The handled infants were found to be more active, regained their initial birth weight faster, appeared to cry less, and after seven to eight

months were found to be more active and healthier as measured by growth and motor development. Though the sample is very small these findings agree with those of Hasselmeyer, who found that premature infants who received
increased sensory, tactile, and kinesthetic stimulation were
significantly more quiescent, especially before feedings, than
unstimulated controls.

The self-rocking commonly seen among patients in mental
hospitals has often been remarked, and is frequently observed as an act of self-comfort in grief among individuals
who do not otherwise rock. Among many Semitic-language-
speaking peoples, including orthodox Jews, body-rocking
often accompanies prayer, grief, and study. It is quite clearly
a comforting form of behavior.

The behavior and motivations of all mammalian infants
are directed towards maintaining contact with the mother.
Contact seeking is the foundation upon which all subsequent behavior develops. When such contact seeking is frustrated the infant resorts to such behaviors as self-clasping, fingersucking, rocking, or swaying. These behaviors constitute
a regression to the passive movement-stimulation experienced in the womb, the swaying, rocking motions, and the
sucking of fingers with forearms pressed against the body.
Self-rocking and similar repetitive activities represent substitutes for passive movement-stimulation, just as self-clasping
and fingersucking substitute self-stimulation for social stimulation. Dr. William A. Mason and his colleague Dr. Gershon
Berkson of the Delta Regional Primate Research Center of
Tulane University, New Orleans, tested the presumed relationship between self-rocking and the quality of maternal
stimulation. They compared two groups of rhesus monkeys,
both separated from their mothers at birth. One group was

reared with a cloth-covered social substitute that moved freely about the cage on an irregular schedule; the other group was reared with a device identical to the moving dummy, except that it was stationary. The three monkeys reared with stationary dummies all developed stereotyped rocking as a persistent pattern, whereas those reared with the moving robots showed no evidence of such behavior.

Thus it would seem probable that self-rocking represents a form of substitute satisfaction of the need for passive movement-stimulation which would normally be obtained from a mother to whom one could cling or who carried one in contact with her body.

Solomon's view that the rocking motion stimulates the vestibular apparatus is undoubtedly sound, but misses the point that, in rocking, the skin itself undergoes a complex series of motions, not to mention the motions of proprioceptors and interoceptors, and the motions of internal organs. All of this is eroticising. Rocking or swaying represents a kind of self-caressing, a self-comforting, and as such it is often observed in grief and mourning. It is significant that the region of America in which the rocking chair remains most popular should be New England—the land of the cod and the cold fish.

ROCKING, MUSIC, AND THE DANCE

But O' for the touch of a vanish'd hand
And the sound of a voice that is still!

Was Tennyson, when he wrote those poignant words, unconsciously or consciously recalling his early experiences of his mother? It has been said that music utters the things that cannot be spoken. In much music there is a very pervasive tactile quality. Wagner's *Liebestod* is said to represent a musical version of coitus leading to orgasm and postcoital subsidence. Debussy's *L'Après-Midi d'un Faune* conveys the most tactile of sexual nuances. In the "rock" music of our day, so aptly named, for the first time in the history of the dance in the Western world the participating couples no longer touch each other at any time but remain separated throughout the dance, dancing most of the time to deafeningly loud music of which the lyrics, usually addressed to one's parents, or generally to the older generation, only too often say, "You do not understand," "Where were you when I needed you?" or words to that effect.

Lawrence K. Frank, in a brilliant paper on tactile communication, writes, "The potency of music, with its rhythmical patterning and varying intensities of sounds, depends in large measure upon the provision of an auditory surrogate for the primary tactile experiences in which . . . rhythmic patting, is peculiarly effective in soothing the baby."

Can it be that dances like the Twist and later ones of the same rock variety, together with rock music, represent, at least in part, reactions to a lack of early tactile stimulation, to a deprivation suffered in the antiseptic, dehumanized environments created by obstetricians and hospitals? Where but in such a setting should we enact this most important of all dramatic events: the birth and welcoming of a new member into "the bosom of the family"?

The most involved and the larger part of the constituency of the rock groups are adolescents. This is not surprising. For it is they who remain closest to the conditions they are protesting through their music, their dances, and their other forms of expression. Under the circumstances it is highly desirable that the young should protest in these ways against the conditions they find so intolerable. But unfortunately the young are not always clear as to the nature of all the things that need to be changed. This would be too much to expect. However, in the areas in which they are most perceptive, child rearing, education and human relations, they often see far beyond their elders. *Love* is a word which has come to be meaningful to them, to mean a great deal more than it does to most adults, and if they will demonstratively act it out, they may yet succeed in remaking the world.

The tactual sensitivity with which the baby is born has already undergone much preparatory development in the womb. We know that the fetus is capable of responding both to pressure and to sound, and that the beating of its own heart at about 140 beats per minute and the beating of its mother's heart, with a frequency of 70, provides it with something of a syncopated world of sound. Given the knowledge that the baby is laved by the amniotic fluid to the symphonic beat of two hearts, it is not surprising to learn that the soothing effect of rhythmical sounds has been connected, in the hypotheses of some researchers, with the feeling of well-being assumed to exist *in utero* in relation to the mother's heartbeat.

Dr. Lee Salk has shown that, both in monkeys and in the human species, the mother has a marked preference for holding her infant on the left side. Because the apex of the heart is more exposed on the left side, it is reasoned that the preference which these primate mothers show for holding the baby's head against that side is related to the need of the baby to continue to hear the solacing rhythm of its mother's heartbeat. Since, however, most mothers are right-handed, they are most likely to hold the infant in the left arm, thus leaving the right hand free and putting the infant's head opposite the apex of the heart. This may be the real explanation for the manner in which most mothers hold the infant on the left side.

On the assumption that exposure to a normal heartbeat sound immediately following birth would tend to buffer the trauma of birth by providing the infant with the continuity of a familiar security-giving stimulus, Dr. Salk exposed a number of babies in a hospital nursery to the tape recording of normal authentic heartbeat sounds at 72 paired beats per minute. The results were most interesting. A significantly larger number, 69.6 percent of babies who were exposed to the heartbeat sounds, gained weight after the first twenty-four hours of age, whereas only 33.0 percent of the unexposed group gained weight. One or more babies were crying 38.4 percent of the time during the heartbeat phase of the experiment, but 59.8 percent of the time when the sound was not present. Breathing was deeper and more regular among the heartbeat babies than among the controls. Respiratory and gastrointestinal difficulties decreased during the heartbeat period.

Dr. Salk concluded that the sound of a normal heartbeat during the early days and weeks of its postnatal life may well contribute to the infant's better emotional adjustment later in life. Because of its deep-rooted biological significance as the first sound, the constant security-giving sound, the sound experienced when closest to the mother, the heartbeat sound or its equivalent later succeeds in allaying fear where all else might fail.

What connection, if any, does the mother's heartbeat and that of the fetus have to the beat and rhythms of music? "Zwei Herzen in Dreiviertel Takt"—"Two Hearts in Three-quarter Time," was a highly successful film in the early thirties. Its theme-song, from which the film took its title, was a waltz written, as are all waltzes, in three-quarter time, 1. 2. 3—the baby's heart having beaten, most of its time *in utero*, twice for every one beat of the mother's heart. It is possible that such a juxtaposition of meanings represents a reverberation of uterine or infantine experiences? Dr. Joost Meerloo thinks it likely.

Every mother [he writes] intuitively knows that in order to put her baby to sleep she has to rock it, thereby repeating the nirvanic dance [of the fetus in the womb]. The lullabye "Rock-a-bye Baby" unobtrusively takes the child's memory back to the world it has just left. Rock 'n' Roll does the same for older children. It is just as simple as that! Rhythm and whirling around take each of us back to reminiscences of nirvanic equanimity.

But listen well. This does not imply that the dance means no more than a regressive reminiscing, even though in many of us syncopated rhythms, music and counterpoint at regular intervals cause a deep oceanic yearning and a longing for maternal protection, which once was the happy world we lived in.

Dr. Meerloo also draws attention to what he calls "The Milk Dance," the rhythmic interaction between mother and child during the baby's suckling at the mother's breast. The kind of experience the infant has had at the breast, Dr. Meerloo believes, will influence the individual's later rhythmic interests and moods. Nursing deprivations, being brought too late to the breast or getting no breastfeeding at all, may cause the repressed rhythms to come to the fore inappropriately. "As a result of this so-called early oral frustration these children may withdraw desolately in a corner, spontaneously showing the milk dance, while rocking and rolling in a void. These are the children whom doctors give the sophisticated label of being early schizophrenics. Indeed, some of these children can remain such dancing zombies for the rest of their lives, always searching, in a frozen rhythm and unrest, for the lost Nirvana."

Dr. Meerloo considers it important to describe these early biological roots of the dance, because in his clinical practice he has met "many a dance student who used her or his dance aspirations not only to create beauty of gesture and movement, but also as a means to return unobtrusively to frustrated, desperate moods carried over from childhood."

"The charm," he adds, "and the seduction imposed on us by these vibrant reminiscences can drag us into the despair of continuous repetition of sad memories just as easily as they can lead us into the highest triumph of freely creating a new counter-gesture: the dance. From then on our movements become lighter than air, ethereal gestures into space, away from all heaviness."

In the dance, Dr. Meerloo thinks, man's earliest existence is revealed. "Whenever rhythm, cadence, syncopation reach ear and eye man is unobtrusively dragged back into the very beginning of his existence; together with others he undergoes a common regression. The clue of mental contagion is the inadvertent common regression *all* people undergo when special sounds and rhythms reach their ears. That is the reason why tapping, rhythmic calling, musical shouting, jazz, etc., are so infectious."

There is no genetically determined predisposition to tap, or for rhythmical calling or music or the dance. The manner in which all these things are developed is culturally determined, learned. For example, keeping time to music by tapping with the foot is a culturally learned activity, mostly as a result of unconscious imitation. Most of us are unaware that we are beating time in this way to music. I remember, many years ago, reading the autobiography of the great Hungarian philologist Arminius Vambery apropos of this point. Vambery was an extraordinarily gifted linguist. His Arabic was perfect. This enabled him, in disguise as an Arab, to make the pilgrimage to Mecca when that was still a forbidden city to infidels like him. In Mecca he was honored with a feast by one of the local chieftains, as a visiting Arab dignitary from distant parts. While music was being played the chieftain approached Vambery, and good-humoredly said to him, "You are a European." Vambery was astonished. "How did you find out?" he inquired. "I observed," the chieftain replied, "that during the playing of the music you beat time with your foot. No Arab ever does that." *

There does appear to be a natural predisposition for rhythmical movement in man. The manner of that movement is, however, culturally conditioned. The body contact characteristic of ballroom dancing represented a formalized closeness in rhythm which would not in other situations be permitted except between husband and wife or parents and children. Then in the twenties in America, cheek leaning was added to body contact in dancing. Again, this was a formalized act which would not otherwise have been allowed except between relatives. Did this cheek leaning represent an attempt to achieve the cutaneous contact that had been denied the cheek leaners earlier in life? May it not also be that rock 'n' roll and other popular contemporary varieties of music and the dance represent a like response? At least in part, but in a very fundamental way, may not these forms derive from a periphrastic response to an early insufficient experience of comforting, rocking, rolling, and cutaneous stimulation?

* I quote the story from memory. It will be found in Arminius Vambery, *The Story of My Struggles* (London: Fisher Unwin, 1904).

In the cradle-rockingless, lullabyeless, strife-torn world of the twentieth century, rock 'n' roll music and plaintive lullabies, often very beautiful, sometimes stridently percussive, are possibly compensatory effects of the lack of solicitude which parents have in the past exhibited for their children's cutaneous needs. Ignorance concerning the experience of such needs is widespread. But this does not mean that it is uncorrectable. The music of a segment of the population and of a period may sometimes bear a direct relation to the kind of early conditioning experiences, or lack of them, the individual has undergone in his early life. Whether or not this is true in the present instance, in relation to the skin, cannot be decided until a great deal more research has been done on this engaging subject. It is an interesting conjecture, and it is worth pursuing if only for the light it might throw on the micro-mechanics of human development, which is to say the light it might throw on human nature.

CLOTHES AND THE SKIN. Our discussion has considered the possible relation of the kinds of experiences of early cutaneous stimulation and the kinds of music and dance that may develop, especially in response to the lack of adequate rocking and cutaneous stimulation. This brings us to another interesting question, namely the relationships of clothes, skin, and behavior.

Irwin and Weiss have found that activity was significantly less in infants when they were clothed than when they were unclothed. This raised the question whether the reduced activity was due to mechanical restraint by the clothes or possibly the elimination of self-stimulation, or perhaps the alleviation of hunger contractions, or finally, whether the clothing perhaps reduced or offered insulation against incoming stimuli.

The correct answer to these questions is probably that all four factors are operative, but that the last is the most important, namely the insulation that clothing produces against incoming stimuli.

It is difficult to say whether or not the habit of dressing the infant in clothes early in his life bears any relation to the development of behavioral differences, distinguishing those behaviors from behaviors found in cultures in which neither children nor adults wear clothes. Clothes, and different kinds of clothes, probably affect the skin differently enough to result in behavior directly traceable to the effects exercised through the skin. It may be conjectured that the remarkable innovations in dress worn by young people, and such phenomena as long hair, beards, and other hispid facial embellishments in the male, have some connection with early kinds of tactile or lack of tactile experiences. Hair is an important appendage of the skin, and indeed constitutes the avenue through which much of its stimulation is initiated. Possibly the hair that young men began to sport on their heads and faces in the late 1960's in some measure represents an expression of the need for love which was earlier denied them because of the stroking and patting and caressing they failed to receive in infancy. The highly successful musical play, *Hair,* is emphatically, among other things, devoted to long hair and, for a bit, to nudity. Perhaps it would not be putting too great a strain on the imagination to offer the exegesis that what the play is pleading for is more love, for being stroked the right way rather than being rubbed the wrong.

During World War I, when women began to bob their hair and shorten their skirts, Eric Gill, the distinguished English type designer, typographer and sculptor, penned the following quatrain:

If skirts should get much shorter
Said the flapper with a sob,
There'll be two more cheeks to powder
And one more place to bob.

One wonders what he would have thought of miniskirts, top-less waitresses, see-through dresses, and bikinis?

Allowing for the demise of Anthony Comstock, Mrs. Grundy, and the Censor, as well as for the increasing ampli-tude of our enlarging freedoms, it is possible that the expo-sure of the skin and its integumentary specializations may be related to the needs for cutaneous satisfaction of those who in their earlier lives failed to receive such satisfactions. Clothes largely cut off the experience of pleasurable sensa-tions from the skin, hence, the actual or symbolic shedding of clothes may represent attempts to enjoy experiences that had been earlier denied. Natural skin stimulation, the play of air, sun, and wind upon the body, can be very pleasur-able. Flügel, who conducted an inquiry into the matter, found that such natural skin stimulation was often described in "glowing" terms, as "heavenly," "perfectly delightful," "like breathing in happiness," and in similar expressions of pleasure. The growth of the nudist movement almost cer-tainly reflects the desire for more freedom of communication through the skin.*

This, interestingly enough, takes the form of visual com-munication through the inspection of the nude body. All nudists agree that this greatly reduces sexual tension, and is

* One of the earliest serious discussions of nudism and the disadvan-tages of clothes is to be found in Parmalee, *The New Gymnosophy* (New York: Hitchcock, 1927). See also the book that introduced nud-ism to America, by F. Merrill and M. Merrill, *Among the Nudists* (New York: Garden City Publishing Co., 1931).

of general therapeutic value. Touching, even between husband and wife, was strictly forbidden in all nudist camps, but that rule is today tending to be somewhat relaxed. Hartman, who has made a serious study of nudists, expresses his pleasure in seeing "nudists engaged in various games involving physical contact but not involving any suggestive activities. I had heard so much about the no-touch rule but had been warmly embraced by both males and females during the period of the research and found that such cordiality had nothing to do with sexual arousal. This contact was one of the more pleasurable experiences of the research." Hartman points out that American culture has been regarded as a no-touch one. His observations on nudists lead him to believe that nudists may unwittingly have aggravated the situation. "I believe," he writes, "that much more personal growth would take place among individuals where there is some kind of affectionate touch contact, especially with closely related individuals and generally between all persons. It was my observation that the no-touch rule is on its way out."

The association of nudity with sex is, of course, so strong that where touching of the clothed body is permissible, the same part of the body is taboo to touch when it is unclothed. This rule, however, does not apply to parents and their small children. As the children grow older, physical contact becomes more restrained, and by adolescence is completely terminated. So that adolescents who touch each other while clothed cease to do so when in the nude in camps.

One of the consequences of the habit of wearing clothes from early infancy is that the skin fails to develop the sensitivity it would have done had clothes not been habitually worn. It has been observed, for example, that among nonliterate peoples the skin is very much more responsive to stimuli than it is among Europeans. Kilton Stewart in his book, *Pygmies and Dream Giants,* reports of the Philippine Negritos that they "are very sensitive to creeping things, and were amazed that an ant could crawl up my leg without my being aware of it."

The differences between individuals in skin sensitivity are quite remarkable. There are some who when they touch another feel "a sort of electrical current" passing between them, whereas others experience nothing of the sort. It is also of interest to note that while some individuals retain this sensitivity into old age, others tend to lose it in middle age. Quite possibly in these latter cases hormonal changes may be involved.

The "electricity" that is often, metaphorically speaking, said to pass between people when touching one another, may be something more than a mere metaphor. The skin is an especially good electrical conductor. Electrical changes may be measured at the skin surface in a variety of ways, one of the best known of these being the psychogalvanometer or, as it is commonly miscalled, "the lie detector." Emotional changes acting through the autonomic nervous system usually produce an increase in the electrical conductance of the skin (a decrease in resistance) across the palms of the hands or feet. There can be little doubt that in tactile stimulation electrical changes are transmitted from one individual to the other.

"DERMO-OPTICAL PERCEPTION." Some persons claim to possess skins so sensitive that they are able to see with them. Since the skin is derived from the same embryological ectodermal layer as the eyes, several investigators have maintained that in such individuals the skin has retained some primitive optical properties, and it is this that enables them to see with the skin. This view was forcibly argued by the French novelist Jules Romains in 1919 in his book, *Vision Extra-Rétinienne*. At regular intervals the idea makes its appearance in the press, when some individual is reported with "eyeless sight," or as being able to see from the socket from which his eye was removed, or through his fingers, or through the skin of the face following a thorough sealing of the eyes.

There is, in fact, no evidence whatever that will withstand a moment's critical examination that anyone has ever been able to see with the skin. What appear to be impressive performances are usually due to trickery. Martin Gardner has discussed these alleged cases of dermo-optical perception, and thoroughly disposed of them. The sensory capacities of the skin are remarkable enough to render the making of exaggerated claims for it quite unnecessary. The ability of blind persons like Laura Bridgman and Helen Keller, and Madame de Staël, who used to pass her hands over the faces of her visitors in order to gain some idea of what they looked like, are a matter of record. But no one ever claimed that these ladies were seeing through their skin. We all have stereognostic ability—that is, the ability to perceive objects or forms by touch—and in a metaphoric sense most human beings can almost "see" the form of the object they have touched. The tips of the fingers are the parts of the body which are characterized by the greatest sensitivity in "reading," that is in stereognizing, the form of objects by touch. If any evidence were required to demonstrate the mind of the skin it could rest on the sensory capacities of the fingertips alone. Those capacities, in the form of sensory receptors which pick up the stimuli, transmit them to the brain in the form of conductor substances; through repetition, that is by

learning, capacities become abilities enabling the individual
to make the fine discriminations which endow the particular
sensations with particular meanings. An ability is a trained
capacity, and every human being has to learn how to make
such fine discriminations. Just as he has to learn the ability
of stereognosis so, too, he learns to develop the sensitivities
inherent in his skin, or he does not. That particular variety
of learning is almost entirely determined by the cutaneous
and related experiences he has undergone during infancy
and childhood.

DERMOGRAPHIA. *Dermographia* or *dermatographia* is skin
writing or the raising of wheals by pressure, usually upon
the broad expanse of the back. One may write on the skin
with a blunt instrument. When the wheals show up red, hy-
perreactivity of the vagus nerve (vagotonia) is involved;
when the wheals are predominantly white the sympathetic
nervous system is involved. The wheals themselves are produced by oozing of fluid from capillaries into the surrounding
tissue, the oozing in turn, apparently, resulting from local
dilation of the blood vessels. Everyone's skin will wheal if
stroked sufficiently often or struck sufficiently hard, but in
the abnormal cases mild stroking is sufficient to produce dermographia. Whether or not dermographia has any relation
whatever to early childhood cutaneous experience is at present quite unknown.

Children have for generations played at tracing letters on
each other's backs, competing with each other for the highest
number of correct identifications. Adults can play this game
with varying degrees of competence. The brain, clearly, is capable of translating patterns of stimulated touch receptors
into letters and simple images. No one, so far as I know, has

ever studied the variability in translating such dermatographic messages in different individuals. It would not, I
think, be too rash to predict that significant correlations
would be found between such dermatographic skills and
early cutaneous experience.

Drs. Paul Bach-y-Rita and Carter C. Collins of the Smith-
Kettlewell Institute of Visual Sciences of the University of
the Pacific Graduate School of Medical Sciences in San Francisco, basing themselves on the knowledge of the ability of
the brain to translate dermal messages, have found that such
translation also occurs when the stimuli come from arrays of
electrodes or vibrating points connected to a camera. After a
few hours of training, blind subjects can recognize geometric
figures and objects like chairs and telephones. Additional
training produces the ability to judge distance and even to
recognize faces.

The skin and the retina of the eye are unique in that their
sensory receptors are laid out in a pattern. This enables both
the retina and the skin to pick up regularities and patterns
of stimuli and to convert them readily into images in the
brain. Using an array of electrodes mounted in an elastic matrix, which can be worn on the back or abdomen, under regular clothes, a camera is mounted on the blind person's head
like a miner's lamp. This camera can transmit to the electrodes the information it picks up, which the electrodes in
turn transmit to the skin. The information is then translated
in the brain for what it is. During the course of this research
it was found that the abdominal skin "sees" better than that
of the back or forearms.

The spatio-temporal perceptive capacities of the skin are
quite remarkable. Time is handled almost as well by the
skin as by the ear. The skin can pick up a break of about 10

thousandths of a second in a steady mechanical pressure or
tactile buzz. Eye discriminations are about 25–35 thousandths of a second. The skin picks up the location of dis-
tances on its surface very much more efficiently than the ear
is able to locate sounds at a distance. Utilizing this information Dr. Frank A. Geldard of the Cutaneous Communication
Laboratory at Princeton University has worked out an op-
thohapt alphabet which can be flashed to the skin rapidly
and vividly. The symbols are easy to learn and read, in a language that may be called "body English." Geldard has shown
that Rousseau's envisionment, in 1762, in his treatise on education, *Émile,* of the possibility of communicating through
the skin was, indeed, a remarkable piece of prescience. The
skin, Geldard has demonstrated, is capable of receiving and
reading rapid and sophisticated messages. "There is every
likelihood," he says, "that skin languages of great subtlety
and speed can be devised and used."

Dermo-optical perception is a myth, but perception
through the skin by means of its other properties is a reality.
The skin possesses the ability to respond to a large variety of
modalities. Already electronic devices are available which vi-
brate in an outline identical to the letters of the alphabet,
enabling a blind person, after a little practice, to see. In addition to vibrotactile communication, research is proceeding
on coding alphabets through electropulses. B. von Haller
Gilmer and Lee W. Gregg of the Carnegie Institute of Tech-
nology have been pursuing this approach. They point out
that the skin is rarely if ever "busy," a fact which enables it
to learn, to become habituated to codes that cannot be inter-
fered with under any conditions. The vibrotactile or electro-
tactile signal cannot be shut out. Nor can the skin close its
eyes; it cannot even hold its ears—in this respect it more

closely resembles the ear than the eye. Von Haller Gilmer and Gregg postulate that by its very nature the skin is not handicapped with excess verbiage, as is the written and spoken word. Perhaps the skin has possibilities of codes, they suggest, even superior to other channels because of its "simplicity." The skin may be unique in combining the spatiotemporal dimensions of hearing and vision, the ear being best in the temporal, and the eye in the spatial dimension.

With an apparatus designed by J. F. Hahn to deliver and measure square wave pulses to the skin and its resistance, von Haller Gilmer and Gregg have made exploratory studies on both normal and blind subjects. Given areas of the skin may be stimulated at the rate of one pulse per second with a duration of one milli-second, for up to two hours without report of pain. A pulse language, therefore, becomes possible once the pulses for the code have been worked out. Such an artificial language, the elements of which are defined by cutaneous sensations, has remarkable possibilities. Placing the cutaneous sensations in one-to-one correspondence with the elemental sounds of speech (phonemes), these investigators will be using a programmed computer (the code interpreter) as an analog to the human communications receptor. With the aid of this computer they hope to construct a system that may yield the necessary information upon which a good code can be based.

Touch as interval has never been properly investigated. By an interval in music is meant the difference in pitch between any two notes. The great variety of intervals experienced in touch carries the signals to the brain, which gives them meaning. As in music, so also in tactile experience, intervals can be either concordant or discordant. The psychophysics of the subject has yet to be investigated.

ITCHING AND SCRATCHING. Itching is an irritating cutaneous sensation which provokes the desire to scratch or rub the skin. Scratching, the usual means of relieving itching, is done by scraping with the fingernails. The psychosomatics of itching and scratching are well known. That distinguished polymath William Shakespeare put it this way in *Coriolanus* (I. i. 162), where he makes Caius Marcius say,

> *What's the matter, you dissentious rogues,*
> *That, rubbing the poor itch of your opinion,*
> *Make yourselves scabs.*

An "itch" in the mind, as it were, will often express itself as an itch in the skin. Musaph, who has written a fascinating monograph on the subject of itching and scratching, describes these as derived activities, that is to say, as activities which are derived from the "sparking over" or transduction into a skin response of experiences related to and prepared by the individual's early life. For example, in frustrating situations angry emotions may be converted infra-symbolically into itching and scratching. The various forms of psychosomatic pruritis, that is, functionally induced itching of the skin, often represent the unconscious striving to obtain the attention that was denied in early life, especially the attention that was denied to the skin. Unexpressed feelings of frustration, rage, and guilt, as well as the strong repressed need for love may find symptomatic expression in the form of scratching even in the absence of itching.

Seitz has drawn attention to the clandestine scratching of many persons who feel ashamed because the practice causes them to experience pleasurable sensations of an erotic quality. The erotic quality of much scratching is fairly obvious. An old proverb has it, " 'Tis better than riches to scratch where it itches." No less a person than James I of England declared that "No one but kings and princes should have the itch, for the sensation of scratching is so delightful." And that choleric character, Thomas Carlyle, went so far as to say, "The height of human happiness is to scratch the part that itches." The relief from emotional tension offered by scratching has been portrayed by Samuel Butler (1612–1680) in *Hudibras,*

> *He could raise scruples dark and nice,*
> *And after solve 'em in a trice:*
> *As if Divinity had catch'd*
> *The itch, on purpose to be scratched.* [*I. I. 163*]

Brian Russell points out that deprivation of love often results in itching, an itch to be loved. "The patient with widespread eczema whose skin relapses on the very suggestion of discharge from the hospital, regresses to an infantile stage of dependency with the mute appeal, 'I am helpless; you must care for me.'"

Scratching may be simultaneously a source of pleasure and of displeasure, expressing guilt and a tendency towards self-punishment. Disturbances in sexuality and hostility are almost always present in patients with pruritis.

The pleasures of back scratching are phylogenetically very old; even invertebrates are soothed by gentle back-rubbing, and it is well known that all mammals enjoy it. Also, like man, other mammals enjoy back scratching in the absence of itching even more than they do in its presence. The instrument known as a back scratcher or scratch-back is a very ancient device; the latest electric models are advertised as being "better than a friend, with a hand that jingles up and down like the real thing." Thus, the sheer pleasure-giving qualities of the appropriately stimulated skin testify to its need for pleasurable stimulation. In this sense almost every kind of cutaneous stimulation that is not intended to be injurious is characterized by an erotic component. Under the appropriate circumstances even a touch on the hand can be sexually exciting. It is highly probable that the differences in the degree of cutaneous sensitivity that different individuals exhibit to the pleasures derivable from stimulation of the skin in all states and conditions of being are largely influenced by early experiences of cutaneous stimulation. Certainly the experiments of the Harlows and others abundantly testify to that fact in monkeys, apes, and other mammals, while psychiatric research fully supports that relationship for man.

BATHING AND THE SKIN. The delight which infants take in a warm bath, their joyful splashing and gurgling, and their great reluctance to leave the water testify to the pleasure derived by infants from this aquatic stimulation of the skin. It is perhaps not surprising, therefore, that, especially in America, the bathroom has become the temple of the American household, and the daily bath a ritual celebration of the hymn to self-laving. Women find the bath relaxing; men find the shower stimulating. And both men and women often spend considerably more time in the bath than one would think necessary for the mere purposes of cleanliness. Can it be that in addition to enjoying the pleasures derived from the cutaneous stimulation which each sex obtains in its own way, that these pleasures in part represent a ritual revival of pleasures originally enjoyed in the aquatic environment of the mother's womb, and in the early experiences of bathing during infancy?

It is of great interest that men, and sometimes women,

who seldom otherwise sing will burst out into song in the bathtub or under the shower. What can be the explanation of this? Also, a high proportion of masturbatory activities take place in the bath or shower. Why? Clearly the stimulation of the skin by the water is very different in the shower from what it is in the tub. The sudden and continuing stimulation of the skin by the shower water induces active respiratory changes which in the appropriate subject are likely to result in song. This is much less likely to happen under the more gentle stimulation of the water in the tub. In both cases, however, the rubbing of the skin is likely to induce erotic sensations leading to masturbatory activities.

The enormous increase in the number of private swimming pools, and the rush to the beaches in summer, with bathing incidental to exposure to sun and gentle breezes, further serves to testify to the great pleasure taken in the sensory excitements provided by shedding one's clothes and exposing one's skin to the elements. Years ago Dr. C. W. Saleeby in his book entitled *Sunlight and Health* made eloquent comment on this. Referring to the skin, he wrote,

This admirable organ, the natural clothing of the body, which grows continually throughout life, which has at least four distinct sets of sensory nerves distributed to it, which is essential in the regulation of the temperature, which is waterproof from without inwards, but allows the excretory sweat to escape freely, which, when unbroken, is microbe-proof, and which can readily absorb sunlight—this most beautiful, versatile, and wonderful organ is, for the most part, smothered, blanched, and blinded in clothes and can only gradually be restored to the air and light which are its natural surroundings. Then and only then we learn what it is capable of.

Virtually everyone, from Plato to the present day, who has ever written on the subject has sung the praises of nudity over the clothed body, but contemporary man, and especially woman, quite fail to understand the needs of the skin, and from this ignorance often do themselves great and irreparable damage. The sun-worship in which increasing numbers of people indulge today not only results in drying, wrinkling, and other damage to the skin, but in many cases initiates the development of skin cancer. Most visible signs of skin damage attributed to aging, as Dr. John M. Knox has pointed out, are actually a result of sunlight exposure. Moderate exposure to sunlight is not only desirable but necessary. Immoderate exposure to sunlight is not only unnecessary but dangerous. It is a rather sad reflection on human folly when one thinks of the billions of dollars women spend on the cosmetic care of their skin in the form of lotions, balms, creams, and the like, while at the same time overexposing their skins to the very worst of possible damaging influences, namely excessive sunlight. Twenty minutes of exposure to the midday summer sun can result in sunburned redness of the skin. Most people will spend several hours on a beach exposed to the sun, an exposure which may result in painful blistering sunburn. It is interesting that the notion of tanning as a sign of health came into being in the 1920's. This corresponds to the period when the heavy-handed teachings of the behaviorists were causing parents to approach their children as if they were automata, and caressing and other forms of cutaneous stimulation of the child were being reduced to a minimum. Possibly, here, too, there is a connection. The tanning may symbolically mean, "You see, the sun has continued to smile upon me, and I have basked freely and uninhibitedly in its embracing rays. I have been well and warmly loved."

SKIN AND SLEEP. The skin remains the most alert of the senses in sleep, and is the first to recover on awakening. Sense organs in the skin and the deeper interoceptive sense organs appear to be involved in bringing about the movements of sleep. Skin that is lain on for too long becomes overheated through lack of ventilation, and as a result messages which result in a change of position are communicated to the appropriate centers. Analysis of heartbeat records in normal sleep have shown that some six minutes before the sleeper stirs his heart begins to beat faster. With the change in sleeping position the heartbeat slowly returns to its normal rate.

Anna Freud has commented on the close interrelation between the needs for sleep and for cutaneous contact, "falling asleep being rendered more difficult for the infant who is kept strictly separated from the mother's body warmth." Miss Freud also draws attention to interrelation between sleep and passive body movement, that is, rocking. The relaxed child sleeps, the troubled child suffers from disturbed sleep. Normal sleep is a stimulus barrier. Disturbed sleep is a condition of vulnerability to internally originating excitements. Children who have been briefly separated from their mothers will, during the period of separation, suffer from disturbed sleep. As Heinicke and Westheimer state in their book on the subject, "We find that not only is the most intense fretting for the parents concomitant with the maximum sleep disturbance, but . . . disturbances in sleep are directly connected with longing for the parents." After the third day there would be a pronounced decline in the sleep disturbances of these children, but difficulties in falling asleep and fear of being left alone were noticeably frequent. Furthermore, "more of the children had persistent sleeping difficulties during the period following reunion (or its equivalent) than did those who had not been separated." The separations of these two-year-old children lasted from two weeks to twenty weeks. At some point during the first twenty weeks after reunion, seven of the ten children who had experienced separation had noticeable difficulty in falling asleep or remaining asleep, or both. The duration of the sleeping difficulties persisted from one to twenty-one weeks with the median at four weeks.

Such findings strongly suggest that early interference with the normal mothering process, not only after the infant has made strong identifications with the mother, but even before, may seriously affect the individual's ability to fall asleep or remain asleep. And that, in early infancy especially, the mother's holding, carrying, cuddling, and rocking of the infant constitute acts which play a significant role in the development of later sleep patterns which may persist throughout life.

Deprivation of the tactile need, like deprivation of any other need, causes the infant distress. It will therefore sound the distress signal designed to compel attention to its need, by crying. Aldrich and his co-workers found that among the less generally recognized causes of crying in infants is the need for fondling and rhythmic motion. These investigators found a constant relationship between the amount and frequency of crying and the amount and frequency of nursing care: the more care, the less crying. Infants will continue to cry even when they see that they are being approached or when the mother calls to them. Such infants, however, will cease crying immediately when picked up and fondled. Affectionate tactile stimulation is clearly, then, a primary need, a need which must be satisfied if the infant is to develop as a healthy human being.

FIVE

For touch,
Touch, by the holy powers of the Gods!
Is the sense of the body; whether it be
When something from without makes its way in,
Or when a thing, which in the body had birth,
Hurts it, or gives it pleasure issuing forth
*To perform the generative deeds of Venus.**

SKIN AND SEX

THE FRENCH WIT (quoted in an earlier chapter) who defined sexual intercourse as the harmony of two souls and the contact of two epidermes, elegantly emphasized a basic truth: the massive involvement of the skin in sexual congress. The truth is that in no other relationship is the skin so totally involved as in sexual intercourse. It is principally through stimulation of the skin that both male and female are brought to orgasm in coitus, in the case of the male largely through the sensory receptors in the penis, and in the female

* LUCRETIUS (C. 96 B.C.–C. 53 B.C.) *De Rerum Natura*, II, 434

through the sensory receptors in the vagina and circumvaginal areas of the skin. Both in the male and in the female the pubic and suprapubic areas, which are covered with hair, are highly sensitive, the *mons veneris,* however, being much more sensitive in the female than the corresponding area in the male. In correlation with this it is interesting to note that in the female the hair of the suprapubic region tends to be crinkly, forming a pad, in contrast to the male in whom the hair tends to be longish and uncurled. Also the *mons veneris* contains more fatty tissue than the suprapubic region does in the male. These differences are probably adaptive in response to the male's assumption of the prone horizontal position in intercourse in relation to the female's supine horizontal position.

Several functions are served by these anatomical arrangements. In both sexes chafing or bruising of the skin is thus avoided as well as excessive pressure on the bony pubis, while sexual excitement is enhanced. The suprapubic hairs at their bases, when stimulated, serve to produce those chemo-conductor changes in the nerve endings which, together with those nerve endings directly supplying the skin, induce a heightening of sexual excitement. The perineal region, that is the region extending from the base of the external genitalia to and including the anus, is also supplied with hair and sensory nerves that are highly erotogenic. The nipples in both sexes are similarly highly sensitive, as are the lips. In the female orgasm may be produced by rubbing the *mons veneris*. A similar effect is seldom achievable in the male by rubbing the suprapubic region. Thus the female may masturbate without stimulating the vagina directly, whereas the male masturbates by direct stimulation of the penis.

The question we have to ask is: Do individuals who are maternally adequately cared for differ from those who are not, in the manner in which they respond to cutaneous stimulation in sex relations, in necking, petting, and coitus? Cardinal Newman once said that any fool can ask unanswerable questions. The question we have asked is not unanswerable, but unfortunately not much scientific research has been done which would enable us to answer it. We have seen that the Harlows, in their studies of rhesus monkeys, have got as near that research as anyone. It will be recalled that none of the Harlows' motherless mother-animals ever showed normal female sex posturing and responding. "They were impregnated, not through their own effort, but because of the patience, persistence, and perspicacity of our breeding males." Apparently adequate mothering is necessary for the development of healthy sexual behavior. And what, in our present connection, "adequate mothering" means is the complex of cutaneous stimulations, among other things, which activates the tactile response systems of the infant, and thus early in its life experience prepares it for later adequate functioning in all situations involving tactility. This appears to be especially true of sexual behavior. Just as the individual learns his or her gender role, so, too, each learns or fails to learn the behavioral responses one makes as a result of learning originally initiated through the skin.

"At the beginning of life," writes Anna Freud, "being stroked, cuddled, and soothed by touch libidinizes the various parts of the child's body, helps to build up a healthy body image and body ego, increases its cathexis with narcissistic libido, and simultaneously promotes the development of object love by cementing the bond between child and mother. There is no doubt that, at this period, the surface of the skin in its role as erotogenic zone fulfills a multiple function in the child's growth."

The mother's holding and cuddling of the child plays a very effective and important role in its subsequent sexual development. A mother who loves must enfold the child she loves. She must draw the child to her in a close embrace and, male or female, this is what the adult will want later and be able to demonstrate to anyone he loves. Children who have been inadequately held and fondled will suffer, as adolescents and adults, from an affect-hunger for such attention. Dr. Marc H. Hollender of the Department of Psychiatry of the University of Pennsylvania has reported, as part of a larger study on the need for body contact, on thirty-nine women with relatively acute psychiatric disorders, the most common of which was neurotic depression. In the larger study, Dr. Hollender and his collaborators found that the need to be held and cuddled, like other needs, varies in intensity from person to person and in the same person from time to time. For most women, it was found, body contact is pleasant but not indispensable. However, at one extreme they found women who considered body contact disagreeable and even repugnant, while at the other extreme were women who experienced it as a desire so compelling that it resembled an addiction.

The need for body contact, like oral needs, may become intensified during periods of stress. But while oral longings may be readily satisfied alone, with food, tobacco, alcohol, or the like, body-contact longings can scarcely be satisfied without the participation of another person.

Of the group of thirty-nine women patients, twenty-one, or slightly more than one-half, had used sex to entice a male to hold them. Twenty-six of the women had made direct

requests to be held. Nine women who had made a direct request had not used sex, and four women who had used sex
had not made a direct request.

Clearly, then, such women may entice men to sex relations
when their real desire is to be held or cuddled. As one of
these women put it, in describing her desire to be held, "It's
a kind of an ache . . . It's not like an emotional longing for
some person who isn't there; it's a physical feeling."

Hollender quotes a former call girl who said, "In a way, I
used sex to be held." The resort to sexual intercourse as a
means of obtaining body contact has been referred to by
Blinder in a discussion of depressive disorders. "At best," he
writes, "the sexual experiences of these intensely unhappy
people seem more an attempt to make some sort of human
contact, however incomplete, than to achieve physical satisfaction." Malmquist and his co-workers, in reporting on
twenty women who had three or more illegitimate pregnancies, state, "Eight of the 20 reported that they were consciously aware that sexual activity for them was a price to be
paid for being cuddled and held. Pregenital activity was described by these eight as more pleasurable than intercourse
itself, which was merely something to be tolerated." Similar
observations have been made by other investigators.

Hollender and his co-workers comment, "The desire to be
cuddled and held is acceptable to most people as long as it is
regarded as a component part of adult sexuality. The wish to
be cuddled and held in a maternal manner is felt to be too
childish; to avoid embarrassment or shame, women convert
it into the longing to be held by a man as part of an adult
activity, sexual intercourse" (p. 190).

If one asks why being held by women would not be even
more desirable for these patients, the answer is that they do

often use various devices to persuade women friends to hold them, but when this is achieved they quickly become uncomfortable and draw away, a withdrawal reaction that never occurs with men. Most of these women linked their desire for being held with "adult" sexuality, as very definitely opposed to anything smacking of homosexuality. Overtly, at any rate, they do not want to be taken for lesbians. One woman stated that when she was held by a woman her face reddened and she became afraid that whoever might see her would think she was a homosexual. A third woman said, "I don't want any woman to touch me. I think of lesbians."

Hollender and his co-workers believe that for some women the need to be held or cuddled is a major determinant of promiscuity.

It may well be that such women often have a strong unconscious drive to be held by women, who represent the mother, a need which has been repressed and causes them to seek body contact with men and women on a heterosexual basis, paying the men with their disinterested sexuality, and withdrawing from too close contact with the women for fear that their true motives may be discovered even to themselves. The face-reddening of the one woman is perhaps significant in this connection? Some of the patients in this study were so averse to sexual intercourse with their husbands or anyone else that they would forego the strong desire to be held rather than submit to intercourse.

Hollender and his co-workers have not published anything on the early histories of these women; however, it is highly probable that what is being witnessed in the great longing of these women to be held and cuddled is a response to a need which was largely left unsatisfied in infancy.

Lowen has published a number of case histories of women

who suffered a lack of tactile stimulation in infancy, and who in later life engaged in sexual activities in a desperate attempt to gain some contact with their own bodies. "This compulsive activity," writes Lowen, "may give the impression that these persons are oversexed. They are, if anything, undersexed, for the activity stems from a need for erotic stimulation rather than from a feeling of sexual charge or excitement. Sexual activity of this kind never leads to orgastic satisfaction or fulfillment, but leaves the person empty and disappointed."

These are important points, for they draw attention to the fact that in the Western world it is highly probable that sexual activity, indeed the frenetic preoccupation with sex that characterizes Western culture, is in many cases not the expression of a sexual interest at all, but rather a search for the satisfaction of the need for contact. As Lowen remarks, "An ego that is not grounded in the reality of body feeling becomes desperate."

Strictly speaking, as Freud pointed out, the whole body is an erotogenic zone, and as Fenichel has stated, touch erotism is comparable to the sexual pleasure derivable from looking (scopophilia). Both are brought about by sensory stimuli of a specific kind in specific situations. In the development from pregenital oral and anal satisfactions to genital primacy, in which sexual excitations become genitally oriented and dominant over the extragenital erogenous zones, the sensory stimulations normally "function as instigators of excitement and play a corresponding part in forepleasure. If they have been warded off during childhood they remain isolated, demanding full gratification on their own account and thus disturbing sexual integration."

In Hollender's and in Lowen's women their need for

being held was almost certainly warded off, and has therefore remained isolated and pressing and quite separated from their disturbed and unintegrated need for sexual relations. The only real need they know is the pregenital one of being held and cuddled, and principally loved in this manner. The high intercorrelation between maternal behavior and later child behavior in other variables renders a causal connection between early parental failure and the later longing to be held highly probable.

As Jurgen Ruesch has written,

We know that to secure healthy development any person has to be supplied with the right kind of stimulus at the right time and in the right amount. This is particularly true of children. Quantitatively inappropriate responses of the parents to the infants' primitive messages, such as "I am cold," "I am wet," "I am tired," or "I have had enough" establish deviant feedback circuits. . . . Qualitatively inappropriate responses can produce disturbances which are in no way different from those produced by the quantitatively inappropriate responses. To offer food when thirst is prominent, to offer fluids when excessive cold has to be managed, are self-explanatory examples.

The warding-off or separation between the need to be held and the need for sexual satisfaction in Hollender's women may be accounted for in the recognition (made as long ago as 1898 by Albert Moll) of the sexual impulse as divisible into two components, the one limited to bodily and mental approximation to another individual, the *contrectation impulse* (from *contrectare,* "to touch," "to think about"), and the other insofar as it was confined to the peripheral organs, as the *detumescence-impulse* (from *detumescere,* "to stop swelling," "to subside"). Moll makes it quite clear that each impulse at first operates quite independently of the other, as we may observe in children who are highly tactile but who have no accompanying sexual interest in others until further development has occurred. Should failure to develop contrectation occur as a consequence of inadequate tactile experience, the individual may become fixated on the satisfaction of this need, with consequent exclusion of the development of the need for detumescence.

TOUCH AND COMMUNICATION. It has been remarked that in the final analysis every tragedy is a failure in communication. And what the child receiving inadequate cutaneous stimulation suffers from is the failure of integrative development as a human being, a failure in the communication of the fact that he is being loved. By being stroked, and caressed, and carried, and cuddled, and cooed to, by being loved, he learns to stroke and caress and cuddle, and coo to and love others. In this sense love is sexual in the healthiest sense of that word. It implies involvement, concern, responsibility, tenderness, and awareness of the needs and vulnerabilities of the other. All this is communicated to the infant through his skin in the early months of his life, and gradually reinforced by feeding, sound, and visual cues as the infant develops. The primacy of the infant's first perceptions of reality through the skin can no longer be doubted. The messages he receives through that organ must be security-giving, assuring, and pleasurable if the infant is to thrive. Even in food intake, as Brody has shown in her excellent study of mothering, "save under conditions of body security and comfort no infant, however hungry, appeared to enjoy his feeding."

Such evidence as we have strongly suggests that inadequate communication with the baby through its skin is likely to result in inadequate development of sexual functions.

Freud's view of the skin as an erotogenic zone differentiated into sense organs and special erogenic zones like the anal, oral, and genital, really refers to erogenized tactile zones, and what he calls infantile sexuality appears to be, as Lawrence Frank has observed, largely tactuality. As growth and development proceed, this tactile sensitivity is gradually transformed into interpersonal relations, auto-erotic activities, and eventually into sexual activities. It is to be regretted that in Freud's emphasis, some would say overemphasis, on the erotogenic character of the skin it should have come to be seen principally and almost exclusively as significant for sexual development alone. This erotogenic view of the skin has somewhat impeded the recognition of its role in the development of other behavioral traits.

In this area it would be foolish to pretend to more knowledge than we possess, for while thousands of researches, monographs, books, and articles have been written on virtually every aspect of sex, the role of early cutaneous experience in the mothering situation has been largely neglected. Brody raises the question of "whether earliest skin and muscle erotism has received less than due recognition for the part it plays in gratifications derived from oral erotism and feeling in the first months of life" (p. 338). The answer is that it has, indeed. Hence we are dependent here to a large extent upon conjecture and inference rather than upon the solid ground of research.

The fact that males have projecting external genitalia, penis and scrotum and gonads, makes their handling by the mother, the infant itself, and others, a great deal more inviting and easier than is the case in the female. It is, therefore, likely that male infants in all cultures undergo considerably more genital stimulation than females. This difference in sexual anatomy may also, at least in part, explain the greater frequency of masturbation—self-gratification through skin stimulation—in boys than in girls. The early stimulation of the external genitalia in boys by the mother, or other persons, or both, may have all sorts of later developmental behavioral effects.

"It is notable," wrote Lawrence Frank, "that in our discussions of personality development in children and of sexuality, so little attention has been given to the tactual-cutaneous experiences of the infant. Like all young mammals who are licked, nuzzled, cuddled and kept close to the mother, the human infant likewise has apparently a similar need for close bodily contacts, for patting and caressing, for tactual soothing which calms him and restores his equilibrium when hurt, frightened, or angry." This tactual sensitivity is especially acute in the genitals.

"This infantile tactuality, like his other organic needs, is gradually transformed as the child learns to accept mother's voice as a surrogate, her reassuring words and tones of voice giving him an equivalent for his close physical contacts, or her angry scolding voice serving as punishment and making him cry as if hit. Caressing becomes the chief form of intimacy and expression of affection, with appropriate words and tones of voice. All physical contacts become meaningful and colored by emotion."

Frank then goes on to point out that during the so-called latency period, girls and especially boys are less likely to seek and receive tactual contacts from parents. Tactual sensitivity, however, reappears more strongly than ever at puberty or shortly thereafter, and becomes a major need-objective, to touch and to be touched, not merely as an impersonal sensory stimulation, but as a symbolic fulfillment of the search for intimacy, acceptance, reassurance, and comforting or, in some who have been failed, a continual avoidance of such contacts.

With further development, the need for tactuality

becomes one of the chief components in sexual approaches and intercourse, where the individual's early infantile experiences of adequate tactuality or deprivation may govern his or her capacity for response. The tactual-cutaneous sensitivity of the genitals at puberty becomes more acute and in the male becomes the major focus of his sexuality, while the female seems to retain more of the larger overall tactuality of infancy while exhibiting especial sensitivity in breasts, labiae and clitoris. Auto-erotic practices may serve as both vicarious fulfillments and/or preparation for coitus. [pp. 134–35]

The enormous variety of meanings which sex may have for different individuals, a language which has the kinds of things to say to the other that can be said in no other way, an exchange of love, a means of hurting or exploiting others, a mode of defense, a bargaining point, a way of self-denial or self-assertion, an affirmation or a rejection of masculinity or femininity, and so on, not to mention the abnormal or pathological expressions which sex may take, all, more or less, are influenced by early tactile experience.

As Lowen points out,

The quality of the physical intimacy between mother and child reflects the mother's feelings about the intimacy of sex. If the act of sex is viewed with disgust, all intimate body contact is tainted with this feeling. If a woman is ashamed of her body, she cannot offer it graciously to the nursing infant. If she is repelled by the lower half of her body, she will feel some revulsion in handling this part of the child's body. Each contact with the child is an opportunity for the child to experience the pleasure of intimacy or to be repulsed by the shame and fear of it. When a mother is afraid of intimacy, the child will sense the fear and interpret it as a rejection. The child of a woman who is afraid of intimacy will develop a feeling of shame about its own body.

Early deprivations of tactile experience may lead to behavior calculated to provide substitutes for such tactile deprivations in the form of self-manipulation of various kinds, masturbation and toe, finger, or thumbsucking, pulling or fingering the ears, nose, or hair. It is an interesting fact that among nonliterate peoples who generally give their children all the tactile stimulation they require, fingersucking or thumbsucking seldom occurs. Moloney, for example, writes, "My observations in Africa, Tahiti, and the islands around Tahiti, the Fiji Islands, Islands in the Carribean, Japan, Mexico and Okinawa confirmed for me the fact that most babies in these areas are breast fed and carried on the person of the mother. In these areas I noted that thumbsucking was practically non-existent."

Moloney believes that the thumb becomes a substitute for the mother, just as the pellets of paper do, which schizoid or schizophrenic children so often roll between their fingers. As Lowenfeld has put it, the fingers act like antennae or feelers which probe the surroundings for ensuing motor activities.

The oft-heard complaint directed by women at the clumsiness, crassness, and incompetence of men in their sexual approaches and in sexual intercourse itself, men's lack of skill in foreplay and their failure to understand its meaning, almost certainly substantially reflects the lack of tactile experience that many males have suffered in childhood. The roughness with which many men will handle women and children constitutes yet another evidence of their having been failed in early tactile experience, for it is difficult to conceive of anyone who had been tenderly loved and caressed in infancy not learning to approach a woman or a child with especial tenderness. The very word "tenderness" implies softness, delicacy of touch, caring for. The gorilla, that gentle creature, is the most frequently slandered animal when women wish to describe the sexual approaches of the average male. Sex seems to be regarded as a tension releaser rather than as a profoundly meaningful act of communication in a deeply involved human relationship. In many of its elements the sexual relationship reproduces the loving-mother-child relationship. As Lawrence Frank has put it,

Tactile communication in adult mating, both as foreplay and in intercourse, has been elaborated and refined by some cultures into the most amazing array of erotic patterns which through a variety of tactual stimulation of various parts of the body serve to arouse, prolong, intensify, and evoke communication. Here we see tactile communication, reinforced and elaborated by motor activities and language, by concomitant stimulation, visual, auditory, olfactory, gustatory, and the deeper muscle senses, combined to provide an organic-personality relationship which may be one of the most intense human experiences. It is, or can be, considered an esthetic experience in that there may be little or no instrumental, purposive, or cognitive elements, with greater or less loss of space-time orientation. But the elementary sexual processes of the human organism may be transformed and focused into an interpersonal love relationship with an identified person to whom each is seeking to communicate, using sex not for procreation, as in the mating of a female in heat ready to be fertilized, but as 'another language,' for interpersonal communication. Here we see how the primary tactile mode of communication, which has been largely overlaid and superseded by auditory and visual signs and symbols, is reinstated to function with elementary organic intensity, provided the individuals have not lost the capacity for communication with the self through tactile experiences.

It may well be asked, If men are affected in this manner by lack of early tactual experience, how are women affected? The answer to that question is: Much in the same manner as the women discussed earlier in this chapter, who longed to be held and cuddled. These women were affected by more or less frigidity, a condition which they could easily conceal by pretending to excitements they did not feel, or by a nymphomania which abnormally craves tactual satisfactions. Once again it must be emphasized that it is not being suggested that such conditions are entirely the results of tactual deprivations in early life, but only that they may, in part, be so.

Women have always in great numbers complained of the male's lack of tenderness sexually and in general. May not this deficiency have become rather more epidemic in the recent period as a consequence, again at least in part, of the abandonment of breastfeeding and the reduction in the tactual experiences of the child?

Many mothers early begin to reject demonstrations of love by their sons in the mistaken fear that unless they do so they will cause their sons to become too deeply attached to them. There are many fathers who reject their sons' embraces because, as one such father, a physician, remarked to me, "I don't want him to become a homosexual." The appalling ignorance revealed in such attitudes is very damaging, and would serve to reinforce the male's inability to relate himself tactually to another human being.

To be roughly handled has been considered by many women, especially women of the working classes, an indispensable evidence of love. There is, for example, the well-known feminine Cockney supplication to her man which illustrates this: "If ya loves us, chuck us abaht." The sexual element was very evident in the flagellation epidemics of medieval times, as a penance which the church at first approved and then forbade, when it realized the sensuality involved. That the participants in such flagellation episodes were more than anxious to receive the caresses of the whip suggests that a great many infants in medieval times received an inadequate amount and quality of tactile stimulation.

Slapping infants as a form of discipline or for other reasons turns the skin into an organ of pain rather than pleasure. For reasons which are not too difficult to discern, the buttocks have constituted a preferred locus for spanking the child. This region is closely related to the sexual organs, and supplied by sensory nerves which form part of the nervous plexus associated with the sexual functions. Hence spanking on the buttocks may produce distinctively erotic sensations in children, including sexual orgasm. Children have been known to misbehave deliberately in order to receive such desired "punishment," pretending to be distressed while receiving it.

Rousseau relates that when he was eight (he was actually ten) he learned to know sexual pleasure from the spankings administered by his governess, who used to lay him over her knees in order to attend to him *a posteriori*. Far from being distressed by these assaults upon his integrity, he tells how he welcomed them, and how his bed was removed from his governess's room when she became aware of the effects her punishments were having upon her charge.

Whether or not some element of perverted sadism is present in the personality of a particular discipliner, the early conditioning of the association between pain and sexual

pleasure produced by spanking may result in a permanent
pathology,* the disorder known as *algolagnia*. Algolagnia is a
condition in which pain and cruelty provoke voluptuous
sexual pleasure. It may be either active or passive. Masochis-
tic algolagnia renders the experience of pain, disgust, or humiliation one which produces sexual excitement. Sadistic
algolagnia is the opposite, making the infliction of pain,
discomfort, fear, or humiliation upon others the source of
sexual pleasure in oneself.

Spanking and slapping with the open hand in order to
punish children is still too often indulged. Inflicting pain
upon them in this manner deprives children of the comfort
the skin usually means to them; as a result, they may come to
associate their own skin and that of others with fear of contact and pain, and thus may avoid skin contacts in later life.

Quite often biting, pinching, scratching, and gripping caresses, even to the point of pain, are intermixed with normal
sexuality and are enjoyed by one or both partners. In pathological sexuality such behavior is often intensified, and the
skin becomes a dominant factor in the experience of sexual
pleasure. Flagellation, generally on the buttocks and thighs,
has been a most frequent form of sexual perversion, with
every kind of whip imaginable used for this purpose. Estab-
lishments have long existed on the continent of Europe especially, and doubtless have existed or continue to exist in
North and South America, in which the clients—for a
consideration—are all but flayed alive in the search for sexual satisfaction.

The pinching of women's buttocks by "dirty old men"

* For a good discussion of the pathological effects of spanking see J. F.
Oliver, *Sexual Hygiene and Pathology* (Philadelphia: Lippincott,
1965), pp. 63–67.

constitutes an example of a sexual perversion which society has clearly understood and found not unamusing. Interestingly enough, there are women who similarly exhibit their sexual interest in a male by pinching with such passion that it leaves him black and blue. Some women, in the midst of orgasm, will cry out to be hurt and will enjoy the pain inflicted upon them—a pain always inflicted upon and experienced through the skin. Others will indulge in "love-bites." As Van de Velde says, "Women are conspicuously more addicted to love-bites than are men. It is not at all unusual for a woman of passionate nature to leave a memento of sexual union on the man's shoulder in the shape of a little slanting oval outline of tooth-marks. The bite occurs almost without exception *during coitus* or immediately afterwards, while the generally gentler, slighter, or at least less noticeable love-bites given by the man to his partner, are part of the erotic play before, or the final stage after, coitus." In the case of the male "many blue marks or bruises on women's arms are witnesses of the man's *tourbillon*." Van de Velde believes that the feminine inclination to bite during the sexual act arises mainly from the wish to give a kiss more intense than is humanly possible. It is a wish, as it were, to make a permanent integumentary impression, the intensification of the tactile sensation. "Indeed," writes Van de Velde, "both the active and passive partner feel a peculiarly keen, erotic pleasure in the tiny, delicate, gentle or sharp but never really painful nips man and woman exchange as the love-play quickens, especially when such caresses are applied in rapid succession and in adjacent places" (p. 155). The line between the normal and the abnormal is a thin one here, a subject which has been admirably discussed by Havelock Ellis and others.

The extraordinary frequency with which individuals with

abnormalities of sexuality suffer from pathologies of the skin suggest not merely a centrifugal psychosomatic effect, but a centripetally originating one. This is evidenced by the frequency with which such individuals strive to solve their sexual conflicts by securing a close, dependable, and passive relationship to the mother or a mother surrogate. It may be postulated that failure of adequate mothering, and especially adequate communication through the skin, almost certainly occurred in the early lives of such individuals.

Scopophilia, to which reference has already been made, the pleasure in looking, may become a perversion, which is then known as *voyeurism*. The voyeurism may be restricted exclusively to the genitals, or be connected with the overriding of disgust, as in looking on excretory functions. Or instead of being preparatory to the sexual aim, it may supplant it, as in exhibitionism.

During the first year of life the association between looking at objects, touching them, and taking them into the mouth is a closely linked one. The association between looking and touching is especially closely connected. The experiences of urination and defecation are pleasantly relieving ones and warming. If, however, the oral needs are unsatisfactorily satisfied, and come to be characterized by greed, hunger, insatiety, with fears of the ensuing hostile aspects of these processes, the visual functions may come to have a similar compulsive, devouring quality, and later tend to be defended by complex inhibitory systems of various sorts. Instead of libidinal oral, anal, tactile, and visual functions being harmoniously integrated, these functions become anarchically and dysfunctionally associated. Thus, looking comes to replace normal sexual outlets as in scopophilia, as does touching, often in abnormal ways such as pinching, scratching, or biting, with or without the accompanying desire to inflict pain, or the various forms of exhibitionism. Women do not usually expose the genital region in exhibitionism, but they will expose breasts or buttocks. This, of course, they have done, with the vagaries of fashion, quite normally for millennia. Exposure of the breasts in ancient Crete was customary, and at various periods in the Western world, devices drawing attention to the breasts as well as to the buttocks have been the vogue. But what appears to be the boldest attempt of all, the attempt to draw attention to the external genitalia, namely, the miniskirt, is a development of the 1960's. Topless dresses have not become the fashion, but see-through dresses have gained a limited popularity.

These phenomena, however, are not in any sense pathological evidences of sexual disturbance. What they are evidence of is the expression of the need for love; and since love and sex have come to be identified in the Western world, sexual attractiveness becomes a means of achieving "love." In this manner love establishes itself as "skin-deep." The more skin she exposes the more loveable the female becomes. This kind of scopophilia has become normal for most males in the Western world who, upon the perception of a female possessing the proper curvilinear properties will phototropically migrate in her direction. Hence the emphasis upon nudity. In such cases it is not so much skin as sex that is involved. The true exhibitionist, however, may be an extreme prude insofar as nudity is concerned, and may never allow either himself or his wife to see the other in the nude. Puritanical attitudes of this kind are well known to be characteristic of the families of exhibitionists. In such families cutaneous as well as related deprivations are common throughout childhood.

The motivations of strippers appear to confirm our views. Skipper and McCaghy studied thirty-five strippers, and found that some 60 percent came from broken or unstable homes in which the father was in some way inadequate. Lacking the strong response from a father, these girls had to settle for substitutes. In baring their bodies strippers may be merely asking for the attention and affection denied them by their fathers. The girls in this study estimated that between 50 and 75 percent of strippers are lesbians. This fact further tends to confirm the view the the stripper still nurses the feeling of paternal rejection she suffered in childhood.

SEX DIFFERENCES IN TACTUALITY. The female, at all ages, appears to be very much more responsive to tactile stimuli than the male, and more dependent upon touch for erotic arousal than the male, who depends more upon visual stimuli. The difference seems to be, at least in part genetic, but cultural differences undoubtedly also play a significant role in the development of tactual responsiveness as between the sexes.

Tactile stimulation is much more meaningful to females than it is to males. As Fritz Kahn says, bodily contact is to a woman an act of great intimacy and a far-reaching concession. Hence, a woman who refuses intimate connection with a man is roused to indignation if he touches her against her will, and repulses him with the memorable words, "How dare you touch me!"

SEX DIFFERENCES IN TACTILE EXPERIENCES. With the exception of the United States, there is little information of any value available relating to the differences between civilized societies, in the tactile experience to which each of the sexes is exposed. Margaret Mead has drawn attention to the fact that

American mothers tend to be closer to their daughters than to their sons, an observation that has been confirmed by the findings of a number of investigators. Erikson draws a picture, based on his clinical experience, of the American mother as one who in her son's "early childhood . . . deliberately understimulated him sexually and emotionally," with "a certain determined lack of maternalism." Sears and Maccoby, in their retrospective study of child-rearing patterns in the United States, found that baby girls received more demonstrations of affection than boys, and that mothers seemed to be happier about having girl babies than they were about having boy babies. It was also found, as in the Fischers' study of a New England town, that girls were weaned later than boys, suggesting that the later weaning indicated a more indulgent attitude towards girls. Clay, in her study of American mother-infant tactile interactions, also found that female children received more tactile stimulation than male children.

Perhaps this difference in tactile experience, at least in part, accounts for the American female being so much less uptight about tactuality than the American male.

SIX

*Man is a growing animal, and his
birthright is development.*—ANON

GROWTH
AND DEVELOPMENT

GROWTH is increase in dimension. Development is increase
in complexity. What role, if any, does tactile experience play
in the growth and development of the organism? The evidence, both for animals in general and man in particular, is
unequivocally clear: tactile experience plays a fundamentally
important role in the growth and development of all mammals thus far studied, and probably also in non-mammals.

Lawrence Casler has drawn attention to the fact that the
ill effects of maternal deprivation so ably discussed by
Bowlby and others are probably the result of perceptual deprivations, principally tactile, visual, and probably vestibular. (The vestibule is the central part of the inner ear connecting in front with the cochlea, the essential organ of

hearing, and above and behind with the semicircular canals, which give us our sense of balance.) This seems most likely to be the case. When we have learned appreciably more than we know at present concerning the components of maternal love, we shall undoubtedly be able to describe it as a function of biochemical, physiological, kinesic, tactile, visual, auditory, and other factors. From observations made on nonhuman animals we may gain some insight into the manner in which tactile experience, with which we are here mainly concerned, may affect the growth and development of man. So we will begin with a discussion of the findings on animals other than man, and then proceed to the evidence for the effects of tactile experience upon man himself.

THE EVIDENCE FROM OTHER ANIMALS. In a series of experiments carried out by Dr. John D. Benjamin of the University of Colorado Medical School, one group of twenty laboratory rats, supplied with exactly the same kinds and amounts of food and living conditions, were caressed and cuddled by the investigator, while the other group was treated coldly. "It sounds silly," one investigator is reported to have remarked, "but the petted rats learned faster and grew faster."

Far from sounding silly, this is exactly what we would expect. The living organism depends to a very large extent upon the stimulation of the external world for its growth and development. Those stimuli must for the most part be pleasurable ones, just as they must be in learning. Hence, as we would expect, animals that have been handled in infancy later tend to be less emotional in open field tests, showing less defecation and urination, and more willingness to explore a strange environment, than those animals who have not been handled in the pre-weaning period. Also they are better able to learn a conditioned avoidance response. Handling before weaning also results in a heavier weight of the brain, and in greater development of the cortex and subcortex. More cholesterol and cholinesterase have been found in the brains of gentled rats than ungentled ones, thus indicating a more advanced stage of neural development, especially in the formation of myelin sheaths.

Gentled rats show greater liveliness, curiosity, and problem-solving ability than ungentled rats. They also tend to be more dominant than ungentled rats.

Skeletal and body growth are more advanced in gentled than in ungentled control rats, food is better utilized, and we have cited the evidence earlier, showing that gentled experimental animals show less emotionality in stressful situations.* Attention has also already been drawn to the fact that gentled animals show, as adults, a more efficiently developed immunological system than rats that have been ungentled in infancy. This is a really quite remarkable finding. How this works is at present unknown, but it has been suggested that environmentally responsive hormones may affect the development of thymic function, which plays a significant role in the establishment of immunologic competency. The hypothalamus, which is known to play a role in the regulation of immunity, may also play a role here.

Gentling leads to more rapid maturation of the pituitary-adrenal axis, that is to say, the alarm-reaction system of the body. Rats so gentled in infancy recover from electroconvulsive shock highly significantly more effectively than ungentled rats.

We would expect that early tactile stimulation would in

* See pp. 25–27.

most respects be more important than later tactile stimulation in the development of the organism, and this, indeed, is experimentally found to be the case. Thus, Levene found that handled rats exhibited greater emotional stability, as measured by excretory activity, general activity, and so forth, than nonhandled rats. Furthermore, extra-handled rats, those receiving more than ordinary handling, are better at learning and retention than ordinarily handled or unhandled rats.

While there can be little doubt that genetic factors enter into the structure of the behavior with which animals respond to handling or gentling, the evidence is unequivocally clear that all animals respond favorably to handling or gentling, and respond more effectively to whatever tests or trials they are put to than animals which have not undergone such tactile experience. Urie Bronfenbrenner has summed up the findings very well. "First, the effects are generally salutary for the organism both physiologically and psychologically. Thus, handling has been shown to enhance the organism's later capacity to withstand stress, its general activity level, and its learning ability. Second, the presence or absence of handling has its maximal impact during the first ten days of life, although significant effects have been reported for animals handled as late as fifty days of age."

On the organismic level, growth and development are controlled by endocrine and neural factors. It is well known that emotional factors are capable of influencing the growth and development of the organism, principally through the differential action of hormones. Animals that have enjoyed adequate tactile experiences will respond very differently from those who have been failed in such experiences. The differences will be measurable, emotionally, in neural, glandular, biochemical, muscular, and cutaneous changes. Such differences have been measured in handled and nonhandled animals, and the findings have been in the expected direction, namely that in all these respects the handled animals are more advanced than the nonhandled animals.

The inadequately gentled animal, we may, I believe, safely assume, is an emotionally unsatisfied creature. The satisfaction of tactile needs has not hitherto been considered a basic need, a basic need being defined as one which must be satisfied if the organism is to survive. But the fact is that the need for tactuality *is* a basic need, since it must be satisfied if the organism is to survive. With complete cessation of skin stimulation the organism would die. An organism deprived of its skin cannot live. What we are, of course, generally concerned with is quality, quantity, frequency, and critical periods when the organism must receive certain amounts and qualities of tactile stimulation, rather than with all-or-none considerations. And what the evidence abundantly indicates is that there are critical periods in the development of every organism possessing a skin during which that outer integument must receive sufficient stimulation if the organism is to develop in a healthy manner.

The pre-weaning period, whenever that may occur, is critically important here, for the new complexities of existence introduced into the life of the newborn and neonate confront it with the kind of insecurities that the beetle placed on its back experiences when its feet lose contact with the earth. The infant wants tangible evidence of security, the experience of reassuring contacts with another body.

THE EVIDENCE IN INFANTS. The early development of the nervous system of the infant is to a major extent dependent upon the kind of cutaneous stimulation it receives. There can be no doubt that tactile stimulation is necessary for its healthy development. As Clay says:

The need for peripheral skin stimulation and contact exists throughout life, but it appears to be most intense and crucial in the early phase of reflex attachment. Ribble goes so far as to say that the nervous system of the infant requires some sort of stimulus feeding at this early period. Certainly the young child needs an optimum period for the gratification of his sensual needs, which are both oral and tactile. This is why the preverbal years are considered a critical period for tactile learning. From this time on the needs for tactile contact decline, but tactile stimulation must still be age-graded according to the developmental needs of the human organism.

The evidence indicates clearly that the skin is the primary sense organ of the human infant, and that during its reflex attachment period it is its tactile experience that is critical for its continued growth and development. This may be seen in a variety of ways, but most particularly in the growth and development of tactile sensitivity in the infant receiving an adequate amount of tactile stimulation as compared with the infant who has received an inadequate amount.

There is every reason to believe that, just as the salamander's brain and nervous system develops more fully in response to peripheral stimulation, so does the brain and nervous system of the human being.

Yarrow, in an investigation of the effects of early maternal care on babies, states that perhaps the most striking finding was the extent to which developmental progress during the first six months appeared to be influenced by maternal stimulation. The amount of stimulation and the quality of stimulation were highly correlated with maternal I.Q. "These data suggest," writes Yarrow, "that mothers who give much and intense stimulation and encouragement to practice developmental skills tend to be successful in producing infants who make rapid developmental progress." The conclusion is reinforced, suggests Yarrow, that in institutions it is stimulus deprivation in early infancy that is a causative factor in developmental retardation.

Yarrow also reports on several children who, as a consequence of contact failures in infancy, reacted with disturbances in tactility to any difficulty in the mother-child relationship.

Province and Lipton, comparing seventy-five institutionalized infants with seventy-five infants reared in families, found that institutionalized infants reacted peculiarly to being held, engaged in much rocking behavior, and were usually quiet and slept excessively. "They did not adapt their bodies well to the arms of the adults, they were not cuddly, and one noted a lack in pliability. . . . They felt something like sawdust dolls; they moved, they bent easily at the proper joints, but they felt stiff or wooden." By the age of five to six months rocking appeared in most infants and by eight months was present in all of them. Province and Lipton distinguish four types of rocking: (1) a transient rocking as a normal reaction to frustration; (2) rocking as an autoerotic activity in children who have suffered some degree of maternal deprivation; (3) rocking as withdrawal of attention and extreme preoccupation in children suffering from infantile psychoses; and (4) rocking which serves the purpose of discharge or self-stimulation.

Shevrin and Toussieng of the Menninger Clinic, observing the disturbed tactile behavior of their juvenile patients, postulated the existence of a need for optimum tactile stimulation in early infancy, which had somehow been denied them. "Such major disturbances were found," they write, "in the history of all the children we have studied thus far." When infants receive too little or too much tactile stimulation, according to these investigators, conflicts are generated which interfere seriously with psychic development. The course of these conflicts can be traced in the thoughts and actions of severely disturbed children of all ages. The main way these children cope with tactile conflicts is not by repression or other psychic defenses. It is either by a defensive raising of thresholds for all stimuli emanating from the environment or from inside the body, or through protective fluctuations in the physical distance between themselves and other people. The fantasy productions of these children yield strong evidence of the conflict, which usually assumes the form of an elaborate denial of the need for closeness. But in spite of this the need for tactile stimulation persists. Shevrin and Toussieng hypothesize that certain rhythmic behavior, such as rocking, is used to prevent a total loss of tactile stimulation resulting from excessive raising of thresholds.

The infant's need for body contact is compelling. If that need is not adequately satisfied, even though all other needs are adequately met, it will suffer. Because the consequences of the lack of satisfaction of such basic needs as hunger, thirst, rest, sleep, bowel and bladder elimination, and avoidance of dangerous and painful stimuli are fairly obvious, we are conscious of the importance of satisfying them. In the case of the tactile needs the consequences of failing to satisfy them are far from obvious, and so these needs have been mostly overlooked. It is important that we begin to understand how necessary it is for the healthy growth and development of the child that its tactile needs be adequately satisfied.

We do not have much evidence of a direct kind that tactile stimulation or its absence affects the growth and development, physical or psychological, of the human infant. Such direct evidence is largely lacking for the simple reason that it has never been sought in man. We do, however, have as we have seen, plenty of direct evidence of this sort for nonhuman animals. Also, we have a great deal of direct evidence in human infants which thoroughly supports the extrapolation that tactile stimulation is at least as important in the physical and psychological growth of the human infant as it is in the nonhuman infant.

The failure to satisfy tactile needs in the human infant shows how damaging such deprivations can be, and how important such early satisfactions are.

The maternal deprivation syndrome, consisting of the effects of a minimum amount of mothering, unquestionably involves substantial tactile deprivations, among others. It is an interesting fact that almost invariably the skin of such children, instead of exhibiting the roseate firm character of the healthy infant, shows instead a deep pallor and loss of tone, as well as, usually, various disorders of the skin.

Patton and Gardner have published detailed records of children who had been maternally deprived and shown how severely their physical as well as their mental growth had been disturbed, a three-year old child's bone growth in such a maternally deprived situation being just half that of the bone growth of a normal child. Emotionally deprived children everywhere suffer serious retardations in growth, both physical and behavioral. The literature on this subject is now extensive.

It has been demonstrated that children who are emotionally disturbed as a result of an unfavorable home environment tend to suffer from hypopituitarism, with deficiencies in ACTH and growth hormone the commonest defects, associated with short stature. When such children are removed to favorable environments they show a spectacular increase in growth and the development of normal growth hormone secretion.

The physiological mechanisms involved in tactile deprivation appear to be clearly related to those involved in maternal deprivation and emotional disturbances in whatever way induced. All these mechanisms add up to the one complex series of processes expressed in the word *shock*.

The process of birth represents a prolonged series of shocks which every infant experiences, and nothing exists more powerfully calculated to assuage the effect of those shocks than the fondling and nursing the mother is designed to give the child as immediately after its birth as possible. When afforded such reassurance through the skin, the effects of the shock of birth are gradually mitigated. But if the infant is not afforded such an alleviation of his shock, the effects of that shock will continue, and will more or less affect his subsequent growth and development.

Today we know a great deal more about the nature of shock and its effects than was the case only a few years ago. Indeed, we are today in a position to discuss the nature of shock on a cellular level.

Essentially shock is a molecular disorder producing metabolic derangements revolving around aerobic glucose metabolism, resulting in increased amounts of lactic acid which greatly contribute to anxiety, and the production of amino acids, fatty acids, and phosphoric acids. The deficient metabolism of acids produces disruption in the membranes of the sacs of digestive and lytic enzymes known as lysosomes, with resulting death of the cell. The energy upon which the cell is dependent, ATP (adenosine triphosphate) is decreased, with a consequent derangement of protein synthesis and cell membrane pump function. The derangement in protein synthesis interferes with growth and the ability to withstand shock, and the derangement in cell pump function results in swelling.* The circulation tends to slow down, blood pressure falls, red blood cells tend to agglutinate, oxygen supply to the tissues of the body is reduced, there is a general wasting away, until the heart stops and the brain is no longer excited. This is, of course, the extreme end-effect of unrelieved shock; it is, however, very likely that all these processes occur to some extent in varying degrees in infants receiving inadequate cutaneous stimulation. And, just as in shock, the process is usually reversible by the use of blood volume, antacids, oxygen, corticosteroids, vasodilators, and energy production solutions like glucose, potassium, and insulin, so the consequences of inadequate cutaneous stimulation in the infant can be reversed by giving him all the tender, loving care he needs, principally in the form of what he best and most immediately understands: warm, fondling, embracing tactuality. The effects upon the infant of such satisfactions of his tactile needs are remarkable.

Temerlin and co-workers, in a study of thirty-two nonverbal retarded males of a median age of nine years, found that the children who received active mothering and maximum skin contact made significantly higher weight gains during the period of the experiment than the subjects in the control groups.

* For a detailed discussion see W. Schumer and R. Sperling, "Shock and Its Effect on the Cell," *Journal of the American Medical Association,* vol. 205 (1968), pp. 215–19.

WHAT THE INFANT FEELS. In fullterm infants pain and touch are not well differentiated. McGraw remarks, "When only a few hours or days old some infants exhibit no overt response to cutaneous irritation such as pinprick. It is impossible to know whether such absence of response should be attributed to an undeveloped sensory mechanism or to lack of connection between sensory and somatic centers, or between receptor centers and those mechanisms governing crying. Such infants usually do respond to deep pressure stimulation. In any event, this period of hypaesthesia is brief; by the end of the first week or ten days most infants respond to cutaneous irritation."

The relative insensibility of the newborn to cutaneous stimulation has been noted by many investigators.

With growth the number of sensory receptors increase in the skin over a wider area and in close proximity. Part of the newborn's reduced sensibility may be due, as Greenacre suggests, to sensory birth fatigue.

At first the infant's tactile sense is very generalized; it acts as a mass effect rather than as a sharply discriminating critical point effect. Touch and pain are not well differentiated, and the development of critical discrimination of tactile stimuli follows much the same path as the development of returning sensation after a nerve has been cut, the physiology of which Henry Head, the distinguished English neurologist, described in some detail. As sensation begins to return it is experienced in a very generalized way; this is termed *protopathic* sensation. The touch which at first is only distinguishable for the area in general, in time becomes more localized, more critical, so that one can locate it exactly; this Henry Head termed *epicritic*. At first the newborn's tactile sense is largely protopathic; only gradually does it develop the epicritic ability which enables it to localize the point of the stimulus precisely.

It is only between seven and nine months of age, approximately, that specific localization really begins to develop, and becomes well established by between twelve and sixteen months.

Infants probably differ in skin sensitivity. As Escalona has said, "There can be no doubt that something like skin awareness, or sensations of the kind generated by the skin, are sharp and frequent throughout the day for some babies and less intense for others." And she goes on to point out that just such skin-sensitive babies will receive an inordinate amount of attention and handling. Such babies tend to receive a considerable amount of tactile stimulation for the greater part of their waking and half-waking hours. In the Western world it is perhaps a great advantage for an infant to have a sensitive skin or diaper-rashes or some other dermatological disorder, for then, at least, it can be assured of receiving an adequate amount of cutaneous stimulation. Ribble believes that diapering, at least in America, is "invariably overdone." She considers that the desire to keep the baby dry in the first months is misplaced, "except for the comfort of the adults handling the child." And she adds that the frequent diaper-changing may focus the child's attention on this area, "and thus foster later emotional reactions which become deeply involved with the function of elimination." In many cases this may well be so. Escalona points out that there are extraordinary differences in the amount and kind of tactile stimulation to which babies are exposed, and that "the baby's life is largely a succession of sharply felt touches, sounds, sights, movements, temperatures, and the like" (p. 19).

Escalona's reference to "sharply felt touches" almost certainly does not accurately describe what the newborn and young infant feels. The evidence, on the other hand, indicates that the baby tends to feel rather more protopathically than epicritically, and only gradually learns to discriminate discrete point sensations. It would seem to be an admirably adaptive provision that the baby should not at first feel "sharply," but for the most part only in a generalized way, for it is such a general rather than a "sharp" or specific sensing of assurance that he requires in his early days. Not that the infant is incapable of discriminating and localizing discrete point sensations. This he is undoubtedly able to do, but almost certainly in most cases not "sharply." It is on the foundation of his generalized tactile experience that he subsequently learns and refines the sharply felt touches, sounds, sights, movements, temperatures, and the like, into specific, recognizably distinctive and meaningful modalities.

More than three hundred years ago Thomas Hobbes wrote, "For there is no conception in man's mind, which hath not first been begotten upon the organs of Sense." The shape and form and space of the outer world of reality, its figures and the background from which they emerge are gradually built by the infant out of the building blocks of its experience, entering through all its senses, always contingent, correlated, measured, and evaluated by the criterion of touch. If this object that holds me so pleasurably does so long and consistently enough I come to identify her face and eventually all its tangibly visible parts with pleasure. It is, however, my skin which primarily tells me that this face is pleasure giving, since, as a baby, it is only through the skin that I can make that judgment. And so it is with all the other sensations I experience.

How does this sensation, whatever it is, "feel"? Since the

various senses are really skin receptors of different sorts, the eyes and ears and nose and certainly the tongue, at first "feel" rather than see, hear, smell, and taste. As soon as he is able, the baby will put to the test whatever he can, by putting it into his mouth, and what he there feels with hand and mouth will tell him what he desires to know. Gradually he will come to increase the distance between what he tactually feels and what he experiences through the other senses, until he is eventually able to recognize each experience or object as separate and distinct from others, and by its own attributes rather than by reference to the verdict of the skin.

As Sylvester has stated, "The mother's sensitivity and selectivity of response facilitates the transition from prevalent orientation by close receptors to orientation by distance receptors. In the earliest stages, the infant's security is a matter of skin contact and kinesthetic sensations of being held and supported. Later, security is derived also from orientation by sight and sound and from the infant's ability to maintain contact with his mother through these perceptive modalities." Sometimes, Sylvester goes on to say, the infant continues to depend upon skin contact, and fails to develop the ability to use sight and sound for orientation and communication. This can occur because of "primary maternal attitudes," or as the result of conditions leading to increased skin sensitization (such as infantile eczema, or the loss or absence of other sensory organs). Often, according to Sylvester, the beginnings of "habitual defects in orientation or body image" can be traced to such early difficulties.

The mother mutually adapted to her child will respond in rhythm to her child's needs. Her flexibility will reflect itself in the child's perceptual development. The mother, as the main source of the infant's ebb and flow of incoming stimuli,

is thereby also the main source of his comfort and the per-
former of the tasks that will later be assumed by his ego. According to Sylvester, "if a mother prevents her child from
regulating approach and retreat autonomously, he may react
to threats by drawing closer to or by taking flight from inanimate objects. It is possible that such enforced substitution
of gadgets for people is one of the roots of human mechanization."

"From his first day onward," writes Escalona, "the baby is
reacted to and himself reacts to other persons. The nature of
these contacts, more frequent, varied, and complex the older
he gets, is perhaps the single most important determinant of
how he shall experience his world and of the kind of human
relationships which he will be able to have as he grows up"
(p. 33).

The infant will develop a sense of trust or mistrust depending upon his sensory impression, received mainly
through the skin, whether gratifying or not. The infant's
sense of space, time, and reality are all of a piece, being experienced first as whatever is durably gratifying, then as what
is perceptually meaningful, and later as events which can be
anticipated. Chronologic time remains meaningless until
much later in the infant's development. The earliest steps in
the development of mastery of time and space have been
imagined by Escalona to be something like this:

At first, the world is a succession of different sensations and feeling states. What varies is the quality and distribution and intensity of sensations. Except for the difference in the nature of the
sensations involved, hunger, which we say originates from within,
and a sharp sound or cold breeze, which we cannot imagine except as something that reaches us from outside, are indistinguishable. There is no awareness of such things as approach,
withdrawal, or direction of any sort. Even if the baby turns his

head toward the nipple and grasps it, his sensation is that the
nipple comes or is; no other state with which to contrast this exists. Light and darkness; harshness and softness; cold and
warmth; sleep and waking; the contours of mother's face as seen
from below, vis-à-vis, or even from above; being grasped and released; being moved and moving; the sight of moving people, cur-
tains, blankets, toys; all these recede and approach and comprise
the totality of experience in whatever constellation they occur at
each split second in time. With recurrence, there develop islands
of consistency. For instance, a certain way of being grasped, certain kinesthetic sensations, and the change in visual environment
afforded by the vertical position combine into an awareness of
being lifted, being moved, as an entity.

The importance of recurring experiences of the same kind
is of the essence of this developmental process, and Escalona
believes that such "islands of consistency," with a definite
rhythm and sameness to them, in respect to such important
experiences as feeding and bathing, may enable infants to acquire a sense of themselves as entities to whom things happen and who can make things happen. "The one who is not
held, moved about, and rocked is less likely to become aware
of himself through the sensation of passive motion and less
likely to recognize his mother's characteristic touch and
tempo" (p. 26).

The infant is at first not only lacking in psychic structure
but also in psychic and somatic boundaries. He is unable to
distinguish between inside and outside, between "I" and
"not-I" ; in brief, he is in a state of psychic nondifferen-
tiation. In this stage the primary identifications he makes are
with his need gratifications as part of his own body. And, as
Spitz points out, primary identification is made difficult by
mothers who withhold from their children the need gratification inherent in being touched.

They extensively restrict the occasions for primary identification through withholding tactile experiences. Yet, if the infant is to differentiate himself from his mother, these primary identifications, tactile and otherwise, have to be dealt with, severed and overcome. Action-directed motility first, and locomotion later, are the child's devices for dealing with primary identification and achieving differentiation. When differentiation from the mother has been accomplished, the infant can form those secondary identifications which pave the way to autonomy and independence.

Tennyson, in his magnificent elegiac poem, *In Memoriam,* refers to the process of individuation, which he clearly fully understood. Though published in 1850, the poem was written much earlier.

> *The baby new to earth and sky*
> *What time his tender palm is prest*
> *Against the circle of the breast,*
> *Has never thought that "this is I."*
>
> *But as he grows he gathers much,*
> *And learns the use of "I" and "me,"*
> *And finds "I am not what I see,*
> *And other than the things I touch."*
>
> *So rounds he to a separate mind*
> *From whence clear memory may begin,*
> *As thro' the frame that binds him in*
> *As isolation grows defined.*
>
> *This use may lie in blood and breath,*
> *Which else were fruitless of their due,*
> *Had man to learn himself anew*
> *Beyond the second birth of Death.*   [XLV]

The process of what Mahler has called individuation-separation leads to individuation through secondary identifications. By taking over the mother's techniques of caring for him through identification with them the infant makes the first steps toward ego-formation, the stage of secondary identification, beginning in the second half of the first year. In this stage the infant acquires the techniques and devices by means of which he achieves independence from his mother. In these first six months tactile experiences are fundamental in the development of the stage of primary identification and the mechanism of secondary identification.

Erasmus Darwin, in his *Zoonomia*, published in 1794, had arrived at much the same conclusion. He wrote:

The first ideas we become acquainted with, are those of the sense of touch; for the foetus must experience some varieties of agitation, and exert some muscular action, in the womb; and may with great probability be supposed thus to gain some ideas of its own figure, of that of the uterus, and of the tenacity of the fluid, that surrounds it . . .

Many of the organs of sense are confined to a small part of the body, as the nostrils, ear, or eye, whilst the sense of touch is diffused over the whole skin, but exists with a more exquisite degree of delicacy at the extremities of the fingers and thumbs, and in the lips. The sense of touch is thus very commodiously disposed for the purpose of encompassing smaller bodies, and for adapting itself to the inequalities of larger ones. The figure of small bodies seem to be learnt by children by their lips as much as by their fingers; on which account they put every new object to their mouths, when they are satiated with food, as well as when they are hungry. And puppies seem to learn their ideas of figure principally by the lips in their mode of play.

We acquire our tangible ideas of objects either by the simple pressure of this organ of touch against a solid body, or by moving our organ of touch along the surface of it. In the former case we learn the length and breadth of the objects by the continuance of this pressure on our moving organ of touch.

It is hence, that we are very slow in acquiring our tangible ideas, and very slow in recollecting them; for if I now think of the tangible idea of a cube, that is, if I think of its figure, and the solidity of every part of that figure, I must conceive myself as passing my fingers over it, and seem in some measure to feel the idea, as I formerly did the impression at the ends of them, and thus am very slow in distinctly recollecting.

The modalities of space, time, and reality, shape, form, depth, quality, texture, and the like, are almost certainly developed in large part on the basis of the infant's tactile experiences. As Escalona has put it,

Awareness of the body in space, and of space surrounding the self must come about in a thousand ways. As the baby's legs kick and stretch, the pressure of the diaper increases, his feet contact the blanket, gown, or end of the crib. As he flails his arms, he encounters the side of the crib, nothing, the surface on which he lies, or portions of his own body. As he is lifted, he temporarily feels the absence of contact with anything firm except the part of the body where his mother is grasping him. Simultaneously, kinesthetic sensations are quite different from before, the contours and range of his visual field change strangely as he is brought to the vertical position. It is at about the time when visual coordination and focusing occur more easily that purposive body movement begins to emerge.

As we shall see in the next chapter, the differences in the kinds of cutaneous experiences to which children are exposed, within one culture and cross-culturally, make very significant differences in the rates at which they mature and the ways in which they relate to their fellows.

Landauer and Whiting have produced some interesting evidence suggesting that the handling which results in increase in size in rodents, as a consequence, they assume, of stress effects, is similarly operative in the human species. In order to throw some light on this matter they studied cross-culturally the relation between apparently stressful infant care practices and the stature of adult males in some eighty different societies for which appropriate information was available. The stresses they studied were:

1. *Piercing:* Nose, lips, circumcision, infibulation, etc.
2. *Molding:* Stretching arms, legs, shaping head, etc.
3. *External:* Heat, hot baths, fire, intense sunlight, etc.
4. *Extreme cold:* Baths, exposure to snow, cold, etc.
5. *Internal stressors:* Emotions, irritants, enemas
6. *Abrasions:* Rubbing with sand, etc.
7. *Intense sensory stimulation*
8. *Binding:* Swaddling

Upon analysis it was found that "In societies in which the heads or limbs of infants were repeatedly molded or stretched, or where their ears, noses, or lips were pierced, where they were circumcised, vaccinated, inoculated, or had tribal marks cut or burned in their skin, the mean adult male stature was over two inches greater than in societies where these customs were not practiced."

Here the question may well be raised as to the difference between "handling" and "gentling." Most investigators have interpreted "handling" to signify the equivalent of a stressful experience, while "gentling" has been regarded as a comforting, reassuring experience for the animal exposed to it. The practices used as criteria by Landauer and Whiting were undoubtedly largely stressful. There remains, however, the very real question whether they were not in part also pleasurable. The practices which these investigators found most significantly correlated with increased growth are for the most part associated with elevations in status, the passage from one grade into another, greater attractiveness, and therefore greater self-esteem. Thus, whether as a direct or an indirect result of the stressful tactile experience, the subsequent pleasurable rewards of these operations are very considerable. In numberless societies the decoration of the skin by incision, puncture, the rubbing of dirt in the wounds, tattooing, and the like, though painful, has nevertheless been voluntarily sought for its rewarding end-effects. Even in rodents who have been handled, reward is not missing, for the release unharmed from the handling to the freedom of the cage must be considered to constitute a reward. In human beings the combination of the stressful cutaneous experience with the highly rewarding experiences which follow probably constitutes a factor in the observed increase in growth.

Physiologically, the involvement of the sympathetico-adrenal axis, with added secretion of pituitary growth hormone, in the colligation of conditions described, would be sufficient to explain the results observed.

Developmental abnormalities which are thought to be the direct result of lack of adequate contacts with the maternal figure often express themselves in reactive skin disorders. As Flanders Dunbar put it, in summarizing the evidence, "It may well be said that the skin, like other sense organs, is likely to become sick when contact of the sufferer with his parents and with the outside world has been disturbed at an early age, and it appears that many skin disorders are relieved when emotional contact with the outer world is improved." Many skin sufferers have experienced early prohibitions of tactile expression and experience. D. W. Winnicott says, "The smallest skin lesion, if it concerns the feelings, concerns the whole body. Prohibitions relative to tactile experience are those in the area of: 'No, no; don't touch!', and, by way of corollary, 'Don't let yourself be touched.' " *Noli me tangere*. Because the skin is the organ of embrace and contact, many skin disorders can be understood as the expression of ambivalence relating to such intimate tactual experience.

Since tactile communication is essentially an interactional process, from the first contact with the hands of the person who has delivered the baby to the contact with the mother's body, any significant failure in the experience of such contacts may lead to a profound failure or disorder in later interactional relationships, which may sometimes express itself in schizophrenia, as well as in a variety of other behavioral disorders, not to mention such respiratory disorders as asthma and the like.

Alexander Lowen has written the best account of the failure of early tactile experience and its relationship to schizophrenia in his book, *The Betrayal of the Body*. Based on the clinical study of many schizophrenics, Lowen shows that the feeling of identity arises from a feeling of contact with the body. To know who one is, the person must be aware of what he feels. This is precisely what is wanting in the schizophrenic. There is a complete loss of body contact to such an extent that, broadly speaking, the schizophrenic doesn't know who he is. He is out of touch with reality. He is aware that he has a body, and is therefore oriented in time and space. "But since his ego is not identified with his body and does not perceive it in an alive way, he feels unrelated to the world and to people. Similarly, his conscious sense of identity is unrelated to the way he feels about himself." There is a dissociation between image and reality in the schizoid state. The healthy person has an image of himself which agrees with the way he feels and looks, for normally images derive their reality from association with feeling and sensation. Loss of touch with the body results in loss of touch with reality. Personal identity has substance and structure only insofar as it is based on the reality of bodily feeling.

The fundamental trauma of the schizoid personality, Lowen states, is the absence of pleasurable physical intimacy between mother and child. "The lack of erotic body contact is experienced by the child as abandonment. If the child's demands for this contact are not met with a warm response, it will grow up with the feeling that no one cares" (pp. 105–106). In order to cut off unpleasant feelings and sensations, the child will hold his breath, suck in his belly, and immobilize his diaphragm. He will lie very still to avoid being afraid. In short, he will "deaden" his body in order not to feel pain, and by these means abandon reality. By such dissociation, especially when fear of the body becomes unendurably terrifying, the ego dissociates from the body, completely splitting the personality into two contradictory identities. One of these identities is based on the body, the other is based on the ego image.

As Otto Fenichel has pointed out, "A lack of emotions which is due not to mere repression but to real loss of contact with the objective world gives the observer a specific impression of 'queerness.'" Sometimes these individuals "seem normal because they have succeeded in substituting 'pseudo contacts' of manifold kinds for a real feeling contact with other people; they behave 'as if' they had feeling relations with people." And as Lowen adds, pseudo contacts often take the form of words, which serve as substitutes for touch. Another form of pseudo contact is role playing, which serves as a stand-in for emotional involvement. The main complaint of the schizoid personality is that, as Herbert Weiner puts it, he is unable to feel any emotions; he is estranged from others, withdrawn, and detached.

Involvement and identity become established by involvement and identification between mother and infant, and this mainly through touch. Tactile failure in infancy results only too often in estrangement, uninvolvement, lack of identity, detachment, emotional shallowness, and indifference—all marks of the schizoid or schizophrenic personality.

In the matter of allergic disorders, Dr. Maurice J. Rosenthal made a direct test of the "thesis that eczema arises in certain predisposed infants because they fail to obtain from their mother or mother-substitute adequate physical soothing contact (caressing and cuddling)." Towards this end he investigated twenty-five mothers with children under two years of age suffering from eczema, and found that, indeed, the hypothesis he set out to test was abundantly confirmed. The majority of these infants had mothers who had failed to give them an adequate amount of cutaneous contact.

In discussing a case of infantile eczema, Spitz raises an interesting question. "We might ask ourselves," he writes, "whether this cutaneous reaction represents an adaptive effort, or alternatively, a defense. The child's reaction could be in the nature of a demand addressed to the mother to incite her to touch him more frequently. It could also be a form of narcisstic withdrawal, in the sense that through the eczema the child would be giving himself the stimuli in the somatic sphere which his mother denies him. We do not know."

Cheek patting, hair patting, and chucking under the chin are, in the Western world, forms of behavior indicating affection, and all are tactile.

The "laying on of Hands," "the King's touch," for the cure

of specific diseases like scrofula, "the King's evil," was widely practiced, and often very effective.

The use of the skin as a tension-reliever takes many forms, perhaps the most familiar in Western cultures being head scratching in men. Women do not usually behave in this manner; indeed, the sexual differences in the use of the skin are marked. In states of perplexity men will rub their chins with their hand, or tug at the lobes of their ears, or rub their forehead or cheeks or back of the neck. Women have very different gestures in such states. They will either put a finger on their lower front teeth with the mouth slightly open or pose a finger under the chin. Other masculine gestures in states of perplexity are: rubbing one's nose, placing the flexed fingers over the mouth, rubbing the side of the neck, rubbing the infraorbital part of the face, rubbing the closed eyes, and picking the nose. These are all masculine gestures; so is rubbing the back of the hand or the front of the thigh, and pursing of the lips.

These all appear to be self-comforting gestures, designed to relieve or reduce the tension. Similarly, in states of alarm or grief the wringing of hands, the holding on to oneself by clasping or grasping one's hands is comforting. In ancient Greece it was customary, and is still so in much of Asia, to carry a smooth-surfaced stone, or amber, or jade, sometimes called a "fingering-piece." Such a "worrybead," as it is also named, by its pleasant feel, serves to produce a calming effect. The telling of beads by religious Catholics seems to produce a similar result. "Worrybeads" in the United States have, in recent years, enjoyed increasing sales. Apropos of "worrybeads," it is of more than passing interest to note here that during World War II Dr. Jenny Rudinesco, who provided sanctuary for orphaned schizoid children, observed that many of them rolled a small pellet of paper between thumb and index finger. And J. C. Moloney, in his interpretation of these rolled pellets of paper as "stand-ins" for the absent mothers, points out that "they are 'mothers' that can be controlled by the emotionally disturbed child because they are 'mothers' created by the child."

Rubbing of thumb and index finger together is often observed in persons under tension. This may also be extended to rubbing all the fingers simultaneously against the palm of the same hand.

In the matter of skin disorders, Dr. S. Hammerman of the Department of Psychiatry of Temple University Medical School, Philadelphia, has reported to me a case of a girl who suffered very badly from acne, who was cured by treatment involving tactile stimulation in a beauty parlor to which she was sent by a perceptive physician when every other form of orthodox medical treatment had failed.

For those who have not been lovingly and securely held in infancy the fear of falling is a not unexpected development in later life. Lowen points out that the fear of falling, whether from high places or falling asleep, is related to the fear of falling in love. Indeed, the patient who presents any one of these anxieties is usually found to be susceptible to the others, the common factor in all three being an anxiety about the loss of full control of the body and its sensations. Such patients experience these fears as a "sinking" sensation, and they can be terrifying and utterly immobilizing. Such sensations "are the delight of little children, who seek these sensations on their swings, slides, and similar amusements. The healthy child loves to be thrown into the air and to be caught by the waiting arms of a parent."

In the matter of distance, it is of interest that in the

theatre certain directors tell their actors not to touch each other when playing comedy, but certainly not to refrain from doing so when playing tragedy. It is like the difference between extraversion and introversion. In comedy distance is required, noninvolvement, hence one refrains from touching. In tragedy it is the very reverse, involvement is what must be communicated, hence touching is encouraged. Again, gestures may be vertical in comedy, but they should be horizontal in tragedy. In comedy such vertical gestures are or tend to be manic, in tragedy horizontal gestures tend to suggest sympathy, embrace. Thus, Helen Hayes has said, "In comedy I have found that I must keep myself up, arms must be held higher, gestures must be of an upward nature. In tragedy just the reverse."

Sexual differences in cutaneous behavior are very marked in probably all cultures. Females are very much more apt to indulge in every sort of delicate tactile behavior than males. Also females appear to be much more sensitive to the tactile properties of objects, as for example, when they will pass their hands over a fabric in order to appreciate its texture or quality, something males seldom do. Fondling and caressing are largely feminine activities, as is gentleness of approach on every level. Backslapping and handshake crushing are specifically masculine forms of behavior. Cultural differences in these respects are also marked. As Hall points out, the Japanese are very conscious of the significance of texture. "A bowl that is smooth and pleasing to the touch communicates not only that the artisan cared about the bowl and the person who was going to use it but about himself as well." Hall goes on to add that the rubbed finishes of their works in wood reflected the medieval craftsman's feeling he had about the importance of touch. "Touch," he writes, "is the most personally experienced of all sensations. For many people, life's most intimate moments are associated with the changing textures of the skin. The hardened, armorlike resistance to the unwanted touch, or the exciting, ever-changing textures of the skin during love-making, and the velvet quality of satisfaction afterward are messages of one body to another that have universal meanings."

Bowlby has postulated certain responses in the infant which function to tie mother and child reciprocally to one another. These responses are sucking, clinging, following, crying, and smiling. The baby initiates the first three responses: the second two are signals to the mother to respond to him. Bowlby found that in his experience the mother's acceptance of clinging and following is consistent with favorable development, even in the absence of breastfeeding, while rejection of clinging and following by the mother, even in the presence of breastfeeding, is apt to lead to emotional distance. Furthermore, it was Bowlby's impression that fully as many psychological disturbances, including the most severe, could be initiated in the second year when clinging and following are at their peak, as in the early months when they are rudimentary.

The psychoanalyst Michael Balint has found that in his patients the need to cling represents a reaction to a trauma, "an expression of, and a defense against, the fear of being dropped or abandoned . . . its aim being the restoration of proximity and touch of the original subject-object identity." This identity, expressed by identity of wishes and interests between subject and object, Balint calls primary object relation or primary love.

Balint divides these patients into two types, the *philobatic,* that is, those who enjoy swings, thrills, trapezes, and the like, and the other the *oncophilic,* those who cannot stand swings, high places, and the like. The philobatic tends to be a loner, relying on his own resources, while the oncophilic constantly struggles with the fear that the object might fail.

The suggestion is that the child who has enjoyed a satisfying primary object relationship, that is, the child who has been satisfyingly tactually stimulated, will not need to cling, and will enjoy high places, thrills, and being swung about, whereas the child who has been failed in his clinging needs, especially during his preverbal reflex period of development, will react to this traumatic experience with an excessive need to hold on, to cling, with fear of the unsteady and of the support that may fail.

Two different perceptual worlds are involved here; one is *sight oriented,* the other is *touch oriented.* The touch-oriented world is more immediate and friendly than the sight-oriented world. In the sight-oriented world space is friendly, but also often horribly empty or filled with dangerous and unpredictable, unsteadying objects. Georges Braque, the great French painter, has remarked that tactile space separates the viewer from objects, while visual space separates objects from each other.

The extraordinary frequency with which one comes upon accounts of breakthroughs brought about by body contact in reaching schizophrenics who had for years been inaccessible to other therapeutic approaches is striking. In May, 1955 the successes with catatonic schizophrenics of Paul Roland, a physical therapist at Veterans Administration Mental Hospital, Chillicothe, Ohio, were reported in the press. Roland began by sitting with the patient and then after a time touching his arm. Before long Roland was able to give the patient a rubdown. Once that occurred rehabilitation proceeded rapidly. Gertrude Schwing has reported how she was able to break through to schizophrenic children by embracing them. Waal has given an excellent description of massage-therapy with an apparently autistic boy, in which "the therapist gives the patient a general soft and maternal massage, with the stimuli of rhythmical petting and very gentle tickling and touching." The solar plexus, the neck, and the whole length of the spine, are massaged while the chest, chin, hands, and palms are tickled very sensitively and cautiously. After this the therapist proceeds to the eyes, and to a second stage in which there is a provocative massage of jaws, chest, shoulders, and eyes again. In this second stage the pressure of the therapists' hands are no longer soft. The patient reacts by screaming and crying and kicking, and is told that these are the reactions of a disappointed baby, and that they are all right. After these outbursts the patient receives soothing and mothering in an uninvolved, objective manner from the therapist. The effect of the therapy, according to Waal, seems to be a bodily maturation and a break in autistic withdrawal, and it seems to have a quicker effect than any other technique thus far attempted.

Similarly, a great deal of cuddling and stroking is involved in the highly successful approach to the treatment of schizophrenics developed by Mr. and Mrs. Morris Schiff of Fredericksburg, Virginia.

TOUCH AND ASTHMA. In 1953 I reported the case of Mrs. C——, a thirty-year-old Englishwoman, of upper-class background, divorced and childless, height 5 feet 4 inches, weight 90 pounds, seen in July 1948, in London. Mrs. C—— was one of identical twins. Both had suffered approximately fort-

nightly episodes of asthma since they could remember. For
the six years prior to 1948 Mrs. C—— had been in and out
of sanitaria for treatment. Her doctor had then informed her
that if she suffered another attack it might be her last. It was
this shocking prognosis that brought me into the case. In
calling upon her at her home in London, Mrs. C——, a
pretty young woman, seemed rather tense but otherwise appeared quite healthy. She greeted her caller with a cold limp
hand, and then folded her forearms over her chest. She then
sat down on a davenport against the back of which she soon,
in a quiet and unobtrusive manner, began rubbing her back.
To the question whether her mother had died early, she replied that her mother had died at her birth, and in some as-
tonishment inquired why I had asked that particular question. I explained that the possibility had occurred to me on
the basis of the following observations: (1) the way she had
limply shaken hands; (2) her folding of her forearms across
her chest; and (3) her rubbing herself against the back of the
davenport. All this had suggested that she might have failed
to receive adequate cutaneous stimulation as an infant; and
since this frequently came about as a result of the early
death of the mother, I had thought of this as one possibility.

The theory of the relationship between tactile stimulation
and the development of the respiratory system was explained, particular pains being taken to emphasize the fact
that this was merely a theory, and that there was nothing
about it that had yet been proven, but that there existed a
certain amount of evidence which suggested such a relationship, and that if she desired she might try testing it. It was
suggested that she might attend a physiotherapy clinic in
London where, according to instructions, she would be ex-
pertly massaged. To this she readily agreed, and several days

later, following her first massage, she was overflowing with enthusiasm. She was then told that the probabilities were high that if she continued with the massage for some time, she would never experience another asthmatic attack unless, possibly, she underwent some serious emotional disturbance. She continued with the treatment for several months, and during the many years which have since elapsed she has not suffered a single serious asthmatic episode.

Mrs. C——'s sister had experienced identical attacks of asthma until she married a famous author, whereupon her attacks declined in frequency although they did not altogether cease. Subsequently there was a divorce, soon after which she died during an asthmatic seizure. In the case of Mrs. C—— her attacks, for all practical purposes, ceased altogether. She subsequently remarried and has lived happily ever after.

There may, of course, be little or no relation in this case between the cessation of the asthma and the cutaneous stimulation Mrs. C—— received. On the other hand, the relation may be a very direct one. In my original paper I wrote, "This case has been cited for its suggestive value. It is to be hoped that those having the adequate opportunities may carry out the observations necessary to show whether or not persons suffering from asthma and other disorders that may be related to inadequate cutaneous stimulation in infancy may be relieved by a course of cutaneous stimulation given them on the theory outlined in this paper."

While that paper aroused a certain amount of interest, it does not appear to have stimulated much research in the indicated direction.

In connection with asthma, it has been noted on an earlier page that putting one's arm around the shoulders of a person during an asthmatic attack is likely to alleviate or bring the attack to a halt.

Sir William Osler once remarked that "Taking a lady's hand gives her confidence in her physician." And, indeed, taking almost anyone's hand under conditions of stress is likely to exert a soothing effect, and by reducing anxiety give both the taken and the taker a feeling of greater security.

How is it, we may ask, that tactile stimulation, in the form of caressing, fondling, cuddling, embracing, stroking, and the like is capable of working such remarkable effects upon emotionally disturbed individuals?

The explanation is quite simple: Tactile stimulation appears to be a fundamentally necessary experience for the healthy behavioral development of the individual. Failure to receive tactile stimulation in infancy results in a critical failure to establish contact relations with others. Supplying that need, even in adults, may serve to give the individual the reassurance he needs, the conviction that he is wanted and valued, and thus involved and consolidated in a connected network of values with others. The individual who is awkward in his contact relations with others, is clumsy in his body relations with others, in shaking hands, in embracing, in kissing, in any, and often all, of his tactile demonstrations of affection, is so principally because he has been failed in his interactive body-contact relations with his mother. His mother has failed him in motherliness, which Garner and Wenar define as maternal gratification of the infant's needs for body care and pleasurable stimulation in ways that also provide the mother herself with satisfaction. Not only does the motherly woman provide her child with gratifications, but she also derives gratification from doing so, as she provides her infant with the close physical contact and protection he needs for growth and development. These investigators show that psychosomatic disorder tends to develop in individuals who have lacked the experience of motherliness —a hypothesis that has been many times confirmed. A basic ingredient of "motherliness" is close physical contact, the hugging, cuddling, caressing, embracing, rocking, kissing, and other tactile stimulations that a motherly mother gives her child.

Body contact is a basic mammalian need which must be satisfied if the individual is to develop those movements, gestures, and body-relatednesses which will be normally developed during the growth of one's experience in relation to one's mother's body. Deprivation of this experience has been experimentally shown to produce the most atypical movements and postures. On an earlier page we saw how this affects sexual behavior, contributing to the awkwardness of the socially deprived male in copulatory behavior. As Mason and others have shown, in such socially deprived individuals, deficiencies in social communication are the rule. While the need is there, one learns to nuzzle, root, cuddle, embrace, kiss, and tenderly and lovingly care for others as a consequence of experiencing such behavior from one's mother. In the absence of such maternal behaviors the need remains but the performance of the behaviors associated with it is left more or less crudely unrealized. Indeed, to a very significant extent, a measure of the individual's development as a healthy human being is the extent to which he or she is freely able to embrace another and enjoy the embraces of others . . . to get, in a very real sense, into touch with others.

The tactually failed child grows into an individual who is

not only physically awkward in his relations with others, but who is also psychologically, behaviorally, awkward with them. Such persons are likely to be wanting in that tact which the *Oxford English Dictionary* defines as the "ready and delicate sense of what is fitting and proper in dealing with others, so as to avoid giving offense, or win good will; skill or judgment in dealing with men or negotiating difficult or delicate situations; the faculty of saying or doing the right thing at the right time."

There appears to be a very distinct carryover from tactile experience in infancy to tactful behavior in later life. It is fascinating that the word *tact,* derived from the Latin word meaning "touch," was not infrequently used in England in place of the word *touch,* down to the middle of the nineteenth century. *Tact,* in its modern sense, was adopted from the French early in the nineteenth century. What the word really means is clearly "to delicately touch" the other. Both the etymological and the psychological relationship of *tact,* in its contemporary meaning, "to touch," have not altogether escaped attention, for we will say of a tactless man that he has a heavy touch. What is so interestingly inherent in the use of the word *tact* in its modern sense is the uncannily clear understanding of the importance of early tactile experience in the development of that delicate sense of fitting and proper behavior implied in the word.

ADAPTIVITY AND REACTIVITY OF THE SKIN. Among the remarkable capacities of the skin is its ability to develop increased acuity and to compensate for deficiencies in other sensory systems. Thus, Zubek, Flye, and Aftenas found that in sixteen hooded students confined to a room in complete darkness for one week there was a marked increase in cutaneous sensitivity as well as in sensitivity to pain. In the blind there is considerable variability in the development of cutaneous sensitivity, some individuals showing increases, others showing decreases. It is a matter worthy of further investigation.

Not only will the skin react to every kind of stimulus with the most appropriate physical changes, but it will also do so behaviorally, for the skin is capable of behaving in very perceptible ways. The reference here is to stimuli originating at the skin surface. The skin is not merely a complex cellular structure, it is an equally complex chemical one; moreover, the substances present on its surface play an important role in the defense system of the body. For example, contact of human plasma or whole blood with the skin accelerates clotting time. If the skin is washed with alcohol the clotting time is prolonged.

Reactivity of the skin to stimuli originating at the skin surface can only occur after mediation of the originating sensory stimuli through the nervous system. It begins to appear that whatever changes are capable of being produced in the skin by stimuli originating in the mind, are also capable of being produced in the skin by changes originating at the level of the skin. Such, for example, are the skin disorders resulting from inadequate tactile stimulation. Clearly, sensory stimuli at the skin level have to be interpreted at the cortical level and the appropriate motor reactions initiated. The skin itself does not think, but its sensitivity is so great, combined with its ability to pick up and transmit so extraordinarily wide a variety of signals, and make so wide a range of responses, exceeding that of all other sense organs, that for versatility it must be ranked second only to the brain itself. This sensitivity can, however, be considerably impaired by the failure to receive the tactile stimuli necessary for its proper development. In this respect, such influences as family, class, and culture play a fundamental role.

SEVEN

Each culture fosters or specifically trains its young as children and as adolescents to develop different kinds of thresholds to tactile contacts and stimulation so that their organic, constitutional, temperamental characteristics are accentuated or reduced.*

CULTURE AND CONTACT

THE EXISTENCE of a wide range of class and cultural differences in attitudes and practices relating to tactile behavior affords a fertile field for the investigation of the relation of such social differences in tactile experience to the development of personality, and to some extent to national traits. In general, while the culture prescribes the customary socializing experiences to which the infant and child shall be exposed, idiosyncratic differences within particular families may substantially depart from the prescribed modes of behavior, with more or less significant consequences for the individuals involved.

* LAWRENCE K. FRANK, "Tactile Communication," p. 241.

There are families in which a great deal of tactile contact occurs, not only between mother and child but also between all the members of the family. There are other families, within the same culture, in which there is a minimal amount of tactile contact between mother and child and all the other members of the family. There are whole cultures which are characterized by a *"Noli mi tangere,"* a "Do not touch me," way of life. There are other cultures in which tactility is so much a part of life, in which there is so much embracing and fondling and kissing it appears strange and embarrassing to the non-tactile peoples. And there are cultures that play every possible variation upon the theme of tactility. In this chapter the attempt will be made to inquire into cultural and individual (familial) differences in attitudes towards tactile contact, the practices to which these attitudes lead and the manner in which they express themselves both in the individual and in his culture.

EXTEROGESTATION AND TACTILITY. Exterogestation constitutes the continuation of the uterogestative process in the environment outside the womb. The exterogestative process is designed to continue the feedback relationships between infant and mother, to continue the development of both, but especially of the infant for its increasingly complicated postnatal functioning in an atmospheric world bounded and unbounded by all sorts of experiences of space. The latter is an important aspect of the organism's experience which has received insufficient recognition.

Within the womb the fetus is enclosed and intimately bounded by the supporting embracing walls of the uterus. This is a comforting and reassuring experience. But with birth the infant experiences a more or less open-ended environment; he must learn to grow accustomed to the very least variations of his environment. To the last day of his postnatal life the most fearful and emotionally most disturbing experience that can befall the individual is the sudden withdrawal of support. The only instinct-like reaction remaining in man, other than the reaction to a sudden loud noise, is the reaction to a sudden withdrawal of support. The uterogestate fetus, embraced, supported, and rocked within his amniotic environment, as an exterogestate requires the continued support of his mother, to be held and rocked in her arms, and in close contact with her body, swallowing colostrum and milk in place of amniotic fluid. He needs to be enclosed in his mother's arms, embraced, in contact with her warm skin, for among other things the newborn is most sensitive to temperature changes, and one of the dangers to which he is often exposed in hospitals is a chilling ambient room temperature, especially in air-conditioned delivery rooms. The professional mode of dealing with this is to place the baby in a heated bassinet—a most inadequate substitute for the warm ambience of the mother's embracing, supportive body.

The boundaries of the uterogestate's world are the walls of the uterus. It is necessary to understand that the neonate is most comfortable when the conditions within the womb are reproduced as closely as possible in the exterogestational state, that is, when the baby is enfolded in his mother's arms at her bosom. The infant needs to learn, on the firm foundation of closeness, what closeness, proximity, distance, and openness mean. In short, he has to learn the meaning, and the manner, of accommodating himself to a great variety and complexity of spatial relationships—all of which is closely bound up with his experiences of tactility, principally in relation to his mother's body.

To remove the newborn baby from its mother and place it on its back or its front on a flat surface, often uncovered, is to fail to understand the newborn's great need for enfoldment, to be supported, rocked, and covered from all sides, and that the infant may only gradually be introduced to the world of more open spaces. From the supporting, continuous, tangible presence of his mother the infant will gradually come to move some distance toward the outside world. One sees this particularly vividly in older infant mammals, and especially in juvenile monkeys and apes, who from tentative proximate separation from the mother gradually increase the distance until they can achieve an independence more or less complete physically, and to some extent emotionally.

TRAUMAS AT SKIN LEVEL. We must ask ourselves here whether, in removing the newborn from his mother, as is customary in hospitals, and placing him in the open space of a bassinet or crib, we are not visiting a seriously disturbing trauma upon the baby, a trauma from which, perhaps, he never completely recovers? A trauma, moreover, which in the civilized world of the West, and those cultures that have been affected by the West's childbirth practices, is repeatedly inflicted upon the infant during the early years of his life. It may be that fear of open spaces (agoraphobia) or of heights (acrophobia), or of sudden drops, may have some connection with such early experiences. It may also be that a preference for having one's bedclothes about one's body rather than tucked in at the foot and sides of the bed reflects a desire to recreate the conditions enjoyed in the womb, in reaction to the lack of body-support experienced in infancy. There are those who like to sleep with their bedroom doors closed; there are others who cannot abide a closed bedroom door. As one might expect, those who like their bedclothes snugly embracing them also tend to prefer their bedroom doors closed, whereas the tucked-in-around-the-bed types prefer their bedroom doors open. What the range of variability is in these matters I do not know. There is a suggestion here for some interesting inquiries in which a good many other variables, such as breastfeeding, maternal affection, deprivations of various sorts, hospital or home deliveries and the like are considered.

It is during the exterogestative period that the infant is first and continuously exposed to the culturalizing effects of his society. And from the moment of birth every society has evolved its own unique ways of dealing with the child. It is on the basis of repeated sensory experiences of the culturally prescribed stimulations that the child learns how to behave according to the requirements of his culture. And it is because of the differences in the kinds and modalities of the individual's tactile experiences within the family, especially in relation to his or her mother, as determined for the most part by particular cultures, that individuals and peoples will differ behaviorally in many fundamental ways from one another.

It should be evident why, during the exterogestative period, the kind of tactile experience the infant undergoes will exert so fundamental an effect upon his development. The explanation is very simple: It is because most of his learning is done during this period through his experiences at the level of the skin. The exterogestative period constitutes a developmental period during which the quality of communication experienced through the skin is critical. It is critical because upon the quality of the tactile communication experienced during that period will depend the kind of psychomotor, the sort of emotional response, the infant learns to make to others. This sort of emotional response will become a fixed and permanent part of his personality, upon which he will subsequently build many learned secondary responses. In view of the fact that the exterogestative tactile learning period has not been adequately recognized as a critical period in the development of every organism, and especially in the human species, we shall have to consider giving children more tactile attention than they have hitherto received.

CULTURE AND TACTILITY. The differences in the quality, frequency, and timing of the tactile experience which the newborn, infant, child, adolescent, and adult undergoes in different cultures run the whole gamut of possible variations. We have already touched upon such differences in several cultures in Chapter Four (pp. 111–124). Here we shall discuss cultural differences in early tactile experience and their relation to personality and to behavior. We can commence with the evidence for nonliterate societies, and then proceed to the discussion of the technologically more advanced societies.

THE NETSILIK ESKIMO. The Netsilik Eskimo live on the Boothia Peninsula in the Canadian Arctic of the Northwest Territories. There they have been studied with particular insight by Richard James de Boer, who lived in a snowhouse among them during the winter of 1966–1967. Maternal-infant caretaking relationships were the focus of Mr. de Boer's interest. The Netsilik mother, even though she lives under the most difficult of conditions, is an unruffled personality who bestows warmth and loving care upon her children. She never chides her infant or interferes with it in any way, except to respond to its needs. De Boer writes:

At parturition and the onset of exterogestation, the Netsilik infant is placed in the back of its mother's attiggi (fur parka) in such a position that its ventral torso is pressed firmly against its mother's back just below the shoulder blades. The infant assumes a sitting posture with its tiny legs around its mother's waist or slightly above and with its head flexed right or left which usually elicits the tonic neck reflex that facilitates the straddling placement of the legs as extensor tonus decreases in either of these limbs. When the infant is in the proper position, the mother ties a sash around the attiggi exterior, across her chest above the breasts and down under the axillae, and where it passes across her back it forms a sling that supports her infant under its buttocks and prevents it from slipping down and out of the garment. The infant wears tiny diapers fashioned from caribou skins, but otherwise it snuggles naked against its mother's skin. Most of the infant's ventral anatomy is in a close tactile and cutaneous contact with its mother and its dorsal body is completely encased in fur, protecting it from the fierce Arctic cold. From outward appearances, the Netsilik mother bearing her infant in this traditional manner presents the appearance of a congenital hunchback, but her awkward appearance is more apparent than real, since her infant's weight is distributed in close proximity to her intrinsic center of gravity. The Netsilik infant is carried about in this fashion until it achieves locomotor ability and thence intermittently until it acquires what the Netsilik Eskimo calls "ihuma" or cognitive sense.

Netsilik mother and child communicate with each other through their skins. When hungry the Netsilik infant roots and sucks on the skin of its mother's back, alerting her to its need. Then it is brought round to the breast and suckled.

Activity needs are satisfied by the various motions to which the infant is subjected in the postural and locomotory and other movements of the mother as she pursues her daily tasks. The rocking movements and contact with the mother's skin promote the sleep the infant so much enjoys. Bowel and bladder elimination occur on the mother's back. The mother's removal of these eliminations serves to prevent any continuing discomfort to the infant. Since the mother anticipates most of the infant's needs with all those sustaining nurturance responses designed to meet his needs, the Netsilik infant seldom cries. The infant's needs are anticipated by the mother tactually.

The Netsilik mother's care of her infant beautifully meets the requirements of its phylogenetically programed needs; the infant's responses are invariably pleasant. This invariability of pleasurable response, de Boer suggests, is the key to the Netsilik Eskimo's stress-coping ability.

The Netsilik Eskimo [writes de Boer] is seldom if ever assaulted by aversive and stress-producing interpersonal stimuli, but he is constantly threatened with the uncertainties of his eco-system. Ecologically stressful situations never upset his emotional homeostasis and he confronts a raging polar bear with the same coolness and equanimity that he exhibits when faced with the threat of food deprivation. The invariability of the homeostatic emotional response does not imply that these responses are stereotypic; on the contrary, homeostasis implies a dynamic life force, but a force that functions below the threshold of disorganization. Evolutionarily, this homeostatic equilibrium has offered the greatest selective advantages to the individual and his group in the struggle for survival.

By the time he is three years of age the Netsilik child has acquired "the only two motivational characteristics necessary to his functioning as a self-regulated human being," namely

pleasant or altruistic responses to interpersonal relationships, and the power of symbolic manipulative ability. Because dominance-subservience relationships are absent in
parental and especially maternal-infant relations a harmonic
balance is achieved between the Netsilik individual and his
society, with the individual in this manner gratifying his
needs for mutually altruistic interpersonal relationships.

It is, of course, not possible to say with certainty that the
altruistic behavior of the Netsilik individual is largely the
product of his experiences in infancy, and especially of those
he undergoes in relation to his mother's body; these experiences are later reinforced by the behavior of almost everyone
else in his small world. The evidence, however, is strongly
suggestive that it is the early experiences that are the most
influential.

The Netsilik infant may defecate and urinate upon his
mother's back without causing any disturbance other than
the mother's cleaning of both the infant and herself. Such relaxed behavior undoubtedly exerts significantly relaxing effects upon the child's responses to its excretory activities.
Such a child would never become an anal-erotic who hoards
his feces or grow to become a niggardly adult. The openness
and generosity of the Eskimo character is, no doubt, in part
at least, due to the unuptightness of his early toilet experiences.

The motions of his mother during her daily activities give
the Eskimo child a view of the world from virtually every
possible angle, a view from which its spatial skills will grow
and be reinforced by its subsequent experiences. The extraordinary spatial faculties of the Eskimo, and probably also
their remarkable mechanical abilities may be closely related
to these early experiences upon the mother's back. Edmund

Carpenter has provided a fascinating account of the remarkable spatial and mechanical abilities of the Aivilik Eskimo of Southampton Island in the northwest boundary of Hudson Bay.

"Aivilik men are first-class mechanics," writes Carpenter. "They delight in stripping down and reassembling engines, watches, all machinery. I have watched them repair instruments which American mechanics, flown into the Arctic for this purpose, have abandoned in despair. Working with the simplest tools, often handmade, they make replacements of metal and ivory. Towtoongie [an Eskimo friend] made a hinge for me. I had to hold it directly before my eyes to see how it worked." And so on.

Carpenter thinks that the explanation for this phenomenal ability lies in the over-all picture of Aivilik time-space orientation, in that the Aivilik do not conceptually separate space and time, but see a situation as a dynamic process; furthermore, they are acutely observant of details. Moreover, they view space not as a static enclosure but as a direction in operation. For example, when handed a copy of an illustrated magazine they will not turn it right side up, indeed they are highly amused when the white man does so, but will look at the pictures whether they are upside-down or horizontal, and see them as if they were right side up!

Whether or not these abilities are related to the tactile, spatial-visual experiences on the maternal back, must, again of course, remain a matter for further research specifically aimed in this direction. It would seem not unlikely. The infant's eye-view from all positions as the mother moves about would suggest the development of a rather special kind of spatial ability. As Carpenter puts it, "Space fluctuates in continuous activity. . . . The visual experience becomes a dy-

namic experience. Thus Aivilik artists do not confine themselves to the reproduction of what can actually be seen in a
given moment from a single vantage point, but they twist
and tilt the various possible visual aspects until they fully explain the object they wish to represent." The twisting and
tilting may very well reflect something of the twistings and
turnings the infant experienced while being carried on the
mother's back.

"In most myths," writes Carpenter, "there is an alternative
shrinking and growing of men and spirits in their mutual relations. Nothing has a static, invariable shape or size. Men,
spirits, animals, have unstable, ever-changing dimensions."
Again, a view of the world very reminiscent of the kinds of
visual experiences the infant undergoes from his dorsal ele-
vated viewpoint, experiences of adults whom he can see face
to face, as well as children, animals, and other things that,
from his high perch in his parka, are small and difficult to
see, but suddenly change in size when mother bends, or
kneels, or assumes a horizontal position.

From his early orientations to the spatial dimensions of
the world the child relies virtually entirely upon its sense of
touch, and by this most primitive of all sensory agencies, by
thigmotropism (from the Greek *thigma,* "touch," and *trope,*
"turn," that is, by responding to contact or touch), it learns
to find its way about in the world of the environment its
mother provides for it. The child's first space is tactile. Initially it is passively tactile, experiencing tactile sensations
which are gradually converted into perceptions, that is, sensations endowed with meanings. With these meanings the
child then actively begins to scan the world for itself. James
Gibson, who has made these distinctions between passive

and active touch, in an experiment designed to judge the accuracy of the information received by each form of touch, found that active touch enabled subjects to reproduce abstract objects that were screened from view with 95 percent accuracy. Only a 49 percent accuracy was achieved with passive touch.

Active touch is stereognostic, that is, it enables one to understand the form and nature of objects. This ability is gradually developed in relation to the mother's body, the grasping of the nipple, the hand resting on the breast, the infant's own lips, nose, eyes, genitals, hands, feet, and other parts of its body. Each of these has its own special characteristics and gradually comes to be recognized through active touch. In its mother's parka the Eskimo child, in addition to receiving communications from her body and body motions, will at first receive also a great many signals from her of an auditory nature, and it will come to associate these with each other. Hence vocal sounds will come to have a soothing tactile quality about them, a repetitive lulling character. One perceives this reflected very clearly in much of the poetry of the Eskimo. Consider such a poem as the following: a dance song, typical of those composed by Eskimos generally, but in this case the creation of a Copper Eskimo of Victoria Island, south of the North Magnetic Pole.

DANCE SONG

I am quite unable
To capture seals as they do, I am quite unable.
Animals with blubber since I do not know how to capture,
To capture seals as they do I am quite unable.
I am quite unable
To shoot as they do, I am quite unable.

I am quite unable,
A fine kayak such as they have I am quite unable to obtain.
Animals that have fawns since I cannot obtain them,
A fine kayak such as they have I am quite unable to obtain.
I am quite unable
To capture fish as they do, I am quite unable.
I am quite unable
To dance as they do, I am quite unable.
Dance songs since I do not know them at all,
To dance as they do I am quite unable.
I am quite unable to be swift-footed as they are,
I am quite unable . . .

This song in its rhythm and metre, as well as its phrasing, repeats something similar to what a child would experience while being carried in a sling on its mother's back. It remains a fascinating and unexplained fact that in many parts of the world many children who were probably never carried in this way will grow up to compose poetry in similar metres and rhythms and phrases. Nevertheless, as we have seen in relation to music, it is a speculation worthy of further inquiry whether there may be a connection between the rhythms and metres of the Eskimos' songs and poetry and their experiences of motion on their mothers' backs.

Song making is highly valued among all Eskimos, and it is the custom to improvise songs for almost every occasion. What can be more humanly beautiful than this song, improvised by Takomaq, an old Iglulik Eskimo woman living on the Melville Peninsula, east of the Netsilik Eskimo? The old lady was about to serve a meal she had prepared for Knud Rasmussen and his companion, when Rasmussen presented her with some tea. This touched her so deeply that she at once joyfully improvised the following song:

Ajaja—aja—jaja.	*All is more beautiful,*
The lands around my dwelling	*All is more beautiful,*
Are more beautiful	*And life is thankfulness.*
From the day	*These guests of mine*
When it is given me to see	*Make my house grand,*
Faces I have never seen before.	Ajaja—aja—jaja.

These likeable people show their friendliness towards those they have never seen before—not strangers, but visitors or guests—by touching and stroking them. Stefansson tells how he and his party were welcomed by the Copper Eskimo in 1913. "Our welcome was as warm and friendly as it could possibly be, and nearly that noisy. Little children jumped up so as to be able to touch our shoulders and men and women stroked and handled us in a very friendly way."

In their snowhouses, where the temperature is often in the vicinity of 100 degrees, and only slightly less at night, Eskimos usually sleep in the nude in close body contact with one another. A man will customarily lend his wife for the night, as an act of courtesy, to the male visitor. The mixture of body odors, burning blubber-oil, and other odors, which white men sometimes find unendurable, is far from unappealing to the Eskimo, whose acute sense of smell has been remarked upon by more than one observer. This trait, too, is perhaps not unrelated to the experiences of the infant in his mother's parka.

Following and in relation to tactility, the sense which is next elaborated is not vision but hearing. The mother hums and sings to the child, while she pats and hugs him, and holds him close to her body in her parka, and in time he learns to identify and respond to her voice as a surrogate for her touch. It is a reflexive form of conditioning, in which the sign of the original stimulus, the voice, replaces the

touch, but the voice always retains its tactile quality, soothing, caressing, reassuring. It stands for the presence of the
loving mother, whose love the infant initially knows primarily through the warmth and support, and yieldingness, and
softness of her skin, and who attends to the infant's needs by
actively as well as passively stimulating its skin, in carrying,
cleaning, and washing it.

Eskimos are not given overmuch to washing, since water is
scarce and ice is melted into water only at the great expense
of burning the difficult-to-come-by blubber. Urine will sometimes be used as a substitute. Among the far northern Ingalik, who are a Northern Athapaskan group who speak both
Ingalik and Eskimo, following the initial bath which a baby
receives soon after birth, the mother licks the face and hands
of the baby with her tongue every morning to clean them,
until the baby is old enough to sit upon the bench. Though
I have found no reference to this practice among Eskimos
proper it is possible that it occurs.

Visual perception almost certainly follows upon the development of auditory perception among the Eskimo. Carpenter confirms this in observing of the Aivilik Eskimo that

they define space more by sound than by sight. Where we might
say, "Let's see what we can hear," they would say, "Let's hear
what we can see." . . . To them, the ocularly visible apparition is
not nearly as important as the purely auditory one. The essential
feature of sound is not its location, but that it *be,* that it fill
space. We say "the night shall be filled with music," just as the
air is filled with fragrance; locality is irrelevant. The concert-goer
closes his eyes.

I know of no example of an Aivilik describing space primarily
in visual terms. They don't regard space as static, and therefore
measurable; hence they have no formal units of spatial measurement, just as they have no uniform divisions of time. The carver

is indifferent to the demands of the optical eye; he lets each piece fill its own space, create its own world, without reference to background or anything external to it. Each carving lives in spatial independence. Size and shape, proportions and selection, these are set by the object itself, not forced from without. Like sound, each carving creates its own space, its own identity; it imposes its own assumptions.

It is perhaps not unreasonable to suppose that this auditory view of reality is related to the Aivilik child's much earlier and longer continued conditioning in vocal than in visual experience. This conditioning is, of course, perpetuated through its oral traditional training.

TOUCH AND SOUND. It has sometimes been remarked, perhaps more as a metaphor than anything else, that sound has a tactile quality. There exists, however, a far deeper relationship between touch and sound than most of us are aware of. The versatility of the skin is such that it is capable of responding to sound waves just as it is to those of pressure. Mirkin, of the Pavlov Institute of Physiology at Leningrad, has shown that the sensory receptors for pressure (deep touch), which are present around muscles, joints, ligaments, and tendons, the Pacinian corpuscles, possess very definite resonance properties. Mirkin subjected Pacinian corpuscles, in mesenteric tissue adjacent to the intestines, to acoustic stimulation in a uniform acoustic field, and found that these receptors possess resonance properties, and that a conditioned connection is obtainable between an optimal frequency of stimulation and periods of bioelectric activity, thus strongly suggesting a biomechanical resonance in Pacinian corpuscles.

Madsen and Mears, using deaf subjects, found that sound vibrations have a significant effect upon the tactile threshold, that a 50 cycles per second tone at both high and low pressure desensitizes the skin and raises the threshold, while a 5,000 cycles per second tone at both high and low pressure levels sensitized the skin.

Gescheider has shown that the skin is able to localize sound waves of different intensities with remarkable accuracy.

Which suggests all sorts of possibilities.

ORDER OF SENSORY DEVELOPMENT. The senses of *Homo sapiens* develop in a definite sequence, as (1) tactile, (2) auditory, and (3) visual. As the child approaches adolescence the order of precedence becomes reversed, as (1) visual, (2) auditory, and (3) tactile. It is much more important to experience tactile and auditory stimulations in the early developing years than it is to experience visual ones. As soon, however, as one has developed through one's tactile and auditory senses the know-how of being human, vision becomes by far the most important of the senses. Yet a vision can only become meaningful on the basis of what it has felt and what it has heard.

Marshall McLuhan speaks of TV as essentially tactile, and he and Parker very cogently remark that "the social, the political and the artistic implications of tactility could only have been lost to human awareness in a visual or civilized culture which is now dissolving under the impact of electric circuitry." These notions have a very real foundation, well understood by the eminent anthropologist, Alfred Kroeber. In a letter to Meyer Shapiro, the art critic, Kroeber wrote with reference to Berenson's "tactile values" in painting, that these can appeal only through the eye, and never actually to the sense of touch, nevertheless they refer to something that under-lies the vision which is at the center of visual art: namely, that feeling by touching precedes sight, phylogenetically and ontoge-netically in every human baby. We all touch first, learn to see later, and in learning erect a nearby visual world on a tactile base, giving a double quality to all perceptions of objects, first within immediate reach, and later within ultimate or potential reach. All children, and many adults, want to handle a new sight. The two senses of course are disparate: they operate through different sense receptors. But what is seen and touched is always made part of ourselves more intensely and more meaning-fully than what is only seen. And so in art representation the rep-resentative picture we *only* see but cannot, in imagination, touch, does not carry the same attraction and concentration of interest as the one we can, imaginatively, handle and touch as well as see clearly.

To this Kroeber added orally, "that perhaps abstractionism of whatever era has a more intellectual, a lesser appeal, the subconscious tactile aspects having been withdrawn and abandoned."

The tactile quality of vision is apparent in the touching of another with the eyes. Hence one avoids looking or staring at strangers, except in certain conventionally accepted situa-tions. It is of great interest to observe here that under natu-ral conditions gorillas avoid looking directly at a stranger, and especially regard a direct look, until friendly relations have been established, with suspicion.

As Ernest Schachtel has pointed out, the distance senses, sight and hearing, both phylogenetically and ontogenetically attain their full development later than the proximity senses, touch, taste, and smell. And, as he rightly states, the proxim-ity senses are neglected and to a considerable extent even tabooed by Western civilization. He adds, "Both pleasure and disgust are more intimately linked with the proximity senses than with the distance senses. The pleasure which a perfume, a taste, or a texture can give is much more of a bodily, physical one, hence more akin to sexual pleasure, than is the more sublime pleasure aroused by sound and the least bodily of all pleasures, the beautiful."

In the daily lives of animals the proximity senses play an important role. In man, if they are not repressed in sexual relations, then they are otherwise tabooed in interpersonal relations, "the more a culture or a group tends to isolate people, to put distance between them, and to prevent spontaneous relationships and the 'natural' animal-like expressions of such relations."

Marcuse remarks that civilization demands the repression of the pleasures to be derived from the proximity senses in order to ensure the desexualization "of the organism required by its social utilization as an instrument of labor."

Perhaps it would be more accurate to say that the taboos on interpersonal tactuality grew out of a fear closely associated with the Christian tradition in its various denominations, the fear of bodily pleasures. One of the great negative achievements of Christianity has been to make a sin of tactual pleasures.

THE GANDA OF EAST AFRICA. Dr. Mary Ainsworth has made a detailed study of rearing practices in infancy among the Ganda of East Africa. Her field study was carried out in a single village some fifteen miles from Kampala. The effects of white contact have long been operative upon the Ganda, but nevertheless the majority of mothers still carried their infants on their backs and enjoyably breast fed them for a year or more. Ganda babies spend most of their waking hours being held by someone. While holding the baby the mother gently patted or stroked him. The total care of this kind given by the mother was very considerable. From her comparative observations, Dr. Ainsworth concludes: "It is better for a baby to be held a lot, to be picked up when he cries, to be given what he wants when he wants it, and to be given much opportunity and freedom to interact than it is for a baby to be kept for long periods in his crib apart from other people, where his signals cannot be perceived and consequently where he cannot experience a sense of predictable consequence and control." The rate of sensorimotor development was accelerated in most babies. They sat, stood, crawled, and walked much earlier than the average baby in Western societies. Ainsworth attributes this to the kind of infant care the Ganda give, "with much physical contact, much interaction between the infant and his mother, much social stimulation, prompt gratification of creature-comfort needs, lack of confinement, and freedom to explore the world."

Unfortunately, Ainsworth's study deals only with the first fifteen months of the Ganda child's development, and tells us nothing at all of the later personality traits of the Ganda adult. The anthropological literature on the Ganda is not much more helpful in this connection, and such other information as is available on this score is largely anecdotal. Audrey Richards emphasizes the fact that there was a remarkable unanimity in the early European visitors' accounts of the Ganda, emphasizing their good manners, politeness, and charm, their cleanliness, neatness, modesty, orderliness, dignity, and intelligence. But it was also observed that they were touchy, competitive, legalistic, capable of cruel behavior, reticent, and difficult to know well. There seem to be many contradictions here, but they may not be really so. It may well be that the congenial qualities of the Ganda adult owe much to the motherliness he has received in his first year or so, and that his less desirable qualities were engendered by later conditionings. It is the etiology of just this kind of differential development that no one seems to have been stimulated to study.

THE DUSUN OF NORTH BORNEO. Williams has made the only anthropological study known to me of tactuality in a non-literate culture. He studied the Dusun of the mountain highlands of North Borneo, an agricultural-hunting people whose principal crop is rice. Williams has emphasized the need for studies devoted to the various ways in which, in different cultures, individuals are required or expected to relinquish particular tactile experiences or practices and develop compensatory symbolic substitutes at different periods in life. "The transformation," he writes, "of tactile experience into abstract conceptualizations would seem crucial to understanding the way some cultural conceptions are acquired by the individual in the course of cultural learning and transmission."

Concern with and recognition of tactile experience, [writes Williams] in Dusun life is complex, but can be observed in both overt behavior and in a variety of linguistic, gesture, and body posture surrogates for touch used in many social situations. Contacts such as "living touch" are distinguished from a "non-living touch" while "touchy," and "touchable," and "touched," each are differentiated from the "act of touching," "tickling," and "touching together." Linguistic uses for specific tactile contacts, including terms denoting limits and acceptability of such experience, comprise a special lexicon. Other surrogates for tactile experience commonly used in Dusun life are in the form of culturally structured gestures meant to be suggestive of particular touch actions; some 40 gestures are used to note emotion, while at least 12 have openly sexual meanings denoting acts of intercourse.* Body posture surrogates for tactile experiences often involve a complex set of actions, including inclinations of the head, facial expression, and hand, arm, and trunk movements. The behavior repertoire of the coquettish Dusun woman includes a variety of such complex body posture surrogates for tactile experience. Such body actions are used generally to indicate approval, or dislike, of displays of body arts, grooming, and decoration as invitations to direct touch experience.

In greeting another no tactile contact is involved in Dusun society, while strict boundaries of permitted tactile contacts exist for various social action situations. It is of interest that the Dusun newborn is isolated for some eight to ten days from all tactile contacts, except those of the mother. Among the phrases used in the several rituals to which the child is exposed during his first year of life, is one saying that "no stranger will be allowed to touch you to bring you harm."

The way in which the members of a culture learn to deal with the sense of touch is culturally defined, and this is made explicitly clear in Williams' excellent study. Williams' plea for further investigation of this important, but most neglected aspect of human behavior, can only be echoed here.

THE TACTILE EXPERIENCE OF THE AMERICAN CHILD. Passing from a nonliterate culture such as that of the Dusun, the

* "Thus, the thumb inserted between the first and second fingers of the same hand is a symbol of intercourse, while the waving of hands alongside the ears, with fingers up and palms forward denotes fright and derision."

TABLE III. CONTACTS AND PATTERNS OF PLAY
BY AGE AND SOCIAL CLASS

For one hour of observation at the beach. Number of children=45

| | Mean Number Contacts | | | | Mean Time in Contact | | | |
Group	W*	M*	U*	Group Average	W	M	U	Group Average
A	4.5	4.2	4.0	4.2	0.0	8.0	9.7	7.5
B	3.1	5.5	15.3	6.3	3.0	8.0	22.3	8.2
C	2.6	3.3	6.0	3.7	1.4	1.3	3.4	1.8
D	—	5.3	4.8	5.0	—	8.3	2.8	4.9
Average for Total	3.1	4.4	7.0	4.9	2.2	5.8	8.2	5.6

* W = Working Class; M = Middle Class; U = Upper Class

Ganda, or the Eskimos to the highly sophisticated culture of the United States, we find that the differences in tactile experience of infants and young children in each culture are very revealing. For the United States there is available an excellent study of the tactile experience of children from infancy to four and a half years of age in working-class, middle-class, and upper-class families. This is an unpublished doctoral dissertation by Vidal Starr Clay entitled, "The Effect of Culture on Mother-Child Tactile Communication." Forty-five mother-child pairs were the subjects of this study, with twenty boys and twenty-five girls. The observations were made on public, country-club, and private beaches. In Table III, the findings are set out for the average tactile contacts by age and class for one hour of observation of children in groups designated *A, B, C,* and *D,* according to the age of the children. From this table it will be seen that tactile con-

	Mean Time Near				Mean Time Away			
Group	W	M	U	Group Average	W	M	U	Group Average
A	4.0	3.0	31.0	27.2	13.0	20.0	20.0	17.7
B	30.5	13.5	19.0	22.9	19.6	30.0	15.7	20.5
C	22.4	22.0	28.7	23.8	23.0	24.0	20.0	22.6
D	—	15.0	25.2	21.1	—	31.3	29.2	30.0
Average for Total	27.4	16.2	25.8	23.3	20.5	27.4	23.2	23.7

SOURCE: Vidal S. Clay, "The Effect of Culture on Mother-Child Tactile Communication" (Ph.D. dissertation, Teachers College, Columbia University, 1966), Table IV, p. 284. By permission.

tact becomes a diminishing factor in the mother-child affectional system with the increasing age of the child. When, however, tactile frequency and duration scores are compared by age and social class a surprising exception occurs in the youngest or infant group, where the highest degree of tactile contact would be expected.

In all three classes, [writes Clay] the tactile frequency scores were less for the youngest children, the neonates and non-walking ones, than they were for the walking children. The duration scores were lower also for the working class and upper class infants than they were for the children just above them in age. Only the middle class duration score shows the pattern we would expect to find: the highest score for the youngest age group. The middle class mothers' duration score was much higher than the duration score for the mothers of the other classes: nearly forty minutes in contact for each child in the hour observed. It was this figure that skewed the duration score average and made it appear that the youngest children in the field study sample received the most time in tactile contact. Therefore the conclusion about tactile contact and age must be rephrased to say that overall tactile contact does decline with age but in this culture, as it was observed in the field study, it is the just walking child who receives the most frequent tactile contact and the contact of longest duration, not the infant and non-walking child. From a high at this time, just walking to two years of age, the amount of contact declines regularly as the child grows older.

It is a general assumption that the neonate and infant receive most tactile stimulation, but the truth seems to be that with the advent of hospital deliveries, bottle-feeding, clothes which form a barrier between the caretaker and the infant's skin, the A-group child, in the group from two months to fourteen months of age, the nonwalkers, receives less tactile experience than the B-group child, the just-walkers from fourteen months to two years. The C group included twelve children between two and three years, and the D group included ten three- and four-year-olds. In view of the actual needs of the infant, this is a very striking and significant finding.

Harlow and his co-workers found that in the rhesus mother-infant affectional system three phases were clearly evident: (1) attachment and protection, (2) ambivalence, and (3) separation. The stage of attachment and protection is characterized by virtually total positive conduct, cuddling, cradling, nursing, grooming, restraining, and retrieving. The stage of ambivalence includes both positive and negative responses, such as mouthing or biting, cuffing or slapping, clasp-pulling the fur, and rejecting attempts to maintain physical contact. The stage of separation results in the termination of contact between mother and infant. There is no doubt that similar stages or phases occur in the maternal affectional development of the human mother, and that the behaviors associated with them are of great consequence for the development of the infant. This is especially clearly most significant in the phase of attachment and protection. It is precisely in this most important of these phases that the American mother seems to fail most. In the rhesus monkey the mother normally exhibits a high degree of interest in her infant for the first thirty days, and then begins to display ambivalent responses. In the human mother the period of attachment is normally of much greater duration. But, as Clay says,

Unlike the primate mother, and mothers of many other societies, the American mother largely omits the phase of close bodily attachment. In this culture, the separation of the bodies of the mother and child at birth is the end for the most part of the mother-child physical symbiosis. Instead of a relationship where the mother's need for intimate physical contact exceeds that of the infant, there is a relationship where the mother shows maternal attachment behavior only in response to the child's gross vocal and kinesthetic demands. This difference in the American maternal pattern in the infant's first four months of life is of course due to the fact that close mother-infant tactile contact is not the norm for this culture. The fact that American mothers did not themselves experience close physical contact with their own mothers no doubt reinforces this behavior. The lack of physical proximity between mother and young child, whereby the mother stimulates the infant and in turn picks up and responds to the cues that the infant gives back to her, also reinforces the cultural pattern of separation.

In America both mother and infant are clothed even during breastfeeding, so that the baby, as he is fed, often experiences little more of her skin than the breast, and perhaps an occasional handstroking. In the bottle-feeding situation, which is the rule in America, the infant experiences the very minimum of reciprocal tactile stimulation. The deprivation of tactile stimulation experienced in this way by both infant and mother explains the institutionalization in American culture of the non-expression of affection, especially between mother and baby, through close physical contact. Tactile contact between the American mother and child expresses caretaking and nurturance, rather than love and affection. This is clearly evident from the fact that mothers in this culture touch their walking children more frequently than they do when their children are nonwalking.

In keeping with the findings of other investigators, Clay found that girl babies received more demonstrative acts of affection than boy babies. Mothers seem to be happier about having girl babies than boy babies, and girl babies tend to be weaned later than boys. Moss, Robson, and Pedersen, in a detailed study of maternal stimulation of infants, in Washington, D.C., found that mothers talked, kissed, and rocked in a rocking-chair their male infants, at the examining age of one month, more than they did their female infants at the same age. These investigators suggest that the difference probably reflects a social-affectionate orientation towards the males, involving behaviors that tend to soothe and modulate rather than excite or activate the infant. The mothers significantly more often resorted to the distance receptors of vision and hearing in dealing with their female children than with their male infants at one month of age. Moss and his collaborators suggest that since female infants develop earlier than male infants, the more expressive mothers may have adjusted the type of stimulation they provided for their infants in consonance with the developmental requirements or status of the child. Thus male infants would have received more talking to, more kissing, and more rocking, whereas female infants with their more advanced developmental status would tend to be stimulated through their active attention and processing of stimuli (auditory and visual) ordinarily associated with higher cortical (cognitive) functioning.

Interestingly enough, the animation of the mother's voice was found to be highly reliably predictive of the amount and type of stimulation she provided her infant at one month and three months of age. The animated mothers were found to give their children more stimulation than the soft-spoken mothers. Less educated mothers tended to provide more physical stimulation than more educated mothers. The better-educated mother tended to spend more time talking to her male infant. Fear of strangers and gaze-averting behavior at eight to nine and a half months of age was definitely found to be related to the type of stimulation the infant received from his mother in earlier infancy. The more stimulation, particularly of the distance receptors, the infant received, the more comfortable the infant appeared to be with a stranger at age eight to nine and a half months. These investigators suggest that children who are accustomed to experiencing novel visual and auditory stimulation may have a better mental organization for coping with and assimilating "strangeness." Since strange stimuli are less novel for such children they tend to evoke less of a sense of subjective uncertainty in them. That is to say, the children who receive more stimulation through the distance receptors become more complex cognitively and therefore have more resources for dealing with unfamiliar auditory or visual stimuli.

Tactile demonstrations of affection between mother and daughter are not as inhibited as they are between mother and son. The very thought of any such demonstration of affection between father and son is something that makes most American fathers squirm. A boy putting his arm around the shoulders of another boy is cause for real alarm. It is simply not done. Even women are reluctant to indulge in such open displays of affection towards members of their own sex. One touches others largely in a sexual context. To touch another out of such context is open to grave misinterpretation, since touching is to a large extent restricted to and associated with sex. When intercourse is completed the male ceases to touch his partner and usually retires to his twin bed to spend the rest of the time in pleasurable lack of contact all by himself.

The replacement of the double bed in which husband and wife sleep together by twin beds in which husband and wife sleep apart may well be significantly correlated with the decline in both breastfeeding and the reduction in maternal-infant tactile stimulation which prevailed in earlier times. I have elsewhere suggested that parents who sleep together in the same bed are likely to develop a quite different relationship to one another and towards their children than parents who habitually sleep in separate beds, and that "same-bed" families tend to be more cohesive. "Keeping in contact" in the same bed comprises a very different experience from the contactless separateness of twin-bed sleeping arrangements. In her novel, *Strange Fruit* Lillian Smith makes Alma, the wife of Dr. Tracy or "Tut," reflect as follows:

Sometimes all she could remember of her's and Tut's nights together was the lifting of his leg off her body. There was something almost *dissipated* about the way Tut slept, letting himself go, so, so uncontrolled, you might say. Alma had thought of twin beds but had never done anything about it, for she doubted in her heart that husbands and wives should sleep separately. It was all a little vague to her, but sleeping together, cold weather or hot, seemed a necessary thread in the fabric of marriage, which, once broken, might cause the whole thing to unravel.

Just how she was not certain. She was convinced, however, that her own mother's custom of sleeping in a room separate from father's had caused their family life to be not as successful as it should have been.

Alma was quite right. Such husbands and wives tend to grow "out of touch" with one another. The subject has been investigated by two American anthropologists working in Japan. Drs. William Caudill and David W. Plath studied the co-sleeping patterns of parents and children in Japanese families in Tokyo and Kyoto. They found that in urban Japan an individual can expect to co-sleep in a two-generation group, first as a child and then as a parent, over approximately half his life. Commencing at birth, this goes on till puberty, and then commences again with the birth of the first child, continuing till about the time of the menopause in the mother, and recurring for a few years in old age. In the intervening years the individual generally sleeps in a one-generation group with a sibling after puberty, with a spouse for a few years after marriage, and again with a spouse in late middle age. Sleeping alone is a reluctant alternative most commonly occurring in the years between puberty and marriage. Caudill and Plath offer the broad generalization that "sleeping arrangements in Japanese families tend to blur the distinctions between generations and between the sexes, to emphasize the interdependence more than the separateness of individuals, and to underplay (or largely ignore) the potentiality for the growth of conjugal intimacy between husband and wife in sexual and other matters in favor of a more general familial cohesion."

The speculation the authors offer "concerns the coincidence of those age periods when sleeping alone is most likely to occur, with the age periods when suicide is most likely to occur in Japan. The rates for both types of behavior are highest in adolescence and young adulthood, and again in old age. It might be that sleeping alone in these two periods contributes to a sense of isolation and alienation for an individual who, throughout the rest of his life cycle, seems to derive a significant part of his sense of being a meaningful person from his sleeping physically close by other family members."

Under the conditions of co-sleeping in Japanese families described by Caudill and Plath the kind of relationships they have postulated may well exist. But under other conditions the opposite effects may be produced. For example, among the working classes of Europe and elsewhere children are often forced to occupy the same bed with strangers taken in by the parents as lodgers. The revulsion caused by such experiences may have enduring effects, resulting in avoidance of any kind of physical contact with strangers, as well as in other forms of rejection and withdrawal.

TACTILE DEPRIVATION AND THE HERITAGE OF PURITANISM. In New England, one would expect that the effect of Puritanism would tend to be characterized by child-rearing practices which reduce reciprocal tactile stimulation between mother and child to a minimum, and this is indeed the case. The Fischers in their study of Orchard Town child-rearing practices found that most babies spent a good part of each day alone in a crib, playpen, or in the yard. "Such contact as a baby has with other human beings is not marked by close bodily contact as in many societies."

New Englanders, in their Puritanism, closely resemble the English from whom they came, and, in common with the English, they suffer from the effects of this Puritanism. The upper-class Englishman—and especially the upper-class

Englishwoman—has notoriously been characterized by an inability to exhibit emotion, and a certain striking lack of warmth.* Not all members of the upper classes are characterized by these traits, and certainly many members of the middle and working classes exhibit them. But such traits are generally due to a lack of parental love, a failure experienced in early infancy and throughout childhood which expresses itself in an inability to relate warmly and affectionately towards others.

The custom among the English upper and middle classes of sending their children away to boarding schools at an early age, of institutionalizing them, as it were, outside the warm ambience of the family, deprives these children of the love and affection so necessary for the development of a healthy personality. The privation of parental love, and especially love in the form of tactile stimulation, during infancy, probably constitutes one of the principal causes of the apparent coldness, the seemingly unemotional character, of the upper-class, and often the middle-class, Englishman. On this aspect of the Englishman's character, E. M. Forster has some illuminating comments:

People talk of the mysterious East, but the West also is mysterious. It has depths that do not reveal themselves at the first glance. We know what the sea looks like from a distance; it is of one color, and level, and obviously cannot contain such creatures as fish. But if we look into the open sea over the edge of a boat, we see a dozen colors, and, depth below depth, the fish swimming in them. That sea is the English character—apparently imperturbable and even. The depth and the colors are the English romanticism and the English sensitiveness—we do not expect to

* Well described by Derek Monsey as "the frigid voluptuousness of the dedicatedly unsatisfied English gentlewoman," in his novel, *Its Ugly Head* (New York: Simon & Schuster, 1960), p. 38.

find such things, but they exist. And—to continue my metaphor —the fish are the English emotions, which are always trying to get up to the surface, but don't quite know how. For the most part we see them moving far below, distorted and obscure. Now and then they succeed and we exclaim, "Why, the Englishman has emotions! He actually can feel!" And occasionally we see that beautiful creature, the flying fish, which rises out of the water altogether into the air and sunlight. English literature is a flying fish. It is a sample of the life that goes on day after day beneath the surface; it is a proof that beauty and emotion exist in the salt, inhospitable sea.

Interesting examples of the upper-class and middle-class types of English cold fish are represented by Sir William Eden, the father of Anthony Eden, and Hugh Walpole, the English novelist. The American counterpart is William Randolph Hearst, whose frightful life was also tellingly and sensitively portrayed in Orson Welles's film, *Citizen Kane*. Yet another casebook history of the unloved child is provided by the victim himself, the English newspaperman Cecil King. All of these individuals, representative of untold thousands like them, were alike in having suffered a lacklove childhood and an inability to behave with affection. This is interesting in the light of the fact that in her study of a group of American mothers Clay found that upper-class mothers gave their infants somewhat more tactile affection—tactile affection being defined as behavior through touch designed to convey love—than both working-class and middle-class mothers.

In the bathing of babies, a situation in which one would expect to find increased magnitudes of tactile stimulation for the infant, this is not necessarily the case. Margaret Mead has pointed out how the attention of the American baby is directed away from the personal relationship to his mother by toys which are introduced into his tub. Thus his attention is focused on things rather than on persons. As Mead says, "The average American woman may never hold a little baby until she nurses her own, and even then she often behaves as though she were still afraid that the infant might break in her hands. In New Guinea and Bali, on the contrary, they know all about babies. Small infants are looked after by child nurses as young as 4 years old, and this familiarity is shown in all their movements."

With the passing of the extended family, in which grandparents, aunts and uncles, cousins and other relatives often gave children large amounts of tactile stimulation of various sorts, that kind of experience is now limited to a rather undemonstrative mother. Clay remarks that she observed a grandmother sitting under a tree next to her grandchild strapped in a plastic carrier. "The grandmother," reports Clay, "told me with a degree of sadness that she wanted to pick up the baby, he wanted it, but his mother had told her he had to learn to be by himself."

TACTILE STIMULATION AND SLEEP. Anna Freud has pointed out that "it is a primitive need of the child to have close and warm contact with another person's body while falling asleep, but this runs counter to all the rules of hygiene which demand that children sleep by themselves and not share the parental bed." She goes on to say, "The infant's biological need for the caretaking adult's constant *presence* is disregarded in our Western culture, and children are exposed to long hours of solitude owing to the misconception that it is healthy for the young to sleep, rest, and later play alone. Such neglect of natural needs creates the first breaks in the smooth functioning of the processes of need and drive fulfillment. As a result, mothers seek advice for infants who have difficulty in falling asleep or do not sleep through the night, in spite of being tired."

In Western culture one constantly encounters the phenomenon of children begging their mothers to lie by their side or at least to stay with them until they fall asleep, a supplication which the mother tends to discourage. The endless calls from the child's bed, the demand for the presence of the mother, for an open door, a drink of water, a light, a story, to be tucked in, and so on, are all symptoms of the child's need for that primary object, his mother, to whom he can securely relate. A cuddly toy, a pet one can take to bed, soft materials, and autoerotic activities such as thumbsucking, rocking, masturbation, are the child's means of facilitating the transition from wakefulness to sleep. When these objects are given up a new wave of difficulties in falling asleep may develop.

It is in his second year that the child experiences the need for the close contact that will enable him to fall asleep. It should be given him. A mother who is involved in the welfare of her child should not find it insuperably difficult, even in the modern world, to lie at bedtime by the side of her child. This will usually be necessary only during the second year. She need stay only until the child falls asleep. It is quite possible that with further discoveries in this area the time which should be devoted to this will be reduced or even eliminated. One possibility has been pioneered by the members of the New Zealand Christchurch Parents Centre. These women became interested in the idea that babies might benefit from lying on the soft, springy fleece of lambskins and derive the same sort of comfort that adult patients obtain from invalid-care sheepskins. The lambskins are specially tanned. At the latest report some twenty-four babies were being nursed on the lambskin rugs. "With nearly all babies there was some indication of added comfort from the rug, and in a number of cases parents reported enthusiastically about the longer hours of sleep, and contentment of the baby . . . The added sleep and contentment and the lessening of strain on the mother that resulted with many babies, has been most encouraging."

Mothers of handicapped, and especially cerebral palsied children, report enthusiastically the extra comfort their babies seem to gain from lying on lambskin rugs.*

It is quite possible that when babies are started off on such a lambskin sleeping rug they may have less difficulty in achieving sleep later on. It is an experiment worth trying.

A further report on lambskins indicates that not all skins are suitable. The best skins must be of large area, with a fine dense fleece such as is grown by Corriedale or Merino breeds or the Southdown Romney cross-lamb. Preliminary tests with the latter type of lambskins indicated that babies were more content and slept longer on them than on conventional sheets and mattresses. When deprived of the skins the babies invariably became restless.

THE TACTILE EXPERIENCE OF THE JAPANESE CHILD. Dr. William Caudill and Mrs. Helen Weinstein have made a valuable comparative study of child-rearing methods in Japan as

* "Lambskin Comfort for Handicapped Children," *Parents Centres* (Auckland, N. Z.), Bulletin 41 (November, 1969), p. 14. The sterilization of baby-care lambskin rugs is also discussed on the same page. The lambskin rugs may be obtained from G. L. Bowron & Co., Ltd., Christchurch, New Zealand; The Sheepskin Rug Co., 33 Queen St., Auckland, New Zealand (bank reference—Credit Department, Southern Region H.Q., Crocker Citizens National Bank, Los Angeles, Calif.); and Donald Macdonald (Antartex) Ltd., Lomond Industrial Estate, Alexandria, Dunbartonshire, Scotland (main U.S.A. warehouse, 120 Greenwich Ave., Greenwich, Conn. 06830—shops in London; New York; Cambridge, Mass.; Geneva, Ill.; and Minneapolis, Minn.).

compared with those in the United States. They studied a selected matched sample of thirty Japanese and thirty American infants, three to four months old, equally divided by sex,
all first born, and all from intact middle-class families in
urban settings. On the basis of previous studies these investigators predicted they would find Japanese mothers spending
more time with their infants, and that they would emphasize
physical contact over verbal interaction, and would have as a
goal a passive and contented baby. The American mothers,
they predicted, would spend less time with their infants,
would emphasize verbal interaction rather than physical contact, and would have as a goal an active and self-assertive
baby. These hypotheses were generally confirmed by the investigators, and indeed they agree fully with those of other
students of Japanese and American culture. Caudill and
Weinstein found that "largely because of different patterns
of interaction with their mothers in the two countries, infants have learned to behave in different and culturally appropriate ways by three to four months of age. Moreover,
these differences in infant behavior are in line with preferred patterns of social interaction at later ages as the child
grows to be an adult in Japan and America."

It is generally agreed that Japanese are more "group" oriented and interdependent in their relations with others,
while Americans are more "individual" oriented and independent. Associated with this is the tendency of Japanese to
be more self-effacing and passive as contrasted with Americans, who tend to be more self-assertive and aggressive. "In
matters requiring a decision, Japanese are more likely to rely
on emotional feeling and intuition, whereas Americans will
go to some pains to emphasize what they believe are the ra-
tional reasons for their action . . . Japanese are more sensitive to, and make conscious use of, many forms of nonverbal

communication in human relations through the medium of gestures and physical proximity, in comparison with Americans, who predominantly use verbal communication within a context of physical separateness."

We have already touched upon the co-sleeping family habits of the Japanese in contrast to the separate sleeping habits of Americans, from the earliest age, and the resulting differences in tactile experience in the two cultures. In keeping with these sleeping habits, at least as significant are the bathing practices of Japanese and Americans. In Japan, from the earliest possible age, approximately at the beginning of the infant's second month, the whole family bathes collectively. The mother or another adult holds the infant in her arms while they bathe together in the deep bathtub (*furo*) at home or in the neighborhood public bath (*sento*). This pattern of shared bathing continues for the Japanese child until he is about ten years old, and even later. In contrast with this, the American mother rarely bathes with an infant, but rather gives him a bath from outside the tub, and communicates with him verbally and by positioning his body. Breast-feeding is still more widespread in Japan than is bottle-feeding, and while babies are started on semi-solid food at the end of the first month in America, this is not the case until the end of the fourth month for Japanese babies. Quite clearly the Japanese infant receives a great deal more reassuring tactile stimulation than does the American infant, and of a kind which by the early age of three to four months has already made a distinctively perceptible behavioral difference in the infants of these two cultures. Caudill and Weinstein summarize their findings as follows:

American infants are more happily vocal, more active, and more exploratory of their bodies and their physical environment, than are Japanese infants. Directly related to these findings, the American mother is in greater vocal interaction with her infant, and stimulates him to greater physical activity and exploration. The Japanese mother, in contrast, is in greater bodily contact with her infant, and soothes him toward physical quiescence, and passivity with regard to his environment. Moreover, these patterns of behavior are in line with the differing expectations for later behavior in the two cultures as the child grows to be an adult.

Caudill and Weinstein predict that when they have analyzed their data on two-year-olds and six-year-olds from each culture they will find that these early patterns of behavior will jell and persist.

As Douglas Haring says,

One outstanding fact not stressed in the literature but amply verified involves the almost uninterrupted bodily contact of Japanese infants with mother or nursemaid. Practically never is a baby left to lie alone quietly. Always he rides on someone's back or sleeps close to someone. When he is restless his bearer sways or jiggles from one foot to the other. Some writers deem this jiggling a fearsome experience for the infant. . . . My own unsystematic observations indicate that most Japanese think it soothes the child. At any rate the infant almost constantly feels the reassuring touch of human skin. When he cries he is given the breast, and in lower-class families his sexual organs are manipulated until he falls asleep. Many better-educated Japanese repudiate the latter practice, but they employ nursemaids versed in the folkways rather than in the niceties of genteel refinement.

Then when the child reaches walking age he is quite drastically left on his own a great deal of the time, and must learn to conform to the implicit taboo on touching other people.

As Haring points out, the sudden break in the infant's habitual basic dependence on contact with other persons involves frustration, and frustration will result in emotional behavior designed to compel attention to the need that has been frustrated. In the Japanese boy this takes the form of temper tantrums, the expression of which, either in verbal or physical abuse, is permitted upon the body of the mother, but not upon the father. The expression of temper in girls is strictly forbidden. In the rigidly defined situation of Japanese life no adequate outlets are provided for the effects of frustration, except in childhood abuse of animals and of the mother for boys, and also perhaps through alcoholic intoxication. Girls must repress their expressions of frustration. "Long postponed revenge for childhood frustration—a motivation of which the individual is unconscious—may be accomplished either in suicide or in the sadistic outbursts of war and torture of the helpless. In males these latter outbursts receive social approval. Females apparently live with their repressions, unless the common neurotic malady called *hisuteri* (derived from the English hysteria—usually nymphomania) may be regarded as a consequence."

Undoubtedly related to the sudden cessation of tactility, and especially the relaxing manipulation of the external genitalia of the small child, is the reactive behavior of adolescent and adult males towards their own bodies and those of others. All the visceral functions that received such lavish attention in infancy, in the older Japanese male come to symbolize frustration. Sexual functions, even though they may provide occasion for boasting, are repudiated in disgust. "The unconscious conflict within the growing boy finds in sex a symbol of frustrated aggression and longing for dominance. Behavior related to sex is tinged with sadistic violence; the fierce obscenity of Japanese schoolboys, homosexuality, contempt for wives, and sexual mutilation of helpless enemies all stem perhaps from these unresolved conflicts."

While these socialization processes and the behavioral responses to them characterize pre–World War II Japan, to varying degrees they remain true of large segments of Japanese society today.*

Quite clearly the differences in tactile stimulation undergone by Japanese and American infants play a considerable role in the development of their behavioral differences. What these behavioral differences are has already been suggested in the studies we have cited.

NATIONAL AND CULTURAL DIFFERENCES IN TACTILITY. National and cultural differences in tactility run the full gamut from absolute non-touchability, as among upper-class Englishmen, to what amounts to almost full expression among peoples speaking Latin-derived languages, Russians, and many nonliterate peoples. Those who speak Anglo-Saxon-derived languages stand at the opposite pole in the continuum of tactility to the Latin peoples. In this continuum Scandinavians appear to occupy an intermediate position. I do not propose here a calculus of tactile variations among the peoples of the world. The necessary information for such a discussion is simply not available. Clay's study on a small sample of the population of one local region in North America is the only one of its kind. However, from general observation of the marked differences in tactility observable among different peoples today it is possible to draw certain obvious conclusions.

* For pre-World War II Japan see Alice Bacon, *Japanese Girls and Women,* Boston: Houghton Mifflin Co., 1902; R. F. Benedict, *The Chrysanthemum and the Sword* (Boston: Houghton Mifflin Co., 1946); B. S. Silberman, ed., *Japanese Character and Culture.* (Tucson: University of Arizona Press, 1962); G. DeVos and H. Wagatsuma, *Japan's Invisible Race: Caste and Culture in Personality* (Berkeley: University of California Press, 1966); R. J. Smith and R. K. Beardsley, *Japanese Culture: Its Development and Characteristics* (Viking Fund Publications in Anthropology, vol. 34, 1962).

There exist not only cultural and national differences in tactile behavior but also class differences. In general it seems possible to say that the higher the class, the less there is of tactility, and the lower the class, the more there is. As we have seen, this was not found to be the case by Clay in her American sample, in which the upper-class mothers seemed to be more at ease with tactility than the lower-class mothers. It is possible that this finding could be generalized for the American population as a whole, with exceptions represented by blacks and other "minority" groups. Whereas in Europe, for example, and especially in England, the upper classes are likely to be hereditary and long entrenched in their ways, in America social mobility is so great that one can move from lower to upper-class status in a single generation. Parents of the second generation move very much more freely than their own parents did, not only in the class achieved for them by earlier generations, but in their ideas on such important matters as child-rearing practices. Hence, in America, new members of the upper classes will often give their children more rationalized attention than the members of other classes. Whatever the explanation may be for Clay's sample, there does seem to exist a highly significant correlation between class membership and tactility, and this appears to be largely due to early conditioning.

Among the upper classes of England relationships between parents and children were, and continue to be, distant from birth till death. At birth the child was usually given over to a nurse, who either wetnursed it for a brief period or bottle fed it. Children were generally brought up by governesses and then at an early age sent away to school. They received a minimum amount of tactile experience. It is, therefore, not difficult to understand how, under such conditions, non-touchability could easily become institutionalized as part of the way of life. A well-bred person never touched another without his consent. The slightest accidental brushing against another required an apology, even though the other might be a parent or a sibling. Too often a lacklove childhood combined with a minimum of tactile stimulation, compounded by the experience of a Public School (which in England is so called because the public is not admitted to it), produced a rather emotionally arid human being who was quite incapable of warm human relationships. Such individuals made efficient governors of the British Empire, since they were seldom capable of understanding genuine human need.

It is quite fascinating that not a single book by a member of the upper classes reveals the slightest insight into the nature of these conditions; the few writings produced on the subject were all by members of the middle classes.* It is not that the members of the middle classes necessarily required more tactile affection than members of the upper classes, but that they were simply, in some cases, more articulate about the losses and the indignities they had suffered.

The English public schools, as is well known, were breeding-grounds for homosexuality, for these were all-boy schools and all the teachers were males, and usually the only love a boy ever received was from another boy or a master. The parental inadequacies from which many of these boys suffered produced a high rate of homosexuality. Such famous figures as Algernon Swinburne, J. A. Symonds, Oscar Wilde, Lord Alfred Douglas, and numerous others, were all products of such parents, and such schools. It is not to be won-

* One of the best of these is George Orwell's *Such, Such Were the Joys* (New York: Harcourt, Brace, 1953).

dered at that parentally abandoned children sought to find some human relationship in sexual friendship with others in the same predicament as themselves.

The conditioning in non-tactility received by so many Englishmen of the upper classes seems to have produced a virtual negative sanction on tactility in English culture. This was so much the case that the sense of touch and the act of touching have both been culturally defined as vulgar. The public demonstration of affection is vulgar, touching is vulgar, and only men who are quite outside the pale, like Latin types, Russians, and the like, would ever dream of putting their arms around one another, not to mention such indecencies as kissing one another upon the cheek!

Even more far gone in non-tactility, if such a thing can be imagined, than the English, are the Germans. The emphasis upon the warrior virtues, the supremacy of the hardheaded martinet father, and the complete subordination of the mother in the German family made for a rigidified, unbending character which renders the average German, among other things, a not very tactile being.

Austrian males, however, unlike Germans, are tactually more demonstrative, and will embrace close friends. In Germany this rarely occurred, except among men of Jewish extraction—but that is quite another thing, for among Jews tactility is highly developed.

The Jews, as a tribe, culture, or people, are characterized by a high degree of tactility. "The Jewish mother" has become a byword, for her deep and unremitting care for her children. This meant that until recent times the children were breast fed on demand, that there was a great deal of fondling of children by mother, father, and siblings. Hence, Jews tend to be tactually very demonstrative, and it is considered perfectly normal for an adult male to continue to greet his father with a kiss and an embrace and to do so also on parting. In forty years of close observation I have only once seen an adult American male (in this case in his middle twenties) publicly greet his father with a kiss. Of what cultural origins this American male may have been I do not know.

Americans of Anglo-Saxon origin are not quite as untactual as the English or the Germans, but they do not lag far behind. American boys neither kiss nor embrace their fathers after they have "grown up,"—"grown up" in this sense is generally taken to be about ten years of age. Nor do American males embrace their friends as Latin Americans do.

There are clearly contact peoples and non-contact peoples, the Anglo-Saxon peoples being among the latter. Curious ways in which non-contactuality expresses itself are to be seen in the behavior of members of the non-contact cultures in various situations. It has, for example, been observed that the way an Anglo-Saxon shakes hands constitutes a signal to the other to keep his proper distance. In crowds this is also observable. For example, in a crowded vehicle like a subway, the Anglo-Saxon will remain stiff and rigid, with a blank expression on his face which seems to deny the existence of other passengers. The contrast on the French Metro, for example, is striking. Here the passengers will lean and press against others, if not with complete abandon, at least without feeling the necessity either to ignore or apologize to the other against whom they may be leaning or pressing. Often the leaning and lurching will give rise to good-natured laughter and joking, and there will be no attempt to avoid looking at the other passengers.

While waiting for a bus Americans will space themselves

like sparrows on a telephone wire, in contrast to Mediterranean peoples who will push and crowd together.

Sydney Smith, "The Smith of Smiths," the great English wit, writing in 1820, amusingly described the varieties of the handshake. "Have you noticed," he wrote, "how people shake your hand? There is the *high-official*—the body erect, and a rapid, short shake, near the chin. There is the *mortmain*—the flat hand introduced into your palm, and hardly conscious of its contiguity. The *digital*—one finger held out, much used by the high clergy. There is the *shakus rusticus,* where your hand is seized in an iron grasp, betokening rude health, warm heart, and distance from the Metropolis; but producing a strong sense of relief on your part when you find your hand released and your fingers unbroken. The next to this is the *retentive shake*—one which, beginning with vigour, pauses as it were to take breath, but without relinquishing its prey, and before you are aware begins again, till you feel anxious as to the result, and have no shake left in you. Worse, there is the *pisces*—the damp palm like a dead fish, equally silent, equally clammy, and leaving its odour in your hand."

The reference to the handshake brings us to the matter of tactile salutations in general. These represent a form of tactile behavior which has received very little attention. The handshake is clearly an evidence of friendliness. Ortega y Gasset has elaborated an anthropologically quite unsound theory of the origin of the handshake. In this he sees the submission of the vanquished or of the slave to his master. The theory is not by any means novel, but, as Westermarck points out, handshaking in many cases seems to have the same origin as other ceremonies consisting in bodily contact. Salutatory gestures may express not only absence of evil intentions but positive friendliness. Whatever its origins the handshake is quite obviously a tactile communication. So is the placing together of the palms of the hands, placing the hand on the heart, nose rubbing, embracing, kissing, and even the backslapping, cheek-tweaking, and hair-mussing in which some people indulge. Westermarck long ago recognized that these various forms of salutation by contact "are obviously direct expressions of affection." He goes on to add that "we can hardly doubt that the joining of hands serves a similar object when we find it combined with other tokens of good will. Among some of the Australian natives, friends, on meeting after an absence, 'will kiss, shake hands, and sometimes cry over one another.' * In Morocco equals salute each other by joining their hands with a quick motion, separating them immediately; and kissing each his own hand. The Soolimas, again, place the palms of the right hands together, carry them to the forehead, and from thence to the left side of the chest (p. 151)."

Cheek patting, head patting, chin chucking are all, in the Western world, forms of behavior indicating affection, and all are tactile. Such tactile salutations, as evidence of friendliness or affection, are probably founded on the earliest experiences of tactile affection received from the mother (and others) as a child.

Sexual differences in salutations are of interest here. For example, in the Western world it is customary for men to shake hands, but not for women to do so; they kiss or embrace when they are friends, and shake hands only when meeting for the first time or as casual acquaintances. Men do

* For an account of weeping as a form of salutation see W. G. Sumner, A. G. Keller, and M. R. Davie, *The Science of Society* (4 vols., New Haven: Yale University Press, 1927), vol. 4, pp. 568–70.

not shake hands with women, but bow, unless the woman extends her hand, when in the English-speaking world it will be shaken, and in the Latin-speaking world kissed. In recent years, in their growing affection for women, men have taken to kissing them where formerly they would merely have bowed or shaken hands. Different times, different mores. In Elizabethan England kissing as a greeting was extended to all members of the same class, whether friends or strangers. Erasmus (1466?–1536) in one of his letters comments on this delightful custom of the English. It would not be too bold an inference from this that perhaps the English, as children, received a great deal more tender loving care in Elizabethan days than they did in a period like that of Victoria and her son Edward, a period, as Rupert Brooke put it, so full of impalpable restraints.

It is of great interest that in the middle 1960's something of the importance of the skin should have been rediscovered by so-called "encounter," "Marathon," and "Sensitivity Training" groups. These groups usually consist of adults or older adolescents. A principal emphasis in such groups is on touching. All diffidence is dropped and one is encouraged to embrace others, caress them, hold hands with them, bathe in the nude with them, and even be massaged.

Everyone enjoys having his back scratched, and to be massaged constitutes one of the supreme pleasures. But these are physical gratifications. These various groups are concerned with much more than physical pleasures. What they seek to achieve is a greater behavioral aliveness to their own and others' presence, relatedness to the environment; they seek to put people who have become dissociated back into touch with their fellow man and the world in which they are living.

The idea is a good one even though it comes late in the day for many of the participants. It runs counter to the Freudian notion that touching should comprise no part of therapy. Freud himself was a bit of a cold fish, and one cannot avoid the suspicion that he was insufficiently fondled when he was an infant. However that may be, the rediscovery of the skin as an organ which, in its own way, requires just as much attention as the mind, is long overdue. The therapeutic benefits resulting from the experiences in these various groups in which tactility plays a significant role have been reported to be appreciable.

Canadians of Anglo-Saxon origins perhaps even outdo the English in their non-tactuality. On the other hand, French Canadians are as tactually demonstrative as their counterparts are in their land of origin.

The manner in which Frenchmen will embrace and kiss their male friends, and the embracing and kissing that takes place on ceremonial occasions, as when a general conferring a decoration upon another officer will embrace and kiss him ceremonially on both cheeks, embarrasses Anglo-Saxons into deprecatory giggles. Whereas the non-tactuality of Anglo-Saxons means to most tactual peoples that they are unemotional and cold.

The Russians, who are a highly tactual people, receive a great deal of cutaneous stimulation when they are young, and continue in the habit of tactility all through their lives. The swaddling which most Russians customarily underwent as infants ensured them a great deal of tactile stimulation, for they were usually unswaddled in order to be breast fed, otherwise fed, bathed, cleaned, and in other ways attended, a fact which seems to have been overlooked by the proponents of the "swaddling hypothesis" who claimed that many of the national traits of Great Russians (Central and Northeastern Russians) could be explained by the restraints such children suffered as infants as a consequence of swaddling. The child was kept isolated from its parents, with only siblings and maids for human contact, and was only brought out of the nursery or children's quarters in order to perform in some manner such as the recitation of poetry, the playing of a musical instrument, or singing. During infancy, according to the swaddling hypothesis, the swaddling inhibits muscular activity, while the release from swaddling in order to be fed and otherwise cared for becomes associated with an "all or none" feeling toward pleasure which the Russian adult displays in his emotional life, an emotional life in which gratification is experienced as orgiastic.

There has been much misunderstanding concerning the nature of swaddling. It takes skill to do it. As Peter Wolff has written, "*Swaddling* is a very effective method to quiet a fussy baby, provided it is done by someone who knows how, and who sees to it that the baby is immobilized. When the swaddling is done unskillfully so that the clothing simply restricts the range of movement without inhibiting it totally, the procedure has a marked arousal effect and may provoke the 'mad cry.' The critical difference is probably that 'poor' swaddling generates a constant background of *variable* proprioceptive feed-back, whereas 'good' swaddling generates a constant background of tactile stimulation."

The swaddling hypothesis has been severely criticized and found wanting on virtually every ground. Under the Soviet system swaddling has been largely abandoned throughout the Russias.

In *The Study of Culture at a Distance,* edited by Mead and Métraux, there is a valuable account of the sense of

touch among the Russians, written by a sensitive woman informant in the Research on Contemporary Cultures project.
It is well worth reproducing here in its entirety.

The Dictionary of the Russian Language defines the sense of
touch as follows: "In reality all five senses can be reduced to one
—the sense of touch. The tongue and palate sense the food; the
ear, sound waves; the nose, emanations; the eyes, rays of light."
That is why in all textbooks the sense of touch is always mentioned first. It means to ascertain, to perceive, by body, hand, or
fingers.

There are two words to express the idea "to feel." If one feels
with some outer part of the body, it is *ossyazat;* but to feel without touching, without direct contact, is *oschuschat* physically,
morally, or spiritually: "I feel (*oschuschat*) too cold or cold", or
"I feel (*oschuschat*) happiness." But when I feel something with
my fingers, I *ossyazat*—I don't really feel, I finger, grope.

Though there exists an adverb *ossyasatelny* (tangible), Russians avoid using it. I have never heard anybody using it, nor
have I come across it in literature. Tangible evidence in Russian
will be "material proof." Touch is not considered the right way
of exploration. One does not have to finger a thing when one can
see it with one's eyes. One of my [Russian] college professors
complained that his students were "savages." When he showed
them a bone, drawing their attention to a cavity, the majority of
the students poked their fingers into it. Children were taught not
to touch things. They learned very quickly, and when you
handed a child something you wanted him to feel—like a piece
of velvet or a kitten—the child picked it up and put it against
his cheek.

The standard joke among lower-class people was for a man to
ask a woman, "Nice calico you are wearing. How much did you
pay a yard?" And under the pretext of feeling the material, he
would pinch the woman.

Russians in general touch each other much less than Americans do. There is hardly any horseplay, slapping on the back,
patting, fondling of children. The exception is when somebody is

very happy or drunk. Then he hugs somebody. But that is not touching. He opens his arms wide as if to embrace the whole world, and then presses you against his breast. The breast is the dwelling place of the soul, and this gesture means that he has taken you to his heart.

These are interesting observations, though not entirely internally consistent. For example, if Russians are non-tactile why is it that the students poked their fingers into the cavity of the bone? In spite of the fact that this informant states that hugging is not touching, the fact is that it is very much so. Soviet officials when they meet embrace and often kiss each other, and may behave in this manner toward nationals of other countries, if one may depend upon what one sees in TV news reports and photographs.

Several students have reported the emphasis they believe Russians place on visual experience. Thus Leites writes of their "desire to translate all the abstractions visually." Haimson believes that in contrast with the "objective" thinking that characterizes Western society, and which he believes is largely founded on motor activity and tactile manipulation of external objects, the visual thinking of Great Russians is singularly lacking in specificity, especially when evaluated by the measure of manipulation. The suggestion is that tactual manipulation is important in the development of abstract and conceptual thought. These students suggest that an element is lacking in Russian abstract thought, present in the concrete situation, and which may be approached through tactual or physical manipulation. Combined with the supposed effects of swaddling upon the kinesthetic movements of the child, the lack of the tactual/manipulative approach to experience is somehow seen to affect the Russian's ability to grasp the essentials of a given whole, to break up a given whole in parts, to isolate and synthesize them. The "whole," on the contrary, is likely to be seen as consisting of overlapping and contradictory items, all of which being lumped together, constitute one diffused whole, to which one responds with "emotion and intensity." Russian thinking is declared to be deficient in logical simplicity, consistency, and completeness.

Interesting as these observations are, it would be of value to have them explored further, and to have the comments of informed students of the childhood and development of "Great Russians."

MOTHER, FATHER, CHILD, AND SKIN. In the symbiotic relationship in which the infant is programmed to continue with his mother, skin contact, as we have seen, plays a fundamental role. It is a communication which the father is also designed to make through the skin, if not in quite as massive and continuous a manner as the mother. But in civilized societies men are even more enveloped by clothes than women and so this important cutaneous means of early communication between father and child tends to be nullified by this artificial barrier. A basic factor in the development of the ability to love is the growing reciprocal involvement in the source from which the pleasure-giving sensory stimulations are received. Between mother and child there is normally an exchange of pleasure-giving experiences. The father, in civilized societies, is to a large extent deprived of the possibility of such direct reciprocal pleasure-giving exchanges. It is, therefore, not surprising that children in these societies should develop such close identifications with the mother.

The male in all societies is at greater risk in this, as in all other connections. As Ritchie has pointed out, "The female, as she grows and develops, has before her in more or less continuous direct relationship, the model of her mother. The man, as he goes through life, begins his life also in primary relationship to a maternal object but he has to give it up, he has to leave off identification with the mother, he has to take on the full male role. Males have to switch identification during development, and all sorts of things can go wrong in this." And, unfortunately, they frequently do. The male has a much harder time than the female does, in growing up and separating himself from the loving mother, and in identifying himself with a father with whom he is nowhere nearly as deeply involved as he remains with the mother; this often puts some strain upon him. The switch in identification he is called upon to make results in something of a conflict. This he usually seeks to resolve by, in part, rejecting the mother and relegating her to a status inferior to that into which he has, so to speak, been thrust. Masculine anti-feminism can be regarded as a reaction-formation designed to oppose the strong unconscious trend towards mother-worship. When the male's defenses are down, when he is *in extremis,* when he is dying, his last, like his first word, is likely to be "mother," in a resurgence of his feeling for the mother he has never really repudiated, but from whom he has been forced, at the overt level, to disengage himself.

If in our culture we could learn to understand the importance of fathers as well as mothers giving their infants adequate tactile satisfactions, we would be taking a considerable step towards the improvement of human relations. There is nothing to prevent a father from bathing his infant child, from drying it, fondling it, caressing it, cuddling it, changing its diapers and cleaning it, from holding it, rocking it, carrying it, playing with it, and continuing to give it a good deal of affectionate tactile stimulation. The only thing that stands in the way of such behavior on the part of males is the ancient and outmoded tradition that such conduct is feminine and therefore unbecoming a male. Fortunately, this is a tradition which is rapidly breaking down and increasingly one sees young fathers involved with their children very much more deeply and in all sorts of "feminine" ways which only a generation or so ago were considered beneath the dignity of a "real" male. Dignity, as Laurence Sterne pointed out, is usually a mysterious carriage of the body calculated to conceal the infirmities of the mind.

Winnicott has observed that the physical holding of the child is a form of loving, that it is, in fact, perhaps the only way in which a mother can show the infant her love for it. This is equally true for the father or, for the matter of that, for anyone else. And as Winnicott says, "There are those who can love an infant and there are those who cannot; the latter quickly produce in the infant a sense of insecurity, and distressed crying."

TACTILE STIMULATION AND THE EXPRESSION OF HOSTILITY. During the nineteenth century, and probably also in earlier centuries, males in the Western world often indulged in the peculiar custom of greeting children with noxious manipulations of their skin. Such practices lasted well into the twentieth century. The victims of these assaults must have been sorely puzzled by such behavior and in some cases probably developed some strange ideas concerning the relationships between skin, pain, and the putative demonstration of affection. It is of interest to note that males exclusively were guilty of such sadistic practices, and then usually only towards male children, although girls with braids did not entirely escape their attentions. A favorite trick was to grasp the child's cheek between thumb and forefinger and give it a thorough tweak, or the ear might be so treated or pulled or given an even more painful flick with a finger. Hair mussing, pinching, a spank on the bottom or a push were among the other engaging indignities to which children, all in the guise of affection, were subjected. A hearty slap on the back was usually reserved for older adolescent boys and males up to middle age. Such demonstrations of affection by painful attacks on the skin could only have been performed by individuals who had themselves been the victims of such abnormal treatment.

Just as those who have been inadequately loved, or have been frustrated in their need for love as infants will exhibit a great deal of hostility in their verbal activities, so, too, those who have been failed in the experience of tactile affection will often be awkward and crude in their attempts at demonstrations of such affection. There are men who almost crush the hand they shake when introduced to another male, who with their familiars punch them in the chest or abdomen, as a mark of affection. The same males tend to be rough, awkward, and crude with "the gentler sex." Since a lacklove infancy and the privation of tactile affection generally go together, it is not surprising to find that the unloved child grows up to be not only awkward in his demonstrations of love but also awkward in his body relationships towards others. Such persons rub others the wrong way because they have been failed in the experience of being stroked the right way.

There has been a great change in the earlier forms of hostile demonstration of "affection" towards boys, but what remains is the expression of anger towards the child in the form of aggressive tactilisms, such as slapping, spanking, or shoving. "Corporeal punishment" is still widely practiced throughout the Western world, and the skin not only made a target and a vehicle for the experience of pain, but an organ which is directly associated with anger, punishment, sin, aggression, naughtiness, and evil. As Lawrence Frank has remarked,

Spanking and slapping are often used to punish a child, utilizing this tactual sensitivity as the chief mode of making him suffer, thus depriving him of his usual comforting, and giving instead painful contacts.

This infantile tactuality, like his other organic needs, is gradually transformed as the child learns to accept mother's voice as a surrogate, her reassuring tones of voice giving him an equivalent for his close physical contacts, her angry scolding voice serving as a punishment and making him cry as if hit.

An unkind remark "hurts" just as if it were a slap or a painful blow to the body. A cutting remark causes its target to "bleed" just as if his skin were slashed. Words may also "sting to the quick."

Class differences in the use of angry words containing the threat of tactile punishment were very marked in Clay's study. The working-class mothers used words harshly, the middle class used them sparingly, while the upper class "used them most often in a kind of affectionate play and, more than the other classes, they combined touch and words."

Some parents, particularly fathers, make it a point to tell their children before they strap them why they are being punished. One can thus learn to dissociate the infliction of bodily pain from the display of any emotion at all. The Nazis were particularly adept at this, and there can be little doubt, as we have seen, that their affectless inhumanity was in no little part due to their early conditioning, with tactile experience largely neglected or else restricted to a punishing kind. This would seem to be an especially undesirable form of conditioning.

The canings, usually administered by senior prefects, customary in English public schools, during which any display of emotion on the part of either the caner or his victim was strictly tabooed, undoubtedly served to produce a dissociation between pain and emotion. Hence, one could remain not only uninvolved with the pain of others, but inflict it upon them without in any way feeling that one was being anything but just. Hence, the great pleasure educated Englishmen have often taken in wit that was cruel, and the complete indifference and lack of understanding of the consequences of their conduct.*

One wonders whether tattooing in the Western world may not be related to an exhibitionistic desire to reward oneself and one's skin through a regressively painful experience resulting in a permanent embellishment of the abused organ.

In immediate anticipation of a spanking and during the assault the child is often terrified, exhibiting all the accompaniments of extreme fear, pallor, muscle rigidity, accelerated heartbeat, and weeping. In later years, under conditions of emotional upset persons who have undergone such childhood experiences will frequently exhibit similar reactions. Or in an effort to defend themselves against the autonomic discharge of feeling, they will "bite their lips," grow rigid, or clasp one hand with the other in a firm grip. This is a method, like keeping "a stiff upper lip," of preventing one's

* This was strikingly exhibited in the English film *If,* widely seen in the United States in 1969.

emotions from expressing themselves, of holding back the tears, of bracing oneself for the blow by employing muscle tension. Muscle tension as a method of keeping emotionally disturbing feelings under control has been remarked by many observers. Or one can dig one's nails into the palms of one's hands until they bleed, in an effort to counteract the expression of emotion, or use the skin ambivalently as a means of both drawing attention to one's needs and at the same time rejecting the other. As Clemens Benda has put it, "Skin diseases vividly demonstrate the difficulties of maintaining contact—a sore skin, a running nose, an infected mouth—each area of external or internal contact is a possible spot for an interference with the even flow of human exchange."

It is here being suggested that behavior of this kind is significantly related to the tactile experiences of the individual during infancy and childhood.

The weeping which is usually associated with physical punishment in childhood may, in later years, express itself in weeping through the skin. Kepecs and his co-workers in a series of ingenious experiments have shown that in emotional weeping the visible expression "is not limited in its effects to the lacrimal glands, but also finds expression in other parts of the body, including the skin." Having, under hypnosis, induced an artificial cantharides blister in the skin of their experimental subjects, the investigators then induced various emotional states in them and measured the amount of fluid exudation into the blister site. Emotional states were associated with a rise in the exudation rate, especially in weeping; the heavier the weeping the higher the exudation rate. Interestingly enough, as would be expected, inhibition of weeping was associated first with a fall and then with a great rise in exudation rate. Thus, the male of the English-speaking world who is everywhere taught that "a little man" doesn't cry, having repeatedly been caused to repress his desire to weep until he has become incapable of weeping from his lacrimal glands, often begins, in later life, to weep through his skin or his gastrointestinal tract. It is now well established that in a large proportion of cases of atopic dermatitis there is associated a strong but inhibited desire to weep.

INFANT-DIRECTED TACTILE BEHAVIOR TOWARDS THE MOTHER. Harlow has made it clear, in his studies of rhesus monkeys, that the most important of the young animal's experiences, for its subsequent development, is bodily contact with its mother, and so it is with the young of *Homo sapiens.*

The four phases of the child-mother affectional system, in both human infants and infant monkeys, are: (1) a reflex stage in which the infant reacts automatically to the stimuli presented by the mother; (2) a stage of affectionate attachment; (3) a security stage, and (4) a stage of independence. The reflex stage lasts only a few weeks in rhesus monkeys and a few months in human infants. The phase of affectionate attachment begins in the human infant at between two and three months of age, and develops gradually during the first year. By smiling, cuddling, gurgling, and the like the baby begins to show active voluntary affection for its mother. The primary tie to the mother appears to operate, in the rhesus monkey, through the two systems of nursing and contacting; these are primarily operative during the first year. Clinging and following, that is, visual and auditory responsiveness to the mother, are at their peak in the second year.

The third stage, the security stage, follows shortly after the commencement of the attachment phase. The so-called six-months anxiety is thought to mark the beginning of this phase, which is considered to be the period at which the infant begins to experience visually induced fear reactions. Among the maternal responses to the infant at this stage are acts of comfort, protection, and reassurance in all situations in which the infant feels fearful and insecure. Under such conditions little monkeys run to their mother and attach to her. "Within minutes or even seconds after attaching, the subject's hands and body relax and the monkey (or child) will visually explore the frightening stimulus with little or no sign of anxiety." In time, the security responses of the infant, derived from the security-giving satisfactions his mother has given him, enable the young monkey to leave the mother, and explore the world tentatively at first, and later, more securely, for himself.

As Clay puts it, "The mother can be thought of as the center or pivot of the small child's security. As the child becomes able to move about he no longer wants to remain physically in contact with the mother; visual contact is sufficient. The concept of behavior distance can be used to explain the distance from the mother that the mobile child is able to experience comfortably." As a child grows older in the socialization process, behavior distance is increased.

In her study Clay found that it was the non-walking toddlers who spent most time in contact with their mothers. It was at this period that the children's affectionate attachment to their mothers was at its height. As soon as the child is able to walk his independent forays away from the mother in the "exhilaration of his new mobility and excitement of learning about the world around him" grow more frequent.

His independence, however, is tentative, for he must maintain visual contact with his mother or know where she is in order to feel safe.

The child, Clay found, who had not experienced satisfactory tactile contact with his mother did not make any tactile approaches to her. There were two examples of this behavior, both of them in children in the crawling stage, who stayed away from their mothers during the period when affectionate attachment is usually at its height. However, it appeared that children who had experienced a highly satisfactory tactile relationship with the mother did not come to the mother for more. Finally, overanxious children tended to have very high tactile needs, a condition which showed itself in the physical use of the mother as a haven of security. One of these children had suffered from inadequate maternal responsiveness, while two others appeared to be reacting to marital difficulties between their parents. "Like the infant monkeys, all three children clung to their mothers and were unable, except for relatively short sallies, to go out, explore and play in the environment."

In Clay's group middle-class children expressed more tactual affection towards their mothers than did the children of the other two classes. Clay suggests that this may have been due to the greater duration of tactile contact they received in the neonate and just-walking stages of development.

The Harlows remark that "all the mother-infant interactions relating to nursing, bodily contact, and following-imitation contribute to security, although there is evidence that sheer bodily contact-comfort is the dominant variable in the rhesus monkey." This appears also to be the case in the human infant.

CONTACT AND PLAY. The importance of play in learning is now recognized by almost everyone, and, as Harlow has pointed out, all forms of play behavior reduce to expressions of the fundamental motive of exploration and manipulation. "Social play is preceded by exploration of the physical environment and play with inanimate objects, and apparently social exploration and play take precedence over environmental exploration and play because of the greater regard and feedback given by animate rather than inanimate objects."

Among the monkeys observed by the Harlows, object exploration preceded social exploration, and each involved three identifiable components: (1) a visual exploration, in which the monkey orients closely to, and peers intently at, the object or other animal; (2) an oral exploration, a gentle mouthing response; and (3) a tactual exploration, limited to a transient clasp, either of a physical object or of another animal. Here, once more, we perceive that the tactile sense remains the dominant one, and it is important to note that these components are not separate but interrelated, so that when one speaks of visual exploration, this is not to be construed as a behavior unrelated to the tactual-oral explorations, but coordinated with them.

In the rhesus monkey close physical ties between infant and mother must cease before play can develop with agemates and peers. Here, too, three stages may be identified: (1) a reflex stage, (2) a manipulation stage, and (3) a stage of interactive play. In the reflex stage during the early weeks of life infants will fixate each other visually and make approach attempts. If they contact each other, they cling to one another reflexly as they do to their mothers. When two infants are involved they cling in a ventral-to-ventral manner, if more than two are involved they will cling in a typical "choo-choo" pattern. In the manipulation stage, beginning at the end of the first month, the infants explore each other as they would objects, with eyes, hands, mouth, and body, alternating manipulation of age-mates with manipulation of the physical environment. Like the preceding stage, this is a presocial period in peer relationships, the exploratory activity characterizing it persisting into the stage of interactive play. As they come to learn more from their experiences of each other they gradually begin to respond to one another as social rather than as physical objects, and social play emerges from the matrix of manipulatory play. The third stage, interactive play, marks the development of genuine social interactions between peers. This occurs at about three months of age, and overlaps with manipulatory play and sequence of exploration of the physical environment. Interactive play develops in the human infant during the second year of life.

Clay observed a pattern of development of play behavior in her subjects consisting of alternating periods of mother-child interaction, followed by periods of play at a distance from the mother, with a subsequent return to her for further communication.

As the child grows older and extends his behavior distance, the time actually in contact with the mother, or next to her, decreases and the time spent away from her increases. The kinds of contact and the kinds of feedback that the child requires from the mother for his emotional well-being change also. Where at first the small child or toddler might want to sit upon the mother's lap for several minutes, the actively mobile child may just run up to his mother and say, "Hi!" This kind of psychological tagging in at the source of security is a pattern that was observed for almost all the children. It was especially noticeable among the older children whose mothers allowed them a larger circle of play.

The "tagging in" is especially important in making certain that contact is still maintained, especially when one is beginning to explore other parts of the world for oneself. As Clay found, with time the child comes to depend less and less upon his mother for physical contact, and devotes more and more time to play away from her. At the younger ages he is still not ready to play independently at any remove from her for more than short periods of time. He still needs the reassurance of contact with her, to keep in touch both physically and visually.

As Clay emphasizes, the young of all mammals must learn to play. The development of the ability to play in relation to the mother will depend upon whether or not the infant's tentatively playful approaches are rewarded. Working-class mothers apparently do not encourage their young to play with them as much as middle-class and upper-class mothers do—the upper-class children, in Clay's study, make more tactile play approaches to their mothers than do middle-class children.

Interestingly, Clay found that mothers who did not give their youngsters much tactile stimulation nevertheless encouraged their children to play with them. It was almost as though the direct physical contact and the feelings it arouses were considered uncomfortable, but that physical contact, through games, mediated often through objects like a ball, a picnic spoon, or a popsicle stick were acceptable substitutes.

Clay refers to Williams' study of tactility among the Dusun of Borneo, in which he called attention to the need to study ". . . ways in which individuals are required, or expected, to relinquish particular tactile experiences and develop compensatory symbolic substitutes at different periods in enculturation." This kind of learning of symbolic substitutes for tactility is seen in the behavior of the children who approached their mothers with various play objects. And it is important to understand that a great many other forms of symbolic learning of a similar kind constitute but an extension of the learning based on the mind of the skin.

Tsumori has shown how important the prolonged experience of exploratory play activities is in the development and discovery of new adaptive behaviors in Japanese macaques, and Hall makes it quite clear that much of the later behavior of the nonhuman primate is learned in social situations and practiced in play.

These observations hold true with even greater force in the human species.*

The separation or detachment from the mother in all mammals plays an important role in the initiation and extension of the infant's contacts with the rest of the world. As Rheingold and Eckerman point out, even when the infant is carried about, his contacts with the world are necessarily circumscribed. It is only when he leaves his mother's side by himself that many new kinds of learning can occur.

The infant comes in contact with an increasing number and variety of objects. Through touching them he learns their shapes, dimensions, slopes, edges, and textures. He also fingers, grasps, pushes, and pulls, and thus learns the material variables of heaviness, mass, and rigidity, as well as the changes in visual and auditory stimuli that some objects provide. He moves from place to place within a room, and from one room to another. From the

* For two valuable books on play see J. Huizinga, *Homo Ludens* (New York: Roy Publishers, 1950), and H. C. Lehman and P. A. Witty, *The Psychology of Play Activities* (New York: A. S. Barnes Co., 1927).

consequent changes in visual experience, coupled with his own kinesthetic sensations, he learns the position of objects relative to other objects. He also learns the invariant nature of many sources of stimulation. In a word, he learns the properties of the physical world, including the principles of object constancy and the conservation of matter.

CONTACT, INDIVIDUATION, AND AFFECTION. Awareness of self is largely a matter of tactile experience. Whether we are walking, standing, sitting, lying, running, or jumping, whatever the other messages we receive from muscle, joint, and other tissue, the first and most extensive of these messages are received from the skin. Long before body temperature either falls or rises from external causes, it is the skin that will register the change and communicate to the cortex the necessary messages designed to initiate those behaviors which will lead to the appropriate response.

In separating himself from the mother the exploratory activities in which the infant engages, though based on what he sees, fundamentally constitute an extension of learning through tactile experience. Vision endows the tactile experience with a formal meaning, but it is the tactile meanings which endow the objects seen with form and dimension.

In summarizing the results of her study Clay concludes: "The question that we have been pursuing in this project, whether the amount and kind of tactile stimulation and contact that American mothers give their babies and young children is adequate to their physiological and emotional needs, must therefore be answered negatively." The mothers observed at the beach were not so much concerned with holding, cradling, cuddling, caressing or expressing love to their babies and young children, as with controlling their behavior and attending to their nurturance needs. "Comforting, playing and giving tactile affection were maternal behaviors of much less importance and frequency." Repeatedly Clay observed that tactile contact between mothers and preverbal children most often expressed caretaking and nurturance, rather than love and affection.

The impersonal child-rearing practices which have long been the mode in the United States, with the early severance of the mother-child tie, and the separation of mothers and children by the interposition of bottles, blankets, clothes, carriages, cribs, and other physical objects, will produce individuals who are able to lead lonely, isolated lives in the crowded urban world with its materialistic values and its addiction to things. Clay properly feels that perhaps a higher degree of closeness within the family, commencing with the primary mother-child tactile tie, would help Americans to feel somewhat more anchored in the family, while an acceptance of the importance of emotional tactile needs beyond childhood might help them to withstand the impersonal pressures of our times and the inevitable vicissitudes of life.

This is, perhaps, expecting too much of touch relationships within the family, but the common adoption of such tactile practices is certainly a consummation devoutly to be wished. The contemporary American family constitutes only too often an institution for the systematic production of mental illness in each of its members, as a consequence of its concentration on making each of them a "success." Which means that the individual is gradually converted into a mechanism with a built-in design for achievement in accordance with the prevailing requirements, entailing the suppression of emotion, the denial of love and friendship, the ability to trade with whatever serves him for a conscience, while conveying an unvarying appearance of rectitude. Towards this end, parents feel that they must not give their children "too much" affection, even in the reflex and affectionate stages when children literally cannot receive too much affection, they are so much in need of it. All sorts of reasons and rationalizations are produced: the child will be spoiled, he will become too dependent upon others, he will develop abnormal interests in his mother, or in other boys or even girls, he will become feminine, and so on. The cultural goal is to make "a he-man" of the male, and a successful manipulator of her world of the female. Given the emphasis on such goals, whether consciously or unconsciously followed, the success-oriented American would still constitute the problem he presents, no matter how adequate the tactile experience of the young might be. The importance of tactility in the socialization process, therefore, is not likely to be overemphasized, nor should it be, as it has been, underemphasized.

The importance of tactile experience, especially in the preverbal stages of human development, cannot, in fact, be overemphasized, and it is the burden of this book to convey that message.

ENVOI

Camerado, this is no book,
Who touches this touches a man.
Walt Whitman, So Long!

IN THE PRECEDING pages we have seen that the human significance of touching is considerably more profound than has
hitherto been understood. The skin as the sensory receptor
organ which responds to contact with the sensation of touch,
a sensation to which basic human meanings become attached
almost from the moment of birth, is fundamental in the development of human behavior. The raw sensation of touch
as stimulus is vitally necessary for the physical survival of the
organism. In that sense it may be postulated that the need
for tactile stimulation must be added to the repertoire of
basic needs in all vertebrates, if not in all invertebrates as
well.

Basic needs, defined as tensions which must be satisfied if
the organism is to survive, are the needs for oxygen, liquid,
food, rest, activity, sleep, bowel and bladder elimination, escape from danger, and the avoidance of pain. It should be
noted that sex is not a basic need since the survival of the organism is not dependent upon its satisfaction. Only a certain

number of organisms need satisfy sexual tensions if the species is to survive.* However that may be, the evidence points unequivocally to the fact that no organism can survive very long without externally originating cutaneous stimulation.

Cutaneous stimulation may take innumerable forms, such as those of temperature or radiation, liquid or atmospheric stimulation, pressure, and the like. Such cutaneous stimulation is clearly necessary for the physical survival of the organism. Yet even this elementary fact does not seem to have been adequately recognized. Important as such cutaneous stimulation is, the form with which we have been principally concerned in this book is tactile stimulation, that is, touching. By touching is meant the satisfying contact or feeling of another's or one's own skin. Touching may take the form of caressing, cuddling, holding, stroking or patting with the fingers or whole hand, or vary from simple body contact to the massive tactile stimulation involved in sexual intercourse.

As we have seen, in our very brief survey, different cultures vary in both the manner in which they express the need for tactile stimulation and the manner in which they satisfy it. But the need is universal and is everywhere the same, though the form of its satisfaction may vary according to time and place.

The evidence presented in these pages suggests that adequate tactile satisfaction during infancy and childhood is of fundamental importance for the subsequent healthy behavioral development of the individual. The experimental and other research findings on other animals, as well as those on humans, show that tactile deprivation in infancy usually re-

* For a discussion of the basic needs see A. Montagu, *The Direction of Human Development* (Revised edition, New York: Hawthorn Books, 1970).

sults in behavioral inadequacies in later life. Significant as these theoretic findings are, it is their practical value that is of principal interest to us. In short, how may these findings be utilized in the raising of healthy human beings?

It should be evident that in the development of the person tactile stimulation should begin with the newborn baby. The newborn should, whenever possible, be placed in his mother's arms, and allowed to remain by her side as long as she may desire. The newborn should be put to nurse at his mother's breast as soon as possible. The newborn should not be removed to a "nursery" nor placed in a crib. The cradle should be restored to universal usage as the best auxiliary and substitute for cradling in the mother's arms ever invented. Fondling of the infant can scarcely be overdone—a reasonably sensible human being is not likely to overstimulate an infant—hence, if one is to err in any direction it were better in the direction of too much rather than too little fondling. Instead of baby carriages infants should be carried on their mother's backs, and also on their fathers' backs, in the equivalent of the Chinese *madai* or Eskimo parka.*

Any abrupt cessation of fondling should be avoided, and it is recommended that in cultures of the Western world, and in the United States particularly, parents express their affection for each other and for their children more demonstratively than they have in the past. It is not words so much as acts communicating affection and involvement that children, and, indeed, adults, require. Tactile sensations become

* Such a baby-carrier may be obtained from the La Leche League, 9616 Minneapolis Avenue, Franklin Park, Illinois, 60131, from Mrs. Anne Marshall, 260 Woodham Road, Linwood, Christchurch 6, New Zealand, and from Gerry Designs Inc., Boulder, Colorado. The Gerry Designs baby-carrier is obtainable in many retail shops throughout the United States.

tactile perceptions according to the meanings with which they have been invested by experience. When affection and involvement are conveyed through touch, it is those meanings as well as the security-giving satisfactions, with which touch will become associated. Inadequate tactile experience will result in a lack of such associations and a consequent inability to relate to others in many fundamental human ways. Hence, the human significance of touching.

REFERENCES

Page and Line

Chapter One

1 : 7–11   D. Hooker, *The Prenatal Origin of Behavior* (Lawrence, Kansas: University of Kansas Press, 1952), p. 63.

2 : 21–25   C. M. Jackson, "Some Aspects of Form and Growth," in W. J. Robbins, ed., *Growth* (New Haven: Yale University Press, 1928), pp. 125–27; G. R. De Beer, *Growth* (London: Arnold, 1924), pp. 10, 34.

   : 28 to   L. Carmichael, "The Onset and Early Development of Be-
3 : 1   havior," in L. Carmichael, ed., *Manual of Child Psychology*, (2nd ed., New York: Wiley, 1954) pp. 97–98; E. T. Raney and L. Carmichael, "Localizing Responses to Tactual Stimuli in the Fetal Rat in Relation to the Psychological Problem of Space Perception," *Journal of Genetic Psychology*, vol. 43 (1934), pp. 3–21; A. W. Angulo y Gonzalez, "The Prenatal Development of Behavior in the Albino Rat," *Journal of Comparative Neurology*, vol. 55 (1932), pp. 395–442; E. A. Swenson, "The Development of Movement of the Albino Rat Before Birth," (Ph.D. diss. University of Kansas, 1926); W. Preyer, *Specielle Physiologie des Embryo* (Leipzig: Grieben, 1885); A. Peiper, *Cerebral Function in Infancy and Childhood* (New York: Consultants Bureau, 1963), pp. 34–40.

   : 3–4   S. Rothman, ed., *The Human Integument* (Washington, D.C.: American Association for the Advancement of Science, 1959).

   : 7–9   H. Strughold, "Ueber die Dichte und Schwellen der Schmerzpunkte der Epidermis in den verschiedenen Körperregionen," *Zeitschrift der Biologie,* vol. 80 (1924), p. 367.

   : 9–11   C. Ingbert, "On the Density of the Cutaneous Innervation

Page and Line

in Man," *Journal of Comparative Neurology*, vol. 13 (1903), pp. 209–222.

3 : 19–22 E. F. DuBois, *Basal Metabolism in Health and Disease* (Philadelphia: Lea & Febiger, 1936), pp. 125–44.

: 22–23 S. Rothman, *Physiology and Biochemistry of the Skin* (Chicago: University of Chicago Press, 1954), pp. 493–514.

: 27–28 H. Yoshimura, "Organ Systems in Adaptation: The Skin," in D. B. Dill et al., eds., *Adaptation to Environment* (Washington, D. C.,: American Physiological Society, 1964), p. 109.

: 29 to R. F. Rushmer et al., "The Skin," *Science*, vol. 154 (1966),
4 : 3 pp. 343–48.

: 5–10 Rothman, *Physiology and Biochemistry of the Skin*; W. Montagna, *Structure and Function of Skin* (New York: Academic Press, 1956); D. Sinclair, *Cutaneous Sensation* (New York: Oxford University Press, 1967); H. Piéron, *The Sensations* (London: Miller, 1956); Rothman, *The Human Integument*.

6 : 6–20 G. H. Bishop, "Neural Mechanisms of Cutaneous Sense." *Physiological Reviews*, vol. 26 (1946), pp. 77–102.

: 20–32 W. Penfield and T. Rasmussen, *The Cerebral Cortex of Man* (New York: The Macmillan Co. 1950), p. 214.

7 : 21–25 A. R. Luria, "The Functional Organization of the Brain." *Scientific American*, vol. 222 (1970), pp. 66–78.

9 : 1–4 A. Montagu, "The Sensory Influences of the Skin," *Texas Reports on Biology and Medicine*, vol. 2 (1953), pp. 291–301.

10 : 16–22 W. J. O'Donovan, *Dermatological Neuroses* (London: Kegan Paul, 1927).

: 22–25 M. E. Obermayer, *Psychocutaneous Medicine* (Springfield, Illinois: Charles C Thomas, 1955). See also J. A. Aita, *Neurocutaneous Diseases* (Springfield, Illinois; Charles C Thomas, 1966); H. C. Bethune and C. B. Kidd, "Psychophysiological Mechanisms in Skin Diseases," *The Lancet*, vol. 2 (1961), pp. 1419–1422.

12 : 16–18 F. S. Hammett, "Studies in the Thyroid Apparatus: I," *American Journal of Physiology*, vol. 56 (1921), pp. 196–204, p. 199.

13 : 20–31 F. S. Hammett, "Studies of the Thyroid Apparatus: V," *Endocrinology*, vol. 6 (1922), pp. 221–29.

14 : 1–3 M. J. Greenman and F. L. Duhring, *Breeding and Care of the Albino Rat for Research Purposes* (2nd ed., Philadelphia: Wistar Institute, 1931).

Page and Line

15 : 29 to   J. A. Reyniers, "Germ-Free Life Studies," *Lobund Re-*
16 : 4   *ports,* University of Notre Dame, No. 1 (1946); No. 2
              (1949).

   : 7–12   Ibid. No. 1, p. 20.

   : 14–28   Personal communication 10 November 1950.

   : 33 to   R. A. McCance and M. Otley, "Course of the Blood Urea
17 : 2   in Newborn Rats, Pigs and Kittens," *Journal of Physi-*
              ology, vol. 113 (1951), pp. 18–22.

   : 10–17   L. Rhine, "One Little Kitten and How it Grew," *McCall's*
              Magazine, 10 July 1953, pp. 4–6.

   : 24–25   R. W. Schaeffer and D. Premack, "Licking Rates in In-
              fant Albino Rats," *Science,* vol. 134 (1962), pp.
              1980–1981.

   : 26 to   J. S. Rosenblatt and D. S. Lehrman, "Maternal Behavior
18 : 19   of the Laboratory Rat," in H. L. Rheingold, ed., *Mater-*
              nal Behavior in Mammals (New York: Wiley, 1963) p.
              14; T. C. Schneirla, J. S. Rosenblatt, and E. Tobach,
              "Maternal Behavior in the Cat," ibid, in Rheingold,
              ref. 31, p. 123; H. L. Rheingold, "Maternal Behavior in
              the Dog," ibid., pp. 179–81; P. Jay, "Mother-Infant Re-
              lations in Langurs," ibid., p. 286; I. DeVore, "Mother-
              Infant Relations in Free-Ranging Baboons," ibid., pp.
              310–11.

19 : 10–29   L. L. Roth and J. S. Rosenblatt, "Mammary Glands of
              Pregnant Rats: Development Stimulated by Licking,"
              Science, vol. 151 (1965), pp. 1403–1404.

   : 30 to   H. G. Birch, "Source of Order in the Maternal Behavior
20 : 8   of Animals." *American Journal of Orthopsychiatry,* vol.
              26 (1956), pp. 279–84; T. C. Schneirla, "A Considera-
              tion of Some Problems in the Ontogeny of Family Life
              and Social Adjustments in Various Infrahuman Ani-
              mals," in M. J. E. Senn ed., *Problems of Infancy and*
              Childhood (New York: Josiah Macy Jr. Foundation,
              1951), p. 96.

   : 28 to   G. F. Solomon, S. Levine, and J. K. Kraft, "Early Experi-
21 : 5   ences and Immunity." *Nature,* vol. 220 (1968), pp.
              821–23.

   : 7–12   G. F. Solomon, and R. H. Moos, "Emotions, Immunity,
              and Disease," *Archives of General Psychiatry,* vol. 2
              (1964), pp. 657–74.

   : 18–23   O. Weininger, "Mortality of Rats Under Stress as a Func-
              tion of Early Handling," *Canadian Journal of Psychol-*
              ogy, vol. 7 (1953), pp. 111–14; O. Weininger, W. J.
              McClelland, and R. K. Arima, "Gentling and Weight

Page and Line

Gain in the Albino Rat," *Canadian Journal of Psychology*, vol. 8 (1954), pp. 147–51; L. Bernstein and H. El-rick, "The Handling of Experimental Animals as a Control Factor in Animal Research—a Review," *Metabolism*, vol. 6 (1957), pp. 479–82; S. Levine, Stimulation in Infancy," *Scientific American*, vol. 202 (1960), pp. 81–86; W. R. Ruegamer, L. Bernstein, and J. D. Benjamin, "Growth, Food Utilization, and Thyroid Activity in the Albino Rat as a Function of Extra Handling," *Science*, vol. 120 (1954), pp. 184–85.

21 : 27 to   G. Alexander and D. Williams, "Maternal Facilitation of
22 : 6   Sucking Drive in Newborn Lambs." *Science*, vol. 146 (1964), pp. 665–66.

    : 10–15   H. Blauvelt, "Neonate-Mother Relationship in Goat and Man," in B. Schaffner, ed., *Group Processes* (New York: Josiah Macy, Jr. Foundation, 1956), pp. 94–140; p. 116; ibid. p. 116, H. S. Liddell.

    : 15–24   R. A. Maier, *Maternal Behavior in the Domestic Hen; III: The Role of Physical Contact*, Loyola Behavior Laboratory Series, vol. 3, No. 3 (1962–1963), pp. 1–12.

    : 26–29   W. H. Burrows and T. C. Byerly, "The Effects of Certain Groups of Environmental Factors Upon the Expression of Broodiness," *Poultry Science*, vol. 17 (1938), pp. 324–30; Y. Saeki and Y. Tanabe, "Changes in Prolactin Content of Fowl Pituitary During Broody Periods and Some Experiments on the Induction of Broodiness," *Poultry Science*, vol. 34 (1955), pp. 909–19.

    : 29–31   D. S. Lehrman, "Hormonal Regulation of Parental Behavior in Birds and Infrahuman Mammals," in W. C. Young, ed., *Sex and the Internal Secretions* (2 vols., Baltimore: Williams & Wilkins, 1961), vol. 2, pp. 1268–1382; A. T. Cowie and S. J. Folley, "The Mammary Gland and Lactation," ibid., pp. 590–642.

    : 32 to   N. E. Collias, "The Analysis of Socialization in Sheep and
23 : 3   Goats." *Ecology*, vol. 37 (1956), pp. 228–39.

    : 18–24   L. Hersher, A. U. Moore, and J. B. Richmond, "Effect of Postpartum Separation of Mother and Kid on Maternal Care in the Domestic Goat." *Science*, vol. 128 (1958), pp. 1342–1343.

    : 25–30   L. Hersher, J. B. Richmond, and A. U. Moore, "Modifiability of the Critical Period for the Development of Maternal Behavior in Sheep and Goats." *Behaviour*, vol. 20 (1963), pp. 311–20.

    : 31 to   B. M. McKinney, "The Effects Upon the Mother of Re-

Page and Line

24 : 7   moval of the Infant Immediately After Birth," *Child-Family Digest,* vol. 10 (1954), pp. 63–65.

: 8–11   H. F. Harlow, M. K. Harlow, and E. W. Hansen, "The Maternal Affectional System of Rhesus Monkeys," in Rheingold. *Maternal Behavior in Mammals,* p. 268.

: 32 to
25 : 7   V. H. Denenberg and A. E. Whimbey, "Behavior of Adult Rats Is Modified by the Experience Their Mothers Had as Infants," *Science,* vol. 142 (1963), pp. 1192–1193.

: 8–12   R. Ader and P. M. Conklin, "Handling of Pregnant Rats: Effects on Emotionality of Their Offspring," *Science,* vol. 142 (1963), pp. 412–13.

: 13–17   J. Werboff, A. Anderson, and B. N. Haggett, "Handling of Pregnant Mice: Gestational and Postnatal Behavioral Effects," *Physiology and Behavior,* vol. 3 (1968), pp. 35–39.

: 18–29   A. Sayler and M. Salmon, "Communal Nursing in Mice: Influence of Multiple Mothers on the Growth of the Young," *Science,* vol. 164 (1969), pp. 1309–1310.

26 : 14–20   H. Selye, *The Physiology and Pathology of Exposure to Stress.* (Montreal: Acta, 1950); C. Newman, ed., *The Nature of Stress Disorder* (Springfield, Illinois: Charles C Thomas, 1959); H. G. Wolff, *Stress and Disease.* (2nd ed., Springfield, Illinois: Charles C Thomas, 1968).

: 21 to
27 : 2   O. Weininger, "Physiological Damage Under Emotional Stress as a Function of Early Experience," *Science,* vol. 119 (1954), pp. 285–86.

: 16–20   J. L. Fuller, "Experiential Deprivation and Later Behavior," *Science,* vol. 158 (1967), pp. 1645–1652.

: 21–27   L. Hersher, J. B. Richmond, and U. Moore, "Maternal Behavior in Sheep and Goats," in Rheingold, *Maternal Behavior in Mammals,* p. 209.

: 27–30   D. H. Barron, "Mother-Newborn Relationship in Goats," in Schaffner, *Group Processes,* pp. 225–26.

28 : 1–4   G. G. Karas, "The Effect of Time and Amount of Infantile Experience Upon Later Avoidance Learning" (M. A. thesis, Purdue University, 1957).

: 4–10   S. Levine and G. W. Lewis, "Critical Period for the Effects of Infantile Experience on Maturation of Stress Response," *Science,* vol. 129 (1959), p. 42.

: 10–14   R. W. Bell, G. Reisner, and T. Linn, "Recovery From Electroconvulsive Shock as a Function of Infantile Stimulation," *Science,* vol. 133 (1961), p. 1428.

: 14–17   V. H. Denenberg and G. G. Karas, "Effects of Differential Handling Upon Weight Gain and Mortality in the Rat

Page and Line

and Mouse," Science, vol. 130 (1959), pp. 629–30; V. H. Denenberg and G. G. Karas, "Interactive Effects of Age and Duration of Infantile Experience on Adult Learning," Psychological Reports, vol. 7 (1960), pp. 313–22; V. H. Denenberg and G. G. Karas, "Interactive Effects of Infant and Adult Experience Upon Weight Gain and Mortality in the Rat," Journal of Comparative and Physiological Psychology, vol. 54 (1961), pp. 658–89.

29 : 1–8   G. Hendrix, J. D. Van Valck, and W. E. Mitchell, "Early Handling by Humans Is Found to Benefit Horses," New York Times, 27 December 1968.

   : 28 to   A. F. McBride and H. Kritzler, "Observations on Preg-
30 : 7   nancy, Parturition, and Post-Natal Behavior in the Bottlenose Dolphin," Journal of Mammalogy, vol. 32 (1951), pp. 251–66.

   : 8–21   A. Gunner, "A London Hedgehog," The Listener (London), 16 February 1956, p. 255.

31 : 11–14   H. F. Harlow, "The Nature of Love," The American Psychologist, vol. 13 (1958), pp. 673–85.

32 : 8 to 34 : 6   Ibid. p. 676.

34 : 28–32   H. F. Harlow, M. K. Harlow, and E. W. Hansen, "The Maternal Affectional System of Rhesus Monkeys," in Rheingold Maternal Behavior in Mammals; p. 260.

35 : 22–28   Ibid. pp. 260–61.

   : 29 to   P. Jay, "Mother-Infant Relations in Langurs;" in Rhein-
36 : 3   gold, Maternal Behavior in Mammals, p. 286.

   : 5–6   H. Hediger, Wild Animals in Captivity (London: Butterworth, 1950).

   : 11–14   A. Jolly, Primate Behavior (New York: Macmillan, 1971).

   : 14–18   T. R. Anthoney, "The Ontogeny of Greeting, Grooming, and Sexual Motor Patterns in Captive Baboons (Superspecies Papio cynocephalus)," Behaviour, vol. 31 (1968), pp. 358–72; J. Sparks, "Allogrooming in Primates: A Review," in Desmond Morris, ed., Primate Ethology (Chicago: Aldine Publishing Co., 1967) pp. 148–75.

   : 21–27   J. Van Lawick-Goodall, "Mother-Offspring Relationships in Free-Hanging Chimpanzees," ibid., pp. 287–346.

   : 28–32   Jolly, Primate Behavior.

   : 32 to 37 : 2   Anthoney, "Patterns in Captive Baboons," pp. 358–72.

                Chapter Two

39 : 16–27   May Sarton, "An Informal Portrait of George Sarton," Texas Quarterly, Autumn, 1962, p. 105.

44 : 23–25   R. W. Jondorf, R. P. Maichel, and B. B. Brodie, "Inabil-

Page and Line

ity of Newborn Mice and Guinea Pigs to Metabolize Drugs," *Biochemical Pharmacology*, vol. 1 (1958), pp. 352–54.

44 : 28–30   I. D. Ross and I. F. Deforges, "Further Evidence of Deficient Enzyme Activity in the Newborn Period," *Pediatrics*, vol. 23 (1959), pp. 718–25.

: 30 to   C. Smith, *The Physiology of the Newborn Infant* (3rd ed.,
45 : 2   Springfield, Illinois: Charles C Thomas, 1960); E. H. Watson and G. H. Lowrey, *Growth and Development of Children* (5th ed. Chicago: Yearbook Medical Publishers, 1967), pp. 203–204; C. A. Villee, "Enzymes in the Development of Homeostatic Mechanisms," in G. W. Wolstenholme and M. O'Connor, eds., *Somatic Stability in the Newly Born* (Boston: Little, Brown, 1961), pp. 246–78; H. F. R. Prechtl, "Problems of Behavioral Studies in the Newborn Infant," in D. S. Lehrman, R. A. Hinde, and E. Shaw, eds., *Advances in the Study of Behavior*. (2 vols., New York: Academic Press, 1965), vol. 1, p. 79.

: 30 to   A. Montagu, *The Human Revolution* (New York: Bantam
46 : 8   Books, 1967), pp. 126–38. A. Montagu, "Time, Morphology and Neoteny in the Evolution of Man," *American Anthropologist*, vol. 57 (1955), pp. 13–27. A. Montagu, "Neoteny and the Evolution of the Human Mind," *Explorations*, No. 6 (Toronto, 1956), pp. 85–90; G. De Beer, *Embryos and Ancestors* (3rd ed. New York: Oxford University Press, 1958). F. Kovács, "Biological Interpretation of the Nine Months Duration of Human Pregnancy," *Acta Biologica Magyar*, vol. 10 (1960), pp. 331–61; A. Portmann, *Biologische Fragmente* (Basel: Benno Schwalbe & Co., 1944).

46 : 14–16   J. Bostock, "Exterior Gestation, Primitive Sleep, Enuresis and Asthma: A Study in Aetiology," *Medical Journal of Australia*, vol. 2 (1958), pp. 149–53; 185–88.

49 : 6–19   A. Montagu, *Prenatal Influences* (Springfield, Illinois: Charles C Thomas, 1962), pp. 413–14; P. Gruenwald, "The Fetus in Prolonged Pregnancy," *American Journal of Obstetrics and Gynecology*, vol. 89 (1964), pp. 503–505; P. B. Mead, "Prolonged Pregnancy." *American Journal of Obstetrics and Gynecology*, vol. 89 (1964). pp. 495–502; W. E. Lucas, "The Problems of Postterm Pregnancy," *American Journal of Obstetrics and Gynecology*, vol. 91 (1965), pp. 241–50; M. Zwerdling, "Complications of Prolonged Pregnancies," *Journal of the*

300TWO: THE WOMB OF TIME

American Medical Association, vol. 195 (1966), pp.
39–40; R. L. Naeye, "Infants of Prolonged Gestation,"
Archives of Pathology, vol. 84 (1967), pp. 37–41.

50 : 16–20   A. Montagu, *Prenatal Influences;* A. Montagu, *Life Before
Birth* (New York: New American Library, 1964); N. J.
Berrill, *The Person in the Womb* (New York: Dodd,
Mead), 1968.

55 : 18–23   C. M. Drillien, "Physical and Mental Handicap in the
Prematurely Born," *Journal of Obstetrics and Gynaecol-
ogy of the British Empire,* vol. 66 (1959), pp. 721–28;
See also B. Corner, *Prematures* (Springfield, Illinois:
Charles C Thomas), 1960.

: 24 to   M. Shirley, "A Behavior Syndrome Characterizing Prema-
56 : 19   turely-Born Children," *Child Development,* vol. 10
(1939), pp. 115–28.

: 23–32   A. J. Schaffer, *Diseases of the Newborn* (Philadelphia: W.
B. Saunders, 1965), pp. 45–46.

57 : 1–3   A. P. Kimball and R. J. Oliver, "Extra-Amniotic Caesarean Section in the Prevention of Fatal Hyaline Membrane Disease," *American Journal of Obstetrics and Gynecology,* vol. 90 (1964), pp. 919–24.

: 9–11   R. J. McKay, Jr., and C. A. Smith, in W. E. Nelson, ed.,
Textbook of Pediatrics (7th ed., Philadelphia: W. B.
Saunders, 1959), p. 286.

: 12–24   G. W. Meier, "Behavior of Infant Monkeys: Differences
Attributable to Mode of Birth," *Science,* vol. 143 (1964),
pp. 968–70.

: 30 to   S. Segal, in T. K. Oliver, Jr., ed., *Neonatal Respiratory
58 : 3   Adaptation* (Bethesda, Maryland: U. S. Dept. of Health,
Education, and Welfare, National Institutes of Health
(1966), pp. 183–88.

: 4–7   T. K. Oliver, Jr., A. Demis, and G. D. Bates, "Serial
Blood-Gas Tensions and Acid-Base Balance During the
First Hour of Life in Human Infants," *Acta Paediatrica*
vol. 50 (Stockholm, 1961), pp. 346–60.

: 8–16   M. Cornblath et al., "Studies of Carbohydrate Metabolism
in the Newborn Infant," *Pediatrics,* vol. 27 (1961), pp.
378–89.

: 19–22   L. J. Grota, V. H. Denenberg, and M. X. Zarrow, "Neonatal Versus Caesarean Delivery: Effects Upon Survival
Probability, Weaning Weight, and Open-Field Activity," *Journal of Comparative and Physiological Psychology,* vol. 61 (1966), pp. 159–60.

Page and Line

59 : 11–32   W. J. Pieper, E. E. Lessing, and H. A. Greenberg, "Personality Traits in Cesarean-Normally Delivered Children," *Archives of General Psychiatry*, vol. 2 (1964), pp. 466–71.

60 : 13–15   M. Straker, "Comparative Studies of Effects of Normal and Caesarean Delivery Upon Later Manifestations of Anxiety," *Comprehensive Psychiatry*, vol. 3 (1962), pp. 113–24.

: 15–18   W. T. Liberson and W. H. Frazier, Evaluation of EEG Patterns of Newborn Babies. *American Journal of Psychiatry*, vol. 118 (1962), pp. 1125–1131.

: 23 to   D. H. Barron, "Mother-Newborn Relationships in Goats,"
61 : 4   in B. Schaffner, ed., *Group Processes* (New York: Josiah Macy, Jr. Foundation, 1955), p. 225.

: 5–21   Ibid. p. 226.

: 22–25   Meier, "Behavior of Infant Monkeys . . .", *Science*, vol. 143 (1964), pp. 968–70.

: 25–31   R. A. McCance and M. Otley, "Course of the Blood Urea in Newborn Rats, Pigs and Kittens," *Journal of Physiology*, vol. 113 (1951), pp. 18–22.

62 : 5–7   H. B. Pack, "Mother-Newborn Relationship in Goats," in B. Schaffner, ed., *Group Processes* (New York: Josiah Macy, Jr. Foundation, 1955), p. 228.

: 8–9   Editorial, "The Gut and the Skin," *Journal of the American Medical Association*, vol. 196 (1966), pp. 1151–1152.

: 10–11   M. E. Obermayer, *Psychocutaneous Medicine* (Springfield, Illinois, 1955), pp. 376–77; L. Fry, S. Shuster, and R. M. H. McMinn, "The Small Intestine in Skin Disease," *Archives of Dermatology*, vol. 93 (1966), pp. 647–53; M. L. Johnson and H. T. H. Wilson, "Skin Lesions in Ulcerative Colitis." *Gut*, vol. 10 (1969), pp. 255–63.

: 12–21   F. Reitzenstein, "Aberglauben," in M. Marcuse, ed., *Handwörterbuch der Sexualwissenschaft*, (2nd ed., Bonn: Marcus & Weber, 1926), p. 5.

            Chapter Three

64 : 1–4   O. Rank, *The Trauma of Birth* (London: Allen & Unwin), 1929.

67 : 28 to   *Infant Care* (Washington, D. C.: U. S. Government Print-
68 : 5   ing Office, 1963), p. 16.

70 : 2–4   T. Smith and R. B. Little, "The Significance of Colostrum to the New-Born Calf," *Journal of Experimental Medicine*, vol. 36 (1922), pp. 181–98.

Page and Line

70 : 4–10   J. A. Toomey, "Agglutinins in Mother's Blood, Mother's
             Milk, and Placental Blood," *American Journal of Di-
             seases of Children,* vol. 47 (1934), pp. 521–28; J. A.
             Toomey, "Infection and Immunity," *Journal of Pediat-
             rics,* vol. 4 (1934), pp. 529–39.

72 : 4–6   T. J. Cronin, "Influence of Lactation Upon Ovulation,"
             The Lancet, vol. 2 (1968), pp. 422–24; R. Gioiosa, "Inci-
             dence of Pregnancy During Lactation in 500 Cases,"
             American Journal of Obstetrics and Gynecology, vol. 70
             (1955), pp. 162–74; I. C. Udesky, "Ovulation and Lac-
             tating Women," *American Journal of Obstetrics and
             Gynecology,* vol. 59 (1950), pp. 843–51; Solien de Gon-
             zales, N. L., "Lactation and Pregnancy: A Hypothesis,"
             American Anthropologist, vol. 66 (1964), pp. 873–78.

  : 8–15   E. R. Kimball, "How I Get Mothers to Breastfeed,"
             ob/gyn's Supplement in *Physician's Management,* June,
             1968.

  : 16–24   C. Hoefer and M. C. Hardy, "Later Development of
             Breast Fed and Artificially Fed Infants," *Journal of the
             American Medical Association,* vol. 96 (1929), pp.
             615–19.

  : 26 to   "Phenotype: Postnatal Development," *Science,* vol. 159
73 : 13   (1968), pp. 658–59.

  : 23 to   F. M. Pottenger, Jr., and B. Krohn, "Influence of Breast
74 : 2   Feeding on Facial Development," *Archives of Pediatrics,*
             vol. 67 (1950), pp. 454–61; F. M. Pottenger, Jr., "The
             Responsibility of the Pediatrician in the Orthodontic
             Problem," *California Medicine,* vol. 65 (1946), pp.
             169–70.

  : 3–4   D. L. Raphael, "The Lactation-Suckling Process within a
             Matrix of Supportive Behavior" (Ph. D. diss., Columbia
             University, 1966) p. 246.

  : 4–8   See Chapter 2 of the above work for a survey of the etho-
             logical evidence.

  : 8–10   For further discussion of this subject see F. H. Richard-
             son, *The Nursing Mother* (New York: Prentice-Hall,
             1953); M. P. Middlemore, *The Nursing Couple* (Lon-
             don: Cassell & Co., 1953); La Leche League Interna-
             tional, *The Womanly Art of Breastfeeding* (Franklin
             Park, Illinois, 1963); B. M. Caldwell, "The Effects of
             Infant Care," in M. L. Hoffman and L. W. Hoffman,
             eds., *Review of Child Development Research,* New York:
             Russell Sage Foundation, 1964) vol. 1, pp. ii–41.

Page and Line

75 : 1–23   M. King, *Truby King the Man* (London: Allen & Unwin, 1948), pp. 170–78.

76 : 11–19   Ibid. p. 167.

: 24 to   H. Moltz, R. Levin, and M. Leon, "Prolactin in the Post-
77 : 7   partum Rat: Synthesis and Release in the Absence of Suckling Stimulation," *Science,* vol. 163 (1969), pp. 1083–1084.

: 13–15   S. Lorand and S. Asbot, "Uber die durch Reizüng der Brustwarze reflektorischen Uterus Kontraktionen," *Zentralblatt für Gynäkologie,* vol. 74 (1952), pp. 345–52.

78 : 9–23   E. Darwin, *Zoonomia, or the Laws of Organic Life* (4 vols., 3rd ed., London: J. Johnson, 1801), vol. 1, p. 206.

: 30 to 79 : 10   Ibid., p. 210.

79 : 23–34   R. St. Barbe Baker, *Kabongo* (New York: A. S. Barnes & Co., 1955), p. 18.

                   Chapter Four

81 : 3 to   J. L. Halliday, *Psychosocial Medicine: A Study of the Sick*
82 : 19   *Society* (New York: W. W. Norton, 1948), pp. 244–45.

: 25–28   H. D. Chapin, "A Plea for Accurate Statistics in Children's Institutions," *Transactions of the American Pediatric Society,* vol. 27 (1915), p. 180.

83 : 2–11   F. Talbot, "Discussion," *Transactions of the American Pediatric Society,* vol. 62 (1941), p. 469.

: 15–17   L. E. Holt, *The Care and Feeding of Children* (15th ed. New York: Appleton-Century, 1935); E. Holt, Jr., *Holt's Care and Feeding of Children* (New York: Appleton-Century, 1948).

84 : 9–11   J. Brennemann, "The Infant Ward," *American Journal of Diseases of Children,* vol. 43 (1932), p. 577.

: 11–15   H. Bakwin, "Emotional Deprivation in Infants," *Journal of Pediatrics,* vol. 35 (1949), pp. 512–21.

85 : 1–16   M. H. Elliott and F. H. Hall, *Laura Bridgman* (Boston: Little, Brown, 1903). Helen Keller, *The Story of My Life* (New York: Doubleday, 1954).

: 17 to   K. Davis, "Extreme Social Isolation of a Child," *American*
86 : 4   *Journal of Sociology,* vol. 45 (1940), pp. 554–65; K. Davis, "Final Note on a Case of Extreme Isolation," *American Journal of Sociology,* vol. 52 (1947), pp. 432–37; M. K. Mason, "Learning to Speak after Six and One Half Years," *Journal of Speech Disorders,* vol. 7 (1942), pp. 295–304.

: 26 to 87 : 5   The historian Salimbene (13th Century), in J. B. Ross

Page and Line

                    and M. M. McLaughlin, eds., *A Portable Medieval
                    Reader* (New York: Viking Press, 1949), p. 366.

87 : 11–18   H. Bakwin, "Emotional Deprivation in Infants," *Journal
                    of Pediatrics*, vol. 35 (1949), pp. 512–21.

   : 21–25   "Annotation, Perinatal Body Temperatures," *The Lancet*,
                    vol. 1 (1968), p. 964.

   : 29   B. D. Bower, "Neonatal Cold Injury," *The Lancet*, vol. 1
                    (1962), p. 426.

88 : 3–17   O. Fenichel, *The Psychoanalytic Theory of Neurosis* (New
                    York: W. W. Norton, 1945), pp. 69–70.

   : 18–25   Editorial, "At What Temperature Should You Keep a
                    Baby?" *The Lancet*, vol. 2 (1970), p. 556.

89 : 3–6   L. Glass, "Wrapping Up Small Babies," *The Lancet*, vol.
                    2 (1970), pp. 1039–1040.

   : 7–8   F. A. Geldard, *The Human Senses* (New York: Wiley,
                    1953), pp. 211–32.

   : 7–14   T. P. Mann and R. I. K. Eliot, "Neonatal Cold Injury
                    Due to Accidental Exposure to Cold," *The Lancet*, vol.
                    1 (1957), pp. 229–34; W. A. Silverman, J. W. Fertig,
                    and A. P. Berger, "The Influence of the Thermal En-
                    vironment upon the Survival of Newly Born Premature
                    Infants," *Pediatrics*, vol. 22 (1958), pp. 876–86.

   : 19–27   E. N. Hey, S. Kohlinsky, and B. O'Connell, "Heat-Losses
                    from Babies During Exchange Transfusion," *The Lan-
                    cet*, vol. 1 (1969), pp. 335–38.

   : 27–28   C. P. Boyan, "Cold or Warmed Blood for Massive Trans-
                    fusions," *Annals of Surgery*, vol. 160 (1964), pp. 282–
                    86.

90 : 19–21   M. S. Elder, "The Effects of Temperature and Position
                    on the Sucking Pressure of Newborn Infants," *Child
                    Development*, vol. 41 (1970), pp. 94–102.

   : 21–24   R. E. Cooke, "The Behavioral Response of Infants to
                    Heat Stress," *Yale Journal of Biology and Medicine*,
                    vol. 24 (1952), pp. 334–40.

91 : 7–10   T. Schaefer, Jr., F. S. Weingarten, and J. C. Towne,
                    "Temperature Change: The Basic Variable in the Early
                    Handling Phenomenon?" *Science*, vol. 135 (1962), pp.
                    41–42.

   : 10–13   R. Ader, "The Basic Variable in the Early Handling Phe-
                    nomenon," *Science*, vol. 136 (1962), pp. 580–83; also G.
                    W. Meier, pp. 583–84, and T. Schaefer, Jr., et al.,
                    "Temperature Change . . .", *Science*, pp. 584–587.

92 : 26–28   R. G. Patton and L. I. Gardner, *Growth Failure in Ma-

Page and Line

ternal Deprivation (Springfield, Illinois: Charles C
Thomas, 1963).

93 : 6–8   R. L. Birdwhistell, "Kinesic Analysis of Filmed Behavior
of Children," in B. Schaffner, ed. *Group Processes* (New
York: Josiah Macy Jr. Foundation, 1956), p. 143.
R. L. Birdwhistell, *Kinesics and Context* (Philadelphia:
University of Pennsylvania Press, 1970); J. Fast, *Body
Language* (New York: M. Evans, 1970).

94 : 1–3   P. Lacombe, "Du Role de la Peau dans l'Attchment
Mere-Enfant," *Revue Francaise du Psychoanalyse,* vol.
23 (1959), pp. 83–101.

: 9 to   P. F. D. Seitz, "Psychocutaneous Conditioning During
95 : 23   the First Two Weeks of Life," *Psychosomatic Medicine,*
vol. 12 (1950), pp. 187–88.

97 : 22 to   M. A. Ribble, "Disorganizing Factors of Infant Personal-
98 : 2   ity," *American Journal of Psychiatry,* vol. 98 (1941), pp.
459–63.

: 15–16   L. S. Kubie, "Instincts and Homeostasis," *Psychosomatic
Medicine,* vol. 10 (1948), pp. 15–30.

99 : 3–6   D. B. Dill, *Life, Heat, and Altitude* (Cambridge: Harvard
University Press, 1938).

: 25–28   V. V. Rozanov, *Solitaria* (London: Wishart, 1927).

100 : 29 to   M. I. Heinstein, "Behavioral Correlates of Breast-Bottle
101 : 7   Regimes under Varying Parent-Infant Relationships,"
*Monographs of the Society for Child Growth and De-
velopment,* Serial No. 88, vol. 28, no. 4 (1963); M. I.
Heinstein, "Influence of Breast Feeding on Children's
Behavior," *Children,* vol. 10 (1963), pp. 93–97.

102 : 13–18   G. Stanley Hall, "Notes on the Study of Infants," *Peda-
gogical Seminary,* vol. 1 (1891), pp. 127–38.

: 21 to   S. Freud, *Three Essays on the Theory of Sexuality* [1905]
103 : 2   (London: Imago, 1949), p. 60.

: 22–26   S. Rado, "The Psychical Effects of Intoxication," *Psychoanalytic Review,* vol. 18 (1931), pp. 69–84.

104 : 5–21   H. F. Harlow and M. K. Harlow, "The Effect of Rearing
Conditions on Behavior," in John Money, ed., *Sex Re-
search: New Developments* (New York: Holt, Rinehart
& Winston, 1965), pp. 161–75.

: 30–32   G. W. Henry, *All The Sexes* (New York: Rinehart, 1955);
R. J. Stoller, *Sex and Gender* (New York: Science
House, 1968); S. Brody, *Patterns of Mothering* (New
York: International Universities Press, 1956).

105 : 7–11   L. J. Yarrow, "Maternal Deprivation: Toward an Empiri-

Page and Line

cal and Conceptual Re-valuation," *Psychological Bulletin*, vol. 58 (1961), pp. 459–90; p. 485. See also John Bowlby, *Attachment and Loss*, vol. 1, *Attachment* (New York: Basic Books, 1969).

105 : 19–26   E. Gamper, "Bau und Leistung eines menschlichen Mittelhirnwesens, II," *Zeitschrift für die Gesammte Neurologie und Psychiatrie*, vol. 104 (1926), pp. 48 et seq.

106 : 5–9   R. A. Spitz, *No and Yes* (New York: International Universities Press 1957), pp. 21–22.

: 11–19   I. DeVore, "Mother-Infant Relations in Free-Ranging Baboons," in H. L. Rheingold ed., *Maternal Behavior in Mammals* (New York: Wiley, 1963), p. 312.

: 23–25   Ibid. pp. 314, 317–18.

107 : 26–31   W. Ong, *The Presence of the Word* (New Haven: Yale University Press, 1967), pp. 169–70.

108 : 1–15   José Ortega y Gasset, *Man and People* (New York: W. W. Norton, 1957), pp. 72 et seq.

: 26–30   M. A. Ribble, *The Rights of Infants* (2nd ed. New York: Columbia University Press).

109 : 6–10   W. Hoffer, "Mouth, Hand, and Ego-Integration," in A. Freud, et al., eds., *The Psychoanalytic Study of the Child*, vols. 3/4 (New York: International Universities Press, 1949), pp. 49–56; W. Hoffer, "Development of the Body Ego," in *The Psychoanalytic Study of the Child*, vol. 5 (New York: International Universities Press, 1950), pp. 18–23.

111 : 27 to   R. Rubin, "Maternal Touch," *Child and Family*, vol. 4
112 : 8   (1965), p. 8.

: 23–24   R. Rubin, "Basic Maternal Behavior," *Nursing Outlook*, vol. 9 (1961), pp. 683–86.

: 24–27   R. Rubin, "Maternal Touch," *Child and Family*, vol. 4 (1965), pp. 8–9.

113 : 19–27   Ibid. p. 10.

114 : 28–32   M. H. Klaus, J. H. Kennell, N. Plumb, and S. Zuehlke, "Human Maternal Behavior at the First Contact with Her Young," *Pediatrics*, vol. 46 (1970), pp. 187–92.

115 : 4–9   C. R. Barnett, P. H. Leiderman, R. Grobstein, and K. Marshall, "Neonatal Separation: the Maternal Side of Interactional Deprivation," *Pediatrics*, vol. 45 (1970), pp. 197–205.

: 9–10   C. P. S. Williams and T. K. Oliver, Jr., "Nursery Routines and Staphylococcal Colonization of the Newborn," *Pediatrics*, vol. 44 (1969), pp. 640–46.

Page and Line

115 : 13–31   Editorial, "Mothers of Premature Babies," *British Medical Journal*, 6 June 1970, p. 556.

116 : 1–12   G. Bateson and M. Mead, *Balinese Character* (Special Publication, New York: New York Academy of Sciences, 1942), p. 30.

117 : 8–10   R. S. Illingworth, *The Development of the Infant and Young Child* (Edinburgh: Livingstone, 1960), pp. 130–32.

118 : 28–32   M. Mead and F. C. Macgregor, *Growth and Culture* (New York: G. P. Putnam's Sons, 1951), pp. 42–43.

119 : 4–8   C. McPhee, quoted in Mead and Macgregor, *Growth and Culture*, p. 43. See also C. McPhee, *Music in Bali* (New Haven: Yale University Press), 1966.

     : 8–12   B. Nettl, *Ethnomusicology* (New York: Free Press, 1964).

121 : 16–19   Mead and Macgregor, *Growth and Culture*, p. 50.

122 : 24 to   J. Zahovsky, "Discard of the Cradle," *Journal of Pediat-*
123 : 2   *rics*, vol. 4 (1934), pp. 660–67.

126 : 29 to   B. Chisholm, *Prescription For Survival* (New York: Col-
127 : 36   umbia University Press 1957), pp. 37–38.

128 : 31 to   E. Sylvester, "Discussion," in M. J. E. Senn, ed., *Problems*
129 : 7   *of Infancy* (New York: Josiah Macy, Jr. Foundation, 1953), p. 29.

     : 15–17   A. B. Bergman, J. B. Beckwith, and C. G. Ray, eds., *Sudden Infant Death Syndrome* (Seattle: University of Washington Press, 1970).

130 : 8–14   A. Peiper, *Cerebral Function in Infancy and Childhood* (New York: Consultants' Bureau, 1963), p. 606.

     : 18–20   G. R. Forrer, *Weaning and Human Development* (New York: Libra Publishers, 1969).

131 : 19–28   Zahovsky, "Discard of the Cradle," pp. 660–70; See also Ashley Montagu, "What Ever Happened to the Cradle?" *Family Weekly* (New York), 14 May 1967.

132 : 13–31   M. A. Powell, "Riverside Is Rockin' Along With Old-Fashioned Rhythm," *Toledo Blade Sun*, 2 February 1958, p. 13.

133 : 19 to   J. C. Solomon, "Passive Motion and Infancy," *American*
134 : 3   *Journal of Orthopsychiatry*, vol. 29 (1959), pp. 650–51.

     : 4–15   W. J. Greene, Jr., "Early Object Relations, Somatic, Affective, and Personal," *The Journal of Nervous and Mental Disease*, vol. 126 (1958), pp. 225–53.

     : 24 to   W. J. Greene, Jr., quoted by A. P. Shasberg, "Of Reading,
135 : 1   Rocking, and Rollicking," *New York Times Magazine*, 5 January 1969.

Page and Line

135 : 9–16   D. G. Freedman, H. Boverman, and N. Freedman, "Effects of Kinesthetic Stimulation on Weight Gain and Smiling in Premature Infants," paper presented at the meeting of the American Orthopsychiatry Association, San Francisco, April, 1960.

: 21 to
136 : 2   N. Sokoloff, S. Yaffe, D. Weintraub, and B. Blase, "Effects of Handling on the Subsequent Development of Premature Infants," *Developmental Psychology*, vol. 1 (1969), pp. 765–68.

: 2–7   E. G. Hasselmeyer, "The Premature Neonate's Response to Handling," *Journal of the American Nurses Association*, vol. 2 (1964), pp. 14–15.

: 27 to
137 : 7   W. A. Mason, "Early Deprivation in the Nonhuman Primates: Implications for Human Behavior," in D. C. Glass, ed., *Environmental Influences* (New York: The Rockefeller University Press, 1968), pp. 70–101.

138 : 13–18   L. K. Frank, "Tactile Communication," *Genetic Psychology Monographs*, vol. 56 (1957), p. 227.

140 : 4–24   L. Salk, "The Effects of the Normal Heartbeat Sound on the Behavior of the Newborn Infant: Implications for Mental Health," *World Mental Health*, vol. 12 (1960), pp. 1–8.

141 : 8–19   J. A. M. Meerloo, *The Dance* (Philadelphia: Chilton Co., 1960), pp. 13–14.

: 25 to 142 : 15   Ibid. pp. 15–16.
142 : 16–24   Ibid. p. 35.
144 : 24–31   O. C. Irwin and L. Weiss, "The Effect of Clothing and Vocal Activity of the Newborn Infant," in W. Dennis, ed., *Readings in Child Psychology* (New York: Prentice-Hall, 1951).

146 : 18–22   J. C. Flügel, *The Psychology of Clothes* (London: Hogarth Press, 1930), p. 87. J. C. Flügel, "Clothes Symbolism and Clothes Ambivalence," *International Journal of Psychoanalysis*, vol. 10 (1929), p. 205.

147 : 3–19   W. E. Hartman, M. Fithian, and D. Johnson, *Nudist Society* (New York: Crown, 1970), pp. 289, 293.

148 : 1–5   K. Stewart, *Pygmies and Dream Giants* (New York: W. W. Norton, 1954), p. 105.

149 : 1–3   Jules Romains, *Vision Extra-Rétinienne* (Paris, 1919; English translation, *Eyeless Sight*, New York: Putnam, 1924).

: 12–14   M. Gardner, "Dermo-Optical Perception: A Peek Down the Nose," *Science*, vol. 151 (1966), pp. 654–57.

Page and Line

150 : 17–20   M. R. Ostrow, "Dermographia: A Critical Review," *Annals of Allergy*, vol. 25 (1967), pp. 591–97.

151 : 6–29   P. Bach-y-Rita, "System May Let Blind 'See With Their Skins,' " *Journal of the American Medical Association*, vol. 207 (1967), pp. 2204–2205.

152 : 3–17   F. A. Geldard, "Body English," *Readings in Psychology Today* (Del Mar, California: CRM Associates, 1969), pp. 237–41; F. A. Geldard, "Some Neglected Possibilities of Communication," *Science*, vol. 131 (1960), pp. 1583–1588. See also J. R. Hennessy, "Cutaneous Sensitivity Communication," *Human Factors*, vol. 8 (1966), pp. 463–69; G. A. Gescheider, "Cutaneous Sound Localization," (Ph.D. diss. University of Virginia, 1964); G. von Bekesy, "Similarities Between Hearing and Skin Sensation," *Psychological Reviews*, vol. 66 (1959), pp. 1–22.

: 21–23   "Replacing Braille?" *Time*, 19 September 1969.

: 23 to   B. von Haller Gilmer and L. W. Gregg, "The Skin as a
153 : 6   Channel of Communication," *Etc.*, vol. 18 (1961), pp. 199–209.

: 9–10   J. F. Hahn, "Cutaneous Vibratory Thresholds for Square-Wave Electrical Pulses," *Science*, vol. 127 (1958), pp. 879–80.

154 : 12–19   H. Musaph, *Itching and Scratching: Psychodynamics in Dermatology* (Philadelphia: F. A. Davis Co., 1964).

: 19–26   P. F. D. Seitz, "Psychocutaneous Aspects of Persistent Pruritis and Excessive Excoriation," *Archives of Dermatology and Syphilology*, vol. 64 (1951), pp. 136–41; M. E. Obermayer, *Psychocutaneous Medicine* (Springfield, Illinois: Charles C Thomas, 1955); S. Ayres, "The Fine Art of Scratching," *Journal of the American Medical Association*, vol. 189 (1964), pp. 1003–1007; J. G. Kepecs and M. Robin, "Studies on Itching," *Psychosomatic Medicine*, vol. 17 (1955), pp. 87–95; B. Russell, "Pruritic Skin Conditions," in C. Newman, ed., *The Nature of Stress Disorder* (Springfield, Illinois, 1959), pp. 40–51.

: 27–30   Seitz, "Psychocutaneous Aspects of Persistent Pruritis . . . ," *Archives of Dermatology and Syphilology*, vol. 64 (1951), pp. 136–41.

155 : 13–18   Russell, "Pruritic Skin Conditions," in Newman, *The Nature of Stress Disorder*, p. 48.

310   FOUR: TENDER, LOVING CARE

Page and Line

155 : 19–22   E. Stern, "Le Prurit," Étude Psychosomatique, *Acta Psychotherapeutica*, vol. 3 (1955), pp. 107–116.

157 : 21–31   C. W. Saleeby, *Sunlight and Health* (London: Nisbet, 1928), p. 67.

: 32–35   Plato, *The Republic,* Book 5; G. V. N. Dearborn, "The Psychology of Clothing," *Psychological Monographs*, vol. 26 (1918/19), no. 1 (1928), p. 64; Hilaire Hiler, *From Nudity to Raiment* (London: Simpkin Marshall, 1930); Maurice Parmelee, *The New Gymnosophy* (New York: Hitchcock, 1927); Flügel, *The Psychology of Clothes;* L. E. Langner, *The Importance of Wearing Clothes* (New York: Hastings House, 1959).

158 : 6–8   J. M. Knox, Symposium on Cosmetics, "The Sunny Side of the Street Is Not the Place to Be," *Journal of the American Medical Association*, vol. 195 (1966), p. 10.

: 8–11   A. L. Lorincz, "Physiological and Pathological Changes in Skin from Sunburn and Suntan," *Journal of the American Medical Association*, vol. 173 (1963), pp. 1227–1231; R. G. Freeman, "Carcinogenic Effects of Solar Radiation and Prevention Measured," *Cancer*, vol. 21 (1968), pp. 1114–1120; A. M. Kligman, "Early Destructive Effect of Sunlight on Human Skin," *Journal of the American Medical Association*, vol. 210 (1969), pp. 2377–2380.

159 : 6–9   C. Pincher, *Sleep,* (London: Daily Express, 1954), pp. 18–19; G. G. Luce and J. Segal, *Sleep and Dreams* (London: Heinemann, 1967).

: 10–15   Anna Freud, "Psychoanalysis and Education," *The Psychoanalytic Study of the Child*, vol. 9 (1954), p. 12.

: 21 to   C. M. Heinicke and I. Westheimer, *Brief Separations*
160 : 5   (New York: International Universities Press, 1965), pp. 165, 266.

: 6–14   Fenichel, *The Psychoanalytic Theory of Neurosis*, pp. 120–21.

: 18–26   A. Aldrich, Chieh Sung, and C. Knop, "The Crying of Newly Born Babies," *Journal of Pediatrics*, vol. 27 (1945), p. 95.

                   Chapter Five

162 : 15–18   A. Montagu, *The Human Revolution* (New York: Bantam Books, 1967), pp. 150–51.

163 : 10–15   H. F. Harlow, M. K. Harlow, and E. W. Hansen, "The Maternal Affectional System of Rhesus Monkeys," in H. L. Rheingold, ed., *Maternal Behavior in Mammals* (New York: Wiley, 1963), pp. 277–78.

Page and Line
163 : 22–23   R. J. Stoller, *Sex and Gender* (New York: Science House, 1968).

: 26 to   A. Freud, *Normality and Pathology in Childhood* (New
164 : 2   York: International Universities Press, 1965), p. 199.

: 11 to   M. H. Hollender, L. Luborsky, and T. J. Scaramella,
165 : 8   "Body Contact and Sexual Excitement," *Archives of General Psychiatry*, vol. 20 (1969), pp. 188–91; M. H. Hollender, "The Wish To Be Held," *Archives of General Psychiatry*, vol. 22 (1970), pp. 445–53.

: 9–10   M. H. Hollender, "Prostitution, the Body, and Human Relations," *International Journal of Psychoanalysis*, vol. 42 (1961), pp. 404–413.

: 10–16   M. G. Blinder, "Differential Diagnosis and Treatment of Depressive Disorders," *Journal of the American Medical Association*, vol. 195 (1966), pp. 8–12.

: 16–22   C. P. Malmquist, T. J. Kiresuk, and R. M. Spano, "Personality Characteristics of Women with Repeated Illegitimate Pregnancies: Descriptive Aspects," *American Journal of Orthopsychiatry*, vol. 36 (1966), pp. 476–84.

: 22–23   A. Moll, *The Sexual Life of the Child* (London: Allen & Unwin, 1912); H. Graff and R. Mallin, "The Syndrome of the Wrist Cutter," *American Journal of Psychiatry*, vol. 124 (1967), pp. 36–42.

166 : 32 to   A. Lowen, *The Betrayal of the Body* (New York: Collier
167 : 10   Books, 1969), p. 102.

: 16–18   Ibid. p. 24.

: 19–20   S. Freud, *An Outline of Psychoanalysis* (New York: W. W. Norton, 1949), p. 24.

: 20–31   O. Fenichel, *The Psychoanalytic Theory of Neurosis* (New York: W. W. Norton, 1945), p. 70

168 : 6–7   E. S. Schaefer and Nancy Bayley, "Maternal Behavior, Child Behavior, and Their Intercorrelations from Infancy Through Adolescence," *Monographs of the Society for Research in Child Development*, vol. 28, no. 3, pp. 1–117, 1963.

: 11–21   J. Ruesch, *Disturbed Communication* (New York: W. W. Norton, 1957), pp. 31–32.

: 22–31   Moll, *The Sexual Life of the Child*, pp. 29–31.

169 : 25–29   S. Brody, *Patterns of Mothering* (New York: International Universities Press, 1956), p. 340.

170 : 4–8   S. Freud, *Introductory Lectures On Psycho-Analysis* (London: Allen & Unwin, 1922), pp. 269–84.

171 : 10–19   L. K. Frank, "Genetic Psychology and its Prospects,"

Page and Line

                          American Journal of Orthopsychiatry, vol. 21 (1951), p.
                          517.
171 : 20–28   L. K. Frank, "The Psychosocial Approach in Sex Re-
                          search," *Social Problems*, vol. 1 (1954), p. 134.
172 : 18–20   J. S. Plant, *Personality and the Cultural Pattern* (New
                          York: The Commonwealth Fund, 1937), p. 22.
      : 21   W. A. Weisskopf, *The Psychology of Economics* (Univer-
                          sity of Chicago Press, 1955), p. 147.
      : 23–24   Frank, "The Psychosocial Approach in Sex Research," *So-
                          cial Problems*, vol. 1 (1954), p. 137.
      : 28 to 173 : 6   Lowen, *The Betrayal of the Body*, p. 105.
173 : 14–20   J. C. Moloney, "Thumbsucking," *Child and Family*, vol. 6
                          (1967), pp. 29–30.
      : 23–25   V. Lowenfeld, *Creative and Mental Growth* (New York:
                          Macmillan, 1947).
174 : 14 to   L. K. Frank, "Tactile Communication," *Genetic Psychol-
175 : 2   ogy Monographs*, vol. 56 (1957), pp. 209–255; p. 233.
176 : 2–5   R. von Krafft-Ebing, *Psychopathia Sexualis* (New York:
                          Putnam, 1965); G. R. Taylor, *Sex in History* (New
                          York: Vanguard Press, 1954).
      : 22–29   J. J. Rousseau, *Confessions*, Book 1, 1782.
178 : 9–19   Th. Van de Velde, *Ideal Marriage* (New York: Simon &
                          Schuster, 1932), p. 159.
      : 29–31   H. Ellis, *Studies in the Psychology of Sex* (New York:
                          Random House), 1936.
      : 32 to   M. A. Obermayer, *Psychocutaneous Medicine* (Springfield,
179 : 6   Illinois: Charles C Thomas, 1955), p. 244 et seq.; J. T.
                          McLaughlin, R. J. Shoemaker, and W. B. Guy, "Person-
                          ality Factors in Adult Atopic Eczema," *Archives of Der-
                          matology and Syphilology*, vol. 68 (1953), p. 506; I.
                          Rosen, ed., *The Pathology and Treatment of Sexual
                          Deviation* (New York: Oxford University Press), 1964.
      : 10–16   I. Rosen, "Exhibitionism, Scopophilia and Voyeurism," in
                          Rosen, ed., *The Pathology and Treatment of Sexual
                          Deviation*, p. 308.
      : 22–27   S. Freud, "Three Essays on the Theory of Sexuality"
                          [1905], in *Complete Psychological Works of Sigmund
                          Freud* (Standard Edition, 24 vols., London: Hogarth
                          Press, 1953), vol. 7, pp. 120–243.
181 : 2–4   J. K. Skipper, Jr. and C. H. McCaghy, "Stripteasers: The
                          Anatomy and Career Contingencies of a Deviant Occupa-
                          tion," *Social Problems*, vol. 17 (1970) , pp. 391–405.
      : 11–16   A. C. Kinsey et al., *Sexual Behavior in the Human Fe-
                          male* (Philadelphia: W. B. Saunders, 1953), pp. 570–90,
                          p. 688; J. Money, "Psychosexual Differentiation," in J.

Page and Line

| | Money, ed., *Sex Research: New Developments* (New York: Holt, Rinehart & Winston, 1965), p. 20. |

181 : 21–26   F. Kahn, *Our Sex Life* (New York: A. A. Knopf, 1939), p. 70.

: 27 to   M. Mead, *Male and Female* (New York: William Morrow
182 : 2   & Co., 1949), Chapter 7.

: 2–3   R. R. Sears, E. E. Maccoby, and H. Levin, *Patterns of Child Rearing* (New York: Row, Peterson & Co., 1957), pp. 56–57, p. 402.

: 3–7   E. H. Erikson, *Childhood and Society* (2nd ed., New York: W. W. Norton, 1963), p. 309.

: 12–15   J. L. Fischer and A. Fischer, "The New Englanders of Orchard Town, U. S. A.," in B. B. Whiting, ed., *Six Cultures* (New York: Wiley, 1963).

: 15–18   V. S. Clay, "The Effect of Culture on Mother-Child Tactile Communication," (Ph.D. diss., New York: Teachers College, Columbia University, 1966), pp. 219 et seq.

Chapter Six

183 : 8–12   L. Casler, "Maternal Deprivation: A Critical Review of the Literature," *Monographs of the Society for Research in Child Development,* vol. 26, no. 2, 1961.

: 10   J. Bowlby, *Maternal Care and Mental Health* (Geneva: World Health Organization, 1961).

184 : 15–22   Cited in G. W. Gray, "Human Growth," *Scientific American,* vol. 189 (1953), pp. 65–67.

: 27–32   V. H. Denenberg and J. R. C. Morton, "Effects of Environmental Complexity and Social Groupings upon Modification of Emotional Behavior," *Journal of Comparative Psychology,* vol. 55 (1962), pp. 242–46.

185 : 1–3   S. Levine, "A Further Study of Infantile Handling and Avoidance Learning," *Journal of Personality,* vol. 25 (1962), pp. 242–46; V. H. Dennenberg and C. G. Karas, "Interactive Effects of Age and Duration of Infantile Experience on Adult Learning," *Psychological Reports,* vol. 7 (1960), pp. 313–22.

: 1–5   J. T. Tapp and H. Markowitz, "Infant Handling: Effects on Avoidance Learning, Brain Weight, and Cholinesterase Activity," *Science,* vol. 140 (1963), pp. 486–87.

: 8–9   L. Bernstein, "A Note on Christie's 'Experimental Naiveté and Experiential Naiveté,'" *Psychological Bulletin,* vol. 49 (1952), pp. 38–40.

: 10   J. Rosen, "Dominance Behavior as a Function of Early

Page and Line

Gentling Experience in the Albino Rat" (M.A. thesis, University of Toronto, 1957).

185 : 11–12   O. Weininger, W. J. McClelland, and K. Arima, "Gentling and Weight Gain in the Albino Rat," *Canadian Journal of Psychology*, vol. 8 (1954), pp. 147–51.

: 12   W. R. Ruegamer, L. Bernstein, and J. D. Benjamin, "Growth, Food Utilization, and Thyroid Activity in the Albino Rat as a Function of Extra Handling," *Science*, vol. 120 (1954), pp. 184–85.

: 19–24   G. F. Solomon, "Early Experience and Immunity," *Nature*, vol. 220 (1968), pp. 821–22.

: 25–27   S. Levine, M. Alpert, and G. W. Lewis, "Infantile Experience and the Maturation of the Pituitary Adrenal Axis," *Science*, vol. 126 (1957), p. 1347.

: 27–29   R. W. Bell, G. Reisner, and T. Linn, "Recovery From Electroconvulsive Shock as a Function of Infantile Stimulation," *Science*, vol. 133 (1961), p. 1428.

186 : 3–6   S. Levine, "Noxious Stimulation in Infant and Adult Rats and Consummatory Behavior," *Journal of Comparative and Physiological Psychology*, vol. 51 (1958), pp. 230–33.

: 6–9   L. Bernstein, "The Effects of Variation in Handling Upon Learning and Retention," *Journal of Comparative and Physiological Psychology*, vol. 50 (1957), pp. 162–67.

: 10–16   J. A. King, "Effects of Early Handling Upon Adult Behavior in Two Subspecies of Deermice, *Peromyscus maniculatus*," *Journal of Comparative and Physiological Psychology*, vol. 52 (1959), pp. 82–88.

: 16–24   U. Bronfenbrenner, "Early Deprivation in Mammals: A Cross-Species Analysis," in G. Newton and S. Levene, eds., *Early Experience and Behavior* (Springfield, Illinois: Charles C Thomas, 1968), p. 661; L. Bernstein, "A Note on Christie's 'Experimental Naiveté and Experiential Naiveté,' " *Psychological Bulletin*, vol. 49 (1952), pp. 38–40; L. Bernstein, "The Effects of Variations in Handling Upon Learning and Retention," *Journal of Comparative and Physiological Psychology*, vol. 50 (1957), pp. 162–67; V. H. Dennenberg, "A Consideration of the Usefulness of the Critical Period Hypothesis as Applied to the Stimulation of Rodents in Infancy," in Newton and Levine, *Early Experience and Behavior*, 1968, pp. 42–167.

187 : 1–5   Ruegamer et al., "Growth, Food Utilization, and Thyroid

Page and Line

Activity in the Albino Rat . . . ," *Science,* vol. 120 (1954), pp. 184–85.

187 : 23–27 W. von Buddenbrock, *The Senses* (Ann Arbor: The University of Michigan Press, 1958), p. 127.

188 : 3–13 V. S. Clay, "The Effect of Culture on Mother-Child Tactile Communication" (Ph.D. diss., Teachers College, Columbia University, New York, 1966), p. 308.

: 14–21 M. Ribble, *The Rights of Infants* (2nd ed. New York: Columbia University Press, 1965), p. 54, et seq.

: 22–24 G. E. Coghill, *Anatomy and the Problem of Behaviour* (New York & London: Cambridge University Press, 1929; Reprinted New York: Hafner Publishing Co., 1964).

: 26 to
189 : 10 L. J. Yarrow, "Research in Dimension of Early Maternal Care," *Merrill-Palmer Quarterly,* vol. 9 (1963), pp. 101–122.

: 11–28 S. Province and R. C. Lipton, *Infants in Institutions* (New York: International Universities Press), 1962.

: 29 to
190 : 19 H. Shevrin and P. W. Toussieng, "Vicissitudes of the Need for Tactile Stimulation in Instinctual Development," *The Psychoanalytic Study of the Child,* vol. 20 (1965), pp. 310–39; H. Shevrin and P. W. Toussieng, "Conflict Over Tactile Experiences in Emotionally Disturbed Children," *Journal of the American Academy of Child Psychiatry,* vol. 1 (1962), pp. 564–90.

191 : 17–21 R. Spitz, *The First Year of Life* (New York: International Universities Press, 1965); Ribble, *The Rights of Infants.*

: 22–27 R. G. Patton and L. I. Gardner, *Growth Failure in Maternal Deprivation* (Springfield, Illinois: Charles C Thomas, 1963).

: 27–30 E. M. Widdowson, "Mental Contentment and Physical Growth," *The Lancet,* vol. 1 (1951); L. J. Yarrow, "Maternal Deprivation: Toward an Empirical and Conceptual Revaluation," *Psychological Bulletin,* vol. 58 (1961), pp. 459–90.

: 31 to
192 : 6 G. F. Powell, J. A. Brasel, and R. M. Blizzard, "Emotional Deprivation and Growth Retardation Simulating Idiopathic Hypopituitarism," *New England Journal of Medicine,* vol. 276 (1967), pp. 1271–1278; G. F. Powell, J. A. Brasel, S. Raiti, and R. M. Blizzard, "Emotional Deprivation and Growth Retardation Simulating Hypopituitarism," *New England Journal of Medicine,* vol. 276 (1967), pp. 1279–1283; J. B. Reinhardt and A. L.

Page and Line

            Drash, "Psychosocial Dwarfism: Environmentally In-
            duced Recovery," *Psychosomatic Medicine,* vol. 31
            (1969), pp. 165–72. See also C. Whitten et al., "Evi-
            dence that Growth Failure from Maternal Deprivation
            is Secondary to Undereating," *Journal of the American
            Medical Association,* vol. 209 (1969), pp. 1675–1682.

193 : 24–29   M. K. Temerlin, et al., "Effects of Increased Mothering
            and Skin Contact on Retarded Boys," *American Jour-
            nal of Mental Deficiency,* vol. 71 (1967), pp. 890–93.

194 : 2–12   M. McGraw, *Neuromuscular Maturation of the Human
            Infant* (New York: Columbia University Press, 1943), p.
            102.

   : 13–14   P. Greenacre, *Trauma, Growth, and Personality* (New
            York: W. W. Norton, 1952), pp. 12–14; M. Sherman
            and I. C. Sherman, "Sensorimotor Response in Infants,"
            Journal of Comparative Psychology, vol. 5 (1925), pp.
            53–68; A. Thomas, et al., *Examen Neurologique du
            Nourrison* (Paris: La Vie Medicale, 1955); E. H. Watson
            and G. H. Lowrey, *Growth and Development of Chil-
            dren* (5th ed., Chicago: Year Book Medical Publishers,
            1967).

   : 15   E. Dewey, *Behavior Development in Infants* (New York:
            Columbia University Press, 1935).

   : 16   D. Sinclair, *Cutaneous Sensation* (New York: Oxford Uni-
            versity Press, 1967), p. 38.

   : 19–31   H. Head, *Studies in Neurology* (Oxford: Oxford Univer-
            sity Press, 1922).

195 : 7–11   S. Escalona, "Emotional Development in the First Year of
            Life," in M. J. E. Senn, ed., *Problems of Infancy and
            Childhood* (New York: Josiah Macy, Jr. Foundation,
            1953), p. 17.

   : 20–26   Ribble, *The Rights of Infants,* p. 57.

196 : 2–5   Watson and Lowrey, *Growth and Development of Chil-
            dren,* pp. 220–21.

197 : 12–28   E. Sylvester, "Discussion," in Senn, *Problems of Infancy
            and Childhood,* p. 29.

198 : 3–8   Ibid.

   : 24 to   Escalona, "Emotional Development in the First Year of
199 : 13   Life," in Senn, *Problems of Infancy and Childhood,* p.
            25.

199 : 28 to 200 : 9   Spitz, *The First Year of Life,* pp. 232–33.

   : 31   M. S. Mahler, "On Two Crucial Phases of Integration
            Concerning Problems of Identity: Separation-Individua-
            tion and Bisexual Identity," *Journal of the American*

Page and Line

Psychoanalytic Association, vol. 6 (1958), pp. 136–42.

201 : 9 to   E. Darwin, *Zoonomia, Or The Laws of Organic Life* (2
202 : 5   vols., London: J. Johnson, vol. 1, 1794), pp. 109–111.

: 9–21   Escalona, "Emotional Development in the First Year
             . . . ," in Senn, *Problems of Infancy and Childhood,* p.
             24.

: 27 to   T. K. Landauer and J. W. M. Whiting, "Infantile Stimu-
203 : 20   lation and Adult Stature of Human Males," *American
             Anthropologist,* vol. 66 (1964), pp. 1007–1028.

204 : 18–20   D. H. Williams, "Management of Atopic Dermatitis in
             Children," Control of the Maternal Rejection Factor,
             Archives of Dermatology and Syphilology, vol. 63
             (1951), pp. 545–60.

: 20–27   F. Dunbar, *Emotions and Bodily Changes* (4th ed. New
             York: Columbia University Press, 1954), p. 647.

: 28 to   D. W. Winnicott, "Pediatrics and Psychiatry," *British
205 : 1   Journal of Medical Psychology* vol. 21 (1948), pp.
             229–40.

: 8–11   R. Spitz, *The First Year of Life* (New York: International
             Universities Press, 1965); M. E. Allerhand et al., "Per-
             sonality Factors in Neurodermatitis," *Psychosomatic
             Medicine,* vol. 12 (1950), pp. 386–90; E. Wittkower
             and B. Russell, *Emotional Factors in Skin Disease* (New
             York: Hoeber, 1955).

: 11–12   M. E. Obermayer, *Psychocutaneous Medicine* (Springfield,
             Illinois: Charles C Thomas, 1955).

: 12–13   H. C. Bethune and C. B. Kidd, "Physiological Mecha-
             nisms in Skin Diseases," *The Lancet,* vol. 2 (1961), pp.
             1419–1422; J. G. Kepecs et al., "Atopic Dermatitis," *Psy-
             chosomatic Medicine,* vol. 13 (1951), pp. 2–9; Dunbar,
             Emotions and Bodily Changes, p. 647.

: 16–28   A. Lowen, *The Betrayal of the Body* (New York: Collier
             Books, 1969), pp. 2–3.

206 : 20–27   O. Fenichel, *The Psychoanalytic Theory of Neurosis* (New
             York: W. W. Norton, 1945), p. 445.

: 31 to   H. Weiner, "Diagnosis and Symptomatology," in L. Bel-
207 : 2   lak, ed., *Schizophrenia* (New York: Logos Press, 1958),
             p. 120.

: 9–18   M. J. Rosenthal, "Psychosomatic Study of Infantile
             Eczema," *Pediatrics,* vol. 10 (1952), pp. 581–93.

: 19–27   R. Spitz, *The First Year of Life,* p. 24.

: 31 to   W. E. A. Axon, "King's Evil," in J. Hastings, ed., *Encyclo-
208 : 2   paedia of Religion and Ethics* (New York: Scribners,
             1914), pp. 736–38.

Page and Line

209 : 2–6   J. C. Moloney, "Thumbsucking," *Child and Family*, vol. 6
                 (1967), p. 28.

    : 20–31   Lowen, *The Betrayal of the Body*, pp. 187–88.

210 : 8–14   M. Eustis, ed., *Players at Work* (New York: Theater Arts,
                 1937).

    : 25 to   E. T. Hall, *The Hidden Dimension* (New York: Double-
211 : 7   day, 1966), p. 59.

    : 8–22   J. Bowlby, "The Nature of the Child's Tie to His
                 Mother," *International Journal of Psychoanalysis*, vol.
                 39 (1958), pp. 364–65; J. Bowlby, *Attachment and Loss.*
                 vol. 1, *Attachment* (New York: Basic Books, 1969).

    : 23 to   M. Balint, "Friendly Expanses—Horrid Empty Spaces,"
212 : 5   *International Journal of Psychoanalysis*, vol. 36 (1955),
                 pp. 225–41.

    : 27 to   D. Secrest, " 'Catatonics' Cure is Found," *International
213 : 2   News Service*, 27 May 1955.

    : 2–4   G. Schwing, *A Way to the Souls of the Mentally Ill*
                 (New York: International Universities Press, 1954).

    : 4–22   N. Waal, "A Special Technique of Psychotherapy with an
                 Autistic Child," in G. Caplan, ed., *Emotional Problems
                 of Early Childhood* (New York: Basic Books, 1955), pp.
                 443–44.

    : 23–26   N. Ickeringill, "An Approach to Schizophrenia that is
                 Rooted in Family Love," *New York Times*, 28 April
                 1968, p. 44.

    : 28 to   A. Montagu, "The Sensory Influences of the Skin," *Texas
215 : 27   Reports on Biology and Medicine*, vol. 2 (1953), pp.
                 291–301.

216 : 27 to   A. M. Garner and C. Wenar, *The Mother-Child Interac-
217 : 2   tion in Psychosomatic Disorders* (Urbana, Illinois: Uni-
                 versity of Illinois Press, 1959).

    : 18–20   W. M. Mason, "Early Social Deprivation in the Nonhu-
                 man Primates: Implications for Human Behavior," in
                 D. C. Glass, ed., *Environmental Influences* (New York:
                 Rockefeller University Press, 1968), pp. 70–101.

    : 30–33   J. P. Zubek, J. Flye, and M. Aftanas, "Cutaneous Sensitiv-
                 ity after Prolonged Visual Deprivation," *Science*, vol.
                 144 (1964), pp. 1591–1593.

    : 33 to   S. Axelrod, *Effects of Early Blindness* (New York: Ameri-
218 : 3   can Foundation for the Blind, 1959).

219 : 11–14   D. Ogston, C. M. Ogston, and O. D. Ratnoff, "Studies on
                 Clot-Promoting Effect of the Skin," *Journal of Labora-
                 tory and Clinical Medicine*, vol. 73 (1969), pp. 70–77.

Page and Line

Chapter Seven

226 : 1–31   R. James de Boer, "The Netsilik Eskimo and the Origin of Human Behavior," MSS, 1969, p. 8.

227 : 15–30   Ibid. p. 15.

228 : 32 to   E. Carpenter, "Space Concepts of Aivilik Eskimos," *Explo-*
229 : 13   *rations Five,* June 1955, pp. 131–45.

230 : 30 to   J. Gibson, "Pictures, Perspective and Perception," *Daeda-*
231 : 6   *lus,* Winter, 1961.

   : 25 to   H. H. Roberts and D. Jenness, *Eskimo Songs, Report of*
232 : 12   *the Canadian Arctic Expedition, 1913–18* (Ottawa) vol. 14 (1925), pp. 9, 12.

   : 28 to   K. Rasmussen, *The Intellectual Culture of the Iglulik Es-*
233 : 6   *kimos* (Copenhagen: Gyldendalske boghandel, 1929), p. 27.

   : 9–14   V. Stefansson, *The Friendly Arctic* (New York: The Macmillan Co., 1943), p. 418; V. Stefansson, *My Life With the Eskimo* (New York: The Macmillan Co., 1915).

234 : 11–18   C. Osgood, "Ingalik Social Culture," *Yale University Publications in Anthropology,* no. 53 (1958), p. 178.

   : 20 to   E. Carpenter, F. Varley, and R. Flaherty, *Eskimo: Explo-*
235 : 6   *rations Nine* (Toronto: University of Toronto Press, 1959), p. 32.

   : 19–30   A. S. Mirkin, "Resonance Phenomena in Isolated Mechanoreceptors (Pacinian Bodies) With Acoustic Stimulation," *Biofizika,* vol. 2 (1966), pp. 638–45 (in Russian).

   : 31 to   C. K. Madsen and W. G. Mears, "The Effect of Sound
236 : 4   Upon the Tactile Threshold of Deaf Subjects," *Journal of Music Therapy,* vol. 2 (1965), pp. 64–68.

   : 5–7   G. A. Gescheider, 'Cutaneous Sound Localization" (Ph.D. diss., University of Virginia, 1964; *Dissertation Abstracts,* vol. 25 [1964], no. 6, 3701).

   : 22–27   M. McLuhan and H. Parker, *Through the Vanishing Point* (New York: Harper & Row, 1969), p. 265.

   : 27 to   T. Kroeber, *Alfred Kroeber: A Personal Configuration*
237 : 19   (Berkeley: University of California Press, 1970), pp. 267–68.

   : 27 to   E. G. Schachtel, "On Memory and Childhood Amnesia,"
238 : 7   in P. Mullahy, ed., *A Study of Interpersonal Relations* (New York: Hermitage Press, 1949), pp. 23–24.

   : 9–14   Ibid. pp. 25–26.

   : 15–18   H. Marcuse, *Eros and Civilization* (Boston: Beacon Press, 1955), p. 39.

Page and Line

239 : 4–12   M. D. S. Ainsworth, *Infancy in Uganda* (Baltimore; Johns
                    Hopkins Press, 1967), p. 451. See also L. K. Fox, ed.,
                    East African Childhood (New York: Oxford University
                    Press, 1970).

: 15–20   Ibid. p. 330.

: 26 to   A. I. Richards, "Traditional Values and Current Political
240 : 1   Behavior," in L. A. Fallers, ed., *The King's Men: Lead-
                    ership and Status in Modern Buganda* (New York: Ox-
                    ford University Press, 1964), pp. 297–300.

: 14–23   T. R. Williams, "Cultural Structuring of Tactile Experi-
                    ence in a Borneo Society," *American Anthropologist*,
                    vol. 68 (1966), pp. 27–39.

: 24 to 241 : 11   Ibid. p. 29.

242 : 25   V. S. Clay, "The Effect of Culture on Mother-Child Tac-
                    tile Communication" (Ph.D. diss., Teachers College,
                    Columbia University, New York, 1966).

243 : 23 to 244 : 9 Ibid. pp. 199–201.

: 20–24   H. F. Harlow, M. K. Harlow, and E. W. Hansen, "The
                    Maternal Affectional System of Rhesus Monkeys," in H.
                    L. Rheingold, ed., *Maternal Behavior in Mammals*
                    (New York: Wiley, 1963), pp. 258 et seq.

245 : 10–26   Clay, "The Effect of Culture . . . ," pp. 201–202.

246 : 10–14   R. E. Sears, E. E. Maccoby, and H. Levin, *Patterns of
                    Child Rearing* (White Plains: Row, Petersen & Co.,
                    1957), pp. 56–57, 402; J. L. Fischer and A. Fischer,
                    "The New Englanders of Orchard Town, U. S. A.," in
                    B. B. Whiting, ed., *Six Cultures* (New York: Wiley,
                    1963), p. 941.

: 14 to   H. A. Moss, K. S. Robson, and F. Pedersen, "Determi-
247 : 4   nants of Maternal Stimulation of Infants and Conse-
                    quences of Treatment for Later Reactions to Stran-
                    gers," *Developmental Psychology*, vol. 1 (1969), pp.
                    239–46; H. A. Moss and K. S. Robson, "Maternal Influ-
                    ences in Early Social-Visual Behavior," *Child Develop-
                    ment*, vol. 38 (1968), pp. 401–08.

: 5–28   R. H. Walters and R. D. Parke, "The Role of the Dis-
                    tance Receptors in the Development of Social Respon-
                    siveness," in L. P. Lipsitt and C. C. Spiker, eds., *Ad-
                    vances in Child Development and Behavior* (New York:
                    Academic Press, 1965).

248 : 12–21   A. Montagu, "Some Factors in Family Cohesion," *Psychia-
                    try*, vol. 7 (1944), pp. 349–52.

: 24 to 249 : 4   L. Smith, *Strange Fruit* (New York: Reynal, 1944), p. 74.

249 : 8–29   W. Caudill and D. W. Plath, "Who Sleeps by Whom?

Page and Line

          Parent-Child Involvement in Urban Japanese Families,"
          Psychiatry, vol. 29 (1966), p. 363.
249 : 30 to 250 : 7   Ibid. p. 363.
250 : 24–28   See Fischer and Fischer, "The New Englanders . . . ," in
          Whiting, *Six Cultures*, p. 947.
251 : 19 to   E. M. Forster, *Abinger Harvest* (New York: Harcourt,
252 : 10   Brace, 1947).
    : 11–13   Timothy Eden, *The Tribulations of a Baronet* (London:
          Macmillan, 1933).
    : 13   R. Hart-Davis, *Hugh Walpole: A Biography* (New York:
          Macmillan, 1952).
    : 14   W. A. Swanberg, *William Randolph Hearst* (New York:
          Macmillan, 1961).
    : 18   Cecil King, *Strictly Personal* (London: Weidenfield & Ni-
          colson), 1969.
    : 27 to   M. Mead, "Cultural Differences in the Bathing of Ba-
253 : 8   bies," in K. Soddy, ed., *Mental Health and Infant De-
          velopment* (New York: Basic Books, vol. 1, 1956), pp.
          170–71.
    : 13–18   Clay, "The Effect of Culture . . . ," p. 273.
    : 20 to   A. Freud, *Normality and Pathology in Childhood* (New
254 : 2   York: International Universities Press, 1965), p. 155.
    : 3–10   Ibid. p. 156.
    : 26 to   Editorial, "Baby-Care Lambskin Rugs," *Parents Centres*
255 : 6   (Auckland, N. Z.), Bulletin 38, March 1969, p. 8. See
          also Bulletin 35, June 1968.
    : 13–20   N. F. Roberts, "Baby Care Lambskin Rugs." *Parents
          Centres* (Auckland, N. Z.), Bulletin 39, June 1969, pp.
          12–18.
    : 22 to   W. Caudill and H. Weinstein, "Maternal Care and Infant
256 : 22   Behavior in Japan and America," *Psychiatry*, vol. 32
    : 28 to   (1969), pp. 12–43; p. 13.
257 : 4   Ibid. pp. 14–15.
    : 15–17   E. F. Vogel, *Japan's New Middle Class: The Salary Man
          and His Family in a Tokyo Suburb* (Berkeley: Univer-
          sity of California Press, 1963).
    : 29 to   Caudill and Weinstein, "Maternal Care and Infant Be-
258 : 6   havior . . . ," *Psychiatry*, vol. 32 (1969), p. 42.
    : 11–24   D. G. Haring, "Aspects of Personal Character in Japan,"
          in D. G. Haring, ed., *Personal Character and Cultural
          Milieu* (Syracuse: Syracuse University Press, 1956), p.
          416.
259 : 8–16   Ibid. p. 417.
    : 24–30   Ibid.

322 SEVEN: CULTURE AND CONTACT

Page and Line

263 : 14–20   B. Schaffner, *Father Land* (New York: Columbia University Press, 1948).

265 : 3–21   E. A. Duyckinck, ed., *Wit and Wisdom of the Rev. Sydney Smith* (New York: Widdleton, 1866) p. 426.

: 25–28   Ortega y Gasset, *Man and People* (New York: W. W. Norton, 1957), pp. 192–221.

: 29–31   E. Westermarck, *The Origin and Development of the Moral Ideas.* (2 vols., London: Macmillan, 1917), vol. 2, pp. 150–51.

267 : 10–15   I. Pinchbeck and M. Hewitt, *Children in English Society,* Vol. 1: *From Tudor Times to the Eighteenth Century* (London: Routledge & Kegan Paul, 1970); L. L. Schucking, *The Puritan Family* (London: Routledge & Kegan Paul, 1970); P. Aiès, *Centuries of Childhood* (New York: A. A. Knopf, 1962).

268 : 1–11   W. E. Hartman, M. Fifthian, and D. Johnson, *Nudist Society* (New York: Crown, 1970), pp. 278–86. See also J. Howard, *Please Touch* (New York: McGraw-Hill, 1970); M. Shepard and M. Lee, *Marathon 16* (New York: G. P. Putnam's Sons, 1970); B. L. Austin, *Sad Nun at Syanon* (Holt, Rinehart & Winston, 1970).

: 24 to
269 : 14   M. Mead and R. Métraux, eds., *The Study of Culture at a Distance* (University of Chicago Press, 1953), pp. 107–115, 352–53; G. Gorer and J. Rickman, *The People of Great Russia: A Psychological Study* (New York: Chanticleer Press, 1950).

: 16–26   P. H. Wolff, "The Natural History of Crying and Other Vocalizations in Early Infancy," in E. B. Foss, ed., *Determinants of Infant Behavior* (London: Methuen & Co., 1969), vol. 4, p. 92.

: 27–30   H. Orlansky, "Infant Care and Personality," *Psychological Bulletin,* vol. 46 (1949), pp. 1–48.

270 : 5   V. Dal, *The Dictionary of the Living Great Russian Language (Tolkovyi slovar Velikomusskavo Yazkaya* [St. Petersburg, 1903]).

: 5 to
271 : 5   Mead and Métraux, *The Study of Culture at a Distance,* p. 163.

: 16–17   N. Leites, *The Operational Code of the Politburo* (New York: McGraw-Hill, 1951).

: 17 to
272 : 7   L. H. Haimson, "Russian 'Visual Thinking,'" in Mead and Métraux, p. 247.

: 32 to
273 : 8   J. E. Ritchie, "The Husband's Role," *Parents Centres* (Auckland, N. Z.), Bulletin 38, March 1969, pp. 4–7.

Page and Line

274 : 12–19   D. W. Winnicott, "The Theory of Parent-Infant Relationship," *International Journal of Psychoanalysis,* vol. 41 (1958), p. 591.

276 : 6–15   L. K. Frank, "The Psychological Approach in Sex Research," *Social Problems,* vol. 1 (1954), pp. 133–39.

: 21–26   Clay, "The Effect of Culture . . . ," p. 278.

: 27–30   L. M. Stolz, *Influences on Parent Behavior* (Stanford: Stanford University Press, 1967), p. 141.

278 : 3–5   F. Dunbar, *Psychosomatic Diagnosis* (New York: Hoeber, 1943), pp. 86–87; J. G. Kepecs, "Some Patterns of Somatic Displacement," *Psychosomatic Medicine,* vol. 15 (1953), pp. 425–32.

: 9–14   C. E. Benda, *The Image of Love* (New York: Free Press, 1961), p. 162.

: 20 to   J. G. Kepecs, M. Robin, and M. J. Brunner, "Relationship between Certain Emotional States and Exudation
279 : 1   into the Skin," *Psychosomatic Medicine,* vol. 13 (1951), pp. 10–17.

: 6–9   J. G. Kepecs, A. Rabin, and M. Robin, "Atopic Dermatitis: A Clinical Psychiatric Study," *Psychosomatic Medicine,* vol. 13 (1951), pp. 1–9; H. C. Bethune and C. B. Kidd, "Psychophysiological Mechanisms in Skin Diseases," *The Lancet,* vol. 2 (1961), pp. 1419–1422.

: 12–15   H. F. Harlow and M. K. Harlow, "Learning to Love," *American Scientist,* vol. 54 (1966), pp. 244–72, and numerous other papers.

: 16–20   H. F. Harlow, "Primary Affectional Patterns in Primates," *American Journal of Orthopsychiatry,* vol. 30, (1960), pp. 676–77; M. K. Harlow and H. F. Harlow, "Affection in Primates," *Discovery,* vol. 27, January 1966.

280 : 9–12   Harlow, "Primary Affectional Patterns in Primates," *American Journal of Orthopsychiatry,* vol. 30 (1960), p. 683.

: 17–23   Clay, "The Effect of Culture . . . ," pp. 281–82.
281 : 17–20   Ibid. p. 286.
: 26–30   H. F. Harlow and M. K. Harlow, "Learning to Love," *American Scientist,* vol. 54 (1966), p. 250.

282 : 2–10   H. F. Harlow, "Development of the Second and Third Affectional Systems in Macaques Monkeys," in T. T. Tourlentes, S. L. Pollack, and H. E. Himwich, eds., *Research Approaches to Psychiatric Problems* (New York: Grune & Stratton, 1962), pp. 209–229.

Page and Line

283 : 24 to 284 : 3   Clay, "The Effect of Culture . . . ," p. 290.

284 : 30 to   T. R. Williams, "Cultural Structuring of Tactile Experi-
285 : 3   ence in a Borneo Society," *American Anthropologist*,
                       vol. 68 (1966), pp. 27–39.

: 9–12   A. Tsumori, "Newly Acquired Behavior and Social Inter-
                       actions of Japanese Monkeys," in S. A. Altmann, ed., *So-
                       cial Communication Among Primates* (Chicago: Univer-
                       sity of Chicago Press, 1967), pp. 207–219.

: 12–14   K. R. L. Hall, "Observational Learning in Monkeys and
                       Apes," *British Journal of Psychology*, vol. 54 (1963), pp.
                       201–206; K. R. L. Hall, "Social Learning in Monkeys,"
                       in P. Jay, ed., *Primates* (New York: Holt, Rinehart &
                       Winston, 1969), pp. 383–97.

: 19 to   H. L. Rheingold and C. O. Eckerman, "The Infant Sepa-
286 : 6   rates Himself from His Mother," *Science*, vol. 168
                       (1970), pp. 78–83.

: 3   R. Held and A. Hein, "Movement-Produced Stimulation
                       in the Development of Visually Guided Behavior,"
                       Journal of Comparative and Physiological Psychology,
                       vol. 56 (1963), pp. 872–76.

: 23 to 287 : 19   Clay, "The Effect of Culture . . . ," pp. 308, 322.

INDEX